50% OFF
Online Social Work
ASWB Clinical Prep Course!

By Mometrix

Dear Customer,

We consider it an honor and a privilege that you chose our LCSW Study Guide. As a way of showing our appreciation and to help us better serve you, we are offering **50% off our online Social Work ASWB Clinical Prep Course**. Many LCSW courses are needlessly expensive and don't deliver enough value. With our course, you get access to the best LCSW prep material, and **you only pay half price**.

We have structured our online course to perfectly complement your printed study guide. The LCSW Prep Course contains **in-depth lessons** that cover all the most important topics, **20+ video reviews** that explain difficult concepts, over **1,000 practice questions** to ensure you feel prepared, and more than **400 digital flashcards**, so you can study while you're on the go.

Online Social Work ASWB Clinical Prep Course

Topics Included:

- Human Development, Diversity, and Behavior in the Environment

- Assessment, Diagnosis, and Treatment Planning

- Psychotherapy, Clinical Interventions, and Case Management

- Professional Values and Ethics

Course Features:

- LCSW Study Guide
  - Get content that complements our best-selling study guide.
- Full-Length Practice Tests
  - With over 1,000 practice questions, you can test yourself again and again.
- Mobile Friendly
  - If you need to study on the go, the course is easily accessible from your mobile device.
- LCSW Flashcards
  - Our course includes a flashcard mode with over 400 content cards to help you study.

To receive this discount, visit us at mometrix.com/university/aswbc/ or simply scan this QR code with your smartphone. At the checkout page, enter the discount code: **LCSW50off**

If you have any questions or concerns, please contact us at support@mometrix.com.

SCAN HERE

FREE Study Skills Videos/DVD Offer

Dear Customer,

Thank you for your purchase from Mometrix! We consider it an honor and a privilege that you have purchased our product and we want to ensure your satisfaction.

As part of our ongoing effort to meet the needs of test takers, we have developed a set of Study Skills Videos that we would like to give you for <u>FREE</u>. These videos cover our *best practices* for getting ready for your exam, from how to use our study materials to how to best prepare for the day of the test.

All that we ask is that you email us with feedback that would describe your experience so far with our product. Good, bad, or indifferent, we want to know what you think!

To get your FREE Study Skills Videos, you can use the **QR code** below, or send us an **email** at <u>studyvideos@mometrix.com</u> with *FREE VIDEOS* in the subject line and the following information in the body of the email:

- The name of the product you purchased.
- Your product rating on a scale of 1-5, with 5 being the highest rating.
- Your feedback. It can be long, short, or anything in between. We just want to know your impressions and experience so far with our product. (Good feedback might include how our study material met your needs and ways we might be able to make it even better. You could highlight features that you found helpful or features that you think we should add.)

If you have any questions or concerns, please don't hesitate to contact me directly.

Thanks again!

Sincerely,

Jay Willis
Vice President
jay.willis@mometrix.com
1-800-673-8175

LCSW
Clinical Exam
Study Guide
2021 and 2022

Social Work ASWB Clinical
Secrets Prep

3 Full-Length
Practice Tests

Detailed Answer
Explanations

2nd Edition Book

Written and edited by the Mometrix Social Worker Certification Test Team

Printed in the United States of America

This paper meets the requirements of ANSI/NISO Z39.48-1992 (Permanence of Paper).

Mometrix offers volume discount pricing to institutions. For more information or a price quote, please contact our sales department at sales@mometrix.com or 888-248-1219.

Mometrix Media LLC is not affiliated with or endorsed by any official testing organization. All organizational and test names are trademarks of their respective owners.

ISBN 13: 978-1-5167-1822-1
ISBN 10: 1-5167-1822-4

DEAR FUTURE EXAM SUCCESS STORY

First of all, **THANK YOU** for purchasing Mometrix study materials!

Second, congratulations! You are one of the few determined test-takers who are committed to doing whatever it takes to excel on your exam. **You have come to the right place.** We developed these study materials with one goal in mind: to deliver you the information you need in a format that's concise and easy to use.

In addition to optimizing your guide for the content of the test, we've outlined our recommended steps for breaking down the preparation process into small, attainable goals so you can make sure you stay on track.

We've also analyzed the entire test-taking process, identifying the most common pitfalls and showing how you can overcome them and be ready for any curveball the test throws you.

Standardized testing is one of the biggest obstacles on your road to success, which only increases the importance of doing well in the high-pressure, high-stakes environment of test day. Your results on this test could have a significant impact on your future, and this guide provides the information and practical advice to help you achieve your full potential on test day.

Your success is our success

We would love to hear from you! If you would like to share the story of your exam success or if you have any questions or comments in regard to our products, please contact us at **800-673-8175** or **support@mometrix.com**.

Thanks again for your business and we wish you continued success!

Sincerely,
The Mometrix Test Preparation Team

> **Need more help? Check out our flashcards at:**
> **http://mometrixflashcards.com/ASWB**

TABLE OF CONTENTS

Introduction

Thank you for purchasing this resource! You have made the choice to prepare yourself for a test that could have a huge impact on your future, and this guide is designed to help you be fully ready for test day. Obviously, it's important to have a solid understanding of the test material, but you also need to be prepared for the unique environment and stressors of the test, so that you can perform to the best of your abilities.

For this purpose, the first section that appears in this guide is the **Secret Keys**. We've devoted countless hours to meticulously researching what works and what doesn't, and we've boiled down our findings to the five most impactful steps you can take to improve your performance on the test. We start at the beginning with study planning and move through the preparation process, all the way to the testing strategies that will help you get the most out of what you know when you're finally sitting in front of the test.

We recommend that you start preparing for your test as far in advance as possible. However, if you've bought this guide as a last-minute study resource and only have a few days before your test, we recommend that you skip over the first two Secret Keys since they address a long-term study plan.

If you struggle with **test anxiety**, we strongly encourage you to check out our recommendations for how you can overcome it. Test anxiety is a formidable foe, but it can be beaten, and we want to make sure you have the tools you need to defeat it.

Review Video Directory

As you work your way through this guide, you will see numerous review video links interspersed with the written content. If you would like to access all of these review videos in one place, click on the video directory link found on the bonus page: **mometrix.com/bonus948/swclinical**

Secret Key #1 – Plan Big, Study Small

There's a lot riding on your performance. If you want to ace this test, you're going to need to keep your skills sharp and the material fresh in your mind. You need a plan that lets you review everything you need to know while still fitting in your schedule. We'll break this strategy down into three categories.

Information Organization

Start with the information you already have: the official test outline. From this, you can make a complete list of all the concepts you need to cover before the test. Organize these concepts into groups that can be studied together, and create a list of any related vocabulary you need to learn so you can brush up on any difficult terms. You'll want to keep this vocabulary list handy once you actually start studying since you may need to add to it along the way.

Time Management

Once you have your set of study concepts, decide how to spread them out over the time you have left before the test. Break your study plan into small, clear goals so you have a manageable task for each day and know exactly what you're doing. Then just focus on one small step at a time. When you manage your time this way, you don't need to spend hours at a time studying. Studying a small block of content for a short period each day helps you retain information better and avoid stressing over how much you have left to do. You can relax knowing that you have a plan to cover everything in time. In order for this strategy to be effective though, you have to start studying early and stick to your schedule. Avoid the exhaustion and futility that comes from last-minute cramming!

Study Environment

The environment you study in has a big impact on your learning. Studying in a coffee shop, while probably more enjoyable, is not likely to be as fruitful as studying in a quiet room. It's important to keep distractions to a minimum. You're only planning to study for a short block of time, so make the most of it. Don't pause to check your phone or get up to find a snack. It's also important to **avoid multitasking**. Research has consistently shown that multitasking will make your studying dramatically less effective. Your study area should also be comfortable and well-lit so you don't have the distraction of straining your eyes or sitting on an uncomfortable chair.

 The time of day you study is also important. You want to be rested and alert. Don't wait until just before bedtime. Study when you'll be most likely to comprehend and remember. Even better, if you know what time of day your test will be, set that time aside for study. That way your brain will be used to working on that subject at that specific time and you'll have a better chance of recalling information.

Finally, it can be helpful to team up with others who are studying for the same test. Your actual studying should be done in as isolated an environment as possible, but the work of organizing the information and setting up the study plan can be divided up. In between study sessions, you can discuss with your teammates the concepts that you're all studying and quiz each other on the details. Just be sure that your teammates are as serious about the test as you are. If you find that your study time is being replaced with social time, you might need to find a new team.

Secret Key #2 – Make Your Studying Count

You're devoting a lot of time and effort to preparing for this test, so you want to be absolutely certain it will pay off. This means doing more than just reading the content and hoping you can remember it on test day. It's important to make every minute of study count. There are two main areas you can focus on to make your studying count.

Retention

It doesn't matter how much time you study if you can't remember the material. You need to make sure you are retaining the concepts. To check your retention of the information you're learning, try recalling it at later times with minimal prompting. Try carrying around flashcards and glance at one or two from time to time or ask a friend who's also studying for the test to quiz you.

To enhance your retention, look for ways to put the information into practice so that you can apply it rather than simply recalling it. If you're using the information in practical ways, it will be much easier to remember. Similarly, it helps to solidify a concept in your mind if you're not only reading it to yourself but also explaining it to someone else. Ask a friend to let you teach them about a concept you're a little shaky on (or speak aloud to an imaginary audience if necessary). As you try to summarize, define, give examples, and answer your friend's questions, you'll understand the concepts better and they will stay with you longer. Finally, step back for a big picture view and ask yourself how each piece of information fits with the whole subject. When you link the different concepts together and see them working together as a whole, it's easier to remember the individual components.

Finally, practice showing your work on any multi-step problems, even if you're just studying. Writing out each step you take to solve a problem will help solidify the process in your mind, and you'll be more likely to remember it during the test.

Modality

Modality simply refers to the means or method by which you study. Choosing a study modality that fits your own individual learning style is crucial. No two people learn best in exactly the same way, so it's important to know your strengths and use them to your advantage.

For example, if you learn best by visualization, focus on visualizing a concept in your mind and draw an image or a diagram. Try color-coding your notes, illustrating them, or creating symbols that will trigger your mind to recall a learned concept. If you learn best by hearing or discussing information, find a study partner who learns the same way or read aloud to yourself. Think about how to put the information in your own words. Imagine that you are giving a lecture on the topic and record yourself so you can listen to it later.

For any learning style, flashcards can be helpful. Organize the information so you can take advantage of spare moments to review. Underline key words or phrases. Use different colors for different categories. Mnemonic devices (such as creating a short list in which every item starts with the same letter) can also help with retention. Find what works best for you and use it to store the information in your mind most effectively and easily.

Secret Key #3 – Practice the Right Way

Your success on test day depends not only on how many hours you put into preparing, but also on whether you prepared the right way. It's good to check along the way to see if your studying is paying off. One of the most effective ways to do this is by taking practice tests to evaluate your progress. Practice tests are useful because they show exactly where you need to improve. Every time you take a practice test, pay special attention to these three groups of questions:

- The questions you got wrong
- The questions you had to guess on, even if you guessed right
- The questions you found difficult or slow to work through

This will show you exactly what your weak areas are, and where you need to devote more study time. Ask yourself why each of these questions gave you trouble. Was it because you didn't understand the material? Was it because you didn't remember the vocabulary? Do you need more repetitions on this type of question to build speed and confidence? Dig into those questions and figure out how you can strengthen your weak areas as you go back to review the material.

Additionally, many practice tests have a section explaining the answer choices. It can be tempting to read the explanation and think that you now have a good understanding of the concept. However, an explanation likely only covers part of the question's broader context. Even if the explanation makes perfect sense, **go back and investigate** every concept related to the question until you're positive you have a thorough understanding.

As you go along, keep in mind that the practice test is just that: practice. Memorizing these questions and answers will not be very helpful on the actual test because it is unlikely to have any of the same exact questions. If you only know the right answers to the sample questions, you won't be prepared for the real thing. **Study the concepts** until you understand them fully, and then you'll be able to answer any question that shows up on the test.

It's important to wait on the practice tests until you're ready. If you take a test on your first day of study, you may be overwhelmed by the amount of material covered and how much you need to learn. Work up to it gradually.

On test day, you'll need to be prepared for answering questions, managing your time, and using the test-taking strategies you've learned. It's a lot to balance, like a mental marathon that will have a big impact on your future. Like training for a marathon, you'll need to start slowly and work your way up. When test day arrives, you'll be ready.

Start with the strategies you've read in the first two Secret Keys—plan your course and study in the way that works best for you. If you have time, consider using multiple study resources to get different approaches to the same concepts. It can be helpful to see difficult concepts from more than one angle. Then find a good source for practice tests. Many times, the test website will suggest potential study resources or provide sample tests.

Practice Test Strategy

If you're able to find at least three practice tests, we recommend this strategy:

UNTIMED AND OPEN-BOOK PRACTICE

Take the first test with no time constraints and with your notes and study guide handy. Take your time and focus on applying the strategies you've learned.

TIMED AND OPEN-BOOK PRACTICE

Take the second practice test open-book as well, but set a timer and practice pacing yourself to finish in time.

TIMED AND CLOSED-BOOK PRACTICE

Take any other practice tests as if it were test day. Set a timer and put away your study materials. Sit at a table or desk in a quiet room, imagine yourself at the testing center, and answer questions as quickly and accurately as possible.

Keep repeating timed and closed-book tests on a regular basis until you run out of practice tests or it's time for the actual test. Your mind will be ready for the schedule and stress of test day, and you'll be able to focus on recalling the material you've learned.

5

Secret Key #4 – Pace Yourself

Once you're fully prepared for the material on the test, your biggest challenge on test day will be managing your time. Just knowing that the clock is ticking can make you panic even if you have plenty of time left. Work on pacing yourself so you can build confidence against the time constraints of the exam. Pacing is a difficult skill to master, especially in a high-pressure environment, so **practice is vital**.

Set time expectations for your pace based on how much time is available. For example, if a section has 60 questions and the time limit is 30 minutes, you know you have to average 30 seconds or less per question in order to answer them all. Although 30 seconds is the hard limit, set 25 seconds per question as your goal, so you reserve extra time to spend on harder questions. When you budget extra time for the harder questions, you no longer have any reason to stress when those questions take longer to answer.

Don't let this time expectation distract you from working through the test at a calm, steady pace, but keep it in mind so you don't spend too much time on any one question. Recognize that taking extra time on one question you don't understand may keep you from answering two that you do understand later in the test. If your time limit for a question is up and you're still not sure of the answer, mark it and move on, and come back to it later if the time and the test format allow. If the testing format doesn't allow you to return to earlier questions, just make an educated guess; then put it out of your mind and move on.

On the easier questions, be careful not to rush. It may seem wise to hurry through them so you have more time for the challenging ones, but it's not worth missing one if you know the concept and just didn't take the time to read the question fully. Work efficiently but make sure you understand the question and have looked at all of the answer choices, since more than one may seem right at first.

Even if you're paying attention to the time, you may find yourself a little behind at some point. You should speed up to get back on track, but do so wisely. Don't panic; just take a few seconds less on each question until you're caught up. Don't guess without thinking, but do look through the answer choices and eliminate any you know are wrong. If you can get down to two choices, it is often worthwhile to guess from those. Once you've chosen an answer, move on and don't dwell on any that you skipped or had to hurry through. If a question was taking too long, chances are it was one of the harder ones, so you weren't as likely to get it right anyway.

On the other hand, if you find yourself getting ahead of schedule, it may be beneficial to slow down a little. The more quickly you work, the more likely you are to make a careless mistake that will affect your score. You've budgeted time for each question, so don't be afraid to spend that time. Practice an efficient but careful pace to get the most out of the time you have.

Secret Key #5 – Have a Plan for Guessing

When you're taking the test, you may find yourself stuck on a question. Some of the answer choices seem better than others, but you don't see the one answer choice that is obviously correct. What do you do?

The scenario described above is very common, yet most test takers have not effectively prepared for it. Developing and practicing a plan for guessing may be one of the single most effective uses of your time as you get ready for the exam.

In developing your plan for guessing, there are three questions to address:

- When should you start the guessing process?
- How should you narrow down the choices?
- Which answer should you choose?

When to Start the Guessing Process

Unless your plan for guessing is to select C every time (which, despite its merits, is not what we recommend), you need to leave yourself enough time to apply your answer elimination strategies. Since you have a limited amount of time for each question, that means that if you're going to give yourself the best shot at guessing correctly, you have to decide quickly whether or not you will guess.

Of course, the best-case scenario is that you don't have to guess at all, so first, see if you can answer the question based on your knowledge of the subject and basic reasoning skills. Focus on the key words in the question and try to jog your memory of related topics. Give yourself a chance to bring the knowledge to mind, but once you realize that you don't have (or you can't access) the knowledge you need to answer the question, it's time to start the guessing process.

It's almost always better to start the guessing process too early than too late. It only takes a few seconds to remember something and answer the question from knowledge. Carefully eliminating wrong answer choices takes longer. Plus, going through the process of eliminating answer choices can actually help jog your memory.

Summary: Start the guessing process as soon as you decide that you can't answer the question based on your knowledge.

7

How to Narrow Down the Choices

The next chapter in this book (**Test-Taking Strategies**) includes a wide range of strategies for how to approach questions and how to look for answer choices to eliminate. You will definitely want to read those carefully, practice them, and figure out which ones work best for you. Here though, we're going to address a mindset rather than a particular strategy.

Your odds of guessing an answer correctly depend on how many options you are choosing from.

Number of options left	5	4	3	2	1
Odds of guessing correctly	20%	25%	33%	50%	100%

You can see from this chart just how valuable it is to be able to eliminate incorrect answers and make an educated guess, but there are two things that many test takers do that cause them to miss out on the benefits of guessing:

- Accidentally eliminating the correct answer
- Selecting an answer based on an impression

We'll look at the first one here, and the second one in the next section.

To avoid accidentally eliminating the correct answer, we recommend a thought exercise called **the $5 challenge**. In this challenge, you only eliminate an answer choice from contention if you are willing to bet $5 on it being wrong. Why $5? Five dollars is a small but not insignificant amount of money. It's an amount you could afford to lose but wouldn't want to throw away. And while losing $5 once might not hurt too much, doing

it twenty times will set you back $100. In the same way, each small decision you make—eliminating a choice here, guessing on a question there—won't by itself impact your score very much, but when you put them all together, they can make a big difference. By holding each answer choice elimination decision to a higher standard, you can reduce the risk of accidentally eliminating the correct answer.

The $5 challenge can also be applied in a positive sense: If you are willing to bet $5 that an answer choice *is* correct, go ahead and mark it as correct.

Summary: Only eliminate an answer choice if you are willing to bet $5 that it is wrong.

Which Answer to Choose

You're taking the test. You've run into a hard question and decided you'll have to guess. You've eliminated all the answer choices you're willing to bet $5 on. Now you have to pick an answer. Why do we even need to talk about this? Why can't you just pick whichever one you feel like when the time comes?

The answer to these questions is that if you don't come into the test with a plan, you'll rely on your impression to select an answer choice, and if you do that, you risk falling into a trap. The test writers know that everyone who takes their test will be guessing on some of the questions, so they intentionally write wrong answer choices to seem plausible. You still have to pick an answer though, and if the wrong answer choices are designed to look right, how can you ever be sure that you're not falling for their trap? The best solution we've found to this dilemma is to take the decision out of your hands entirely. Here is the process we recommend:

Once you've eliminated any choices that you are confident (willing to bet $5) are wrong, select the first remaining choice as your answer.

Whether you choose to select the first remaining choice, the second, or the last, the important thing is that you use some preselected standard. Using this approach guarantees that you will not be enticed into selecting an answer choice that looks right, because you are not basing your decision on how the answer choices look.

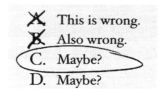

This is not meant to make you question your knowledge. Instead, it is to help you recognize the difference between your knowledge and your impressions. There's a huge difference between thinking an answer is right because of what you know, and thinking an answer is right because it looks or sounds like it should be right.

Summary: To ensure that your selection is appropriately random, make a predetermined selection from among all answer choices you have not eliminated.

Test-Taking Strategies

This section contains a list of test-taking strategies that you may find helpful as you work through the test. By taking what you know and applying logical thought, you can maximize your chances of answering any question correctly!

It is very important to realize that every question is different and every person is different: no single strategy will work on every question, and no single strategy will work for every person. That's why we've included all of them here, so you can try them out and determine which ones work best for different types of questions and which ones work best for you.

Question Strategies

⊘ READ CAREFULLY

Read the question and the answer choices carefully. Don't miss the question because you misread the terms. You have plenty of time to read each question thoroughly and make sure you understand what is being asked. Yet a happy medium must be attained, so don't waste too much time. You must read carefully and efficiently.

⊘ CONTEXTUAL CLUES

Look for contextual clues. If the question includes a word you are not familiar with, look at the immediate context for some indication of what the word might mean. Contextual clues can often give you all the information you need to decipher the meaning of an unfamiliar word. Even if you can't determine the meaning, you may be able to narrow down the possibilities enough to make a solid guess at the answer to the question.

⊘ PREFIXES

If you're having trouble with a word in the question or answer choices, try dissecting it. Take advantage of every clue that the word might include. Prefixes can be a huge help. Usually, they allow you to determine a basic meaning. *Pre-* means before, *post-* means after, *pro-* is positive, *de-* is negative. From prefixes, you can get an idea of the general meaning of the word and try to put it into context.

⊘ HEDGE WORDS

Watch out for critical hedge words, such as *likely, may, can, sometimes, often, almost, mostly, usually, generally, rarely*, and *sometimes*. Question writers insert these hedge phrases to cover every possibility. Often an answer choice will be wrong simply because it leaves no room for exception. Be on guard for answer choices that have definitive words such as *exactly* and *always*.

⊘ SWITCHBACK WORDS

Stay alert for *switchbacks*. These are the words and phrases frequently used to alert you to shifts in thought. The most common switchback words are *but, although*, and *however*. Others include *nevertheless, on the other hand, even though, while, in spite of, despite*, and *regardless of*. Switchback words are important to catch because they can change the direction of the question or an answer choice.

⊘ FACE VALUE

When in doubt, use common sense. Accept the situation in the problem at face value. Don't read too much into it. These problems will not require you to make wild assumptions. If you have to go beyond creativity and warp time or space in order to have an answer choice fit the question, then you should move on and consider the other answer choices. These are normal problems rooted in reality. The applicable relationship or explanation may not be readily apparent, but it is there for you to figure out. Use your common sense to interpret anything that isn't clear.

Answer Choice Strategies

⊘ ANSWER SELECTION

The most thorough way to pick an answer choice is to identify and eliminate wrong answers until only one is left, then confirm it is the correct answer. Sometimes an answer choice may immediately seem right, but be careful. The test writers will usually put more than one reasonable answer choice on each question, so take a second to read all of them and make sure that the other choices are not equally obvious. As long as you have time left, it is better to read every answer choice than to pick the first one that looks right without checking the others.

⊘ ANSWER CHOICE FAMILIES

An answer choice family consists of two (in rare cases, three) answer choices that are very similar in construction and cannot all be true at the same time. If you see two answer choices that are direct opposites or parallels, one of them is usually the correct answer. For instance, if one answer choice says that quantity x increases and another either says that quantity x decreases (opposite) or says that quantity y increases (parallel), then those answer choices would fall into the same family. An answer choice that doesn't match the construction of the answer choice family is more likely to be incorrect. Most questions will not have answer choice families, but when they do appear, you should be prepared to recognize them.

⊘ ELIMINATE ANSWERS

Eliminate answer choices as soon as you realize they are wrong, but make sure you consider all possibilities. If you are eliminating answer choices and realize that the last one you are left with is also wrong, don't panic. Start over and consider each choice again. There may be something you missed the first time that you will realize on the second pass.

⊘ AVOID FACT TRAPS

Don't be distracted by an answer choice that is factually true but doesn't answer the question. You are looking for the choice that answers the question. Stay focused on what the question is asking for so you don't accidentally pick an answer that is true but incorrect. Always go back to the question and make sure the answer choice you've selected actually answers the question and is not merely a true statement.

⊘ EXTREME STATEMENTS

In general, you should avoid answers that put forth extreme actions as standard practice or proclaim controversial ideas as established fact. An answer choice that states the "process should be used in certain situations, if..." is much more likely to be correct than one that states the "process should be discontinued completely." The first is a calm rational statement and doesn't even make a definitive, uncompromising stance, using a hedge word *if* to provide wiggle room, whereas the second choice is far more extreme.

⊘ BENCHMARK

As you read through the answer choices and you come across one that seems to answer the question well, mentally select that answer choice. This is not your final answer, but it's the one that will help you evaluate the other answer choices. The one that you selected is your benchmark or standard for judging each of the other answer choices. Every other answer choice must be compared to your benchmark. That choice is correct until proven otherwise by another answer choice beating it. If you find a better answer, then that one becomes your new benchmark. Once you've decided that no other choice answers the question as well as your benchmark, you have your final answer.

⊘ PREDICT THE ANSWER

Before you even start looking at the answer choices, it is often best to try to predict the answer. When you come up with the answer on your own, it is easier to avoid distractions and traps because you will know exactly what to look for. The right answer choice is unlikely to be word-for-word what you came up with, but it should be a close match. Even if you are confident that you have the right answer, you should still take the time to read each option before moving on.

General Strategies

⊘ TOUGH QUESTIONS

If you are stumped on a problem or it appears too hard or too difficult, don't waste time. Move on! Remember though, if you can quickly check for obviously incorrect answer choices, your chances of guessing correctly are greatly improved. Before you completely give up, at least try to knock out a couple of possible answers. Eliminate what you can and then guess at the remaining answer choices before moving on.

⊘ CHECK YOUR WORK

Since you will probably not know every term listed and the answer to every question, it is important that you get credit for the ones that you do know. Don't miss any questions through careless mistakes. If at all possible, try to take a second to look back over your answer selection and make sure you've selected the correct answer choice and haven't made a costly careless mistake (such as marking an answer choice that you didn't mean to mark). This quick double check should more than pay for itself in caught mistakes for the time it costs.

⊘ PACE YOURSELF

It's easy to be overwhelmed when you're looking at a page full of questions; your mind is confused and full of random thoughts, and the clock is ticking down faster than you would like. Calm down and maintain the pace that you have set for yourself. Especially as you get down to the last few minutes of the test, don't let the small numbers on the clock make you panic. As long as you are on track by monitoring your pace, you are guaranteed to have time for each question.

⊘ DON'T RUSH

It is very easy to make errors when you are in a hurry. Maintaining a fast pace in answering questions is pointless if it makes you miss questions that you would have gotten right otherwise. Test writers like to include distracting information and wrong answers that seem right. Taking a little extra time to avoid careless mistakes can make all the difference in your test score. Find a pace that allows you to be confident in the answers that you select.

⊘ KEEP MOVING

Panicking will not help you pass the test, so do your best to stay calm and keep moving. Taking deep breaths and going through the answer elimination steps you practiced can help to break through a stress barrier and keep your pace.

Final Notes

The combination of a solid foundation of content knowledge and the confidence that comes from practicing your plan for applying that knowledge is the key to maximizing your performance on test day. As your foundation of content knowledge is built up and strengthened, you'll find that the strategies included in this chapter become more and more effective in helping you quickly sift through the distractions and traps of the test to isolate the correct answer.

Now that you're preparing to move forward into the test content chapters of this book, be sure to keep your goal in mind. As you read, think about how you will be able to apply this information on the test. If you've already seen sample questions for the test and you have an idea of the question format and style, try to come up with questions of your own that you can answer based on what you're reading. This will give you valuable practice applying your knowledge in the same ways you can expect to on test day.

Good luck and good studying!

Five-Week Study Plan

On the next few pages, we've provided an optional study plan to help you use this study guide to its fullest potential over the course of five weeks. If you have ten weeks available and want to spread it out more, spend two weeks on each section of the plan.

Below is a quick summary of the subjects covered in each week of the plan.

- Week 1: Human Development, Diversity, and Behavior in the Environment
- Week 2: Assessment, Diagnosis, and Treatment Planning
- Week 3: Psychotherapy, Clinical Interventions, and Case Management
- Week 4: Professional Values and Ethics
- Week 5: Practice Tests

Please note that not all subjects will take the same amount of time to work through.

Three full-length practice tests are included in this study guide. We recommend saving the third practice test and any additional tests for after you've completed the study plan. Take these practice tests without any reference materials a day or two before the real thing as practice runs to get you in the mode of answering questions at a good pace.

Week 1: Human Development, Diversity, and Behavior in the Environment

INSTRUCTIONAL CONTENT

First, read carefully through the Human Development, Diversity, and Behavior in the Environment chapter in this book, checking off your progress as you go:

- ❏ Human Growth and Development
- ❏ Human Behavior in the Social Environment
- ❏ Sexual Orientation
- ❏ Self-Image
- ❏ Stress, Crisis, and Trauma
- ❏ Grief
- ❏ Concepts of Abuse
- ❏ Social and Economic Justice
- ❏ Globalization and Institutionalism
- ❏ Out-of-Home Placement and Displacement
- ❏ Indicators of Substance Abuse
- ❏ Substance Use and Abuse
- ❏ Discrimination
- ❏ Exploitation
- ❏ Culturally Competent Care

As you read, do the following:

- Highlight any sections, terms, or concepts you think are important
- Draw an asterisk (*) next to any areas you are struggling with
- Watch the review videos to gain more understanding of a particular topic
- Take notes in your notebook or in the margins of this book

After you've read through everything, go back and review any sections that you highlighted or that you drew an asterisk next to, referencing your notes along the way.

Week 2: Assessment and Intervention Planning

INSTRUCTIONAL CONTENT

First, read carefully through the Assessment and Intervention Planning chapter in this book, checking off your progress as you go:

- ❑ Biopsychosocial History and Collateral Data
- ❑ Assessment Methods and Techniques
- ❑ Indicators for Risk to Self or Others
- ❑ Risk Management
- ❑ Pharmacologic Interventions
- ❑ Psychiatric Disorders and Diagnosis
- ❑ Research

As you read, do the following:

- Highlight any sections, terms, or concepts you think are important
- Draw an asterisk (*) next to any areas you are struggling with
- Watch the review videos to gain more understanding of a particular topic
- Take notes in your notebook or in the margins of this book

After you've read through everything, go back and review any sections that you highlighted or that you drew an asterisk next to, referencing your notes along the way.

Week 3: Interventions with Clients/Client Systems

INSTRUCTIONAL CONTENT

First, read carefully through the Interventions with Clients/Client Systems chapter in this book, checking off your progress as you go:

- ❑ Therapeutic Relationships and Communication
- ❑ Interventions
- ❑ Family Therapy
- ❑ Group Work
- ❑ Community Organization and Social Planning
- ❑ Program Development and Service Delivery
- ❑ Case Management
- ❑ Consultation and Collaboration
- ❑ Social Policy and Social Change
- ❑ Support Programs
- ❑ Leadership
- ❑ Supervision and Administration

As you read, do the following:

- Highlight any sections, terms, or concepts you think are important
- Draw an asterisk (*) next to any areas you are struggling with
- Watch the review videos to gain more understanding of a particular topic
- Take notes in your notebook or in the margins of this book

After you've read through everything, go back and review any sections that you highlighted or that you drew an asterisk next to, referencing your notes along the way.

Week 4: Professional Values and Ethics

INSTRUCTIONAL CONTENT

First, read carefully through the Professional Values and Ethics chapter in this book, checking off your progress as you go:

- ❏ Legal Issues and Client Rights
- ❏ NASW Code of Ethics
- ❏ Record-Keeping and Documentation
- ❏ Professional Development and the Use of Self

As you read, do the following:

- Highlight any sections, terms, or concepts you think are important
- Draw an asterisk (*) next to any areas you are struggling with
- Watch the review videos to gain more understanding of a particular topic
- Take notes in your notebook or in the margins of this book

After you've read through everything, go back and review any sections that you highlighted or that you drew an asterisk next to, referencing your notes along the way.

Week 5: Practice Tests

Your success on test day depends not only on how many hours you put into preparing, but also on whether you prepared the right way. It's good to check along the way to see if your studying is paying off. One of the most effective ways to do this is by taking practice tests to evaluate your progress. Practice tests are useful because they show exactly where you need to improve. Every time you take a practice test, pay special attention to these three groups of questions:

- The questions you got wrong
- The questions you had to guess on, even if you guessed right
- The questions you found difficult or slow to work through

This will show you exactly what your weak areas are, and where you need to devote more study time. Ask yourself why each of these questions gave you trouble. Was it because you didn't understand the material? Was it because you didn't remember the vocabulary? Do you need more repetitions on this type of question to build speed and confidence? Dig into those questions and figure out how you can strengthen your weak areas as you go back to review the material.

PRACTICE TEST #1

Now that you've read over the instructional content, it's time to take a practice test. Complete Practice Test #1. Take this test with **no time constraints**, and feel free to reference the applicable sections of this guide as you go. Once you've finished, check your answers against the provided answer key. For any questions you answered incorrectly, review the answer rationale, and then **go back and review** the applicable sections of the book. The goal in this stage is to understand why you answered the question incorrectly, and make sure that the next time you see a similar question, you will get it right.

PRACTICE TEST #2

Next, complete Practice Test #2. This time, give yourself **4 hours** to complete all of the questions. You should again feel free to reference the guide and your notes, but be mindful of the clock. If you run out of time before you finish all of the questions, mark where you were when time expired, but go ahead and finish taking the practice test. Once you've finished, check your answers against the provided answer key, and as before, review the answer rationale for any that you answered incorrectly and then go back and review the associated instructional content. Your goal is still to increase understanding of the content but also to get used to the time constraints you will face on the test.

As you go along, keep in mind that the practice test is just that: practice. Memorizing these questions and answers will not be very helpful on the actual test because it is unlikely to have any of the same exact questions. If you only know the right answers to the sample questions, you won't be prepared for the real thing. **Study the concepts** until you understand them fully, and then you'll be able to answer any question that shows up on the test.

Human Development, Diversity, and Behavior in the Environment

Transform passive reading into active learning! After immersing yourself in this chapter, put your comprehension to the test by taking a quiz. The insights you gained will stay with you longer this way. Scan the QR code to go directly to the chapter quiz interface for this study guide. If you're using a computer, simply visit the bonus page at **mometrix.com/bonus948/swclinical** and click the Chapter Quizzes link.

Human Growth and Development

MASLOW'S HIERARCHY OF NEEDS

American psychologist Abraham Maslow defined human motivation in terms of needs and wants. His hierarchy of needs is classically portrayed as a pyramid sitting on its base divided into horizontal layers. He theorized that, as humans fulfill the needs of one layer, their motivation turns to the layer above.

Level	Need	Description
Physiological	Basic needs to sustain life—oxygen, food, fluids, sleep	These basic needs take precedence over all other needs and must be dealt with first before the individuals can focus on other needs.
Safety and security	Freedom from physiological and psychological threats	Once basic needs are met, individuals become concerned about safety, including freedom from fear, unemployment, war, and disasters. Children respond more intensely to threats than adults.
Love/Belonging	Support, caring, intimacy	Individuals tend to avoid isolation and loneliness and have a need for family, intimacy, or membership in a group where they feel they belong.
Self-esteem	Sense of worth, respect, independence	To have confidence, individuals need to develop self-esteem and receive the respect of others.
Self-actualization	Meeting one's own sense of potential and finding fulfillment	Individuals choose a path in life that leads to fulfillment and contentment.

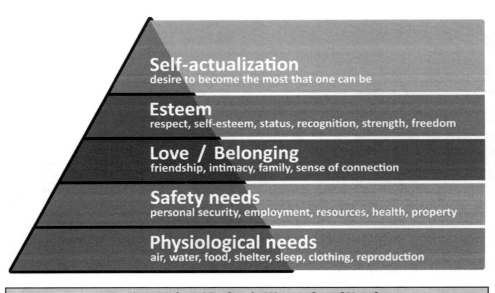

Review Video: Maslow's Hierarchy of Needs
Visit mometrix.com/academy and enter code: 461825

FREUD'S PSYCHOANALYTIC THEORY

MOTIVATIONAL FORCES OF THE UNCONSCIOUS MIND THAT SHAPE BEHAVIOR

Freud's psychoanalytic theory postulates that behavior is influenced not only by environmental stimuli (i.e., physical influences) and external social constrains and constructs (i.e., taboos, rules, social expectations), but also by four specific unconscious elements as well. These elements exist only in the unconscious mind, and individuals remain substantively unaware of all the forces, motivations, and drives that shape their thoughts and behavioral decisions. The **four elements** are:

- Covert desires
- Defenses needed to protect, facilitate, and moderate behaviors
- Dreams
- Unconscious wishes

LEVELS OF THE MIND

The three levels of the mind that Freud proposed include the following:

- The **conscious mind** is comprised of various ideas and thoughts of which we are fully aware.
- The **preconscious mind** is comprised of ideas and thoughts that are outside of immediate awareness, but can be readily accessed and brought into awareness.
- The **unconscious mind** is comprised of thoughts and ideas that are outside of our awareness and that cannot be accessed or brought into full awareness by personal effort alone.

PRIMARY FOCUS OF PSYCHOANALYSIS

The primary focus of psychoanalysis is on the unconscious mind and the desires, defenses, dreams and wishes contained within it. Freud proposed that the key features of the unconscious mind arise from experiences in the past and from problems in the development of the personality. Consequently, a focus on the unconscious mind requires the psychoanalytic process to also focus on the **past**—specifically on those repressed infant and childhood memories and experiences that served to create the desires, defenses, dreams, and wishes that invariably manifest through the thoughts and behaviors of every individual.

FREUD'S STRUCTURAL THEORY OF PERSONALITY DEVELOPMENT

Freud proposed a three-level structure of personality, composed of the id, the ego, and the super-ego:

Id	The level of personality that comprises basic instinctual drives and is the only part of personality present at birth. The id seeks immediate gratification of primitive needs (hunger, thirst, libido) and adheres to the "pleasure principle" (i.e., seek pleasure, avoid pain).
Ego	Develops secondarily and allows for rational thought, executive functions, and the ability to delay gratification. The ego is governed by the "reality principle" and mediates the desires of the id with the requirements of the external world.
Super-ego	Develops last and incorporates the higher concepts of morality, ethics, and justice into the personality, allowing concepts of right, wrong, and greater good to override base instincts and purely rational goals.

SUPER-EGO, CONSCIENCE, AND EGO IDEAL

The **super-ego** is comprised of the conscience and the ego ideal, which are constructed from the restraints and encouragements provided by caregivers (parents, teachers, other role models). The **conscience** focuses on cognitive and behavioral restrictions (i.e., the "should nots") while the **ego ideal** focuses on perfection, including spiritual attainment and higher-order goals (the "shoulds" of thought and behavior).

The super-ego works in opposition to the id, produces feelings of guilt for inappropriate drives, fantasies, and actions, and encourages refinement, aspirations, and higher-order goals. Freud theorized that the super-ego emerges around age five, and is not the dominant feature of the personality in a healthy person (which would result in overly-rigid, rule-bound behavior).

The strongest part of the personality is the ego, which seeks to satisfy the needs of the id without disrupting the super-ego.

Review Video: <u>How do the Id, Ego, and Superego interact?</u> Visit mometrix.com/academy and enter code: 690435

PSYCHOSEXUAL STAGES OF DEVELOPMENT

Freud proposed that children develop through five stages that he referred to as the psychosexual stages of development. They are as follows:

Stage	Description
Oral (Birth to 1.5 years)	Gratification through mouth/upper digestive tract.
Anal (1.5 to 3 years)	The child gains control over anal sphincter and bowel movements.
Phallic (3 to 6 years)	Gratification through genitalia. Major task is resolution of Oedipal complex and leads to development of superego, which begins about age 4. During this time child's phallic striving is directed toward the opposite-sex parent and in competition with same-sex parent. Out of fear and love, child renounces desire for the opposite sex parent and represses sexual desires. Child then identifies with same-sex parent and internalizes their values, etc. This leads to development of superego and ability to experience guilt.
Latency (6 to 10 years)	Sublimation of the oedipal stage, expression of sexual-aggressive drives in socially acceptable forms
Genital (10 years to adulthood)	Acceptance of one's genitalia and concern for others' wellbeing.

ADULT PERSONALITY TYPES

Freud's adult personality types are based on his psychosexual stages and include the following:

Personality Type	Characteristics
Oral	Infantile, demanding, dependent behavior; preoccupation with oral gratification.
Anal	Stinginess, excessive focus on accumulating and collecting. Rigidity in routines and forms, suspiciousness, legalistic thinking.
Phallic	Selfish sexual exploitation of others, without regard to their needs or concerns.

PROCESSES AND STAGES RELEVANT TO DEVELOPMENT OF THE PERSONALITY

Freud identified two primary elements that contribute to the development of the personality:

1. Natural growth and maturational processes (biological, hormonal, and time-dependent processes)
2. Learning and experiential processes (coping with and avoiding pain, managing frustration, reducing anxiety, and resolving conflicts).

According to Freud, psychopathology will result if all 5 stages of psychosexual development are not fully mastered, or if fixation at a particular stage develops (resulting if needs at a particular stage are either over- or under-gratified). If significant developmental frustration is experienced in a later stage, the developmental process may fall back to an earlier stage by means of the defense mechanism known as regression.

CATHEXIS AND ANTI-CATHEXIS

According to Freud's theory, the individual's mental state emerges from the process of reciprocal exchange between two forces: cathexis and anti-cathexis:

- Freud used the term **cathexis** to refer to the psychic energy attached to an object of importance (i.e., person, body part, psychic element). He also used this term to refer to what he called urges, or psychic impulses (e.g., desires, wishes, pain), that drive human behavior.
- In contrast to the driving urges of cathexis, there is a checking force he referred to as **anti-cathexis**. It serves to restrict the urges of the id and also to keep repressed information in the unconscious mind.

ERIK ERIKSON'S PSYCHOSOCIAL STAGES OF DEVELOPMENT

Erik Erikson was one of the first theorists to address human development over the entire life span. The eight developmental stages in his theory of psychosocial development are:

Stage	Description
Trust vs. Mistrust (Birth to 1.5 years)	• Same ages as Freud's oral stage. • Infants develop a sense of trust in self and in others. • Psychological dangers include a strong sense of mistrust that later develops and is revealed as withdrawal when the individual is at odds with self and others.
Autonomy vs. Shame (1.5 to 3 years)	• Same ages as Freud's anal stage. • In this phase, rapid growth in muscular maturation, verbalization, and the ability to coordinate highly conflicting action patterns is characterized by tendencies of holding on and letting go. • The child begins experiencing an autonomous will, which contributes to the process of identity building and development of the courage to be an independent individual. • Psychological dangers include immature obsessiveness and procrastination, ritualistic repetitions to gain power, self-insistent stubbornness, compulsive meek compliance or self-restraint, and the fear of a loss of self-control.
Initiative vs. Guilt (3 to 6 years)	• Same ages as Freud's phallic stage. • Incursion into space by mobility, into the unknown by curiosity, and into others by physical attack and aggressive voice. • This stage frees the child's initiative and sense of purpose for adult tasks. • Psychological dangers include hysterical denial or self-restriction, which impede an individual from actualizing inner capacities.
Industry vs. Inferiority (6 to 11 years)	• Same as Freud's latency stage. • The need of the child is to make things well, to be a worker, and a potential provider. • Developmental task is mastery over physical objects, self, social transaction, ideas, and concepts. • School and peer groups are necessary for gaining and testing mastery. • Psychological dangers include a sense of inferiority, incompetence, self-restraint, and conformity.

Stage	Description
Identity vs. Role Confusion (Adolescence)	• Same age range as Freud's genital stage. • Crucial task is to create an identity, reintegration of various components of self into a whole person—a process of ego synthesis. • Peer group is greatly important in providing support, values, a primary reference group, and an arena in which to experiment with various roles. • Psychological dangers include extreme identity confusion, feelings of estrangement, excessive conformity or rebelliousness, and idealism (a denial of reality, neurotic conflict, or delinquency).
Intimacy vs. Isolation (Early adulthood)	• Task is to enter relationships with others in an involved, reciprocal manner. • Failure to achieve intimacy can lead to highly stereotyped interpersonal relationships and distancing. Can also lead to a willingness to renounce, isolate, and destroy others whose presence seems dangerous.
Generativity vs. Stagnation (Adulthood)	• Key task is to develop concern for establishing and guiding the next generation, and the capacity for caring, nurturing, and concern for others. • Psychological danger is stagnation. Stagnation includes caring primarily for oneself, an artificial intimacy with others, and self-indulgence.
Ego integrity vs. Despair (Late adulthood)	• Task is the acceptance of one's life, achievements, and significant relationships as satisfactory and acceptable. • Psychological danger is despair. Despair is expressed in having the sense that time is too short to start another life or to test alternative roads to integrity. • Despair is accompanied by self-criticism, regret, and fear of impending death.

The stages are hierarchical and build upon each other. The resolution of the fundamental "crisis" of each prior stage must occur before one can move on to the next stage of growth. Although individual attributes are primary in resolving the crisis associated with each stage, the social environment can play an important role as well.

ERIKSON'S EGO STRENGTH

The ego essentially mediates irrational impulses related to the id (drives, instincts, needs). The concept of ego strengths derives from Erikson's (1964, 1985) 8 psychosocial stages and includes hope, will, purpose, competence, fidelity, love, care, and wisdom. Ego strength results from the overcoming of crises in each stage of development and allows the individual to maintain good mental health despite challenges and cope with conflict. Ego strength is assessed through questioning and observation. Characteristics of **ego strength** include the ability to:

- Express a range of feelings and emotions without being overwhelmed by them
- Deal effectively with loss
- Gain strength from loss
- Continue to engage in positive and life-affirming activities
- Exhibit empathy and consideration of others
- Resist temptation and exercise self-control
- Admit responsibility for own actions and avoid blaming others
- Show acceptance of the self
- Set limits in order to avoid negative influences and outcomes

26

JEAN PIAGET'S THEORY OF COGNITIVE AND MORAL DEVELOPMENT

KEY CONCEPTS

Jean Piaget believed that development was progressive and followed a set pattern. He believed the child's environment, their interactions with others in that environment, and how the environment responds help to shape the child's cognitive development. **Key concepts of Piaget's theory of cognitive and moral development** are defined below:

- **Action** is overt behavior.
- **Operation** is a particular type of action that may be internalized thought.
- **Activity in Development** refers to the fact that the child is not a passive subject, but an active contributor to the construction of her or his personality and universe. The child acts on her or his environment, modifies it, and is an active participant in the construction of reality.
- **Adaptation** includes accommodation and assimilation. Accommodation entails adapting to the characteristics of the object. Assimilation is the incorporation of external reality into the existing mental organization.

STAGES OF COGNITIVE AND MORAL DEVELOPMENT

The stages of Piaget's theory of cognitive and moral development are as follows:

Stage	Description
Sensorimotor (Birth to 2 years)	• Infant cannot evoke representations of persons or objects when they are absent—symbolic function. • Infant interacts with her or his surroundings and can focus on objects other than self. Infant learns to predict events (door opening signals that someone will appear). Infants also learn that objects continue to exist when out of sight and learn a beginning sense of causality.
Pre-operational (2 to 7 years)	• Developing of symbolic thought draws from sensory-motor thinking. • Conceptual ability not yet developed.
Concrete operational (7 to 11 years)	• Child gains capacity to order and relate experience to an organized whole. • Children can now explore several possible solutions to a problem without adopting one, as they are able to return to their original outlook.
Formal operational (11 years to adolescence)	• Child/youth can visualize events and concepts beyond the present and is able to form theories.

LAWRENCE KOHLBERG'S THEORY OF MORAL DEVELOPMENT

Lawrence Kohlberg's theory of moral development is characterized as the following:

- Kohlberg formulated his theory to extend and modify the work of Piaget, as he believed that moral development was a longer and more complex process. He postulated that infants possess no morals or ethics at birth and that moral development occurs largely independently of age. Kohlberg asserted that children's experiences shape their understanding of moral concepts (i.e., justice, rights, equality, human welfare).
- Kohlberg suggested a process involving three levels, each with two stages. Each stage reveals a dramatic change in the moral perspective of the individual.
- In this theory, moral development is linear, no stage can be skipped, and development takes place throughout the life span.
- Progress between stages is contingent upon the availability of a role model who offers a model of the principles of the next higher level.

LEVELS AND STAGES OF MORAL DEVELOPMENT

The levels and stages of Kohlberg's theory of moral development are as follows:

Stage	Level	Description
1	Pre-conventional	The individual perspective frames moral judgments, which are concrete. The framework of Stage 1 stresses rule following, because breaking rules may lead to punishment. Reasoning in this stage is egocentric and not concerned with others.
2	Pre-conventional	Emphasizes moral reciprocity and has its focus on the pragmatic, instrumental value of an action. Individuals at this stage observe moral standards because it is in their interest, but they are able to justify retaliation as a form of justice. Behavior in this stage is focused on following rules only when it is in the person's immediate interest. Stage 2 has a mutual contractual nature, which makes rule-following instrumental and based on externalities. There is, however, an understanding of conventional morality.
3	Conventional	Individuals define morality in reference to what is expected by those with whom they have close relationships. Emphasis of this stage is on stereotypic roles (good mother, father, sister). Virtue is achieved through maintaining trusting and loyal relationships.
4	Conventional	In this stage, the individual shifts from basically narrow local norms and role expectations to a larger social system perspective. Social responsibilities and observance of laws are key aspects of social responsibility. Individuals in this stage reflect higher levels of abstraction in understanding laws' significance. Individuals at Stage 4 have a sophisticated understanding of the law and only violate laws when they conflict with social duties. Observance of the law is seen as necessary to maintain the protections that the legal system provides to all.
5	Post-conventional	The individual becomes aware that while rules and laws exist for the good of the greatest number, there are times when they will work against the interest of particular individuals. Issues may not always be clear-cut and the individual may have to decide to disregard some rules or laws in order to uphold a higher good (such as the protection of life).
6	Post-conventional	Individuals have developed their own set of moral guidelines, which may or may not fit with the law. Principles such as human rights, justice, and equality apply to everyone and the individual must be prepared to act to defend these principles, even if it means going against the rest of society and paying the consequences (i.e., disapproval or imprisonment). Kohlberg believed very few, if any, people reached this stage.

PARENTING STYLES

Although children are born with their own temperament, the parenting style they grow up with can influence how this temperament manifests over time.

Authoritarian (autocratic) parents desire obedience without question. They tend toward harsh punishments, using their power to make their children obey. They are emotionally withdrawn from their children and enforce strict rules without discussing why the rules exist. These children tend to have low self-esteem, be more dependent, and are introverted with poor social skills.

28

Authoritative (democratic) parents provide boundaries and expect obedience, but use love when they discipline. They involve their children in deciding rules and consequences, discussing reasons for their decisions, but they will still enforce the rules consistently. They encourage independence and take each child's unique position seriously. These children tend to have higher self-esteem, good social skills, and confidence in themselves.

Indulgent (permissive) parents stay involved with their children, but have few rules in place to give the children boundaries. These children have a difficult time setting their own limits and are not responsible. They disrespect others and have trouble with authority figures.

Indifferent (uninvolved) parents spend as little time as possible with their children. They are self-involved, with no time or patience for taking care of their children's needs. Guidance and discipline are lacking and inconsistent. These children tend toward delinquency, with a lack of respect for others.

ATTACHMENT AND BONDING

Attachment is the emotional bond that develops between an infant and parent/caregiver when the infant responds to the nonverbal communication of the parent/caregiver and develops a sense of trust and security as the infant's needs are met. Nonverbal communication includes eye contact, calm and attentive facial expressions, tender tone of voice, touch, and body language.

Bonding is especially important during the child's first 3 years, and the failure to develop an attachment bond may impact the child's development and the family dynamics. Infants that have bonded generally exhibit stranger anxiety at about 6 months and separation anxiety by one year. While the parent/caregiver can nurture the emotional connection with the child at later ages, those infants who failed to attach in the first year may have increased difficulty doing so later. Children who have bonded with parents/caregivers tend to develop according to expectations, meeting expected milestones, while those who are deprived may exhibit growth and development delays as well as poor feeding.

> **Review Video: Factors in Development**
> Visit mometrix.com/academy and enter code: 112169

LEARNING THEORY AND BEHAVIOR MODIFICATION
PAVLOV'S WORK

Pavlov learned to link experimentally manipulated stimuli (or conditioned stimuli) to existing natural, unconditioned stimuli that elicited a fixed, **unconditioned response**. Pavlov accomplished this by introducing the **conditioned response** just prior to the natural, unconditioned stimulus. Just before giving a dog food (an autonomic stimulus for salivation), Pavlov sounded a bell. The bell then became the stimulus for salivation, even in the absence of food being given. Many conditioned responses can be created through continuing reinforcement.

SKINNER'S WORK

B. F. Skinner developed the **empty organism concept**, which proposes that an infant has the capacity for action built into their physical makeup. The infant also has reflexes and motivations that will set this capacity in random motion. Skinner asserted that the **law of effect** governs development. Behavior of children is shaped largely by adults. Behaviors that result in satisfying consequences are likely to be repeated under similar circumstances. Halting or discontinuing behavior is accomplished by denying satisfying rewards or through punishment. Skinner also theorized about **schedules of reinforcement**. He posited that rather than reinforcing every instance of a correct response, one can reinforce a fixed percentage of correct responses, or space reinforcements according to some interval of time. Intermittent reinforcement will reinforce the desired behavior.

FEMINIST THEORY

Feminist theory views inequity in terms of gender with females as victims of an almost universal patriarchal model in which the sociopolitical, family, and religious institutions are dominated by males. Proponents of feminist theory focus on areas of interest to females, including social and economic inequality, power structures, gender discrimination, racial discrimination, and gender oppression. Feminists often point to the exclusion of women in the development of theories about human behavior, research, and other academic matters. Some feminists believe that oppression of women is inherent to capitalism, where females are often paid less than males, but others believe that it is inherent in all forms of government because they are all based on patriarchal models. Feminists recognize that gender, social class, and race are all sources of oppression with ethnic minorities and those in the lower social classes often suffering the most oppression. Feminists note that the idea that families headed by women are dysfunctional is based on patriarchal ideals.

CAROL GILLIGAN'S MORALITY OF CARE

Carol Gilligan's morality of care is the feminist response to Kohlberg's moral development theory. Kohlberg's theory was based on research only on men. Gilligan purports that a morality of care reflects women's experience more accurately than one emphasizing justice and rights. Key concepts include the following:

- **Morality of care** reflects caring, responsibility, and non-violence, while **morality of justice and rights** emphasizes equality.
- The two types of moralities give two distinct charges, to not treat others unfairly (justice/rights) and to not turn away from someone in need (care). Care stresses interconnectedness and nurturing. Emphasizing justice stems from a focus on individualism.
- **Aspects of attachment**: Justice/rights requires individuation and separation from the parent, which leads to awareness of power differences. Care emphasizes a continuing attachment to parent and less awareness of inequalities, not a primary focus on fairness.

OLDER ADULTHOOD

HOW THE ELDERLY DEAL WITH LIFE TRANSITIONS

Typically, the elderly population seeks to cope with whatever problem comes their way without the benefit of mental health care. In 1991, Butler and Lewis developed a definition for **loss** in relation to the elderly. Elderly can experience a range of emotions whenever loss or death occurs. Examples of loss could be loss of friends, loss of significant others or spouse, a loss of social roles within the community, a loss of work or career, a loss of a prestigious role, a loss of income, a loss of physical vigor, or a loss of health. Some may experience personality changes or changes in sexual appetites. Elderly people may have a situational crisis that puts a strain on their resources. The resiliency of this population is evident by the large number of seniors who live independently with only a little support. Only 4-6% live in nursing homes or assisted living facilities, and 10-15% receive homecare.

FACTORS PREVENTING THE ELDERLY FROM RECEIVING MENTAL HEALTH SERVICES

While mental illness is often overestimated in the elderly population, it is still prevalent, with one in five elderly individuals experiencing some sort of mental illness. The most significant **mental illnesses** experienced by the elderly are anxiety, severe cognitive impairment, and mood disorders. Anxiety is the most prevalent of these problems. These numbers may be skewed by the fact that the elderly may not be seeking help when needed. Sadly, suicide rates are higher in this population than in any other population. The older a person gets, the higher the rate of suicide. Anxiety and depression cause much suffering in the elderly.

There are a number of factors that **prevent the elderly from receiving mental health services**. Part of the problem lies in the strong values which guide the elderly to solve their own problems. Other seniors feel they should keep quiet about private issues. Still others feel a negative connotation from past stigmas attached to those who needed mental health care. Baby boomers approaching old age have been bombarded with literature on psychology and healthy lifestyles. Therefore, the baby boomer generation may take on a healthier attitude about receiving the appropriate mental health care for their needs. A limited number of counselors,

social workers and therapists are trained in geriatric care. Providers for the elderly have difficulties working with payment policies and insurance companies. In addition, seeing the client's aging problems may cause unpleasant personal issues about aging to surface for the provider.

Human Behavior in the Social Environment

PERSON-IN-ENVIRONMENT THEORY

The **person-in-environment** theory considers the influence the client has on their environment and the influence that multiple environments (social, economic, family, political, cultural, religious, work, ethnic, life events) have on the client. This is an interactive model that is central to many professional helping relationships and recognizes the impact of oppression and discrimination on the client. The person-in-environment theory supports the goals of providing personal care for the client and furthering the cause of social justice. The person-in-environment theory is the basis for the strengths-based perspective in which the initial focus is placed on the personal strengths of the client and the strengths within the client's environment. It involves utilizing psychosocial interventions and assessing behavior on the basis of interactions between the client and the environment because the client's life situation results from the relationship between the client and the environment.

HILDEGARD PEPLAU'S THEORY OF INTERPERSONAL RELATIONS

Hildegard Peplau developed the theory of interpersonal relations in 1952, applying Sullivan's theory of anxiety to nursing practice, developing a framework for psychiatric nursing. The model, however, can be applied to other helping disciplines. The relationship comprises the helping professional (counselor, social worker, or nurse) who has expertise and the individual (client or patient) who wants relief from suffering/problems.

According to Peplau, the professional-individual relationship evolves through 4 phases:

Phase	Details
Preorientation	The helping professional prepares, anticipating possible reactions and interventions.
Orientation	Roles and responsibilities are clarified in the initial interview.
Working	The professional and individual explore together and promote the individual's problem-solving skills.
Termination	The final phase consists of summarizing and reviewing.

The helping professional uses process recording, which includes observing, interpreting, and intervening to help the client, but also self-observation to increase self-awareness. Peplau believed that individuals deserved human care by educated helpers and should be treated with dignity and respect. She also believed that the environment (social, psychosocial, and physical) could affect the individual in a positive or negative manner. The helping professional can focus on the way in which clients react to their problems and can help them to use those problems as an opportunity for learning and maturing.

SYSTEMS THEORY

Systems theory derives its theoretical orientation from general systems theory and includes elements of organizational theory, family theory, group behavior theory, and a variety of sociological constructs. Key **principles** include the following:

- Systems theory endeavors to provide a methodological view of the world by synthesizing key principles from its theoretical roots.
- A fundamental premise is that key sociological aspects of clients, families, and groups cannot be separated from the whole (i.e., aspects that are systemic in nature).
- All systems are interrelated, and change in one will produce change in the others.
- Systems are either open or closed: Open systems accept outside input and accommodate, while closed systems resist outside input due to rigid and impenetrable barriers and boundaries.
- Boundaries are lines of demarcation identifying the outer margins of the system being examined.
- Entropy refers to the process of system dissolution or disorganization.
- Homeostatic balance refers to the propensity of systems to reestablish and maintain stability.

ECOSYSTEMS THEORY

Ecosystems (or life model) theory derives its theoretical orientation from ecology, systems theory, psychodynamic theory, behavioral theory, and cognitive theory. Key principles include the following:

- There is an interactive relationship between all living organisms and their environment (both social and physical).
- The process of adaptation is universal and is a reciprocal process by individuals and environments mutually accommodating each other to obtain a "goodness of fit."
- Changes in individuals, their environments, or both can be disruptive and produce dysfunction.
- This theory works to optimize goodness of fit by modifying perceptions, thoughts, responsiveness, and exchanges between clients and their environments.
- On a larger (community) level, treatment interventions by the ecosystems approach are drawn from direct practice and include educating, identifying and expanding resources, developing needed policies and programs, and engaging governmental systems to support requisite change.

IMPACT OF FAMILY ON HUMAN BEHAVIOR
FAMILY TYPES

A **family** consists of a group of people that are connected by marriage, blood relationship, or emotions. There are many different variations when referring to the concept of family.

- The **nuclear family** is one in which two or more people are related by blood, marriage, or adoption. This type of family is typically parents and their children.
- The **extended family** is one in which several nuclear families related by blood or marriage function as one group.
- In a **single-parent structure**, there is only one parent caring for the children in the household.
- In a **blended family**, a parent marries or remarries after they have already had children. Blended families are often referred to as stepfamilies because they consist of a parent, a stepparent, and one or more children.

A **household** consists of an individual or group of people residing together under one roof. The level of interaction with a client's family can range from having essentially no relationship with them to developing a close working relationship with them.

FUNCTIONAL FAMILY

A functional family will be able to change roles, responsibilities, and interactions during a stressful event. This type of family can experience **nonfunctional behaviors** if placed in an acute stressful event; however, they should be able to reestablish their family balance over a period of time. The functional family will have the ability to deal with **conflict and change** in order to deal with negative situations without causing long-term dysfunction or dissolution of the family. They will have completed vital life cycle tasks, keep emotional contact between family members and across generations, over-closeness is avoided, and distance is used to resolve issues. When two members of the family have a conflict, they are expected to **resolve** this conflict between themselves and there is **open communication** between all family members. Children of a functional family are expected to achieve age-appropriate functioning and are given age-appropriate privileges.

FAMILY LIFE CYCLE

The family life cycle comprises the states typical individuals go through from childhood to old age. Stages include:

Stage	Details
Independence	Individuals begin to separate from the family unit and develop a sense of their place in the world. Individuals may begin to explore careers and become increasingly independent in providing for self needs. Individuals often develop close peer relationships outside of the family.
Coupling	Individuals develop intimate relationships with others and may live together or marry, moving toward interdependence, joint goal setting and problem-solving. Individuals learn new communication skills and may have to adjust expectations.
Parenting	Individuals make the decision to have or adopt children and adjust their lives and roles accordingly. Relationships may change and be tested, and parents may shift focus from themselves to their children.
Empty nest	Individuals may feel profound loss and stress at this change, especially since this is also the time when health problems of age and the need to care for parents arise. Relationships with children evolve.
Retirement	Individuals may undergo many changes and challenges and must deal with deaths of family and friends and their own mortality.

CHANGE IN FAMILY ROLES OF MEN AND WOMEN IN UNITED STATES

The family roles of men and women in the United States have changed drastically over the past several decades. Women were traditionally the primary caretakers of children, so they were expected to maintain the household while the men worked to provide for the family. However, this is no longer the case, as there has been a drastic increase in the number of women entering the work force in the recent years. This change is partially due to the fact that it has become more difficult for families to live off of one income. It can be extremely difficult for a family to find the time and money to care for a child, especially if that child has a disability, because both parents are typically required to work.

HOW A FAMILY AIDS THE DEVELOPMENT, EDUCATION, AND FUNCTION OF ITS MEMBERS

A family can aid the development, education, and function of its members in two major ways. First, parents and grandparents typically pass their heritage down to their children and teach them what is considered acceptable through their actions, customs, and traditions. In other words, a person typically acquires culture through their family, and that culture helps the person function in society and interact socially with other people. Second, a person's family can act as an effective support network in many situations. A family may be able to provide some of the emotional, financial, or other types of support a person needs.

EFFECTS OF MENTAL ILLNESS ON FAMILY

Families with a member that has a **chronic mental illness** will provide several functions that those without mentally ill members may not need. These functions can include providing support and information for care and treatment options. They will also monitor the services provided the family member and address concerns with these services. Many times, the family is the biggest **advocate** for additional availability of services for mental health clients. There can often be disagreements between the care providers and the family members concerning the dependence of the client within the family. Parents can often be viewed as overprotective when attempting to encourage a client's independence and self-reliant functioning. They will need support and reassurance if the client leaves home. On the other hand, many parents will provide for their child for as long as they live. Once the primary care provider dies, the client may be left with no one to care for them and they may experience traumatic disruptions.

34

INCONGRUOUS HIERARCHY

An incongruous hierarchy is a family relationship in which a minor figure controls the family dynamic. The control engine may be the exhibition of inappropriate behavior at crucial times. It is a "tail wags the dog" type of scenario. A child throws an entire family into turmoil by ranting and throwing a fit each evening at bedtime. The child's father reacts by attempting to soothe her, offering her candy and letting her stay up late. The child's mother is angry with the father for doing so, and begins shouting at him and withholding affection. An older brother loses sleep because of the daily hysterics, and subsequently performs poorly in school. This type of family dysfunction is called incongruous hierarchy.

FAMILY VIOLENCE

Family violence can include physical, emotional, sexual, or verbal behaviors that occur between members of the same family or others living within the home. This behavior can include both abuse and neglect and involve the elderly, spouses, and children. Family violence is often kept a secret and may be the main issue with many family problems. Many times, actions that would be considered unacceptable to strangers or friends are often the norm between family members. Violence and abuse occur due to the unique interactions between the family members based upon personality differences, situational variations, and sociocultural influences.

CHARACTERISTICS OF VIOLENT FAMILIES

Violent families will often share many of the same characteristics. Many times, the abusive family member will have suffered abuse from their family while growing up. This type of abuse is a **multigenerational transmission** and is a cycle of violence. These abusers have learned to believe that violent behavior is a way to solve problems. Violent families are also usually socially isolated so that others such as friends, teachers, neighbors, or law enforcement officials do not become aware that the abuse is occurring. The abuser will also use and abuse power to **control** the victim. They may be considered a person of authority, such as a parent would be to a child. Power is a very important factor with abuse of an intimate partner. The abuser is often very controlling of their partner and will attempt to dominate every aspect of their life. Another commonality among abusers is **substance abuse**; however, one is not dependent upon the other. Many times, the use of alcohol or drugs may escalate violent behaviors by decreasing inhibitions.

FAMILY LIFE EDUCATION

Family life education, which can include parenting and financial management classes, aims to give people the information and tools they need in order to strengthen family life. Approaches to family life education include:

- **Strength-based**: Assisting clients to identify their strengths and those of their environment in order to increase their sense of personal power and engagement.
- **Cultural**: Focusing on cultural norms and the diverse needs of different populations as well as utilizing communication and activities that correspond to different cultures.
- **Selective**: Aiming at specific groups, such as LGBTQ parents or grandparents, in order to ascertain their unique needs and to provide appropriate education. Some programs may be designed for at-risk groups, such as those in court-ordered education programs because of abuse or neglect.
- **Universal**: Universal education focuses on all members of a particular population, such as all parents, despite differences among the parents. These programs often focus on general information, such as growth and development, and cover a range of topics.

DEVELOPMENTAL MODEL OF COUPLES THERAPY

The developmental model of couples therapy (Bader & Pearson) accepts the inevitable change in relationships and focuses on both individual and couple growth and development. The goal is to assist the couple to

35

recognize their stage of development and to gain the skills and insight needed to progress to the next stage. Problems may especially arise if members of the couple are at different stages. Stages include:

Stage	Details
Bonding	Couples meet, develop a romantic relationship, and fall in love, focusing on similarities rather than differences. Sexual intimacy is an important component.
Differentiating	Conflicts and differences begin to arise, and couples must learn to work together to resolve their problems.
Practicing	Couples become more independent from each other, establish outside friendships, and develop outside interests.
Rapprochement	Couples move apart and then together again, often increasing intimacy and feeling more satisfied with the relationship.
Synergy	Couples become more intimate and recognize the strength of their union.

ANNA FREUD'S DEFENSE MECHANISMS

According to Anna Freud, defense mechanisms are an unconscious process in which the ego attempts to expel anxiety-provoking sexual and aggressive impulses from consciousness. Defense mechanisms are attempts to protect the self from painful anxiety and are used universally. In themselves they are not an indication of pathology, but rather an indication of disturbance when their cost outweighs their protective value. Anna Freud proposed that defense mechanisms serve to protect the ego and to reduce angst, fear, and distress through irrational distortion, denial, and/or obscuring reality. Defense mechanisms are deployed when the ego senses the threat of harm from thoughts or acts incongruent with rational behavior or conduct demanded by the super-ego.

The following are terms that pertain to **Anna Freud's defense mechanisms**:

Compensation	Protection against feelings of inferiority and inadequacy stemming from real or imagined personal defects or weaknesses.
Conversion	Somatic changes conveyed in symbolic body language; psychic pain is felt in a part of the body.
Denial	Avoidance of awareness of some painful aspect of reality.
Displacement	Investing repressed feelings in a substitute object.
Association	Altruism; acquiring gratification through connection with and helping another person who is satisfying the same instincts.
Identification	Manner by which one becomes like another person in one or more respects; a more elaborate process than introjection.
Identification with the Aggressor	A child's introjection of some characteristic of an anxiety evoking object and assimilation of an anxiety experience just lived through. In this, the child can transform from the threatened person into the one making the threat.
Introjection	Absorbing an idea or image so that it becomes part of oneself.
Inversion	Turning against the self; object of aggressive drive is changed from another to the self, especially in depression and masochism.
Isolation of Affect	Separation of ideas from the feelings originally associated with them. Remaining idea is deprived of motivational force; action is impeded and guilt avoided.
Intellectualization	Psychological binding of instinctual drives in intellectual activities, for example the adolescent's preoccupation with philosophy and religion.
Projection	Ascribing a painful idea or impulse to the external world.
Rationalization	Effort to give a logical explanation for painful unconscious material to avoid guilt and shame.
Reaction Formation	Replacing in conscious awareness a painful idea or feeling with its opposite.
Regression	Withdrawal to an earlier phase of psychosexual development.
Repression	The act of obliterating material from conscious awareness. This is capable of mastering powerful impulses.
Reversal	Type of reaction formation aimed at protection from painful thoughts/feelings.
Splitting	Seeing external objects as either all good or all bad. Feelings may rapidly shift from one category to the other.
Sublimation	Redirecting energies of instinctual drives to generally positive goals that are more acceptable to the ego and superego.
Substitution	Trading of one affect for another (e.g., rage that masks fear)
Undoing	Ritualistically performing the opposite of an act one has recently carried out in order to cancel out or balance the evil that may have been present in the act.

Sexual Orientation

SEXUALITY

Sexuality is an integral part of each individual's personality and refers to all aspects of being a sexual human. It is more than just the act of physical intercourse. A person's sexuality is often apparent in what they do, in their appearance, and in how they interact with others. There are four main aspects of sexuality:

- **Genetic identity** or one's chromosomal gender
- **Gender identification** or how one perceives oneself with regard to male or female
- **Gender role** or the attributes of one's cultural role
- **Sexual orientation** or the gender to which one is attracted

Assessing and attempting to conceptualize a person's sexuality will lead to a broader understanding of the client's beliefs and allow for a more holistic approach to providing care.

GENDER IDENTITY

Gender identity is the gender to which the individual identifies, which may or may not be the gender of birth (natal gender). Most children begin to express identification and behaviors associated with gender between ages 2 and 4. The degree to which this identification is influenced by genetics and environment is an ongoing debate because, for example, female children are often socialized toward female roles (dresses, dolls, pink items). Societal pressure to conform to gender stereotypes is strong, so gender dysphoria, which is less common in early childhood than later, may be suppressed. At the onset of puberty, sexual attraction may further complicate gender identity although those with gender dysphoria most often have sexual attraction to those of the same natal gender, so a natal boy who identifies as a girl is more likely to be sexually attracted to boys than to girls. Later in adolescence, individuals generally experiment with sexual behavior and solidify their gender identity.

INFLUENCE OF SEXUAL ORIENTATION ON BEHAVIORS

The degree to which sexual orientation influences behavior may vary widely depending on the individual. For example, some gay males may be indistinguishable in appearance and general behavior from heterosexual males while others may behave in a stereotypically flamboyant manner. The same holds true for lesbians, with some typically feminine in appearance and behavior and others preferring a more masculine appearance. The typical heterosexual model (two people in a stable relationship) is increasingly practiced by homosexual couples while others prefer less traditional practices. Depending on the degree of acceptance that LGBTQ individuals encounter, they may hide their sexual orientation or maintain a heterosexual relationship in order to appear straight. LGBTQ individuals are at higher risk of depression and suicide, especially if they experience rejection because of their sexual orientation or have been taught that it is sinful. LGBTQ individuals with multiple sexual partners (especially males) are at increased risk for STIs, including HIV/AIDS.

COMING OUT PROCESS

The coming out process is the act of revealing LGBTQ sexual orientation to family and friends. This generally occurs during adolescence or early adulthood although some may delay coming out for decades or never do so. Individuals may come out to select groups of people. For example, friends may be aware of an individual's orientation but not family or co-workers. Coming out can be frightening for many people, especially if they have reason to fear rejection or fear for their safety. Stages in coming out typically progress in the following order:

Stage	Actions and feelings involved
Confusion	The individual may be unsure of feelings or be in denial.
Exploration	The individual begins to question orientation and wonder about LGBTQ people.

Stage	Actions and feelings involved
Breakthrough	The individual accepts the likelihood of being LGBTQ and seeks others of the same orientation.
Acceptance	The individual accepts orientation and begins to explore and read about the LGBTQ culture.
Pride	The individual begins to exhibit pride in orientation and may reject straight culture or exhibit stereotypically LGBTQ behaviors.
Synthesis	The individual comes to terms with the reality of the LGBTQ orientation, is at peace with their identity, and is generally out to family, friends, and co-workers.

PRACTICE ISSUES WHEN WORKING WITH LGBTQ CLIENTS

Possible practice issues with LGBTQ clients include, but are not limited to, the following:

- Stigmatization and violence
- Internalized homophobia
- Coming out
- AIDS
- Limited civil rights
- Orientation vs. preference (biology vs. choice)

Problematic treatment models for treating gay and lesbian people include the following:

- The moral model for treatment is religiously oriented and views homosexuality as sinful.
- Reparative or conversion psychotherapy focuses on changing a person's sexual orientation to heterosexual. Traditional mental health disciplines view this type of treatment as unethical and as having no empirical base.

Self-Image

FACTORS INFLUENCING SELF-IMAGE

Factors influencing self-image include the following:

- **Spirituality**: Religious or spiritual beliefs may affect how individuals see their place in the world and their self-confidence. Individuals may gain self-esteem through secure beliefs and membership in a like group, but belief systems with a strong emphasis on sin may impair self-image.
- **Culture**: Individuals are affected (negatively and positively) by cultural expectations, especially if they feel outside of the norm.
- **Ethnicity**: Whether or not the individual is part of the dominant ethnic group may have a profound effect on self-image. Minority groups often suffer discrimination that reinforces the idea that they are less valuable than others.
- **Education**: Those with higher levels of education tend to have a better self-image than those without, sometimes because of greater unemployment and fewer opportunities associated with low education.
- **Gender**: Society often reinforces the value of males (straight) over females and LGBTQ individuals.
- **Abuse**: Those who are abused may often develop a poor self-image, believing they are deserving of abuse.
- **Media**: The media reinforces stereotypes and presents unrealistic (and unattainable) images, affecting self-image.

BODY IMAGE

Body image is the perception individuals have of their own bodies, positive or negative. An altered body image may result in a number of responses, most often beginning during adolescence but sometimes during childhood:

- **Obesity**: Some may be unhappy with their body image and overeat as a response, often increasing their discontent.
- **Eating disorders**: Some may react to being overweight or to the cultural ideal by developing anorexia or bulimia in an attempt to achieve the idealized body image they seek. They may persist even though they put their lives at risk. Their body image may be so distorted that they believe they are fat even when emaciated.
- **Body dysmorphic disorder**: Some may develop a preoccupation with perceived defects in their body image, such as a nose that is too big or breasts or penis that is too small. Individuals may become obsessed to the point that they avoid social contact with others, stop participating in sports, get poor grades, stop working, or seek repeated plastic surgery.

Stress, Crisis, and Trauma

STRESS

RELATIONSHIP BETWEEN STRESS AND DISEASE

Stress causes a number of physical and psychological changes within the body, including the following:

- Cortisol levels increase
- Digestion is hindered and the colon stimulated
- Heart rate increases
- Perspiration increases
- Anxiety and depression occur and can result in insomnia, anorexia or weight gain, and suicide
- Immune response decreases, making the person more vulnerable to infections
- Autoimmune reaction may increase, leading to autoimmune diseases

The body's **compensatory mechanisms** try to restore homeostasis. When these mechanisms are overwhelmed, pathophysiological injury to the cells of the body result. When this injury begins to interfere with the function of the organs or systems in the body, symptoms of dysfunction will occur. If the conditions are not corrected, the body changes the structure or function of the affected organs or systems.

PSYCHOLOGICAL RESPONSE TO STRESS

When stress is encountered, a person responds according to the threat perceived in order to compensate. The threat is evaluated as to the amount of harm or loss that has occurred or is possible. If the stress is benign (typical day-to-day burdens or life transitions) then a challenge is present that demands change. Once the threat or challenge is defined, the person can gather information, resources, and support to make the changes needed to resolve the stress to the greatest degree possible. Immediate psychological response to stress may include shock, anger, fear, or excitement. Over time, people may develop chronic anxiety, depression, flashbacks, thought disturbances, and sleep disturbances. Changes may occur in emotions and thinking, in behavior, or in the person's environment. People may be more able to adapt to stress if they have many varied experiences, good self-esteem, and a support network to help as needed. A healthy lifestyle and philosophical beliefs, including religion, may give a person more reserve to cope with stress.

IMPACT OF DIFFERENT KINDS OF STRESS

Everyone encounters stress in life and it impacts each person differently. There are the small daily hassles, major traumatic events, and the periodic stressful events of marriage, birth, divorce, and death. Of these stressors, the daily stress that a person encounters is the one that changes the health status over time. Stressors that occur suddenly are the hardest to overcome and result in the greatest tension. The length of time that a stressor is present also affects its impact, with long-term, relentless stress, such as that generated by poverty or disability, resulting in disease more often. If there is **ineffective coping**, a person will suffer greater changes resulting in even more stress. The solution is to help clients to recognize those things that induce stress in their lives, find ways to reduce stress when possible, and teach effective coping skills and problem-management.

CRISIS

CHARACTERISTICS OF A CRISIS

A crisis occurs when a person is faced with a highly stressful event and their usual problem solving and coping skills fail to be effective in resolving the situation. This event usually leads to increased levels of anxiety and can bring about a physical and psychological response. The problem is usually an acute event that can be identified. It may have occurred a few weeks or even months before or immediately prior to the crisis and can be an actual event or a potential event. The crisis state usually lasts less than six weeks with the individual then becoming able to utilize problem solving skills to cope effectively. A person in crisis mode does not always

41

have a mental disorder. However, during the acute crisis their social functioning and decision-making abilities may be impaired.

TYPES OF CRISES

DEVELOPMENTAL

There are basically two different types of crises. These types include developmental or maturational crisis and situational crisis. A **developmental crisis** can occur during maturation when an individual must take on a new life role. This crisis can be a normal part of the developmental process. A youth may need to face and resolve crisis to be able to move on to the next developmental stage. This may occur during the process of moving from adolescence to adulthood. Examples of situations that could lead to this type of crisis include graduating from school, going away to college, or moving out on their own. These situations would cause the individual to face a maturing event that requires the development of new coping skills.

SITUATIONAL

The second type of crisis is the **situational crisis**. This type of crisis can occur at any time in life. There is usually an event or problem that occurs, which leads to a disruption in normal psychological functioning. These types of events are often unplanned and can occur with or without warning. Some examples that may lead to a situational crisis include the death of a loved one, divorce, unplanned or unwanted pregnancy, onset or change in a physical disease process, job loss, or being the victim of a violent act. Events that affect an entire community can also cause an individual situational crisis. Terrorist attacks or weather-related disasters are examples of events that can affect an entire community.

COLLECTING A TRAUMA HISTORY

A trauma history should be collected from any client with a known history of physical/emotional abuse, accident involvement, or signs/symptoms of PTSD from known or unknown events. There are several methods of trauma history collection:

- **Trauma History Screen (THS)**: The client self-reports (via questionnaire) by responding with "Yes" or "No" to 14 event types and includes the number of times the event occurred. These events include abuse, accidents/natural disasters, military service, loss of loved ones, and life crises/transitions. Next, the client is prompted to respond to the question, "Did any of these things really bother you emotionally?" If the client responds with "Yes," they are then instructed to provide details about every event that bothered them.
- **Trauma History Questionnaire (THQ)**: Similar to the THS, this questionnaire requires the client to self-report experiences with 24 potentially traumatic events, and then to provide the frequency and details of each experience.

Grief

IMPACT OF GRIEF ON THE INDIVIDUAL

Grief is an emotional response to loss that begins at the time a loss is anticipated and continues on an individual timetable. While there are identifiable stages of grief, it is not an orderly and predictable process. It involves overcoming anger, disbelief, guilt, and a myriad of related emotions. The grieving individual may move back and forth between stages or experience several emotions at any given time. Each person's grief response is unique to their own coping patterns, stress levels, age, gender, belief system, and previous experiences with loss.

KUBLER-ROSS'S FIVE STAGES OF GRIEF

Kubler-Ross taught the medical community that the dying person and their family welcome open, honest discussion of the dying process. She believed that there were certain stages that people go through while experiencing grief. The stages may not occur in order; they may occur out of order, some may be skipped, and some may occur more than once. **Kubler Ross's stages of grief** include the following:

- **Denial**: The person denies the loss and tries to pretend it isn't true. During this time, the person may seek a second opinion or alternative therapies (in the case of a terminal diagnosis) or act as though the loss never occurred. They may use denial until they are better able to emotionally cope with the reality of the loss or changes that need to be made.
- **Anger**: The person is angry about the situation and may focus that rage on anyone or anything.
- **Bargaining**: The person attempts to make deals with a higher power to secure a better outcome to their situation.
- **Depression**: The person anticipates the loss and the changes it will bring with a sense of sadness and grief.
- **Acceptance**: The person accepts the loss and is ready to face it. They may begin to withdraw from interests and family.

> **Review Video: The Five Stages of Grief**
> Visit mometrix.com/academy and enter code: 648794

ANTICIPATORY GRIEF

Anticipatory grief is the mental, social, and somatic reactions of an individual as they prepare themselves for a perceived future loss. The individual experiences a process of intellectual, emotional, and behavioral responses in order to modify their self-concept, based on their perception of what the potential loss will mean in their life. This process often takes place ahead of the actual loss, from the time the loss is first perceived until it is resolved as a reality for the individual. This process can also blend with past loss experiences. It is associated with the individual's perception of how life will be affected by the particular diagnosis as well as the impending death. Acknowledging this anticipatory grief allows family members to begin looking toward a changed future. Suppressing this anticipatory process may inhibit relationships with the ill individual and contribute to a more difficult grieving process at a later time. However, appropriate anticipatory grieving does not take the place of grief during the actual time of death.

DISENFRANCHISED GRIEF

Disenfranchised grief occurs when the loss being experienced cannot be openly acknowledged, publicly mourned, or socially supported. Society and culture are partly responsible for an individual's response to a loss. There is a social context to grief. If a person incurring the loss will be putting himself or herself at risk by expressing grief, disenfranchised grief occurs. The risk for disenfranchised grief is greatest among those whose relationship with the thing they lost was not known or regarded as significant. This is also the situation found among bereaved persons who are not recognized by society as capable of grief, such as young children, or needing to mourn, such as an ex-spouse or secret lover.

43

GRIEF VS. DEPRESSION

Normal grief is self-limiting to the loss itself. Emotional responses will vary and may include open expressions of anger. The individual may experience difficulty sleeping or vivid dreams, a lack of energy, and weight loss. Crying is evident and provides some relief of extreme emotions. The individual remains socially responsive and seeks reassurance from others.

By contrast, **depression** is marked by extensive periods of sadness and preoccupation often extending beyond two months. It is not limited to the single event. There is an absence of pleasure or anger and isolation from previous social support systems. The individual can experience extreme lethargy, weight loss, insomnia, or hypersomnia. Crying is absent or persistent and provides no relief of emotions. Professional intervention is often required to relieve depression.

Concepts of Abuse

CHILD ABUSE
PHYSICAL ABUSE OF CHILDREN

Physical abuse of children is most often in the form of extreme physical discipline that exceeds normative community standards.

Physical indicators of physical abuse:
- Bruises or broken bones on an infant that lack an adequate explanation or that occur in unusual places
- Lacerations
- Fractures
- Burns in odd patterns
- Head injuries
- Internal injuries
- Open sores
- Untreated wounds or illnesses

Behavioral indicators of physical abuse:
- Child may be overly compliant, passive, or undemanding
- Child may be overly aggressive, demanding, or hostile
- Role reversal behavior
- Extremely dependent behavior (increased parental, emotional, and physical needs)
- Developmental delays

SEXUAL ABUSE

Sexual abuse is defined as inappropriate and unsolicited sexual contact, molestation, or rape. Common **signs of sexual abuse** include:

- Genital injuries (abrasions, bruises, scars, tears, etc.)
- Blood in the underwear (from vaginal or rectal injuries)
- Complaints of genital discomfort or excessive grabbing of the genital area
- Any diagnosis of a sexually transmitted infection
- Frequent urinary tract and bladder infections
- Complaints of stomachache when coupled with other signs
- Abrasions or bruises to the thighs and legs
- Enuresis (bed-wetting) or encopresis (fecal soiling)
- Behavioral disturbances (acting out, self-destructive behavior, overly precocious or aggressive sexual behavior, promiscuity, etc.)
- Depression
- Eating disorders
- Fears and phobias
- Dissociation
- Any unexplained or sudden appearance of money, toys, or gifts

CHILD NEGLECT

Child neglect is the failure of a child's parent or caretaker (who has the resources) to provide minimally adequate healthcare, nutrition, shelter, education, supervision, affection, or attention. Also included in the definition of child neglect is the insufficient encouragement to attend school with consistency, exploitation by forcing to work too hard or long, or exposure to unwholesome or demoralizing circumstances.

Indicators of child neglect include the following:

- Abandonment
- Absence of sufficient adult supervision
- Inadequate clothing
- Poor hygiene

- Lack of sufficient medical/dental care
- Inadequate education
- Inadequate supervision
- Inadequate shelter
- Consistent failure, unwillingness, or inability to correct these indicators on the part of the caretaker

ELDERLY AND DISABLED NEGLECT AND ABUSE

The elderly and disabled are at risk for neglect and abuse when they have impaired mental processes or physical deficits that affect their ability to carry out activities of daily living. They are also at risk when there are caregiver problems such as:

- High amount of stress
- Substance abuse
- Physically abusive or violent
- Emotionally unstable or with mental illness
- Dependency on the elderly or disabled person for money, emotional support, or physical support

The social worker should act to help a caregiver cope more effectively to prevent abuse from occurring by providing an outlet for emotions and referring to resources. It's important to ask clients in private whether anyone prevents them from using medical assistive devices or refuses to help them with their daily activities. However, many will not admit to abuse. If there are risk factors present or signs of abuse, the social worker must act to preserve the safety of the individual. Most states require the reporting of elder abuse and neglect. The social worker should assist the person in accessing resources in the community to improve their living situation.

IDENTIFYING AND REPORTING NEGLECT OF THE BASIC NEEDS OF ADULTS

Neglect of the basic needs of adults is a common problem, especially among the elderly, adults with psychiatric or mental health problems, or those who live alone or with reluctant or incapable caregivers. In some cases, **passive neglect** may occur because an elderly or impaired spouse or partner is trying to take care of a client and is unable to provide the care needed, but in other cases, **active neglect** reflects a lack of caring which may be considered negligence or abuse. Cases of neglect should be reported to the appropriate governmental agency, such as adult protective services. Indications of neglect include the following:

- Lack of assistive devices, such as a cane or walker, needed for mobility
- Misplaced or missing glasses or hearing aids
- Poor dental hygiene and dental care or missing dentures
- Client left unattended for extended periods of time, sometimes confined to a bed or chair
- Client left in soiled or urine- and feces-stained clothing
- Inadequate food, fluid, or nutrition, resulting in weight loss
- Inappropriate and unkempt clothing, such as no sweater or coat during the winter and dirty or torn clothing
- A dirty, messy environment

DOMESTIC VIOLENCE

Men, women, elderly, children, and the disabled may all be victims of **domestic violence**. The violent person harms physically or sexually and uses threats and fear to maintain control of the victim. The violence does not improve unless the abuser gets intensive counseling. The abuser may promise not to do it again, but the violence usually gets more frequent and worsens over time. The social worker should ask all clients in private

46

Copyright © Mometrix Media. You have been licensed one copy of this document for personal use only. Any other reproduction or redistribution is strictly prohibited. All rights reserved. This content is provided for test preparation purposes only and does not imply an endorsement by Mometrix of any particular political, scientific, or religious point of view.

about abuse, neglect, and fear of a caretaker. If abuse is suspected or there are signs present, the state may require reporting. The social worker should support the abused by doing the following:

- Give victims information about community hotlines, shelters, and resources
- Urge them to set up a plan for escape for themselves and any children, complete with supplies in a location away from the home
- Assure victims that they are not at fault and do not deserve the abuse
- Try to empower them by helping them to realize that they do not have to take abuse and can find support to change the situation

> **Review Video: Counseling: Domestic Violence**
> Visit mometrix.com/academy and enter code: 530581

ASSESSMENT OF DOMESTIC VIOLENCE

According to the guidelines of the Family Violence Prevention Fund, assessment for domestic violence should be done for all adolescent and adult clients, regardless of background or signs of abuse. While females are the most common victims, there are increasing reports of male victims of domestic violence, both in heterosexual and homosexual relationships. The person doing the assessment should be informed about domestic violence and be aware of risk factors and danger signs. The interview should be conducted in private (special accommodations may need to be made for children <3 years old). The office, bathrooms, and examining rooms should have information about domestic violence posted prominently. Brochures and information should be available to give to clients. Clients may present with a variety of physical complaints, such as headache, pain, palpitations, numbness, or pelvic pain. They are often depressed, may appear suicidal, and may be isolated from friends and family. Victims of domestic violence often exhibit fear of spouse/partner, and may report injury inconsistent with symptoms.

STEPS TO IDENTIFYING VICTIMS OF DOMESTIC VIOLENCE

The Family Violence Prevention Fund has issued guidelines for identifying and assisting victims of domestic violence. There are seven steps:

1. **Inquiry**: Non-judgmental questioning should begin with asking if the person has ever been abused—physically, sexually, or psychologically.
2. **Interview**: The person may exhibit signs of anxiety or fear and may blame oneself or report that others believe they are abused, but they disagree. The person should be questioned if they are afraid for their life or for their children.
3. **Question**: If the person reports abuse, it's critical to ask if the person is in immediate danger or if the abuser is on the premises. The interviewer should ask if the person has been threatened. The history and pattern of abuse should be questioned and if children are involved, whether the children are abused. Note: State laws vary, and in some states, it is mandatory to report if a child was present during an act of domestic violence as this is considered child abuse. The social worker must be aware of state laws regarding domestic and child abuse. All social workers are mandatory reporters.
4. **Validate**: The interviewer should offer support and reassurance in a non-judgmental manner, telling the client that the abuse is not their fault.
5. **Give information**: While discussing facts about domestic violence and the tendency to escalate, the interviewer should provide brochures and information about safety planning. If the client wants to file a complaint with the police, the interviewer should assist the person to place the call.
6. **Make referrals**: Information about state, local, and national organizations should be provided along with telephone numbers and contact numbers for domestic violence shelters.
7. **Document**: Record keeping should be legal, legible, and lengthy with a complete report and description of any traumatic injuries resulting from domestic violence. A body map may be used to indicate sites of injury, especially if there are multiple bruises or injuries.

INJURIES CONSISTENT WITH DOMESTIC VIOLENCE

There are a number of characteristic injuries that may indicate domestic violence, including the following:

- Ruptured eardrum
- Rectal/genital injury (burns, bites, or trauma)
- Scrapes and bruises about the neck, face, head, trunk, arms
- Cuts, bruises, and fractures of the face.

The pattern of injuries associated with domestic violence is also often distinctive. The bathing-suit pattern involves injuries on parts of body that are usually covered with clothing as the perpetrator inflicts damage but hides evidence of abuse. Head and neck injuries (50%) are also common. Abusive injuries (rarely attributable to accidents) are common and include bites, bruises, rope and cigarette burns, and welts in the outline of weapons (belt marks). Bilateral injuries of arms/legs are often seen with domestic abuse.

Defensive injuries are also indicative of abuse. Defensive injuries to the back of the body are often incurred as the victim crouches on the floor face down while being attacked. The soles of the feet may be injured from kicking at perpetrator. The ulnar aspect of hand or palm may be injured from blocking blows.

MANDATORY REPORTING

MANDATED REPORTING IN CASES OF ABUSE

Social work is one of several professions that are under a **legal mandate to report cases of abuse**. It is not necessary to have witnessed the abuse, nor must one have incontrovertible evidence. Rather, there need only be sufficient cause to **suspect** in order for a report to be required. If the report is made in good faith, the reporting party is immune from liability—both from reporting (should the allegations prove unfounded) and from the liability that would otherwise accrue from any failure to report actual abuse. Abuse may be physical, emotional, sexual, or constitute neglect.

All states mandate the reporting of child abuse, and most mandate the reporting of dependent adult abuse (adults who are developmentally delayed and thus mentally infirm or elderly persons unable to protect themselves due to either physical or mental frailty). Where dependent abuse reporting is not mandated, complex situations may occur. Know state laws and seek advice when necessary.

CONCERNS WHEN REPORTING INCIDENTS OR SUSPICIONS OF SEXUAL ABUSE

The following are concerns when reporting incidents or suspicions of sexual abuse:

- Perpetrators of these crimes can be highly motivated to obtain retractions and may threaten or use violence to do so.
- A major concern in developing immediate and long-term strategies for protection and treatment is the role of the non-abusing parent and their ability to protect the child.
- The victim may be safer if the worker does not notify the family when making the report.
- Great care must be taken by the worker with these cases.

FOLLOWING UP AFTER IDENTIFYING CHILD, DEPENDENT ADULT, OR ELDER ADULT ABUSE

After abuse has been determined, a full report must be made to the appropriate agency, initially by telephone with a written report to follow. For social workers employed by such agencies, a follow-up plan of action must be determined. The level of risk must be evaluated, including the perpetrator's relationship to the victim, prior history of abusive behavior, and severity of harm inflicted, as well as the victim's age, health situation, cognitive capacity and psychological status, available support systems, and capacity for self-protection given that the abuse is now in the open.

Follow-up options include the following:

- Reports for criminal prosecution
- Home visits
- Removal from the home
- Alternative caregiver/guardian appointments through courts, etc.

Safety is the primary concern above all else.

EFFECTS OF ABUSE ON INDIVIDUALS

The effects of abuse may vary widely depending on the type and extent of abuse and the resilience of the victim. Effects may include the following:

Physical	Victims may exhibit bruises, fractures, and pain. Long-term physical impairments from injuries may include disabilities from poorly healed fractures, hearing loss, other injuries, and traumatic brain injuries. Some clients may develop PTSD and remain hypervigilant and fearful.
Psychological	Victims may have little self-esteem and appear withdrawn and depressed or angry and aggressive. Over time, clients may become increasingly depressed and engage in self-destructive or antisocial behavior.
Sexual	Victims may try to hide or avoid sexuality or act overly sexualized. Many suffer from low self-esteem and fear, and some may develop PTSD.
Financial	Victims may feel shame for being taken advantage of or confused about what has happened, but if the financial abuse involves a great loss of savings, some victims may be forced to change their life situations, including housing.
Neglect	Victims may be unkempt, malnourished, unclean, and anxious. Victims may be depressed and fearful and may exhibit hoarding to compensate.

Social and Economic Justice

CHILDREN
CHILDREN IN POVERTY IN THE US

The following are basic facts/statistics relating to children in poverty in the US:

- Almost **one in six** children lives in poverty.
- **Minority** children under age six are much more likely than white children of the same age to live in poverty.
- Many of these children in poverty are **homeless** or are in the **child welfare system**.
- Fewer than one-third of all poor children below age six live solely on **welfare**.
- More than half of children in poverty have at least one **working parent**.
- Children of **single mothers** are more likely to live in poverty.
- Poor children have increased risk of **health impairment**.

CHILDREN IN THE FOSTER CARE SYSTEM

The following are some barriers that children in the foster care system face in this country:

- Children in foster care often go through frequent **relocations** due to rejection by foster families, changes in the family situation, returns to biological families and later returns to foster care, agency procedures, and decisions of the court. Additionally, many foster children experience **sexual and physical abuse** within the foster care system.
- Due to frequent changes in their situation, children in foster care may **change schools** multiple times, which can have an adverse impact on their academic achievement.
- Many youths age out of the foster care system at age 18; this can abruptly **end the relationships** with foster families and other supportive structures.
- Compared with children raised with their own families, children who have been through the foster care system have a higher incidence of **behavioral problems**, increased **substance abuse**, and greater probability of entering the **criminal justice system**.

SOCIAL WELFARE ORGANIZATIONS
APPROACHES TO SOCIAL WELFARE POLICY MAKING

The **rational approach to social welfare policy making** is an idealized and structured approach. It includes identifying and understanding a social problem, identifying alternative solutions and their consequences for consumers and society, and rationally choosing the best alternatives. The rational approach minimizes ideological issues.

The political approach recognizes the importance of compromise, power, competing interests, and partial solutions. Those who are most affected by social policies often have the least amount of political power to promote change. Those who have political power are often influenced by interests that are seeking to protect their own position. Policy makers are often concerned with retaining privilege and power. Without aggressive advocacy, the needs of the disadvantaged can become marginalized.

ADMINISTRATIVE CHALLENGES

Administrative challenges unique to social welfare organizations include the following:

- Clinical services can be difficult to assess objectively.
- It is difficult to evaluate prevention programs, as few techniques are able to measure events that have not occurred.
- Staff turnover is high due to low salary and burnout.

- Programs are often dependent on the political environment for funding.
- It can be difficult to implement systematization or routine work due to the flexibility often required when dealing with human problems.

LESSER ELIGIBILITY

This concept of lesser eligibility asserts that welfare payments should not be higher than the lowest paying job in society and derives from Elizabethan Poor Law. It suggests that economic and wage issues underlie the size of benefits and the availability of welfare. Some believe it is a way to control labor and maintain incentives for workers to accept low-paying or undesirable jobs that they might otherwise reject.

CHALLENGES FOR PROGRAMS FOR POOR AND HOMELESS PEOPLE

One criticism of program development supposedly targeting homeless and poor people is that whereas programs affecting the middle class, such as Individual Development Accounts (IDAs), are put into operation upon conception, programs for poor people are first put through testing phases, with implementation taking years, if it happens at all. In program development for the poor, policies at the level of government may be at odds with actually implementing and carrying out a program.

CRIMINAL JUSTICE SYSTEM

The criminal justice system includes agencies and processes involved in apprehending, prosecuting and defending, reaching a verdict, sentencing, and punishing offenders:

- **Law enforcement agencies**: These may include police, sheriffs, highway patrol, US Marshal service, FBI, DEA, ICE, and ATF. Law enforcement agencies may be local, state, or federal. Their purpose is to investigate and apprehend criminals.
- **Court system**: Prosecutors provide evidence against an individual, and defense attorneys attempt to discredit the evidence or otherwise provide a defense against the charges brought. Judges preside over court cases and may, in some cases, determine the verdict and sentence. In some states, judges determine if probable cause for arrest exists (preliminary hearing). A grand jury may meet in other state and federal cases to determine whether the evidence indicates probable cause.
- **Jail/prison systems**: Individuals may be incarcerated in local jails or state or federal prisons for varying duration of sentences.
- **Probation system**: Some individuals may receive probation instead of jail or prison time but must report regularly to probation officers and may have other requirements, such as attending rehab programs. Individuals released from jail or prison on parole may also enter the probation system for a specified period of time.

CRIMINAL JUSTICE PROCESS

The criminal justice process includes the following:

- **Investigation** of a crime by law enforcement officers.
- **Probable cause** of a crime must be established in order to obtain a search warrant unless exigent circumstances exist.
- **Interrogation** may be carried out to obtain information on the suspect after the suspect receives the Miranda warning.
- An **arrest** may be made with or without a warrant in public places and with a warrant in private. After an arrest, the person must be charged or released within 24-48 hours (state laws vary).
- With federal cases and in some states, a grand jury decides whether **evidence supports probable cause**. In some states, this decision is made by a judge in a preliminary hearing.
- **Arraignment** involves presenting the charge in court and reading the charges to the individual.
- **Bail** may be set to allow the individual to remain out of jail.

- The case may be resolved by a **plea bargain or a trial** in which the evidence is presented, a **verdict** reached, and sentence determined.
- The individual may be eligible for **appeal** if found guilty.

IMPACT OF EARLY EXPERIENCE WITHIN THE CRIMINAL JUSTICE SYSTEM

Early experience within the criminal justice system depends to some degree on the action taken. For example, an adolescent arrested for delinquent acts is more likely to reoffend if the sentence is punitive than if it is more lenient. Additionally, the child or adolescent may develop negative attitudes toward law enforcement and authority in general, and is more likely to commit crimes as an adult. Those who are incarcerated in juvenile facilities may suffer bullying and abuse from others, resulting in emotional and physical problems, and may receive inadequate education, limiting future educational and employment opportunities. Children in the juvenile justice system have high rates of depression, but mental health care and rehabilitation programs are often very limited. Children charged as adults may spend many years in juvenile facilities and then prison, and youth incarceration is one of the highest predictors of recidivism. Many youths are in juvenile detention because of non-violent offenses (such as drug use) but may be exposed to and influenced by more serious offenders.

Globalization and Institutionalism

GLOBALIZATION

Globalization refers to the international integration and interaction of multiple systems, such as economics, communications, and trade. Considerations include the following:

- **International integration**: This term most often refers to financial and business affairs related to trade and investments. For example, one company may manufacture in the United States, Europe, and China and do business throughout the world. International integration is most successful when tariffs and quotas are eliminated or restricted in order to allow the free flow of goods. International integration may affect the cost of items to the client and may affect job opportunities.
- **Financial crisis**: Because of international integration, a financial crisis (devaluing currency, recession, inflation) in one country can have a profound effect on other countries. For example, the financial crisis that occurred in 2008-2009 resulted in high rates of unemployment and increased homelessness worldwide. The unemployed were unable to afford goods, causing businesses to fold or suffer losses, increasing unemployment, and increasing prices to the consumer.
- **Interrelatedness of systems**: Something that affects one system is likely to have an effect on other systems. For example, if a person works in a US factory that manufacturers equipment and a disaster occurs in the country from which the factory obtains materials, production may slow down and profits decrease, making it difficult for the company to obtain loans needed to finance operations, and the client may be laid off. Because the person has little or no income, they may be unable to make mortgage payments, resulting in the bank foreclosing, and the person becoming homeless.
- **Technology**: Knowledge flows with technology, and those countries with the most technological progress tend to have stronger economies and higher standards of living. Technology transfers have facilitated international integration and allowed instant sharing of information around the world, making inventory control, manufacturing, and delivery (shipping, ground, and air transport) more efficient.

IMPACT OF GLOBALIZATION ON ENVIRONMENTAL CRISES AND EPIDEMICS

Globalization may have a profound effect on the following crises:

- **Environmental crises**: As industrialization moves into developing countries, pollution and stripping of natural resources follows. The increased worldwide demand for goods means that countries are motivated more by monetary gain than environmental concerns. Forests are decimated, water and air polluted, but the global community has been unable to reach a worldwide agreement on environmental planning, resulting in increasingly common environmental problems.
- **Pandemics**: Because of the rapid increase in international marketing and travel, it is now almost impossible to completely contain an outbreak that at one time may have been local, such as Ebola (which has killed over 11,000 people), HIV (which has killed over 35 million people), and most recently, the COVID-19 pandemic which is still active worldwide, killing half a million Americans in its first year. Additionally, health laws and practices vary widely, so not all populations have adequate preventive care or treatment. Thus, any outbreak can pose a worldwide threat. Viruses especially pose a grave threat because they readily mutate and treatment may be unavailable or inadequate.

PROBLEMS OF GLOBALIZATION CREATED BY MODERNIZATION

Based on the idea that agrarian and impoverished countries would be improved by industrialization, **modernization** has been criticized for contributing to the problems of globalization. In globalization, multinational corporations have relocated their operations and jobs to less-developed regions where poverty remains the norm and average wages are extremely low. These corporations make higher profits, whereas workers in more-developed countries lose their jobs to workers in less-developed countries. Although the merits of this process in regard to workers in the less-developed countries can be debated, the effects on the previously employed workers in the more-developed countries are undeniably negative.

INSTITUTIONALISM

Institutionalism is the idea that social interventions should be state run, and planning should be centralized in government. Reform is initiated through the electoral process, and a benevolent state would oversee reform efforts. Social services would be provided by the state as well. Critiques would include the assumption of a paternalistic and helpful state, run by individuals uninterested in personal power and gain at the expense of others. However, a counterargument may be the success of countries of northern Europe (e.g., Sweden, Denmark, and Norway) where institutionalism provides citizens with healthcare, free education, employment, childcare, and housing benefits.

Out-of-Home Placement and Displacement

OUT-OF-HOME DISPLACEMENT

Out-of-home displacement may have varying effects on clients and client systems:

- **Natural disasters**: Some clients may develop PTSD and have recurring nightmares or fears regarding the disaster, especially if it was particularly frightening or the individual or family members experienced injuries. Some may experience depression and withdrawal. Living situations may change if the home was damaged or destroyed, sometimes forcing clients into sharing homes with others, living in substandard housing, or being homeless. Some may have to move away from schools, neighborhoods, and friends.
- **Homelessness**: Many clients that are homeless develop depression and low self-esteem and may engage in substance abuse. Children may attend school irregularly, have difficulty studying, and lack adequate clothing and nutrition. They may be bullied by other children aware of their circumstances. Families may be separated and children placed in separate shelters or foster care. Risk of injuries and chronic disease increases.

OUT-OF-HOME PLACEMENT

Out-of-home placements may have varying effects on clients and client systems, depending on the age, duration, and reason:

- **Hospitalization**: Both children and adults may feel fearful and anxious. Children, especially, may feel abandoned or rejected and may regress (bed wetting, thumb sucking). Children may be compliant out of fear when alone but cry and express feelings when parents or other caregivers are present. Adolescents may resent the lack of privacy, isolation, and loss of control. Adults may be concerned about the family unit and loss of income.
- **Foster care**: Children may have difficulty attaching and may become depressed or exhibit behavioral issues (anger or aggression). Developmental delays are common, and children often have poor educational backgrounds, resist studying, get low grades, or must repeat grades. Children may act out or become withdrawn after family visits.
- **Residential care**: Those in residential care may suffer from abuse or molestation because of inadequate supervision. Adults may have an increased risk of falls and injuries. Clients of all ages may become withdrawn and regress because of a lack of personal attention and caring. Small children, especially, may exhibit growth and developmental delays.

FOLLOW-UP AFTER PLACING CHILD IN OUT-OF-HOME PLACEMENT

Follow-up after placing a child in out-of-home placement may vary according to the state regulations, age of the child, type of placement, and the child's specific plan of care, but common **follow-up activities** include:

- Making regularly scheduled visits to observe the child and caregivers in the home environment
- Ensuring that the child's special needs, such as for medical care or counseling, are met
- Assessing the caregiver's communication with the child, disciplinary actions, and attention to special needs, such as giving medications and providing a special diet
- Recording compliance with court ordered actions required of the child (such as rehabilitation for an adolescent drug abuser) or the parents (such as attendance at child development or anger management classes or testing free of alcohol and drugs)
- Monitoring health and education, including school records of grades and attendance
- Ensuring that support services are provided to the caregivers as needed
- Sending periodic reports to the court

PERMANENCY PLANNING

Permanency planning for permanent placement should begin when the child is admitted to the care of child protective services (CPS) and the initial plan of care is developed. Permanent placement may include reunification, foster care, kinship placement, adoption, residential care facility, group home, or transition to adult living. **Elements of permanency planning** include:

- Assessing the child and the child's needs as well as those of the potential caregivers
- Reviewing any previous CPS records
- Noting any previous history with the juvenile justice system and reviewing records
- Preparing the child by engaging them in the process as appropriate for their age through explaining options, showing photographs, and asking for the child's input
- Reviewing health and education records (including lists of schools attended and grades) to ascertain the child's needs and the need for interventions or support services
- Establishing permanency goals and target dates
- Attending permanency hearings and providing justification for termination of parental rights when appropriate

Indicators of Substance Abuse

GENERAL INDICATORS OF SUBSTANCE ABUSE

Many people with substance abuse (alcohol or drugs) are reluctant to disclose this information, but there are a number of indicators that are suggestive of substance abuse:

Physical signs include:

- Burns on fingers or lips
- Pupils abnormally dilated or constricted; eyes watery
- Slurring of speech or slow speech
- Lack of coordination, instability of gait, or tremors
- Sniffing repeatedly, nasal irritation, persistent cough
- Weight loss
- Dysrhythmias
- Pallor, puffiness of face
- Needle tracks on arms or legs

Behavioral signs include:

- Odor of alcohol or marijuana on clothing or breath
- Labile emotions, including mood swings, agitation, and anger
- Inappropriate, impulsive, or risky behavior
- Missing appointments
- Difficulty concentrating, short term memory loss, blackouts
- Insomnia or excessive sleeping
- Disorientation or confusion
- Lack of personal hygiene

ALCOHOL

Alcohol is described as follows:

- A liquid distilled product of fermented fruits, grains, and vegetables
- Can be used as a solvent, an antiseptic, and a sedative
- Has a high potential for abuse
- Small-to-moderate amounts taken over extended periods of time may have positive effects on health

POSSIBLE EFFECTS OF ALCOHOL

The following are **possible effects of alcohol use**:

- Intoxication
- Sensory alteration
- Reduction in anxiety

PARTICULAR CHALLENGES OF DIAGNOSIS AND TREATMENT OF ALCOHOL ABUSE

Challenges in **diagnostics and treatment of alcohol abuse** include the following:

- Alcohol is the most available and widely used substance.
- Progression of alcohol dependence often occurs over an extended period of time, unlike some other substances whose progression can be quite rapid. Because of this slow progression, individuals can deny their dependence and hide it from employers for long periods.

- Most alcohol-dependent individuals have gainful employment, live with families, and are given little attention until their dependence crosses a threshold, at which time the individual fails in their familial, social, or employment roles.
- Misuse of alcohol represents a difficult diagnostic problem as it is a legal substance. Clients, their families, and even clinicians can claim that the client's alcohol use is normative.
- After friends, family members, or employers tire of maintaining the fiction that the individual's alcohol use is normative, the individual will be more motivated to begin the process of accepting treatment.

ALCOHOL USE ASSESSMENT TOOLS

The **CAGE tool** is used as a quick assessment to identify problem drinkers. Moderate drinking, (1-2 drinks daily or one drink a day for older adults) is usually not harmful to people in the absence of other medical conditions. However, drinking more can lead to serious psychosocial and physical problems. One drink is defined as 12 ounces of beer/wine cooler, 5 ounces of wine, or 1.5 ounces of liquor.

- **C** – *Cutting down*: "Do you think about trying to cut down on drinking?"
- **A** – *Annoyed at criticism*: Are people starting to criticize your drinking?
- **G** – *Guilty feeling*: "Do you feel guilty or try to hide your drinking?"
- **E** – *Eye opener*: "Do you increasingly need a drink earlier in the day?

"Yes" on one question suggests the possibility of a drinking problem. "Yes" on ≥2 indicates a drinking problem.

The **Clinical Instrument for Withdrawal for Alcohol (CIWA)** is a tool used to assess the severity of alcohol withdrawal. Each category is scored 0-7 points based on the severity of symptoms, except #10, which is scored 0-4. A score <5 indicates mild withdrawal without need for medications; for scores ranging 5-15, benzodiazepines are indicated to manage symptoms. A score >15 indicates severe withdrawal and the need for admission to the unit.

1. Nausea/Vomiting
2. Tremor
3. Paroxysmal Sweats
4. Anxiety
5. Agitation
6. Tactile Disturbances
7. Auditory Disturbances
8. Visual Disturbances
9. Headache
10. Disorientation or Clouding of Sensorium

ALCOHOL OVERDOSE

Symptoms of alcohol overdose include the following:

- Staggering
- Odor of alcohol on breath
- Loss of coordination
- Dilated pupils
- Slurred speech
- Coma
- Respiratory failure
- Nerve damage
- Liver damage
- Fetal alcohol syndrome (in babies born to alcohol abusers)

ALCOHOL WITHDRAWAL AND TREATMENT

Chronic abuse of ethanol (alcoholism) can lead to physical dependency. Sudden cessation of drinking, which often happens in the inpatient setting, is associated with **alcohol withdrawal syndrome**. It may be precipitated by trauma or infection and has a high mortality rate, 5-15% with treatment and 35% without treatment.

Signs and symptoms: Anxiety, tachycardia, headache, diaphoresis, progressing to severe agitation, hallucinations, auditory/tactile disturbances, and psychotic behavior (delirium tremens).

Diagnosis: Physical assessment, blood alcohol levels (on admission).

Treatment includes:

- **Medication**: IV benzodiazepines to manage symptoms; electrolyte and nutritional replacement, especially magnesium and thiamine.
- Use the **CIWA scale** to measure symptoms of withdrawal; treat as indicated.
- Provide an **environment** with minimal sensory stimulus (lower lights, close blinds) and implement fall and seizure precautions.
- **Prevention**: Screen all clients for alcohol/substance abuse, using CAGE or other assessment tool. Remember to express support and comfort to client; wait until withdrawal symptoms are subsiding to educate about alcohol use and moderation.

PSYCHOSOCIAL TREATMENTS FOR ALCOHOL ABUSE

The following are psychosocial treatments for alcohol abuse:

- Cognitive behavioral therapies
- Behavioral therapies
- Psychodynamic/interpersonal therapies
- Group and family therapies
- Participation in self-help groups

CANNABIS

Cannabis is the hemp plant from which marijuana (a tobacco-like substance) and hashish (resinous secretions of the cannabis plant) are produced.

POSSIBLE EFFECTS

Effects of cannabis include:

- Euphoria followed by relaxation
- Impaired memory, concentration, and knowledge retention
- Loss of coordination
- Increased sense of taste, sight, smell, hearing
- Irritation to lungs and respiratory system
- Cancer
- With stronger doses: Fluctuating emotions, fragmentary thoughts, disoriented behavior

OVERDOSE AND MISUSE

Symptoms of cannabis **overdose** include:

- Fatigue
- Lack of coordination
- Paranoia

59

Cannabis **misuse** indications are as follows:

- Animated behavior and loud talking, followed by sleepiness
- Dilated pupils
- Bloodshot eyes
- Distortions in perception
- Hallucinations
- Distortions in depth and time perception
- Loss of coordination

NARCOTICS

Narcotics are drugs used medicinally to relieve pain. They have a high potential for abuse because they cause relaxation with an immediate rush. Possible effects include restlessness, nausea, euphoria, drowsiness, respiratory depression, and constricted pupils.

MISUSE AND SYMPTOMS OF OVERDOSE

Indications of possible **misuse** are as follows:

- Scars (tracks) caused by injections
- Constricted pupils
- Loss of appetite
- Sniffles
- Watery eyes
- Cough
- Nausea
- Lethargy
- Drowsiness
- Nodding
- Syringes, bent spoons, needles, etc.
- Weight loss or anorexia

Symptoms of narcotic **overdose** include:

- Slow, shallow breathing
- Clammy skin
- Convulsions, coma, and possible death

WITHDRAWAL SYNDROME FOR NARCOTICS

The symptoms of narcotic **withdrawal** are as follows:

- Watery eyes
- Runny nose
- Yawning
- Cramps
- Loss of appetite
- Irritability
- Nausea
- Tremors
- Panic
- Chills
- Sweating

DEPRESSANTS

Depressants are described below:

- Drugs used medicinally to relieve anxiety, irritability, or tension.
- They have a high potential for abuse and development of tolerance.
- They produce a state of intoxication similar to that of alcohol.
- When combined with alcohol, their effects increase and their risks are multiplied.

POSSIBLE EFFECTS

Possible effects of depressant use are as follows:

- Sensory alteration, reduction in anxiety, intoxication
- In small amounts, relaxed muscles, and calmness
- In larger amounts, slurred speech, impaired judgment, loss of motor coordination
- In very large doses, respiratory depression, coma, death

Newborn babies of abusers may exhibit dependence, withdrawal symptoms, behavioral problems, and birth defects.

MISUSE, OVERDOSE, AND WITHDRAWAL

The following are indications of possible depressant **misuse**:

- Behavior similar to alcohol intoxication (without the odor of alcohol)
- Staggering, stumbling, lack of coordination
- Slurred speech
- Falling asleep while at work
- Difficulty concentrating
- Dilated pupils

Symptoms of an **overdose** of depressants include:

- Shallow respiration
- Clammy skin
- Dilated pupils
- Weak and rapid pulse
- Coma or death

Withdrawal syndrome may include the following:

- Anxiety
- Insomnia
- Muscle tremors
- Loss of appetite

Abrupt cessation or a greatly reduced dosage may cause convulsions, delirium, or death.

STIMULANTS

Stimulants are drugs used to increase alertness, relieve fatigue, feel stronger and more decisive, achieve feelings of euphoria, or counteract the down feeling of depressants or alcohol.

POSSIBLE EFFECTS

Possible effects include:

- Increased heart rate
- Increased respiratory rate
- Elevated blood pressure
- Dilated pupils
- Decreased appetite

Effects with high doses include:

- Rapid or irregular heartbeat
- Loss of coordination
- Collapse
- Perspiration
- Blurred vision
- Dizziness
- Feelings of restlessness, anxiety, delusions

MISUSE, OVERDOSE, AND WITHDRAWAL

Stimulant **misuse** is indicated by the following:

- Excessive activity, talkativeness, irritability, argumentativeness, nervousness
- Increased blood pressure or pulse rate, dilated pupils
- Long periods without sleeping or eating
- Euphoria

Symptoms of stimulant **overdose** include:

- Agitated behavior
- Increase in body temperature
- Hallucinations
- Convulsions
- Possible death

Withdrawal from stimulants may cause:

- Apathy
- Long periods of sleep
- Irritability
- Depression
- Disorientation

HALLUCINOGENS

Hallucinogens are described below:

- Drugs that cause behavioral changes that are often multiple and dramatic.
- No known medical use, but some block sensation to pain and their use may result in self-inflicted injuries.
- "Designer drugs," which are made to imitate certain illegal drugs, can be many times stronger than the drugs they imitate.

POSSIBLE EFFECTS

Possible effects of use:

- Rapidly changing mood or feelings, both immediately and long after use
- Hallucinations, illusions, dizziness, confusion, suspicion, anxiety, loss of control
- **Chronic use**: Depression, violent behavior, anxiety, distorted perception of time
- **Large doses**: convulsions, coma, heart/lung failure, ruptured blood vessels in the brain
- **Delayed effects**: flashbacks occurring long after use
- **Designer drugs**: possible irreversible brain damage

MISUSE AND OVERDOSE

The following are indications of hallucinogen **misuse**:

- Extreme changes in behavior and mood
- Sitting or reclining in a trance-like state
- Individual may appear fearful
- Chills, irregular breathing, sweating, trembling hands
- Changes in sensitivity to light, hearing, touch, smell, and time
- Increased blood pressure, heart rate, blood sugar

Symptoms of hallucinogen **overdose** include:

- Longer, more intense episodes
- Psychosis
- Coma
- Death

STEROIDS

Steroids are synthetic compounds closely related to the male sex hormone testosterone and are available both legally and illegally. They have a moderate potential for abuse, particularly among young males.

POSSIBLE EFFECTS

Effects include:

- Increase in body weight
- Increase in muscle mass and strength
- Improved athletic performance
- Improved physical endurance

MISUSE AND OVERDOSE

The following are indications of possible **misuse** of steroids:

- Rapid gains in weight and muscle
- Extremely aggressive behavior
- Severe skin rashes
- Impotence, reduced sexual drive
- In female users, development of irreversible masculine traits

Overdose of steroids includes the following:

- Increased aggressiveness
- Increased combativeness

- Jaundice
- Purple or red spots on the body
- Unexplained darkness of skin
- Unpleasant and persistent breath odor
- Swelling of feet, lower legs

WITHDRAWAL SYNDROME

Withdrawal syndrome may include the following:

- Considerable weight loss
- Depression
- Behavioral changes
- Trembling

Substance Use and Abuse

PATHOPHYSIOLOGY OF ADDICTION

Genetic, social, and personality factors may all play a role in the development of **addictive tendencies**. However, the main factor of the development of substance addiction is the pharmacological activation of the **reward system** located in the central nervous system (CNS). This reward systems pathway involves **dopaminergic neurons**. Dopamine is found in the CNS and is one of many neurotransmitters that play a role in an individual's mood. The mesolimbic pathway seems to play a primary role in the reward and motivational process involved with addiction. This pathway begins in the ventral tegmental area of the brain (VTA) and then moves forward into the nucleus accumbens located in the middle forebrain bundle (MFB). Some drugs enhance mesolimbic dopamine activity, therefore producing very potent effects on mood and behavior.

THEORIES OF SUBSTANCE ADDICTION

Theories of substance addiction include the following:

Theory of Addiction	Details
Exposure theory	According to this theory, once individuals begin to introduce a substance into their body, metabolic changes occur that result in increased dosages of the substance, leading to addiction. The exact mechanism as to how this occurs has not been identified.
Genetic theory	Children of individuals who misuse substances (alcohol or drugs) have a 3-4 times higher risk of becoming addicted, suggesting there is an inherited tendency toward addiction. However, the exact genes that may be implicated have not yet been identified and there is some controversy over this theory, which is based on family, sibling, and twin studies. This theory tends to apply to males more than females.
Adaptation theory	This theory postulates that social (peer pressure), environmental (availability, observation), and psychological factors (poor self-image, deficits) can lead individuals to addictions in accordance to their beliefs about the rewards the substances will provide.

> **Review Video: Addictions**
> Visit mometrix.com/academy and enter code: 460412

ETIOLOGIES OF SUBSTANCE ABUSE

Substance abuse refers to the abuse of drugs, medicines, and/or alcohol that causes mental and physical problems for the abuser and family. Abusers use substances out of boredom, to hide negative self-esteem, to dampen emotional pain, and to cope with daily stress. As the abuse continues, abusers become unable to take care of their daily needs and duties. They lack effective coping mechanisms and the ability to make healthy choices. They struggle to identify and prioritize stress or choose positive behavior to resolve the stress in a healthy way. Some family members may act as codependents because of their desire to feel needed by the abuser, to control the person, and to stay with them. The social worker can help the family to confront an individual with their concerns about the person and their proposals for treatment. Family members can enforce consequences if treatment is not sought. Family members may also need counseling to learn new behaviors to stop enabling the abuser to continue substance abuse.

SUBSTANCE ABUSE AND SUBSTANCE DEPENDENCE

Substance abuse alone is considered a less severe condition than substance dependence. Substance abuse is **diagnosed** when:

- Major roles and obligations become impaired at home, school, or work.
- Legal problems ensue (e.g., arrests for driving while intoxicated or disorderly conduct).
- The abuse continues in spite of related interpersonal and social problems.

Substance dependence refers to the increased use of a substance in order to achieve intoxication, the presence of withdrawal symptoms when the substance is not used, and continued use in the face of efforts to stop. Medications that are sometimes prescribed to reduce substance use include disulfiram (Antabuse), which causes negative symptoms if alcohol is ingested and naltrexone (Trexan), a reward/receptor blocker for alcohol and opiates.

SUBSTANCE RELATED DISORDERS

Substance related disorders may be caused by abusing a drug, by medication side-effects, or by exposure to a toxin. These disorders involve substances including the following: caffeine, hallucinogens, alcohol, cannabis, stimulants, tobacco, inhalants, opioids, sedatives, hypnotics, and anxiolytics. Gambling is now also included in substance-related and addictive disorders, as evidence shows that the behaviors of gambling trigger similar reward systems as drugs. The severity of the particular substance use disorder can be determined by the presence of the number of symptoms, which may include substance/activity induced delirium, dementia, psychosis, mood disorders, anxiety disorder, sexual dysfunction, and sleep dysfunction. Substance intoxication or withdrawal includes behavioral, psychological, and physiological symptoms due to the effects of the substance. It will vary depending on type of substance.

FACTORS THAT CONTRIBUTE TO SUBSTANCE USE AND INFLUENCE THE DRUG OF CHOICE

Factors contributing to likelihood of substance abuse include the following:

- Early or regular use of "gateway" drugs (alcohol, marijuana, nicotine)
- Intra-familial disturbances
- Associating with substance-using peers

Factors influencing an individual's **"drug of choice"** include:

- Current fashion
- Availability
- Peer influences
- Individual biological and psychological factors
- Genetic factors (especially with alcoholism)

CLINICAL DISORDERS COMMONLY FOUND IN CLIENTS WITH SUBSTANCE USE DISORDERS

The following are clinical disorders often found in those abusing substances:

- Conduct disorders, particularly the aggressive subtype
- Depression
- Bipolar disorder
- Schizophrenia
- Anxiety disorders
- Eating disorders
- Pathological gambling
- Antisocial personality disorder
- PTSD
- Other personality disorders

HARMS RESULTING FROM SUBSTANCE USE/ABUSE

The following are possible harms resulting from substance abuse:

- Substances that are illegally obtained are often associated with minor crimes, crimes against family members and the community, and prostitution.
- Alcohol is associated with domestic violence, child abuse, sexual misconduct, and serious auto accidents.
- All substances promote behavioral problems that may make it difficult for the individual to obtain/retain employment, or to sustain normal family relationships.

Injuries or illnesses that can result from substance use include:

- Physical damage
- Brain damage
- Organic failure
- Fetal damage when used by pregnant women
- Birth of drug exposed babies who require intensive therapy throughout childhood
- Altering of brain chemistry/permanent brain damage
- Effects on dopamine in brain, which directly effects mood

HARM RELATED TO METHOD OF ADMINISTRATION

Harm from illegal drug use related to their mode of administration includes:

- Unknown dosing, which can lead to drug overdose and death
- Using contaminated needles can cause staph infections, Hepatitis, or HIV/AIDS
- The use of inhalants, which are frequently toxic and can cause brain damage, heart disease, and kidney or liver failure

SUBSTANCE ABUSE TREATMENT

Substance use disorder treatment includes the following components:

- An assessment phase
- Treatment of intoxication and withdrawal when necessary
- Development of a treatment strategy

General treatment strategies include:

- Total abstinence (drug-free)
- Substitution, or the use of alternative medications that inhibit the use of illegal drugs
- Harm reduction

Goals of treatment are:

- Reducing use and effects of substances
- Abstinence
- Reducing the frequency and severity of relapse
- Improvement in psychological and social functioning

Discrimination

SYSTEMIC/INSTITUTIONALIZED DISCRIMINATION

Systemic or institutionalized discrimination is the unfair and unjust treatment of populations because of race, gender, sexual orientation, religion, disability, or any other perceived difference by society in general and by the institutions of society.

Institution	Evidence of racism, sexism, or ageism
Healthcare	Provision and access to care may be unequal. People often lack insurance or depend on Medicaid, which limits access. Lack of prenatal care results in higher rates of infant morbidity/mortality. People often develop chronic illnesses because of poor preventive care.
Employment	Discriminatory hiring practices limit employment and advancement opportunities, resulting in unemployment or low income, which can result in homelessness, substance abuse, or criminal activity.
Finances/Housing	People may be denied loans or face high interest rates, limiting their ability to buy homes, pay for education, and start businesses or resulting in high rates of debt. Low-cost housing is often in areas of high crime and gang activity, which is especially a risk for adolescents and the elderly.
Education	Children may attend substandard schools with few enrichment programs, putting them at a disadvantage as they progress through school and into job market or advanced education programs. Many students graduate without adequate skills or drop out.
Criminal justice	People of color are more likely to be arrested and to receive longer sentences for crimes.

EFFECTS OF DISCRIMINATION ON BEHAVIOR

Discrimination can result in significant effects, primarily negative, on its subjects:

- **Health problems**: Individuals may suffer from increased stress, anxiety, sadness, and depression. Individuals may develop stress-related disorders, such as hypertension or eating disorders. Individuals may not have access to adequate healthcare or insurance and often delay seeking medical help.
- **Substance abuse**: Individuals may seek relief from the stress of discriminatory actions by resorting to the use of alcohol or drugs in order to dull their feelings.
- **Violence/Conflict/Antisocial behavior**: Individuals may respond with anger and seek vengeance against perpetrators of discrimination (or entire groups representing these perpetrators). Adolescents, for example, may join gangs so that they feel accepted. Some individuals may resort to criminal activity, such as robbery.
- **Withdrawal**: Some individuals begin to pull inward and withdraw from social activities or engagement in work or school, leading to increasing failure and even further discrimination. Discrimination in employment and housing may lead to high rates of unemployment and homelessness.
- **Disenfranchisement**: Individuals may feel that they have no voice and may avoid voting or face obstacles to voting, such as lack of proper identification or transportation.

AGEISM AND STEREOTYPES OF THE ELDERLY

Ageism is an attitude toward the capabilities and experiences of old age which leads to devaluation and disenfranchisement. Some **stereotypes of the elderly** include the assumptions that all elderly individuals are:

- Asexual
- Rigid
- Impaired (psychologically)
- Incapable of change

IMPLICATIONS OF BIAS IN HUMAN SERVICE CLINICAL WORK

Health and mental health services express the ideology of the culture at large (dominant culture). This may cause harm to clients or reinforce **cultural stereotypes**. Examples of this include:

- **Minorities and women** often receive more severe diagnoses and some diagnoses are associated with gender.
- **African-Americans** are at greater risk for involuntary commitment.
- **Gay and lesbian people** are sometimes treated with ethically questionable techniques in attempts to reorient their sexuality.

IMMIGRANT CLIENTS

STRESSES ASSOCIATED WITH IMMIGRATION

The process of **immigration introduces many stresses** that must be managed. They include the following:

- Gaining entry into and understanding a foreign culture
- Difficulties with language acquisition
- Immigrants who are educated often cannot find equivalent employment
- Distance from family, friends, and familiar surroundings

CONSIDERATION WHEN ASSESSING IMMIGRANT CLIENTS' NEEDS

The following are considerations when assessing an immigrant's needs:

- Why and how did the client immigrate?
- Social supports the client has or lacks (community/relatives)
- The client's education/literacy in language of origin and in English
- Economic and housing resources (including number of people in home, availability of utilities)
- Employment history and the ability to find/obtain work
- The client's ability to find and use institutional/governmental supports
- Health status/resources (pre- and post-immigration)
- Social networks (pre- and post-immigration)
- Life control: Degree to which the individual experiences personal power and the ability to make choices

KEY CONCEPTS OF DIVERSITY AND DISCRIMINATION

Key concepts of diversity and discrimination include the following:

Race	The concept of race first appeared in the English language just 300 years ago. Race has great social and political significance. It can be defined as a subgroup that possesses a definite combination of characteristics of a genetic origin.
Ethnicity	Ethnicity is a group classification in which members share a unique social and cultural heritage that is passed on from one generation to the next. It is not the same as race, though the two terms are used interchangeably at times.
Worldview	Worldview is an integral concept in the assessment of the client's experience. This can be defined as a way that individuals perceive their relationship to nature, institutions, and other people and objects. This comprises a psychological orientation to life as seen in how individuals think, behave, make decisions, and understand phenomena. It provides crucial information in the assessment of mental health status, assisting in assessment and diagnosis, and in designing treatment programs.
Acculturation	Acculturation is the process of learning and adopting the dominant culture through adaptation and assimilation.
Ethnic identity	Ethnic identity is a sense of belonging to an identifiable group and having historical continuity, in addition to a sense of common customs and mores transmitted over generations.
Social identity	Social identity describes how the dominant culture establishes criteria for categorizing individuals and the normal and ordinary characteristics believed to be natural and usual for members of the society.
Virtual/actual social identity	Virtual social identity is the set of attributes ascribed to persons based on appearances, dialect, social setting, and material features. Actual social identity is the set of characteristics a person actually demonstrates.
Stigma	Stigma is a characteristic that makes an individual different from the group, and is perceived to be an intensely discreditable trait.
Normalization	Normalization describes treating the stigmatized person as if they do not have a stigma.
Socioeconomic status	Socioeconomic status is determined by occupation, education, and income of the head of a household.
Prejudice	Prejudice is bias or judgment based on value judgment, personal history, inferences about others, and application of normative judgments.
Discrimination	Discrimination is the act of expressing prejudice with immediate and serious social and economic consequences.
Stereotypes	Stereotypes are amplified distorted beliefs about an ethnicity, gender, or other group, often employed to justify discriminatory conduct.
Oppressed minority	A group differentiated from others in society because of physical or cultural characteristics. The group receives unequal treatment and views itself as an object of collective discrimination.
Privilege	Advantages or benefits that the dominant group has. These have been given unintentionally, unconsciously, and automatically.
Racism	Generalizations, institutionalization, and assignment of values to real or imaginary differences between individuals to justify privilege, aggression, or violence. These societal patterns have the cumulative effect of inflicting oppressive or other negative conditions against identifiable groups based on race or ethnicity.

Exploitation

CHARACTERISTICS OF PERPETRATORS OF EXPLOITATION

Characteristics of perpetrators of exploitation may vary widely, depending on the type of exploitation, making them difficult to identify.

- Many of those that are involved in **sex trafficking** are part of large criminal enterprises or have a history of criminal acts and antisocial behavior. The perpetrator may exhibit a domineering attitude, speaking for the victims and never leaving the victim unattended.
- Perpetrators of **elder exploitation** are usually family members or caregivers who take advantage of the victims financially. These perpetrators may appear as loving and caring or sometimes abusive. Business people may take advantage of the elderly by overcharging for goods and services, and some people use scams to get victims to pay or invest money.
- Those involved in **exploitation of child labor** are often in agriculture, working children (most often immigrants) for long hours in the fields at low wages.
- Perpetrators of **slavery/involuntary servitude** may come from cultures with different values, or may be individuals with personal values that allow them to take advantage of others.

SEXUAL TRAFFICKING

Risk factors for sexual trafficking include being homeless or a runaway, being part of the LGBTQ community, being African American or Latino, having involvement in the child welfare system, having a substance use disorder, and being an illegal immigrant. **Sexual trafficking** may include the following:

- **Children**: Children may be bought or sold for sexual use or forced by family members, even parents, into sex trafficking. Runaways are often picked up on the street and offered shelter, and some children are lured through internet postings. Children who resist may be beaten or even killed. Young girls especially may serve in prostitution rings or be forced to participate in pornography. Many turn to substance abuse.
- **Adults**: Many adult victims begin as victims of sexual trafficking during childhood and continue into adulthood as part of prostitution rings or the pornography industry which they are afraid of or too dependent on to try to escape. Substance abuse is common, often used to self-treat depression or other mental health conditions. Physical abuse is common, as are high rates of STIs and HIV. Forced abortions are also common.

FINANCIAL EXPLOITATION

Individuals (especially the elderly and disabled) who become unable to manage their own financial affairs become increasingly vulnerable to **financial exploitation**, especially if they have cognitive impairment or physical impairments that impair their mobility. Financial exploitation includes any of the following:

- Outright stealing of property or persuading individuals to give away possessions
- Forcing individuals to sign away property
- Emptying bank and savings accounts
- Using stolen credit cards
- Convincing the individual to invest money in fraudulent schemes
- Taking money for home renovations that are not done

Indications of financial abuse may be unpaid bills, unusual activity at ATMs or with credit cards, inadequate funds to meet needs, disappearance of items in the home, change in the provision of a will, and deferring to caregivers regarding financial affairs. Family or caregivers may move permanently into the client's home and take over without sharing costs. Clients may be unable to recoup losses and forced to live with reduced means and may exhibit shame or confusion about loss.

EXPLOITATION OF IMMIGRATION STATUS

People whose immigration status is illegal are especially at risk of exploitation because they have little recourse to legal assistance that doesn't increase the risk of deportation. Many have paid a high price to "coyotes" to smuggle them into the country and may have been robbed or sexually abused with impunity. Once in the United States, they are often hired at substandard wages and without benefits, including insurance. Many have little access to healthcare and may suffer from dental and health problems. Housing is often inadequate, and children may drop out of school or have poor attendance because parents move from place to place. Immigrants are often fearful of authorities. Mental health problems, such as depression and substance abuse, are common, but little treatment is available, and many immigrants come from cultures that consider mental illness a cause for shame. Legal immigrants who qualify for assistance may face similar problems, especially related to employment and housing, because of poor language skills and societal discrimination.

Culturally Competent Care

THEORY OF CULTURAL RELATIVISM

Key concepts within the theory of cultural relativism include the following:

- Values, beliefs, models of behavior, and understandings of the nature of the universe must be understood within the cultural framework in which they appear.
- The outlines and limitations of normality and deviance are determined by the dominant culture.
- The behavioral norms and expressions of emotional needs of cultural minorities may be defined as abnormal in that they differ from those of the larger, dominant culture.

Behaviors and attitudes may be perceived differently if understood through a unique cultural context. It is important for a social worker to determine whether a client's abnormal or deviant behavior would be considered abnormal or deviant within the client's own culture, as well as in the client's self-assessment.

CULTURAL COMPETENCE
DEVELOPMENT OF CULTURAL COMPETENCE AT THE ORGANIZATIONAL LEVEL

The stages of development of cultural competency at the organization level are as follows:

1. **Cultural destructiveness**: This stage devalues different cultures and views them as inferior.
2. **Cultural incapacity**: The organization becomes aware of a need, but feels incapable of providing the required services, resulting in immobility.
3. **Cultural blindness**: Cultural blindness, or "colorblindness," lacks recognition of differences between cultural groups and denies the existence of oppression and institutional racism.
4. **Cultural pre-competency**: The organization starts to recognize the needs of different groups, seeking to recruit diverse staff and include appropriate training.
5. **Cultural competency**: Diversity issues are addressed with staff and clients. Staff is trained and confident with a range of differences.
6. **Cultural proficiency**: This is the ideal level of cultural competency and is represented by the ability to incorporate and respond to new cultural groups.

MEASURES OF CULTURAL COMPETENCE

Measures of cultural competence include the following abilities:

- Ability to recognize the effects of cultural differences on the helping process
- Ability to fully acknowledge one's own culture and its impact on one's thoughts and actions
- Ability to comprehend the dynamics of power differences in social work practice
- Ability to comprehend the meaning of a client's behavior in its cultural context
- Ability to know when, where, and how to obtain necessary cultural information

ENHANCING CULTURAL COMPETENCE

A social worker can enhance their cultural competence by doing the following:

- Reading applicable practice or scientific professional literature
- Becoming familiar with the literature of the relevant group(s)
- Identifying and consulting with cultural brokers
- Seeking out experiences to interact with diverse groups

Social workers must reflect on themselves, their own cultures, and how their cultures affect their way of thinking and moving in the world. Becoming aware of one's own biases and seeking to be open to differences in other cultures is a critical key in providing culturally competent care.

CULTURAL SENSITIVITY

CULTURALLY SENSITIVE PRACTICE FOR THE INSTITUTION

Culturally sensitive practice for the institution includes practice skills, attitudes, policies, and structures that are united in a system, in an agency, or among professionals and allow that entity to work with cultural differences. It both values diversity (i.e., diverse staff, policies that acknowledge and respect differences, and regular initiation of cultural self-assessment) and institutionalizes diversity (i.e., the organization has integrated diversity into its structure, policies, and operations).

CULTURALLY SENSITIVE PRACTICE FOR INDIVIDUAL SOCIAL WORKERS

Culturally sensitive practice for the individual social worker describes an ability to work skillfully with cultural differences. It includes the following:

- Awareness and acceptance of differences
- Awareness of one's own cultural values
- Understanding the dynamics of difference
- Development of cultural competence
- An ability to adapt practice skills to fit the cultural context of the client's structure, values, and service

Cultural sensitivity is an ongoing process that requires continuing education, awareness, management of transference and counter-transference, and continuous skill development.

CHARACTERISTICS OF CULTURALLY SENSITIVE SOCIAL WORKERS

Characteristics of the culturally sensitive social worker include the following:

- With regard for individuality and confidentiality, the social worker approaches clients in a respectful, warm, accepting, and interested manner.
- The social worker understands that opinions and experiences of both worker and client are affected by stereotypes and previous experience.
- The social worker is able to acknowledge their own socialization to beliefs, attitudes, biases, and prejudices that may affect the working relationship.
- The social worker displays awareness of cross-cultural factors that may affect the relationship.
- The social worker is able to communicate that cultural differences and their expressions are legitimate.
- The social worker is open to help from the client in learning about the client's background.
- The social worker is informed about life conditions fostered by poverty, racism, and disenfranchisement.
- The social worker is aware that a client's cultural background may be peripheral to the client's situation and not central to it.

THEORIES OF CULTURALLY INFLUENCED COMMUNICATION

Interpersonal communication is shaped by both culture and context. According to Hall's theory of communication, **high context communication styles** are used in Asian, Latino, African American, and Native American cultures in the US. In this style, there is a strong reliance on contextual cues and a flexible sense of time. This style is intuitive, and within it, social roles shape interactions, communication is more personal and affective, and oral agreements are binding.

According to Hall's theory, **low context communication styles** are used more in Northern European, white groups in the US. These styles tend to be formal and have complex codes. They tend to show a disregard for contextual codes and a reliance on verbal communication. In these styles, there is an inflexible sense of time, linear logic is used, and relationships are functionally based and highly procedural.

The worker should be aware of the potential for cross-cultural misunderstanding and that all cultures exhibit great diversity within themselves.

75

USE OF LANGUAGE AND COMMUNICATION TO BECOME MORE CULTURALLY SENSITIVE

Methods of communication for the social worker to become more culturally sensitive include the following:

- Learn to speak the target language
- Use interpreters appropriately
- Participate in cultural events of the group(s)
- Form friendships with members of different cultural groups than one's own
- Acquire cultural and historical information about cultural groups
- Learn about the institutional barriers that limit access to cultural and economic resources for vulnerable groups
- Gain an understanding of the socio-political system in the U.S. and the implications for majority and minority groups

LIMITATIONS IN CULTURAL SENSITIVITY

Some cultural differences may be damaging or unacceptable. In these cases, there is a limit to which cultural sensitivity is applied. The worker needs to have a balanced approach to assess cultural norms within the context of American practices, norms, and laws. There are **illegal and unacceptable cultural practices** outside the limits of cultural sensitivity. These may include the following:

- Child labor
- Honor killings
- Private/family vengeance
- Slavery
- Infanticide
- Female genital mutilation
- Wife or servant beating
- Polygamy
- Child marriage
- Denial of medical care
- Abandonment of disabled children
- Extreme discipline of children

BARRIERS TO CROSS-CULTURAL PRACTICE

Barriers to cross-cultural practice include the following:

- **Cultural encapsulation**: Ethnocentrism, color-blindness, false universals
- **Language barriers**: Verbal, nonverbal, body language, dialect
- **Class-bound values**: Treatment, service delivery, power dynamics
- **Culture-bound values**: Religious beliefs/practices, dietary preferences, choice of attire

Chapter Quiz

Ready to see how well you retained what you just read? Scan the QR code to go directly to the chapter quiz interface for this study guide. If you're using a computer, simply visit the bonus page at **mometrix.com/bonus948/swclinical** and click the Chapter Quizzes link.

Assessment, Diagnosis, and Treatment Planning

Transform passive reading into active learning! After immersing yourself in this chapter, put your comprehension to the test by taking a quiz. The insights you gained will stay with you longer this way. Scan the QR code to go directly to the chapter quiz interface for this study guide. If you're using a computer, simply visit the bonus page at **mometrix.com/bonus948/swclinical** and click the Chapter Quizzes link.

Biopsychosocial History and Collateral Data

FOCUSES OF THE SOCIAL WORK ASSESSMENT

The social worker's assessment may focus on any or all of the following:

- **Intrapsychic** dynamics, strengths, and problems
- **Interpersonal** dynamics, strengths, and problems
- **Environmental** strengths and problems
- The **interaction and intersection** of intrapsychic, interpersonal, and environmental factors

The social worker's role in the assessment process is to ask questions, ask for elaboration and description in the client's response, observe client's behavior/affect, and organize data to create a meaningful psychosocial or diagnostic assessment.

> **Review Video: Life Stages in Client Assessment**
> Visit mometrix.com/academy and enter code: 535888

STEPS OF THE INITIAL SOCIAL WORK ASSESSMENT

The initial social work assessment is used to gain information about the client's needs (employment, rehabilitation, monetary support, housing, education, safety). It should include client goals and be the basis for intervention plans. Steps include the following:

1. Schedule an interview and review all pertinent documents (medical records, police reports, housing reports, previous social services records).
2. Utilize a theoretical framework as the basis for the assessment based on the needs of the client.
3. Utilize a standardized form if required by the agency.
4. Ask open-ended questions and avoid "why" questions, rapid questioning, or repeated questioning without pause for reflection. Utilize active listening.
5. Develop a problem list of things that may require intervention.
6. Outline interventions to assist with resolving the client's problems.
7. Assist the client to develop specific time-sensitive goals and outline the client's responsibilities.
8. Summarize the findings of the assessment and review the summary with the client.
9. Set up a follow-up interview.

BIOPSYCHOSOCIAL HISTORY

The social work assessment must gather client information in a comprehensive, accurate, and systematic manner. A history is taken from clients and others (such as family members) to complete the assessment. Information relevant to the client's **biopsychosocial history** includes the following:

- **Appearance** of the client
- **Previous hospitalizations** and experience(s) with healthcare
- **Psychiatric history**: Suicidal ideation, psychiatric disorders, family psychiatric history, history of violence and/or self-mutilation
- **Chief complaint**: Client's perception of the problem
- **Use of complementary therapies**: Acupuncture, visualization, and meditation
- **Occupational and educational background**: Highest level of education, issues while in the school setting, employment record, retirement, and special skills
- **Social patterns**: Family and friends, living situation, typical activities, support system
- **Sexual patterns**: Orientation, practices, and problems
- **Interests and abilities**: Hobbies and sports
- **Current and past substance abuse**: Type, frequency, drinking pattern, use of recreational drugs, and overuse of prescription drugs
- **Ability to cope**: Stress reduction techniques
- **Physical, sexual, emotional, and financial abuse**: Older adults are especially vulnerable to abuse and may be reluctant to disclose out of shame or fear
- **Spiritual/cultural assessment**: Religious/Spiritual importance, practices, restrictions (such as blood products or foods), and impact on health and health decisions
- **Mental status**, gleaned from the following:
  o General attitude: Behavior and reaction to being interviewed
  o Mental activity: Logical or loosely associated
  o Speech profile: Normal, childlike, or pressured
  o Emotional state: Depressed, agitated, or calm
  o Level of consciousness: Alert or stuporous
  o Orientation: Normal or disoriented
  o Thought processes: Pressured thoughts (excessively rapid), flights of ideas, thought blocking, disconnected thoughts, tangentiality and circumstantiality, etc.
  o Judgment: Good, fair, poor, or none
  o Mood: Cooperative or agitated
  o Insight: Good, fair, poor, or none
  o Memory: Intact or presence of deficits

THE ROLE OF OBSERVATION IN ASSESSMENT
LEVELS OF OBSERVATION

One form of assessment involves nonstandard procedures that are used to provide individualized assessments. **Nonstandard procedures** include observations of client behaviors and performance. There are three **levels of observation** techniques that can be applied:

- The first level is **casual informational observation**, where the provider gleans information from watching the client during unstructured activities throughout the day.
- The second level is **guided observation**, an intentional style of direct observation accomplished with a checklist or rating scale to evaluate the performance or behavior seen.
- The third level is the **clinical level**, where observation is done in a controlled setting for a lengthy period of time. This is most often accomplished on the doctoral level with applied instrumentation.

INSTRUMENTS USED DURING THE OBSERVATION PROCESS

The following instruments can be used in an observation:

- The **checklist** is used to check off behaviors or performance levels with a plus or minus sign to indicate that the behavior was observed or absent. The observer can converse with the client as they mark the checklist.
- The **rating scale** is a more complex checklist that notes the strength, frequency, or degree of an exhibited behavior. Likert scales are applied using the following ratings: 1. Never; 2. Rarely; 3. Sometimes; 4. Usually; and 5. Always. The evaluator of the behavior makes a judgment about whatever question has been asked on the rating scale.
- The **anecdotal report** is used to record subjective notes describing the client's behavior during a specified time or in a specified setting and is often applied to evaluate a suspected pattern.

Structured interviews, questionnaires, and personal essays or journals may also be useful in the observation process, depending on the client's ability to participate in these exercises.

INFORMATION SOURCES FOR ASSESSMENT

Information can also be collected from various external sources to contribute to the assessment of the client:

Source	Data Collected
Social services agency	Record of previous contact with the client and interventions made, as well as the reason for termination or continuation of the case.
Employer	History of employment, including the type of work, the duration, attendance record, skills needed for the jobs, problems encountered, and job-related injuries.
Medical records	Names of healthcare providers, diagnoses and treatments prescribed, medication list, history of chronic disorders and need for ongoing treatment and assessment.
Psychological records	Psychosocial assessment, diagnoses of mental health problems, types of therapies utilized, client goals, and recommendations for ongoing care.
Legal records	History of offenses and juvenile detention and adult incarceration/parole. Evidence of history of violence toward self or others.
School records	Attendance records indicate compliance with schooling, grades suggest cognitive ability, disciplinary actions may indicate behavioral problems. 504 plans and IEPs indicate students with disabilities and outline needs for special education and/or accommodations, auxiliary aids, and service.

Assessment Methods and Techniques

METHODS OF PSYCHOLOGICAL TESTING

Various methods of psychological testing exist, which can be used in conjunction with one another, based on the client's needs:

- A **standardized test** is one in which the questions and potential responses from all tests can be compared with one another. Every aspect of the test must remain consistent.
- A **behavioral assessment** assumes that an individual can only be evaluated in relation to their environment. Behavioral assessments must include a stimulus, organism, response, and consequences (SORC).
- A **dynamic assessment** involves systematic deviation from the standardized test to determine whether the individual benefits from education. It is an interactive assessment that includes a process called "testing-teaching-retesting," in which an examinee is provided a problem to solve and their ability to solve it is assessed. They are then provided education to increase their sense of competence on the subject, and finally they are asked to solve the same problem again. In the retest, they are given sequence of stronger support (or "clues) to help solve the problem if needed, until it is solved. This reflects the client's ability to respond to education and apply it in problem solving; therefore, providing insight to the social worker on the client's need for intervention.
- **Domain-referenced testing** breaks evaluation into specific domains of ability—for instance, reading or math ability.

ASSESSMENT OF COMMUNICATION SKILLS

The social worker can assess communication skills through both interview and observation. Additionally, the social worker may provide the client with written information and ask the client to read and discuss the information to determine if the client has adequate ability to read and understand. The social worker should directly ask about which language the client communicates best with and whether there are problems, such as hearing deficit, that may impact communication so that accommodations can be provided. Techniques include the following:

- Ask questions to determine client's ability to understand and respond appropriately.
- Observe for signs of incongruence where words, body language, and tone of voice are inconsistent.
- Ask the client to summarize or restate information according to their understanding.
- Observe the client's ability to initiate and maintain conversation.
- Note the client's ability to understand and/or use metaphoric language.
- Observe the client's turn-taking and response to language cues.
- Note the client's use of appropriate nonverbal language, such as gestures and nodding head.

ASSESSMENT OF COPING ABILITIES

Assessment of coping abilities is done through observation and interview and begins with determining if the client has developed effective coping strategies. The following should be considered as elements required for effective coping:

- **Habits that sustain good health**: Balanced diet, adequate exercise, adequate medical care, leisure activities, relaxation exercises
- **Satisfaction with life**: Work, family, activities, sense of humor, religious/spiritual belief, artistic endeavors
- **Support systems**: Family, friends, religious/spiritual affiliation, clubs, organizations, online supports
- **Healthy response to stressful circumstances**: Problem-solving as opposed to avoidance, utilizing support systems instead of blaming self and taking no positive action, reframing and realistically assessing positives and negatives rather than utilizing wishful thinking that everything will be alright

MENTAL STATUS EXAM

Clients with evidence of dementia or short-term memory loss, often associated with Alzheimer's disease, should have cognition assessed. The **Mini-Mental State Exam (MMSE)** is commonly used. The MMSE requires the client to carry out specified tasks and scores on a scale of 0-9 based on their ability to do so:

Area Assessed	Tasks Performed
Memory	Remembering and later repeating the names of 3 common objects
Attention	Counting backward from 100 by increments of 7 or spelling "world" backward
	Following simple 3-part instructions, such as picking up a piece of paper, folding it in half, and placing it on the floor
Language	Naming items as the examiner points to them
	Repeating common phrases
	Reading a sentence and following directions
	Writing a sentence
Orientation	Providing the date and the location of the examiner's office, including city, state, and street address
Visual-Spatial Skills	Copying a picture of interlocking shapes

Scoring for the MMSE is as follows:

- 24-30: Normal cognition
- 18-23: Mild cognitive impairment
- 0-17: Severe cognitive impairment

INDICATORS OF SEXUAL DYSFUNCTION

Indicators of sexual dysfunction that may present upon assessment include the following:

- **History of promiscuity or prostitution**: Both may indicate that the client was sexually abused at one time or needed to resort to sex to gain income, acceptance, or to pay for drugs or alcohol.
- **Sexualized behavior**: In children and adolescents, this usually indicates sexual abuse. In adults, it often indicates that the individual uses the body as an expression of power.
- **Asexual behavior**: Client may dress or act in such a manner as to appear sexually unattractive as a means of self-protection.
- **Bragging**: Those who feel insecure about their sexuality may resort to bragging about sexual exploits.
- **Paraphilias**: Clients rarely admit to paraphilias (which usually have onset during adolescence), such as sadism, pedophilia, peeping, and exhibitionism, but may come in contact with social services as part of the criminal justice system.
- **Gender dysphoria**: Clients may bind breasts, tuck penis, or cross dress.

PSYCHIATRIC ILLNESS AND SEXUALITY

Many times, psychiatric illness can affect a person's sexuality. Mental illness, such as depression, can often decrease the client's sexual desire, while the manic client will often become hypersexual. Bipolar clients can experience a lack of sexual inhibition and may have many sexual affairs or act very seductively or overtly sexual. Psychotic clients may experience hallucinations or delusions of a sexual nature, and the schizophrenic client may exhibit inappropriate sexual behaviors such as masturbation in public. Clients residing in long-term care facilities must be kept safe from sexually transmitted infections, unwanted pregnancies, and unwanted sexual advances or assaults from others. The social worker must be aware of these risks and provide support and advocacy accordingly.

INDICATORS OF BEHAVIORAL DYSFUNCTION

Indicators of behavioral dysfunction may be present upon assessment, including the following:

Indicator	Manifestations
Unkempt appearance	Sloppily dressed, dirty, smelly
Substance abuse	Burnt fingers, constricted pupils, needle tracks, runny nose, slurred speech, tremors, smell of alcohol
Labile emotions	May have sudden mood swings or outbursts of anger and may appear angry much of the time. May be wildly talkative or withdrawn and silent.
Self-injury	Signs of cutting, excessive piercings, picking at scabs, head banging
Counter-culture identification	May identify with extreme or marginal groups, or dress in the "uniform" of one of these groups.
Attitude	May be disrespectful, scatological, demanding, using expletives, and argumentative. May refuse to follow rules. May refuse to answer questions or respond to social worker.
Dishonesty	May lie and try to deceive. May have a history of stealing (shoplifting is common).
Truancy/Absence	May have a history of skipping classes or failing to attend school at all, running away, or staying out all night.

INDICATORS OF PSYCHOSOCIAL STRESS

Psychosocial stress (which occurs when one perceives a threat as part of social interaction with other individuals) causes a sympathetic nervous system response ("fight or flight") with the release of stress hormones (cortisol, adrenaline, dopamine), which can cause the heart rate and blood pressure to increase. Clients who are facing the need for resocialization (such as after incarceration), role change (after divorce, job loss), or situation change (foster care, rehab) are especially at risk for psychosocial stress. **Indicators** include the following:

Indicator	Manifestation
Self-injury	Signs of cutting, excessive piercings, picking at scabs
Speech alterations	Some may speak very quickly while others may say little or nothing
Demeanor	May be very withdrawn or nervous and agitated
Self-comforting measures	Licking lips, rubbing hands together, sitting with arms folded, taking deep breaths
Substance abuse	Use of alcohol or drugs to alleviate distress and provide an escape from problems
Stress-related ailments	Hypertension, headaches, GI upset
Sleep impairment	Insomnia or excessive drowsiness and sleep periods
Mental health issues	Depression is a common response to stress

NEUROPSYCHOLOGICAL ASSESSMENTS

The following tools are used to assess for psychological deficits caused by neurological disorders:

- The **Benton Visual Retention Test (BVRT)** assesses visual memory, spatial perception, and visual-motor skills in order to diagnose brain damage. The subject is asked to reproduce from memory the geometric patterns on a series of ten cards.
- The **Beery Developmental Test of Visual-Motor Integration (Beery-VMI-6)** assesses visual-motor skills in children; like the BVRT, it involves the reproduction of geometric shapes.

82

- The **Wisconsin Card Sorting Test (WCST)** is a screening test that assesses the ability to form abstract concepts and shift cognitive strategies; the subject is required to sort a group of cards in an order that is not disclosed to them.
- The **Stroop Color-Word Association Test (SCWT)** is a measure of cognitive flexibility; it tests an individual's ability to suppress a habitual reaction to stimulus.
- The **Halstead-Reitan Neuropsychological Battery (HRNB)** is a group of tests that are effective at differentiating between normal people and those with brain damage. The clinician has control over which exams to administer, though they are likely to assess sensorimotor, perceptual, and language functioning. A score higher than 0.60 indicates brain pathology.
- The **Luria-Nebraska Neuropsychological Battery (LNNB)** contains 11 subtests that assess areas like rhythm, visual function, and writing. The examinee is given a score between 0 and 2, with 0 indicating normal function and 2 indicating brain damage.
- The **Bender Visual-Motor Gestalt Test (Bender-Gestalt II)** is a brief examination that involves responding to 16 stimulus cards containing geometric figures, which the examinee must either copy or recall.

ASSESSMENT OF EXECUTIVE FUNCTION

Executive functions are cognitive features that control and regulate all other abilities and behaviors. These are higher-level abilities that influence attention, memory, and motor skills. They also monitor actions and provide the capacity to initiate, stop, or change behaviors, to set goals and plan future behavior, and to solve problems when faced with complex tasks and situations. Executive functions allow one to form concepts and think abstractly. Deficits in executive functioning are evident in the reduced ability to delay gratification, problems with understanding cause and effect (i.e., concrete thinking), poor organization and planning, difficulty following multi-step directions, perseveration with an idea in the face of superior information, and overall poor judgment. Various assessment tools exist to **evaluate executive functioning**, including the following:

- Trail making test
- WAIS-IV
- Clock drawing tests

When combined with observations and the social work assessment, these tests can expose deficiencies in executive function that may disrupt the client's ability to participate in daily activities. From this assessment, the social worker can identify needs and resources to better support the client.

EVALUATION IN THE ASSESSMENT PROCESS

Evaluation is the process of accumulating data in order to improve a person's ability to make a decision based on reliable standards. The accumulated data is given careful consideration and appraisal by the evaluator to ensure that it is complete and accurate. The evaluator must make some kind of interpretation or inference about the data that has been collected. This inference is known as a **value judgment** and is a common task for the social worker who uses a methodical and well-organized system to aid in their evaluation of the assessment process.

Indicators for Risk to Self or Others

COMPONENTS OF A RISK ASSESSMENT

A risk assessment evaluates the client's condition and their particular situation for the presence of certain risk factors. These risks can be influenced by age, ethnicity, spirituality, or social beliefs. They can include risk for suicide, harming others, exacerbation of symptoms, development of new mental health issues, falls, seizures, allergic reactions, or elopement. This assessment should occur within the first interview and then continue to be an ongoing process. The client's specific risks should be prioritized and documented, and then interventions should be put into place to protect this client from these risks.

SUICIDAL IDEATION

Danger to the self or suicidal ideation occurs frequently in clients with mood disorders or depression. While females are more likely to attempt suicide, males actually successfully commit suicide 3 times more than females, primarily because females tend to take overdoses from which they can be revived, while males choose more violent means, such as jumping from a high place, shooting, or hanging. Risk factors include psychiatric disorders (schizophrenia, bipolar disorder, PTSD, substance abuse, and borderline personality disorder), physical disorders (HIV/AIDS, diabetes, stroke, traumatic brain injury, and spinal cord injury), and a previous violent suicide attempt. Passive suicidal ideation involves wishing to be dead or thinking about dying without making plans while active suicidal ideation involves making plans. Those with active suicidal ideation are most at risk. People with suicidal ideation often give signals, direct or indirect, to indicate they are considering suicide because many people have some ambivalence and want help. Others may act impulsively or effectively hide their distress.

SUICIDE RISK ASSESSMENT

A suicide risk assessment should be completed and documented upon initial interview, with each subsequent visit, and any time suicidal ideations are suggested by the client. This risk assessment should evaluate and score the following criteria:

- Would the client sign a contract for safety?
- Is there a suicide plan, and if so, how lethal is the plan?
- What is the elopement risk?
- How often are the suicidal thoughts?
- Have they attempted suicide before?

Any associated symptoms of hopelessness, guilt, anger, helplessness, impulsive behaviors, nightmares, obsessions with death, or altered judgment should also be assessed and documented. A higher score indicates a higher the risk for suicide.

WARNING SIGNS OF SUICIDE

The warning signs of suicide include the following:

- Depression
- Prior suicide attempts
- Family suicide history
- Abrupt increase in substance abuse
- Reckless and impulsive behavior
- Isolation
- Poor coping
- Support system loss
- Recent or anticipated loss of someone special
- Verbal expression of feeling out of control

- Preoccupation with death
- Behavioral changes not otherwise explained (a sudden changed mood from depressed to happy, the giving away of one's personal belongings, etc.)

Where **risk of suicide is suspected**, the client should be questioned directly about any thoughts of self-harm. This should be followed by a full assessment and history (particularly family history of suicide). Where the threat of suicide is not imminent, one commonly used intervention is the no-suicide contract, in which the client signs a written agreement promising to contact the suicide hotline or a counselor, social worker, or other specified professional rather than carry out an act of suicide. While commonly used, these contracts have not been proven to reduce suicide attempts and therefore should not be used in isolation as an intervention for suicide risk, nor should they be used when threat of suicide is high. When a client already has a plan for suicide, or has multiple risk factors, hospitalization must be arranged. If any immediate attempt has already been made, a medical evaluation must occur immediately.

SIGNS AND RISK FACTORS OF CLIENT'S DANGER TO OTHERS

Violence and aggression are not uncommon among clients and pose a danger to others. Risk factors include mental health disorders, access to weapons, history of personal or family violence, abuse, animal cruelty, fire setting, and substance abuse. Violence and aggression should be handled as follows:

- **Violence** is a physical act perpetrated against an inanimate object, animal, or other person with the intent to cause harm. Violence often results from anger, frustration, or fear and occurs because the perpetrators believe that they are threatened or that their opinion is right and the victim is wrong. It may occur suddenly without warning or following aggressive behavior. Violence can result in death or severe injury if the individual attacks, so anyone in the presence of an actively violent client should back away and seek safety.
- **Aggression** is the communication of a threat or intended act of violence and will often occur before an act of violence. This communication can occur verbally or nonverbally. Gestures, shouting, speaking increasingly loudly, invasion of personal space, or prolonged eye contact are examples of aggression requiring the client be redirected or removed from the situation.

FIVE-PHASE AGGRESSION CYCLE

The five-phase aggression cycle is as follows:

Triggering	Client responds to a triggering event with anger or hostility. Client may exhibit anxiety, restlessness, and muscle tension. Other signs include rapid breathing, perspiration, loud angry voice, and pacing.
Escalation	Client's responses show movement toward lack of control. Client's face flushes and they become increasingly agitated, demanding, and threatening, often swearing, clenching fists, and making threatening gestures. Client is unable to think clearly or resolve problems.
Crisis	Client loses emotional and physical control. Client throws objects, hits, kicks, punches, spits, bites, scratches, screams, shrieks, and cannot communicate clearly.
Recovery	Client regains control. Client's voice lowers, muscle tension relaxes, and client is able to communicate more rationally.
Post-crisis	Client may attempt reconciliation. Client may feel remorse, apologize, cry, or become quiet or withdrawn. Client is now able to respond appropriately.

MANAGING ACTIVE THREATS OF HOMICIDALITY BY CLIENTS

A client may be deemed a threat to others if:

- Client makes a serious threat of physical violence.
- The threat is made against one or more specifically named individuals.

When a threat meeting these criteria is made, even in the context of a privileged-communication relationship, a duty to protect is generated. In such a situation, the professional is required not only to notify appropriate authorities and agencies charged to protect the citizenry, but also to make a good-faith effort to warn the intended victim or, failing that, someone who is reasonably believed to be able to warn the intended victim.

The duty to warn stems from the 1976 legal case *Tarasoff v. Regents of the University of California,* where a therapist heard a credible threat and called only law enforcement authorities, failing to notify the intended victim. The murder occurred, and the case was appealed to the California Supreme Court, from which the rubric of duty to protect an intended victim has been established.

Risk Management

INTERNAL CONTROLS THAT MINIMIZE RISK

An agency minimizes risk internally through many different means, ranging from scheduling and infrastructure to excellence in supervision. Some examples of risk management include attending to the physical safety of workers and clients, ensuring that members of staff understand their ethical obligations, creating a work environment where cooperation and self-reflection are encouraged, and developing staff to the highest possible level of competence.

POLICIES AND PROCEDURES THAT MINIMIZE RISK

Policies that help minimize risk may include rules about the number of staff present in the office or at particular interviews, when and how a worker should seek assistance from another staff member or from the police, and how the agency will respond to complaints or threats from clients or their acquaintances. When an issue of risk arises, agencies should have clearly defined ways of handling the problem. Training staff members in procedures concerning suicide prevention is one way to minimize risk; making sure they're current in their understanding of child protection laws is another. Documentation procedures can help an agency defend itself in cases of litigation.

ADDRESSING CRITICAL INCIDENTS AND DEBRIEFING

Posttraumatic stress and vicarious posttraumatic stress can affect even the most balanced, educated worker, and many of the daily events of a social worker's life are difficult, unpleasant, and upsetting. Agencies have a duty to their employees to provide them with supervision, mental health care, and ways to process and work through **critical incidents**. Agencies should either have trained staff to manage debriefings after traumatic events or should contract with outside companies to provide those services. Employee assistance programs (EAPs), on-site supervision sessions targeted to the incident, and policies regarding time off for self-care after critical events are ways agencies can help employees regain and maintain their emotional stability.

SOCIAL WORKERS' RESPONSIBILITIES TO CLIENTS AND COMMUNITY

Social workers have an **ethical obligation** to protect the identity of their clients and the duty to protect vulnerable members of the population. Confidentiality and informed consent documentation tell clients that if they intend to harm themselves or someone else, the social worker's ethical obligation is to get help, even at the expense of confidentiality. In ethical concerns, the word client could be expanded to mean every member of the population; protecting human rights and safety also includes the duty to warn, which extends to anyone the worker believes is in harm's way.

QUALITY ASSURANCE

Quality assurance is an aspect of quality improvement and risk management and includes all processes involved in planning and operations to ensure that care provided is of high quality. **Quality assurance** (also referred to as quality control) includes those methods used to ensure compliance and a specific level of quality in providing services or products. Quality assurance includes devising standards as well as means of ensuring compliance through guidelines, protocols, and written specifications. One of the primary goals of quality assurance is to identify and correct errors that affect outcomes. Quality assurance reviews should be carried out on an ongoing basis, and reports should be issued so that staff members are aware of their progress in eliminating errors and working efficiently. Quality assurance units and personnel should be independent of the programs and processes they are reviewing in order to prevent bias and should use standardized and validated instruments for assessment purposes whenever possible.

Pharmacologic Interventions

DRUGS FOR SCHIZOPHRENIA AND PSYCHOTIC SYMPTOMS

Antipsychotic drugs are the drug of choice used to treat schizophrenia and psychotic symptoms. There are both older first-generation antipsychotic drugs and newer atypical/second generation antipsychotic drugs.

First-Gen Antipsychotics	Atypical/Second-Gen Antipsychotics
Haldol (haloperidol)	Clozaril (clozapine)
Thorazine (chlorpromazine)	Risperdal (risperidone)
Stelazine (trifluoperazine)	Seroquel (quetiapine)
Prolixin (fluphenazine)	Zyprexa (olanzapine)
Navane (thiothixene)	Abilify (aripiprazole)

> **Review Video: Antipsychotic Drugs**
> Visit mometrix.com/academy and enter code: 369601

SIDE EFFECTS AND OTHER RELEVANT FACTORS

A major drawback and potential side effect for the older antipsychotics (which are effective) is **tardive dyskinesia** (TD). TD is irreversible and causes involuntary movements of the face, tongue, mouth, or jaw. Other possible side effects for the older antipsychotics include **Parkinsonian syndrome** (tremor, shuffling gait, or bradykinesia) or **muscle rigidity**; these are reversible and can be counteracted with benztropine.

Among the newer antipsychotics, clozapine requires frequent blood testing due to the risk of **agranulocytosis**, a blood disorder that decreases white blood cells and increases the risk of infection. Though some atypical antipsychotics have much less risk of TD, they are very expensive and can cause weight gain, affect blood sugar, and affect the lipid profile.

DRUGS FOR BIPOLAR DISORDER

Bipolar disorder is treated with **mood stabilizers**:

- Lithium
- Tegretol (carbamazepine)
- Depakote (sodium valproate)
- Lamictal (lamotrigine)

Mood stabilizers can cause weight gain. Regular blood work is necessary to monitor for therapeutic drug levels and for potential side effects. Lithium can cause kidney or thyroid problems, and Tegretol and Depakote can cause problems with liver function.

DRUGS FOR UNIPOLAR DEPRESSION

Medications used for treating unipolar depression include the following:

Drug Classification	Brand Name (generic)
Selective serotonin reuptake inhibitors (SSRIs)	Prozac (fluoxetine)
	Zoloft (sertraline)
	Paxil (paroxetine)
	Luvox (fluvoxamine)
	Celexa (citalopram)
	Lexapro (escitalopram)

Drug Classification	Brand Name (generic)
Atypical antidepressants	Effexor (venlafaxine)
	Wellbutrin (bupropion)
	Cymbalta (duloxetine)
Tricyclic antidepressants	Tofranil (imipramine)
	Elavil (amitriptyline)
MAO inhibitors (MAOIs)	Nardil (phenelzine)
	Parnate (tranylcypromine)
	Eldepryl (selegiline)

SIDE EFFECTS AND OTHER RELEVANT FACTORS

While antidepressants can be extremely effective in the treatment of unipolar depression, they also have many **side effects**, which both the social worker and client must be aware of:

- **SSRIs** have fewer side effects than other antidepressants, and one cannot overdose on SSRIs alone. SSRIs take several weeks to be effective, can cause a loss of libido, and can lose effectiveness after years of usage. In a few individuals, SSRIs can cause agitation, suicidal ideation, or manic symptoms (in which case, the prescriber should discontinue).
- Of the **atypical antidepressants**, Wellbutrin does not cause libido loss and is sometimes prescribed in combination with an SSRI to counter the sexual side effects or to increase the positive antidepressant effect of the SSRI. Cymbalta is recommended for depression linked with somatic complaints.
- **Tricyclic antidepressants** can cause side effects such as dry mouth, and an overdose can result in dangerous complications such as cardiac dysrhythmias. For this reason, tricyclic antidepressants are less commonly used today, but still have their place in treating depression in some clients.
- **MAO inhibitors** are also less commonly used to treat depression due to their required dietary limitations and possibly dangerous side effects (severe hypertension and serotonin syndrome). They are considered a third line treatment of depression for this reason.

DRUGS FOR ANXIETY

Drugs most often used for anxiety are **benzodiazepines**, including the following:

- Ativan (lorazepam)
- Xanax (alprazolam)
- Klonopin (clonazepam)
- Valium (diazepam)

Benzodiazepines are effective, short-acting, and quickly relieve anxiety. They should be used for as short a time as possible and in conjunction with appropriate therapeutic interventions because of their potential for abuse and addiction. In the elderly, long-term use of these drugs can cause psychotic symptoms that can be reversed by discontinuing their usage.

DRUGS USED FOR ATTENTION DISORDERS

Typical drugs used for attention disorders are either amphetamine-like or non-amphetamine like. The **amphetamine-like drugs** can be short- or long-acting and include the following:

- Ritalin (methylphenidate): Short-acting
- Ritalin LA: Long-acting
- Concerta (methylphenidate): Long-acting
- Adderall (dextroamphetamine-amphetamine): Short-acting
- Adderall XR: Long-acting

These medications relieve symptoms quickly and individuals can take them on selected days or partial days if desired. These have potential for abuse, can suppress appetite and cause weight loss, and can cause feelings of edginess similar to that resulting from excessive caffeine. Amphetamine-like drugs can also cause an increased heart rate.

The **non-amphetamine-like drug** most commonly used for attention disorders is Strattera (atomoxetine). Strattera is less appetite-suppressing; therefore, weight loss is less of a problem. This medication takes 2-4 weeks to be effective and must be taken every day. The client must be monitored for a rarely occurring liver problem. This drug has low risk for abuse.

Psychiatric Disorders and Diagnosis

DSM-5-TR CLASSIFICATIONS

The major DSM-5-TR classifications are as follows:

- Neurodevelopmental disorders
- Schizophrenia spectrum and other psychotic disorders
- Bipolar and related disorders
- Depressive disorders
- Anxiety disorders
- Obsessive-compulsive and related disorders
- Trauma- and stressor-related disorders
- Dissociative disorders
- Somatic symptom and related disorders
- Feeding and eating disorders
- Elimination disorders
- Sleep-wake disorders
- Sexual dysfunctions
- Gender dysphoria
- Disruptive, impulse-control, and conduct disorders
- Substance-related and addictive disorders
- Neurocognitive disorders
- Personality disorders
- Paraphilic disorders
- Other mental disorders and additional codes
- Medication-induced movement disorders and other adverse effects of medications
- Other conditions that may be a focus of clinical attention

INTELLECTUAL DISABILITIES

Very few (approximately 5%) cases of intellectual disability are **hereditary**. Hereditary forms of intellectual disability include Tay-Sachs, fragile X syndrome, and phenylketonuria. Most cases of intellectual disability (about 30%) are due to **mutations in the embryo** during the first trimester of pregnancy. Babies born with Down syndrome or those exposed to environmental toxins while in the uterus fall into this category. About 10% of cases of intellectual disability are due to **pregnancy or perinatal problems**, like fetal malnutrition, anoxia, and HIV. About 5% of those with intellectual disability have **general medical conditions** (like lead poisoning, encephalitis, or malnutrition) suffered during infancy or childhood. Approximately 20% are intellectually disabled because of either **environmental factors** or **other mental disorders** (e.g., sensory deprivation or autism). In the remaining 30%, etiology is **unknown**.

PKU

Phenylketonuria (PKU) is one cause of intellectual disability. It occurs when an infant lacks the enzyme to metabolize the amino acid phenylalanine, found in high-protein foods and aspartame sweetener. PKU is a rare recessive genetic disorder diagnosed at birth by a simple blood test. It affects mostly blue-eyed, fair babies. Expectant mothers can reduce the hazard of PKU by maintaining a diet low in phenylalanine. Untreated PKU typically leads to some form of intellectual disability. Some of the symptoms common to individuals with PKU are impaired motor and language development and volatile, erratic behavior. PKU can be treated if it is diagnosed in a timely fashion. Individuals must monitor their diet to keep phenylalanine blood levels at 2-10 mg/dL. Some phenylalanine is required for growth.

DOWN SYNDROME

Down syndrome (Trisomy 21) occurs when a person has three #21 chromosomes instead of two. **Down syndrome** causes 20-30% of all cases of moderate and severe intellectual disability (1:800 births). Around 80% of Trisomy 21 pregnancies end in miscarriage. Classic physical characteristics associated with Down syndrome are slanted, almond-shaped eyes with epicanthic folds; a large, protruding tongue; a short, bent fifth finger; and a simian fold across the palm. Individuals with Down syndrome age rapidly. Medical conditions that often accompany Down syndrome and cause individuals to have a shorter life expectancy than normal, or poor quality of life, include heart lesions, leukemia, respiratory and digestive problems, cataracts, and Alzheimer's disease.

COMMUNICATION DISORDERS

A number of disorders are lumped together under the heading of **communication disorders**:

- Language disorders
- Speech sound disorders
- Childhood-onset fluency disorders (stuttering)
- Social communications disorders

Childhood-onset fluency disorder (stuttering) typically begins between the ages of 2 and 7, and is more common in males than females. Research shows stuttering can be controlled through the removal of psychological stress in the home. Children who are constantly told not to stutter tend to stutter all the more. Many children find success through controlled and regular breathing exercises, accompanied by positive encouragement. In most cases, though, the child will spontaneously stop stuttering before the age of 16.

Many conditions that previously fell under the DSM-IV category of pervasive developmental disorders meet the criteria for communication disorders in DSM-5 and the revised DSM-5-TR. Because autism spectrum disorder has social and communication deficits as part of its defining characteristics, it is important to note that communication disorders should not be diagnosed when there are repetitive behaviors or narrowed interests or activities.

LEARNING DISORDERS AND ASSOCIATED CONDITIONS

A specific learning disorder is diagnosed as learning and academic difficulty, as evidenced by at least one of the following for at least six months (after interventions have been tried):

- Incorrect spelling
- Problems with math reasoning
- Problems with math calculation and number sense
- Difficulty reading
- Problems understanding what is read
- Difficulty using grammar and syntax

A child will be diagnosed with a learning disorder when they score substantially lower than expected on a standardized achievement test and confirmed by a clinical assessment. The expectation for the child's score should be based on age, schooling, and intelligence, and the definition of "substantially lower" is a difference of two or more standard deviations. Learning disorders are frequently attended by delays in language development or motor coordination, attention and memory deficits, and low self-esteem. Learning disorders can be graded by severity as mild, moderate, or severe.

PROGNOSIS AND ETIOLOGY OF LEARNING DISORDERS

Specific learning disorders include specific learning disorder with **impairment in reading**, specific learning disorder with **impairment in mathematics**, and specific learning disorder with **impairment in written expression**. Research has shown that boys are more likely to develop specific learning disorders with

impairment in reading than girls. Although learning disorders are typically diagnosed during childhood or adolescence, they do not go away without treatment, and indeed may become more severe with time. Children who have a learning disorder with impairment in reading are far more likely than others to display antisocial behavior as an adult. At present, many researchers believe that reading disorders derive from problems with **phonological processing**.

Proposed **causes of learning disorders** include:

- Incomplete dominance and other hemispheric abnormalities
- Cerebellar-vestibular dysfunction
- Exposure to toxins, like lead

AUTISM SPECTRUM DISORDER
SYMPTOMS

There are two categories of symptoms necessary for a diagnosis of autism spectrum disorder. The first category is **deficits in social interaction and social communication**, which includes:

- Absence of developmentally appropriate peer relationships
- Lack of social or emotional reciprocity
- Marked impairment in nonverbal behavior
- Delay or lack of development in spoken language
- Marked impairment in the ability to initiate or sustain conversation
- Stereotyped or repetitive use of language or idiosyncratic language
- Lack of developmentally appropriate play

The other category of symptoms necessary for diagnosis of autism spectrum disorder is **restricted, repetitive patterns of behavior (RRBs), interests, and activities**. These include:

- Preoccupation with one or more stereotyped and restricted patterns of interest
- Inflexible adherence to nonfunctional routines or rituals
- Stereotyped and repetitive motor mannerisms
- Persistent preoccupation with the parts of objects

DIAGNOSIS

Both categories of symptoms will be present in the ASD diagnosis. **Severity levels** are: **Level 1** (requiring support), **Level 2** (requiring substantial support), and **Level 3** (requiring very substantial support). Of note, ASD encompasses four disorders that were previously separate under DSM-IV: autistic disorder, Asperger's disorder, childhood integrative disorder, and pervasive developmental disorder. Individuals with ASD associated with other known conditions or language/intellectual impairment should have the diagnosis written: autism spectrum disorder associated with (name of condition/impairment). It should also be specified if catatonia is present.

PROGNOSIS

Autism spectrum disorder (ASD) is frequently first suspected when an infant does not respond to their caregiver in an age-appropriate manner. Babies with ASD are not interested in cuddling, do not smile, and do not respond to a familiar voice. They are often misdiagnosed as profoundly deaf. The current scientific consensus is that four different disorders previously believed to be separate are actually just different **degrees** on the autism spectrum. Many children with ASD severity level 1 may escape diagnosis until a much later age. At the higher end of the spectrum (which was once referred to as Asperger's syndrome), individuals have impairment in social interactions and a limited repertoire of behaviors, interests, and activities, but they do not display other significant delays in language, self-help skills, cognitive development, or curiosity about the environment. They are extremely sensitive to touch, sounds, sights, and tastes, and have strong clothing preferences. The prognosis of the individual with ASD will largely depend on where they are on the spectrum. Unfortunately, even a small degree of improvement in ASD takes a great deal of work. Only one-third of children with autism will achieve some **independence** as adults. Those with ASD who have developed the ability to communicate verbally by age 5-6 and have an IQ over 70 have the best chance for future independence.

CHARACTERISTIC BEHAVIOR PATTERNS

Some very noticeable, specific behavior patterns characteristic of autism spectrum disorder include:

- Lack of eye contact and disinterest in the presence of others
- Infants who rarely reach out to a caregiver
- Hand-flapping
- Rocking
- Spinning
- Echolalia (the imitating and repeating the words of others)
- Obsessive interest in a very narrow subject, like astronomy or basketball scores
- Heavy emphasis on routine and consistency, and violent reactions to changes in their normal environment

One half of people with autism remain mute for their entire lives. The speech that does develop may be abnormal. The majority of people with autism have an IQ in the intellectual disability range.

ETIOLOGY AND TREATMENT

There are a few structural abnormalities in the brain that have been linked to autism spectrum disorders. These include a **reduced cerebellum** and **enlarged ventricles**. Research has also suggested that there is a link between autism and abnormal levels of **norepinephrine**, **serotonin**, and **dopamine**. The support for a genetic etiology of ASD has been increased by studies indicating that siblings of children with autism are much more likely have autism themselves. As for treatment, the most successful interventions focus on teaching individuals with autism the practical skills they will need to survive independently. Therapy should also include development of social skills and the reduction of undesirable behavior. Individuals with autism who reach a moderate level of functioning can be given direct vocational training.

> **Review Video: Autism Spectrum Disorder**
> Visit mometrix.com/academy and enter code: 395410

ADHD

DIAGNOSIS

Attention-deficit/hyperactivity disorder, commonly known as ADHD, can be diagnosed only if a child displays at least six symptoms of inattention or hyperactivity-impulsivity. Their onset must be before the age of 12, and they must have persisted for at least 6 months. The symptoms must not be motivated by anger or the wish to displease or spite others.

Inattentiveness Symptoms (must have 6 for diagnosis for children)	Impulsivity/Hyperactivity Symptoms (must have 6 for diagnosis for children)
• Forgetful in everyday activity • Easily distracted (often) • Makes careless mistakes and doesn't give attention to detail • Difficulty focusing attention • Does not appear to listen, even when directly spoken to • Starts tasks but does not follow through • Frequently loses essential items • Finds organizing difficult • Avoids activities that require prolonged mental exertion	• Frequently gets out of chair • Runs or climbs at inappropriate times • Frequently talks more than peer • Often moves hands and feet, or shifts position in seat • Frequently interrupts others • Frequently has difficulty waiting on turn • Frequently unable to enjoy leisure activities silently • Frequently "on the go" and seen by others as restless • Often finishes other's sentences before they can

ASSOCIATED FEATURES

Even though they are found to have **average or above-average intelligence**, children with ADHD typically score lower than average on **IQ tests**. Almost every child with ADHD will have some trouble in school, with about a quarter having major problems in **reading**. Also, **social adjustment** can be difficult for children with ADHD. Various reports give the co-diagnosis of Conduct Disorder with ADHD occurring 30-90% of the time. Other common co-diagnoses include **Oppositional Defiant Disorder**, **Anxiety Disorder**, and **Major Depression**. About half of all children who are diagnosed with ADHD are also suffering from a learning disorder.

SUBTYPES

There are three subtypes of ADHD:

- **Predominantly Inattentive Type** is diagnosed when a child has six or more symptoms of inattention and fewer than six symptoms of hyperactivity-impulsivity.
- **Predominantly Hyperactive-Impulsive Type** is diagnosed when there are six or more symptoms of hyperactivity-impulsivity and fewer than six of inattention.
- **Combined Type** is diagnosed when there are six or more symptoms of both hyperactivity-impulsivity and inattention.

ADHD is 4-9 times more likely to occur in boys than in girls, although the gender split is about half and half for Predominantly Inattentive Type. The rates of ADHD among adults appear to be about equal for both males and females.

ETIOLOGY

The theory that ADHD is a **genetic disorder** is supported by data that shows slightly higher rates of the disorder occur among biological relatives than among the general population, and there are higher rates among identical twins, rather than fraternal twins. ADHD is associated with structural abnormalities in the brain, like subnormal activity in the frontal cortex and basal ganglia, and a relatively small caudate nucleus, globus pallidus, and prefrontal cortex. Symptoms of ADHD vary widely, depending on the child's environment. Repetitive or boring environments encourage symptoms, as do those in which the child is given no chance to interact. One theory of ADHD asserts that it is the result of an inability to distinguish between important and unimportant **stimuli** in the environment.

PROGNOSIS

The behavior of children with ADHD is likely to remain consistent until **early adolescence**, when they may experience diminished overactivity, but continue to suffer from attention and concentration problems. ADHD adolescents are much more likely to participate in antisocial behaviors and to abuse drugs. More than half of all children who are diagnosed with ADHD will continue to suffer from it as **adults**. These adults are more susceptible to divorce, work-related trouble, accidents, depression, substance abuse, and antisocial behavior. Children with ADHD who are co-diagnosed with Conduct Disorder are especially likely to have these problems later in life.

TREATMENT

Somewhat counterintuitively, central nervous system stimulants like **methylphenidate (Ritalin)** and **amphetamine (Dexedrine)** control the symptoms of ADHD. Side effects include headaches, gastrointestinal upset, anorexia, sleep difficulty, anxiety, depression, blood sugar and blood pressure increase, tics, and seizures. Research has consistently shown that **pharmacotherapy** works best when it is combined with **psychosocial intervention**. Many teachers have used the basic elements of **classroom management** to control the symptoms of ADHD. This involves laying out clear guidelines and contingencies for behavior, so that students do not have to speculate on what will happen in class or what they should be doing. Therapy that tries to increase the child's ability to **self-regulate behavior** has been shown to be less successful. It is always helpful when **parents** are involved in the treatment program.

CONDUCT DISORDER

DIAGNOSIS

Conduct disorder criteria are as follows:

Criteria A	Persistent pattern of behavior in which significant age-appropriate rules or societal norms are ignored, and others' rights and property are violated (theft, deceitfulness); aggression to people and animals and destruction of property are common. To meet diagnosis criteria individuals will display three of the fifteen possible symptoms over the course of a year. All the symptoms can be categorized as belonging to one of the four categories below: • Aggression to people or animals • Destruction of property • Deceitfulness or theft • Serious violations of rules
Criteria B	The patterns of behavior cause academic, social, or other impairments.
Criteria C	The behaviors couldn't better be classified as antisocial personality disorder.

Individuals with conduct disorder persistently violate either the rights of others or age-appropriate rules. They have little remorse about their behavior, and in ambiguous situations, they are likely to interpret the behavior of other people as hostile or threatening.

ETIOLOGY

According to Moffitt, there are two basic **types** of conduct disorder:

- **Life-course-persistent type** begins early in life and gets progressively worse over time. This kind of conduct disorder may be a result of neurological impairments, a difficult temperament, or adverse circumstances.
- **Adolescence-limited type** is usually the result of a temporary disparity between the adolescent's biological maturity and freedom. Adolescents with this form of conduct disorder may commit antisocial acts with friends. It is quite common for children with adolescence-limited conduct disorder to display antisocial behavior persistently in one area of life and not at all in others.

TREATMENT FOR CONDUCT DISORDER AND OPPOSITIONAL DEFIANT DISORDER

Research suggests that conduct disorder **interventions** are most successful when they are administered to preadolescents and include the immediate family members. Some therapists have developed programs of **parent therapy** to help adults manage the antisocial behavior of their children, as this has been demonstrated to have good success. Most programs advise rewarding good behavior and consistently punishing bad behavior.

Oppositional Defiant Disorder is similar to conduct disorder and is characterized by:

- Patterns of negative or hostile behavior towards authority figures
- Frequent outbreaks of temper and rages
- Deliberately annoying people
- Blaming others
- Spite and vindictiveness

This pattern of negative, hostile, defiant behavior, and vindictiveness however, is less serious violations of the basic rights of others that characterize conduct disorders. Behavior is motivated by interpersonal reactivity or resentful power struggle with adults.

MOTOR DISORDERS

Motor disorders are a type of neurodevelopmental disorder. **Motor disorders** can be classified as developmental coordination disorders, stereotypic movement disorders, and tic disorders. **Tic disorders** are further classified as Tourette's disorder, persistent motor or vocal tic disorder, and provisional tic disorder. **Tics** are defined in the DSM as "sudden, rapid, recurrent, nonrhythmic, stereotyped motor movements or vocalizations that feel irresistible yet can be suppressed for varying lengths of time."

TOURETTE'S SYNDROME

Tourette's syndrome is a neurological disorder characterized by at least one vocal tic and multiple motor tics that appear simultaneously or at different times, and appears before the age of 18. Those with **Tourette's syndrome** typically have multiple motor tics and one or more vocal tics. Those with chronic motor or vocal tic disorder have either motor or vocal tics. Individuals with Tourette's syndrome are likely to have obsessions and compulsions, high levels of hyperactivity, impulsivity, and distractibility.

TREATMENT

Most successful treatments for Tourette's syndrome include **pharmacotherapy**. The antipsychotics **haloperidol (Haldol)** and **pimozide (Orap)** are successful in relieving the symptoms of Tourette's syndrome because they inhibit the flow of dopamine in the brain; their success has led many scientists to speculate that Tourette's Disorder is caused by an excess of dopamine. In some cases, psychostimulant drugs amplify the tics displayed by the individual. In these cases, a doctor may treat the hyperactivity and inattention of Tourette's with **clonidine** or **desipramine**. The former of these is a drug usually used to treat hypertension, while the latter is typically used as an antidepressant.

ENURESIS AND ENCOPRESIS

Encopresis and enuresis make up the two major categories of elimination disorders. **Enuresis** is repeated urinating during the day or night into the bed or clothes at least twice a week for three or more months. Most of the time this urination is involuntary. Enuresis is diagnosed only when the child has reached an age at which continence can be reasonably expected (at least age five for DSM-5-TR criteria), and they do not have some other medical condition that could be to blame, like a urinary tract infection. Enuresis is treated with a night alarm, which makes a loud noise when the child urinates while sleeping. This is effective about 80% of the time, especially when it is combined with techniques like behavioral reversal and overcorrection. Desmopressin acetate (DDAVP) nasal spray, imipramine, and oxybutynin chloride (Ditropan) may help control

symptoms. **Encopresis** is the involuntary fecal soiling in children who have already been toilet trained. Encopresis diagnosis cannot be made until the child is at least 4 years of age per DSM-5-TR criteria.

PICA AND RUMINATION DISORDER

Pica is the persistent eating of non-food substances such as paint, hair, sand, cloth, pebbles, etc. Those with **pica** do not show an aversion to food. In order to be diagnosed, the symptoms must persist for at least a month without the child losing an interest in regular food. Also, the behavior must be independent and not a part of any culturally acceptable process. Pica is most often manifested between the ages of 12 and 24 months. Pica has been observed in developmentally disabled children, pregnant women, and people with anemia.

Rumination disorder is the regurgitation and re-chewing of food.

AVOIDANT/RESTRICTIVE FOOD INTAKE DISORDER
DIAGNOSIS

The **criteria for avoidant/restrictive food intake disorder** are as follows:

Criteria A	A disruption in eating evidenced by not meeting nutritional needs and failure to gain expected weight or weight loss, nutritional deficiency requiring nutritional supplementation, or interpersonal interference.
Criteria B	This disruption is not due to lack of food or culture.
Criteria C	There does not appear to be a problem with the individual's body perception.
Criteria D	The disturbance can't be explained by another medical condition.

ANOREXIA NERVOSA
DIAGNOSIS

The characteristics of **anorexia nervosa** are:

Criteria A	Extreme restriction of food, lower than requirements, leading to low body weight
Criteria B	An irrational fear of gaining weight or behaviors that prevent weight gain, despite being at low weight
Criteria C	Distorted body image or a lack of acknowledgement of severity of current weight

A general standard used to determine the minimum healthy body weight is that it should be at least 85% of the norm for the individual's height and weight. People with restricting type anorexia lose weight through fasting, dieting, and excessive exercise. People with binging/purging type anorexia lose weight by eating a great deal and then either vomiting it or inducing immediate defecation with laxatives. People with anorexia are preoccupied with food. The physical symptoms of **starvation** are constipation, cold intolerance, lethargy, and bradycardia. The physical problems associated with **purging** are anemia, impaired renal function, cardiac abnormalities, dental problems, and osteoporosis.

GENDER, AGE, ETIOLOGY, AND TREATMENT

The vast majority of people with anorexia are **female**, and the onset of anorexia is usually in **mid-to-late adolescence**. Onset may be associated with a stressful life event. Some studies associated anorexia with middle- and upper-class families that have a tendency towards competition and success. Girls with anorexia are likely to be introverted, nonassertive, and conscientious. Their mothers are likely to also be very concerned about food intake and weight. The immediate goal of any treatment program is to help the individual gain

weight. Sometimes this requires hospitalization. **Cognitive therapy** is also often employed to correct the individual's misconceptions about healthy weight and nutrition.

BULIMIA NERVOSA

DIAGNOSIS

The characteristics of **bulimia nervosa** are:

Criteria A	Cyclical periods of binge eating characterized by discretely consuming an amount of food that is larger than most individuals would eat in the same time period and situation. The individual feels a lack of control over the eating.
Criteria B	Characterized by binge eating followed by purging via self-induced vomiting/laxatives/fasting/vigorous exercise in order to prevent weight gain
Criteria C	At least one binge eating episode per week for three months
Criteria D	It is marked by a persistent over-concern with body shape and weight.
Criteria E	The eating and compensatory behaviors do not only occur during periods of anorexia nervosa.

Binges are often caused by interpersonal stress and may entail a staggering caloric intake. The **medical complications** associated with bulimia are fluid and electrolyte disturbances, metabolic alkalosis, metabolic acidosis, dental problems, and menstrual abnormalities.

GENDER, AGE, ETIOLOGY, AND TREATMENT

As with anorexia, the vast majority of people with bulimia are **female**. The onset is typically in **late adolescence** or **early adulthood**, and may follow a period of dieting. There are indications of a **genetic etiology** for bulimia. Also, there are links between bulimia and low levels of the endogenous opioid beta-endorphin, as well as low levels of serotonin and norepinephrine. The main point of any treatment for bulimia is encouraging the individual to get control of eating, and modifying unhealthy beliefs about body shape and nutrition. Treatment often involves **cognitive-behavioral techniques** like self-monitoring, stimulus control, cognitive restructuring, problem-solving, and self-distraction. Some antidepressants, like imipramine, have been effective at reducing instances of binging and purging.

ANXIETY DISORDERS

Types of anxiety disorders include the following:

Panic disorder	Recurrent brief but intense fear in the form of panic attacks with physiological or psychological symptoms
Specific phobia	Fear of specific situations or objects
Generalized anxiety disorder	Chronic psychological and cognitive symptoms of distress and excessive worry lasting at least 6 months
Separation anxiety disorder	Excessive anxiety related to being separated from someone the individual is attached to
Selective mutism	Inability to speak in social settings (when it would seem appropriate) though normally able to speak
Social anxiety disorder	Anxiety about social situations
Agoraphobia	Anxiety about being outside of the home or in open places

> **Review Video: Anxiety Disorders**
> Visit mometrix.com/academy and enter code: 366760

PANIC DISORDER

DIAGNOSIS

An individual may be diagnosed with **panic disorder** if they suffer recurrent unexpected panic attacks, and one of the attacks is followed by one month of either persistent concern regarding the possibility of another attack or a significant change in behavior related to the attack. **Panic attacks** are brief, defined periods of intense apprehension, fear, or terror. They develop quickly, and usually reach their greatest intensity after about ten minutes. Attacks must include at least 4 characteristic **symptoms**, which include:

Palpitations or accelerated heart rate (tachycardia)
Sweating
Chest pain
Nausea
Dizziness
Derealization
Paresthesia (pins and needles or numbness)

Shaking
Shortness of breath
Fear of losing control
Fear of dying
Chills or heat sensation
Feeling of choking

PREVALENCE AND GENDER ISSUES

The consensus of research is that 1-2% of the population will suffer panic disorder at some point during their lives, and 30-50% of these individuals will also suffer **agoraphobia**. Panic disorder has a higher rate of diagnostic comorbidity when it is accompanied by agoraphobia. Panic disorder is far more likely to occur in **females** than males, and females with a panic disorder have a 75% chance of also having agoraphobia. There is a great deal of variation in the age of onset, but the most frequent ages of occurrence are in adolescence and the mid-30s. Children can experience the physical symptoms of a panic attack, but are unlikely to be diagnosed with panic disorder because they do not have the wherewithal to associate their symptoms with catastrophic feelings. The individual can be diagnosed with agoraphobia even if they are not diagnosed with panic disorder, but the two are commonly diagnosed together.

TREATMENT AND DIFFERENTIAL DIAGNOSIS

The most effective treatment for panic attacks appears to be controlled in vivo exposure with response prevention, known as **flooding**. Flooding is typically accompanied by cognitive therapy, relaxation, breathing training, or pharmacotherapy. **Antidepressant medications** are often prescribed to relieve the symptoms of panic disorder. If stand-alone drug treatment is used, the risk of relapse is very high. Differential diagnoses for panic disorder include social phobia, and medical conditions like hyperthyroidism, hypoglycemia, cardiac arrhythmia, and mitral valve prolapse. Panic disorder can be distinguished from social phobia by the fact that attacks will sometimes occur while the individual is alone or sleeping.

PHOBIAS

DIAGNOSIS

A specific phobia is a marked and persistent fear of a particular object or situation, other than those associated with social phobia or agoraphobia. When an individual with a phobia is exposed to the feared object or event, they will have a panic attack or some other anxiety response. Adults with a specific phobia should be able to recognize that their fear is irrational and excessive. The onset of a specific phobia is typically in childhood or in the mid-20s. According to the DSM-5-TR, there are five **subtypes** of specific phobia:

- Animal
- Natural environment
- Situational
- Blood-injection-injury
- Other

The blood-injection-injury subtype has different physical symptoms than the others. Individuals with blood-injection-injury phobia have a brief increase in heart rate and blood pressure, followed by a drop in both, often ending in a brief loss of consciousness (fainting). Other phobic reactions just entail the increase in heart rate and blood pressure, without loss of consciousness.

DISTINGUISHING SYMPTOMS OF AGORAPHOBIA

Symptoms that distinguish panic disorder from **agoraphobia** include the fear of being in a situation or place from which it could be difficult or embarrassing to escape, or of being in a place where help might not be available in the event of a panic attack. Agoraphobia usually manifests when the individual is alone outside of the home, is in a crowd, or is traveling in a train or automobile. Those who suffer from agoraphobia will typically go to great lengths to avoid problematic situations, or they will only be able to enter certain situations with a companion and under heavy distress. One of the main problems with agoraphobia is that it causes the individual to severely limit the places they are willing to go. These individuals often become reclusive.

ETIOLOGY AND TREATMENT

The **two-factor theory** proposed by Mower asserts that phobias are the result of avoidance conditioning, when an individual associates a neutral or controlled stimulus with an anxiety-causing, unconditioned stimulus. The phobia reinforces a strategy of avoidance because it prevents anxiety (even though the neutral stimulus was not to blame for the anxiety in the first place). Another theory for the etiology of phobias is offered by **social learning theorists**, who state that phobic behaviors are learned by watching avoidance strategies used by one's parents. As with panic disorder, **in vivo exposure** is considered the best treatment for a specific phobia. **Relaxation and breathing techniques** are also helpful in dispelling fear and controlling physical response.

GENERALIZED ANXIETY DISORDER

Individuals may be diagnosed with generalized anxiety disorder (GAD) if they have excessive anxiety about multiple events or activities. This anxiety must have existed for at least six months and must be difficult for the individual to control. The anxiety must be disproportionate to the feared event. Anxiety must include at least three of the following:

- Restlessness
- Fatigue on exertion
- Difficulty concentrating
- Irritability

- Muscle tension
- Sleep disturbance

The treatment for GAD usually entails a **multicomponent cognitive-behavioral therapy**, occasionally accompanied by pharmacotherapy. **SSRI** antidepressants and the anxiolytic buspirone have both demonstrated success in diminishing the symptoms of GAD.

SEPARATION ANXIETY DISORDER

ONSET

Many children who suffer from separation anxiety disorder will refuse to go to school, and may claim physical ailments to avoid having to leave the home. In some cases, the child will actually develop a headache or stomachache as a result of anxiety about separation from the home or from an individual to whom they are attached. The refusal to go to school may begin as early as 5 or as late as 12. If the separation anxiety occurs after the age of 10, however, it is quite possibly the result of depression or some more severe disorder. There are various treatment plans for separation anxiety disorder, all of which recommend that the child immediately resume going to school on a normal schedule.

SYMPTOMS

Separation anxiety disorder is characterized by age-inappropriate and excessive anxiety that occurs when an individual is separated or threatened with separation from their home or family unit. In order to be diagnosed with separation anxiety disorder, the child must exhibit **symptoms** for at least four weeks and onset must be before the age of 18. Individuals with separation anxiety disorder will manifest some of the following symptoms:

- Excessive distress when separated from home or attachment figures
- Persistent fear of being alone
- Frequent physical complaints during separation

Children with separation anxiety tend to be from loving, stable homes. For many, the disorder begins to manifest after the child has suffered some personal loss.

SOCIAL ANXIETY DISORDER

The characteristics of social anxiety disorder or **social phobia** are a marked and persistent fear of social situations or situations in which the individual may be called upon to perform. Typically, the individual fears criticism and evaluation by others. The response to the feared situation is an immediate panic attack. Those with social phobia either avoid the feared situation or endure it with much distress. The fear and anxiety regarding these social situations have a negative impact on the individual's life, and is present for at least six months. Adults should be able to recognize that their fear is excessive and irrational. As with other phobias, social phobia is best treated with **exposure** in combination with **social skills and cognitive therapy**. Antidepressants and the beta-blocker propranolol are helpful for treating social phobia.

OBSESSIVE-COMPULSIVE DISORDER

The following are the **criteria for obsessive-compulsive disorders:**

Criteria A	The individual exhibits obsessions, compulsions, or both. **Obsession**: continuous, repetitive thoughts, compulsions, or things imagined that are unwanted and cause distress. The individual will try to suppress thoughts, ignore them, or do a compulsive behavior. **Compulsion**: recurrent behavior or thought the individual feels obliged to perform after an obsession to decrease anxiety; however, the compulsion is usually not connected in an understandable way to an observer.
Criteria B	The obsessions and compulsions take at least one hour per day and cause distress.
Criteria C	The behavior is not caused by a substance.
Criteria D	The behavior could not better be explained by a different mental disorder.

Note if the criteria are met with good insight (individual realizes OCD beliefs are not true), poor insight (individual thinks the OCD beliefs are true), or absent insight (individual is delusional, truly believing OCD beliefs are true). Note if the individual has ever had tic disorder.

Other obsessive-compulsive and related disorders include:

- Body dysmorphic disorder
- Hoarding disorder
- Trichotillomania (hair-pulling disorder)
- Excoriation (skin-picking disorder)

GENDER ISSUES, ETIOLOGY, AND TREATMENT

OCD is equally likely to occur in adult males and adult females. The average age of onset is lower for males, so the rates of OCD among male children and adolescents are slightly higher than among females. Evidence suggests that OCD is caused by low levels of **serotonin**. Structurally, OCD seems to be linked to overactivity in the **right caudate nucleus**. The most effective treatment for OCD is exposure with response prevention in tandem with medication, usually either the tricyclic clomipramine or an SSRI. Therapies that provide help with stopping thought patterns seem to be especially successful in battling OCD. When drugs are used alone, there remains a high risk of relapse.

> **Review Video: Obsessive-Compulsive Disorder (OCD)**
> Visit mometrix.com/academy and enter code: 499790

PTSD

DIAGNOSIS

An individual may be diagnosed with post-traumatic stress disorder (PTSD) if they develop symptoms after exposure to an extreme trauma. Examples of extreme trauma include: witnessing the death or injury of another person, experiencing injury to self, learning about the unexpected or violent death or injury of a family member or friend, or repeatedly being exposed to trauma (such as first responders or military soldiers). The

traumatic event must elicit a reaction of intense fear, helplessness, or horror. The **characteristic symptoms** of PTSD are:

- Persistent re-experiencing of the event
- Persistent avoidance of stimuli associated with the trauma
- Persistent symptoms of increased arousal (difficulty concentrating, staying awake, or falling asleep)

These symptoms must have been present for at least a month; symptoms may not begin until three or more months after the event.

TREATMENT

The preferred treatment for PTSD is a **comprehensive cognitive-behavioral approach** that includes:

- Exposure
- Cognitive restructuring
- Anxiety management
- SSRIs to relieve symptoms of PTSD and comorbid conditions

Some psychologists criticize single-session psychological debriefings, because they believe one session amplifies the effects of a traumatic event. Another controversial therapy used to treat PTSD is eye movement desensitization and reprocessing; the positive benefits of this therapy may be more to do with the exposure that goes along with it than with the eye movements themselves.

ACUTE STRESS DISORDER

Acute stress disorder has symptoms similar to those of post-traumatic stress disorder. Acute stress disorder is distinguished by symptoms that occur for more than 3 days and but less than one month. An individual is diagnosed with acute stress disorder when they have 9 or more **symptoms** from any of the following 5 categories, which begin after the trauma:

- Intrusion
- Negative mood
- Avoidance symptoms
- Dissociative symptoms
- Arousal symptoms

An individual with acute stress disorder persistently relives the traumatic event, to the point where they take steps to avoid contact with stimuli that bring the event to mind, and experience severe anxiety when reminiscing about the event.

> **Review Video: Acute Stress Disorder**
> Visit mometrix.com/academy and enter code: 538946

ADDITIONAL TRAUMA- AND STRESSOR-RELATED DISORDERS

Additional trauma- and stress-related disorders include:

Reactive attachment disorder	Child rarely seeks or responds to comfort when upset, usually due to neglect of emotional needs by caregiver (e.g., children who are institutionalized or in foster care). Reactive attachment disorder is characterized by a markedly disturbed or developmentally-inappropriate social relatedness in most settings. This condition typically begins before the age of five. In order to definitively diagnose this disorder, there must be evidence of pathogenic care, which may include neglect or a constant change of caregivers that made it difficult for the child to form normal attachments.
Disinhibited social engagement disorder	Child has decreased hesitations regarding interacting with unfamiliar adults. Does not question leaving normal caregiver to go off with a stranger.
Adjustment disorder	The individual has behavioral or emotional changes occurring within 3 months of a stressor. These changes cause distress for the individual and are disproportional to the actual stressor.

SOMATOFORM DISORDERS

FUNCTIONAL NEUROLOGICAL SYMPTOM DISORDER

Functional neurological symptom disorder (formerly conversion disorder) is a somatoform disorder characterized by either loss of bodily functions or symptoms of a serious physical disease. The individual becomes blind, mute, or paralyzed in response to an acute stressor. Occasionally, individuals develop hyperesthesia, analgesia, tics, belching, vomiting, or coughing spells. These symptoms do not conform to physiological mechanisms, and testing reveals no underlying physical disease. The sensory loss, movement loss, or repetitive physical symptoms are not intentional. The individual is not malingering to avoid work, or factitiously seeking attention. The symptoms of a functional neurological symptom disorder can often be removed with **hypnosis** or **Amytal interview**. Some researchers believe that simply suggesting that these symptoms will go away is the best way to relieve them. The individual can develop complications, like seizures, from disuse of body parts.

PRIMARY GAIN, SECONDARY GAIN, AND DIFFERENTIAL DIAGNOSES

The **etiology of functional neurological symptom disorder** is explained in terms of two psychological mechanisms:

- It may be used for **primary gain** when the symptoms keep an internal conflict or need out of the consciousness.
- It may be used for **secondary gain** when the symptoms help the individual avoid an unpleasant activity or obtain support from the environment.

In order to diagnose a functional neurological symptom disorder, there must be evidence of *involuntary* psychological factors. Functional neurological symptom disorder is occasionally confused with factitious disorder and malingering, both of which are voluntary.

SOMATIC SYMPTOM DISORDER

Somatic symptom disorder is a somatoform disorder, meaning that it suggests a medical condition but is not fully explainable by the medical condition, substance abuse, or other medical disorder. Individuals with somatic symptom disorder often describe their problems in dramatic, overstated, and ambiguous terms. They excessively worry or think about the symptoms and spend much time and energy worrying about health issues. Somatic symptom disorders cause clinically significant distress or impairment, and are not produced

intentionally. A somatic symptom disorder involves recurrent multiple somatic complaints and though no one symptom has to be continuous, some symptoms are present for at least six months. Medical attention has been sought, but no physical explanation has been found.

ILLNESS ANXIETY DISORDER

Individuals with illness anxiety disorder (formerly hypochondriasis) have an unrealistic preoccupation with having or getting a serious illness that is based on a misappraisal of bodily symptoms. This preoccupation is disproportional to symptoms or medical evidence. Individuals with illness anxiety disorder likely know a great deal about their condition, and frequently go to a number of different doctors searching for a professional opinion that confirms their own. They likely either experience frequent health related checks (either by doctors or by self-checks) or avoidance of doctors and healthcare facilities. The symptoms of this disorder have been present for at least six months, however the specific illness that the individual fears may change.

DELIRIUM

Delirium is characterized by a clinically significant deficit in cognition or memory as compared to previous functioning. In order for delirium to be diagnosed, the individual must have disturbances in consciousness and either a change in personality or the development of perceptual abnormalities. These changes in cognition may appear as losses of memory, disorientation in space and time, and impaired language. The perceptual abnormalities associated with delirium include hallucinations and illusions. Delirium usually develops over a few hours or days, and may vary in intensity over the course of the days and weeks. If the cause of the delirium is alleviated, it may disappear for an extended period of time.

The **criteria** for delirium are as follows:

Criteria A	A disturbance in consciousness or attention
Criteria B	Develops over a short period of time, and fluctuates throughout the day
Criteria C	Accompanied by changes in cognition
Criteria D	Not better explained by another condition
Criteria E	Caused by a medical condition or is substance related

Five groups of people at **high risk** for delirium:

- Elderly people
- Those who have a diminished cerebral reserve due to major neurocognitive disorder (formerly dementia), stroke, or some other medical condition
- Those who have recently undergone cardiotomy
- Burn victims
- Individuals who are drug-dependent and in withdrawal

Delirium can also be **caused** by:

- Systemic infections
- Metabolic disorders
- Fluid and electrolyte imbalances
- Postoperative states
- Head trauma
- Long hospital stays, such as those in the intensive care unit

The **treatment** for delirium usually aims at curing the underlying cause of the disorder and reducing the agitated behavior. Antipsychotic drugs can be good for reducing agitation, delusions, and hallucinations, while providing a calm environment can decrease the appearance of agitation.

NEUROCOGNITIVE DISORDERS

Major and minor neurocognitive disorders (NCD) may be due to any of the following: Alzheimer's disease, Frontotemporal lobar degeneration, Lewy body disease, vascular disease, traumatic brain injury, substance or medication use, HIV Infection, prion disease, Parkinson's disease, Huntington's disease, another medical condition, and multiple etiologies. **Criteria** are as follows:

Criteria A	A change in cognitive ability from baseline. This information can be determined by the individual, a well-informed significant other, family member, or caretaker, or it can be determined by neuropsychology testing.
Criteria B	For a major neurocognitive disorder, the cognitive change interferes with ADLs and independence. For a minor neurocognitive disorder, the cognitive change doesn't interfere with normal ADLS and independence, if accommodations are used.
Criteria C	The cognitive change cannot be defined as delirium only.
Criteria D	The cognitive change is not better described as another mental disorder.

DIFFERENTIAL DIAGNOSIS

Some of the cognitive symptoms of major depressive disorder are very similar to those of **neurocognitive disorders**. Indeed, this kind of depression is frequently referred to as pseudodementia. One difference is that the **cognitive deficits** typical of neurocognitive disorders will get progressively worse, and the individual is unlikely to admit that they have impaired cognition.

Pseudodementia, on the other hand, typically has a very rapid onset and usually causes the individual to become concerned about their own health. There are also differences in the quality of memory impairment in these two conditions: Individuals with **neurocognitive disorders** have deficits in both recall and recognition memory, while individuals who are **depressed** only have deficits in recall memory.

DIAGNOSIS

Individuals who suffer from neurocognitive disorders are likely to manifest a few **cognitive deficits**, most notably memory impairment, aphasia, apraxia, agnosia, or impaired executive functioning. Depending on the etiology of the neurocognitive disorders, these deficits may get progressively worse or may be stable.

These individuals could have both **anterograde** and **retrograde amnesia**, meaning that they find it difficult both to learn new information and to recall previously learned information. There may be a decrease in language skill, specifically manifested in an inability to recall the names of people or things. Individuals may also have a hard time performing routine motor programs, and may be unable to recognize familiar people and places. Abstract thinking, planning, and initiating complex behaviors are difficult.

NEUROCOGNITIVE DISORDER DUE TO ALZHEIMER'S DISEASE

Particular kinds of **Alzheimer's disease** have been linked with specific genetic abnormalities. For instance, those with early-onset familial Alzheimer's often have abnormalities on **chromosome 21**, while individuals whose onset is later are likely to have irregularities on **chromosome 19**. Those with Alzheimer's disease have also been shown to have significant **aluminum deposits** in brain tissues, a malfunctioning **immune system**, and a low level of **acetylcholine**. Some of the drugs used to treat Alzheimer's increase the cholinergic activity in the brain. These drugs, which include the trade names **Cognex** and **Aricept**, can temporarily reverse cognitive impairment, though these improvements are not sustained when the drugs are removed.

STAGES OF ALZHEIMER'S DISEASE

Over half of all cases of neurocognitive disorder are caused by Alzheimer's disease. Alzheimer's begins slowly and may take a long time to become noticeable. Researchers have outlined **three stages** of Alzheimer's disease:

- **Stage 1** usually comprises the first 1-3 years of the condition. The individual suffers from **mild anterograde amnesia**, especially for declarative memories. They are likely to have **diminished visuospatial skill**, which often manifests itself in wandering aimlessly. Also common to this stage are indifference, irritability, sadness, and anomia.
- **Stage 2** can stretch between the second and tenth years of the illness. The individual suffers increasing **retrograde amnesia**, restlessness, delusions, aphasia, acalculia, ideomotor apraxia (the inability to translate an idea into movement), and a generally flat mood.
- In **Stage 3** of Alzheimer's disease, the individual suffers **severely impaired intellectual functioning**, apathy, limb rigidity, and urinary and fecal incontinence. This last stage usually occurs between the eighth and twelfth years of the condition.

Alzheimer's disease is quite difficult to diagnose directly, so it is usually only diagnosed once all the other possible causes of major neurocognitive disorder (formerly dementia) have been eliminated. A brain biopsy that indicates extensive neuron loss, amyloid plaques, and neurofibrillary tangles can give solid evidence of Alzheimer's disease. Individuals who develop Alzheimer's disease usually only live about ten years after onset. The disease is more common in females than males, and is more likely to occur after the age of 65.

TREATMENT

Though Alzheimer's disease is a degenerative condition with no known cure, there are a number of different **treatments** that can provide help to those who suffer from the disease:

- Group therapy that focuses on orienting the individual in reality and encourages them to reminisce about past experiences
- Antidepressants, antipsychotics, and other pharmacotherapy
- Behavioral techniques to fight the agitation associated with Alzheimer's
- Environmental manipulation to improve memory and cognitive function
- Involving the individual's family in interventions

NEUROCOGNITIVE DISORDER DUE TO HIV INFECTION

Individuals with AIDS develop a particular form of neurocognitive disorder. In its early stages, the **Human Immunodeficiency Virus** causes major neurocognitive disorder (formerly dementia), which appears as forgetfulness, impaired attention, and generally decelerated mental processes. **Neurocognitive disorders** due to HIV progresses include poor concentration, apathy, social withdrawal, loss of initiative, tremor, clumsiness, trouble with problem-solving, and saccadic eye movements. One of the ways that neurocognitive disorders due to HIV is distinguished is by motor slowness, the lack of aphasia, and more severe forms of depression and anxiety. It shares these features with neurocognitive disorders due to Parkinson's and Huntington's diseases.

NEUROCOGNITIVE DISORDER DUE TO VASCULAR DISEASE

In order to be diagnosed with neurocognitive disorder due to **vascular disease**, the individual must have **cognitive impairment** and either **focal neurological signs** or **laboratory evidence of cerebrovascular disease**. Neurocognitive disorder has varying symptoms, depending on where the brain damage lies. Focal neurological signs may include exaggerated reflexes, weaknesses in the extremities, and abnormalities in gait. Symptoms gradually increase in severity. Risk factors for vascular neurocognitive disorder are hypertension, diabetes, tobacco smoking, and atrial fibrillation. In some cases, an individual may be able to recover from neurocognitive disorder due to vascular disease. Stroke victims, for instance, will notice a great deal of improvement in the first six months after the cerebrovascular accident. Most of this improvement will be in their physical, rather than cognitive, symptoms.

NEUROCOGNITIVE DISORDER DUE TO HUNTINGTON'S DISEASE

Individuals with **Huntington's disease** suffer degeneration of the GABA-producing cells in their substantia nigra, basal ganglia, and cortex. This inherited disease typically appears between the ages of 30 and 40. The **affective symptoms** of Huntington's disease include irritability, depression, and apathy. After a while, these individuals display **cognitive symptoms** as well, including forgetfulness and dementia. Later, **motor symptoms** emerge, including fidgeting, clumsiness, athetosis (slow, writhing movements), and chorea (involuntary quick jerks). Because the affective symptoms appear in advance of the cognitive and motor symptoms, many people with Huntington's are misdiagnosed with depression. Individuals in the early stages of Huntington's are at risk for suicide, as they are aware of their impending deterioration, and will have the loss of impulse control associated with the disease.

NEUROCOGNITIVE DISORDER DUE TO PARKINSON'S DISEASE

The following symptoms are commonly associated with neurocognitive disorder due to **Parkinson's disease**:

- Bradykinesia (general slowness of movement)
- Resting tremor
- Stoic and unmoving facial expression
- Loss of coordination or balance
- Involuntary pill-rolling movement of the thumb and forefinger
- Akathisia (violent restlessness)

Most people with Parkinson's will suffer from **depression** at some point during their illness, and 20-60% will develop major neurocognitive disorder (formerly dementia). Research indicates that those with Parkinson's have a deficiency of **dopamine-producing cells** and the presence of **Lewy bodies** in their substantia nigra. Many doctors now believe that there is some **environmental cause** for Parkinson's, though the etiology is not yet clear. The medication L-dopa (Dopar, Larodopa) alleviates the symptoms of Parkinson's by increasing the amount of dopamine in the brain.

SCHIZOPHRENIA
DIAGNOSIS

Schizophrenia is a psychotic disorder. Psychotic disorders are those that feature one or more of the following: delusions, hallucinations, disorganized speech or thought, or disorganized or catatonic behavior. Schizophrenia **diagnostic criteria** are as follows:

Criteria A	Diagnosis requires at least two of the following symptoms, one being a core positive symptom: • Hallucinations (core positive symptom) • Delusions (core positive symptom) • Disorganized speech (core positive symptom) • Severely disorganized or catatonic behavior • Negative symptoms (i.e., avolition, diminished expression)
Criteria B	Individual's level of functioning is significantly below level prior to onset.
Criteria C	If the individual has not had successful treatment there are continual signs of schizophrenia for more than six months.
Criteria D	Depressive disorder, bipolar disorder, and schizoaffective disorder have been ruled out.
Criteria E	The symptoms cannot be attributed to another medical condition or a substance.
Criteria F	If the individual has had a communication disorder or Autism since childhood, a diagnosis of schizophrenia is only made if the individual has hallucinations or delusions.

ETIOLOGY

Both twin and adoption studies have suggested that there is a **genetic component** to the etiology of schizophrenia. The rates of instance (concordance) among first-degree biological relatives of people with schizophrenia are greater than among the general population. **Structural abnormalities** in the brain linked to schizophrenia are enlarged ventricles and diminished hippocampus, amygdala, and globus pallidus. **Functional abnormalities** in the brain linked to schizophrenia are hypofrontality and diminished activity in the prefrontal cortex. An abnormally large number of the people with schizophrenia in the Northern Hemisphere were born in the late winter or early spring. There is speculation that this may be because of a link between prenatal exposure to influenza and schizophrenia.

SCHIZOPHRENIA AND DOPAMINE

For many years, the professional consensus was that schizophrenia was caused by either an excess of the neurotransmitter **dopamine** or oversensitive **dopamine receptors**. The **dopamine hypothesis** was supported by the fact that antipsychotic medications that block dopamine receptors had some success in treating schizophrenia, and by the fact that dopamine-elevating amphetamines amplified the frequency of delusions. The dopamine hypothesis has been somewhat undermined, however, by research that found elevated levels of norepinephrine and serotonin, as well as low levels of GABA and glutamate in schizophrenics. Some studies have shown that clozapine and other atypical antipsychotics are effective in treating schizophrenia, even though they block serotonin rather than dopamine receptors.

POSITIVE SYMPTOMS

The symptoms of schizophrenia may be **positive, negative,** or **disorganized**. Positive symptoms are **delusions** and **hallucinations**. Delusions are false beliefs that are held despite clear evidence to the contrary. The delusions suffered by a schizophrenic usually fall into one of three categories:

- **Persecutory**, in which the person believes that someone or something is out to get them.
- **Referential**, in which the person believes that messages in the public domain (like song lyrics or newspaper articles) are specifically directed at them.
- **Bizarre**, in which the person imagines that something impossible has happened.

The most common sensory mode for hallucinations is sound, specifically the audition of voices.

DISORGANIZED AND NEGATIVE SYMPTOMS

For many psychologists, the classic characteristic of schizophrenia is **disorganized speech**. Disorganized speech manifests as:

- Incoherence
- Free associations that make little sense
- Random responses to direct questions

Disorganized behavior manifests as:

- Shabby or unkempt appearance
- Inappropriate sexual behavior
- Unpredictable agitation
- Catatonia and decreased motor activity

Negative symptoms of schizophrenia include:

- Restricted range of emotions
- Reduced body language
- Lack of facial expression
- Lack of coherent thoughts
- Inability to make conversation
- Avolition (the inability to set goals or to work in a rational, programmatic manner)

CATATONIA

Criteria for catatonia includes at least three of the following:

- Catalepsy
- Defying or refusing to acknowledge instruction
- Echolalia
- Echopraxia
- Little to no verbal response
- Grimacing
- Agitation
- Semi-consciousness
- Waxy flexibility
- Posturing
- Mannerism
- Stereotypy

Associated Features

Features commonly associated with schizophrenia are:

- Inappropriate affect
- Anhedonia (loss of pleasure)
- Dysphoric mood
- Abnormalities in motor behavior
- Somatic complaints

One of the more troublesome aspects of schizophrenia is that the afflicted individual rarely has any insight into their own condition and so is unlikely to **comply** with treatment. People with schizophrenia often develop substance dependencies, especially to nicotine. Though many people believe that those with schizophrenia are more likely to be violent or aggressive than individuals in the general population, there is no statistical information to support this assertion. The onset of schizophrenia is typically during the ages of 18-25 for males and 25-35 for females. Males are slightly more likely to develop the disorder.

Prognosis and Differential Diagnosis

Individuals typically develop schizophrenia as a **chronic condition**, with very little chance of full remission. Positive symptoms of schizophrenia tend to decrease in later life, though the negative symptoms may remain. The following factors tend to **improve prognosis**:

- Good premorbid adjustment
- Acute and late onset
- Female gender
- Presence of a precipitating event
- Brief duration of active-phase symptoms
- Insight into the illness
- Family history of mood disorder
- No family history of schizophrenia

Differential diagnoses for schizophrenia include bipolar and depressive disorders with psychotic features, schizoaffective disorder, and the effects of prolonged and large-scale use of amphetamines or cocaine.

Treatment

Treatment for schizophrenia begins with the administration of **antipsychotic medication**. Antipsychotics are very effective at diminishing the positive symptoms of schizophrenia, though their results vary from person to person. Antipsychotics have strong side effects, however, including tardive dyskinesia. Medication is more effective when it is taken in combination with psychosocial intervention. Many people with schizophrenia are prone to relapse if they receive a great deal of criticism from family members, so it may be a good idea to initiate **family therapy** in which the level of expressed emotion in the family is discussed. Those who are recovering from schizophrenia also benefit from **social skills training** and **help with employment**.

112

SCHIZOAFFECTIVE DISORDER

The **criteria** for schizoaffective disorder are as follows:

Criteria A	For diagnosis the individual must have at least two of the following symptoms, one being a core positive symptom. The individual will experience the symptoms during a continuous period of illness during which there will also be a significant manic or depressive mood episode. <ul><li>Hallucinations (known as a core positive symptom)</li><li>Delusions (known as a core positive symptom)</li><li>Disorganized speech (known as a core positive symptom)</li><li>Severely disorganized or catatonic behavior</li><li>Negative Symptoms (such as avolition or diminished expression)</li></ul>
Criteria B	Individual experiences hallucinations or delusions for at least two weeks during illness that do not occur during a significant depressive or manic mood episode.
Criteria C	The individual experiences significant depressive or manic mood symptoms for most of the time of the illness.
Criteria D	The symptoms cannot be attributed to another medical condition or a substance.

SCHIZOPHRENIFORM DISORDER

The **criteria** for schizophreniform disorder are as follows:

Criteria A	Diagnosis requires at least two of the following symptoms, one being a core positive symptom: <ul><li>Hallucinations (known as a core positive symptom)</li><li>Delusions (known as a core positive symptom)</li><li>Disorganized speech (known as a core positive symptom)</li><li>Severely disorganized or catatonic behavior</li><li>Negative Symptoms (such as avolition or diminished expression)</li></ul>
Criteria B	An illness of at least one month but less than six months duration.
Criteria C	Depressive disorder, bipolar disorder, and schizoaffective disorder have been ruled out.
Criteria D	The symptoms cannot be attributed to another medical condition or a substance.

BRIEF PSYCHOTIC DISORDER

Brief psychotic disorder is characterized as a delusion that has sudden onset and lasts less than one month. Brief psychotic disorder is a classification of the schizophrenia spectrum and other psychotic disorders.

Criteria A	At least one of the following symptoms: delusions, hallucinations, disorganized speech, or catatonic behavior.
Criteria B	The symptoms last more than one day but less than one month. The individual does eventually return to baseline functioning.
Criteria C	The disorder cannot be attributed to another psychotic or depressive disorder.

DELUSIONAL DISORDER

Delusional disorder is typified by the presence of a persistent delusion. Delusion may be persecutory type, jealous type, erotomanic type (that someone is in love with delusional person), somatic type (that one has physical defect or disease), grandiose type, or mixed.

The following are the **criteria** for delusional disorder:

Criteria A	The individual experiences at least one delusion for at least one month or longer.
Criteria B	The individual does not meet criteria for schizophrenia.
Criteria C	Functioning is not significantly impaired, and behavior except dealing specifically with delusion is not bizarre.
Criteria D	Any manic or depressive episodes are brief.
Criteria E	The symptoms cannot be attributed to another medical condition or a substance.

It should be specified if the delusions are bizarre. Severity is rated by the quantitative assessment measure "Clinician-Rated Dimensions of Psychosis Symptom Severity."

BIPOLAR DISORDERS

DOCUMENTATION AND GENDER INFLUENCES

Bipolar disorders should be documented with current (or most recent) features, whether manic, hypomanic, or major depressive episode noted. The current severity of mild, moderate, or severe should also be noted as well as any applicable specifiers. Partial or full remission should be noted when applicable. Example: bipolar I disorder, current episode manic, moderate severity, with anxious distress. Bipolar **specifiers** include:

- With anxious distress
- With melancholic features
- With peripartum onset
- With seasonal pattern
- With psychotic features
- With catatonia
- With atypical features
- With mixed features
- With rapid cycling

Bipolar II is distinguished from Bipolar I by the fact that the individual has never had either a manic or a mixed episode. Males and females develop Bipolar I disorder equally, but Bipolar II is much more common for females. On average, the age of onset for the first manic episode is the early 20s.

ETIOLOGY AND TREATMENT

Among all mental disorders, Bipolar I and II disorders are the most clearly linked to **genetic factors**. Identical twins are overwhelmingly more likely to develop the disease than are fraternal twins. Research suggests a traumatic event may precipitate the first manic episode, although later manic episodes do not need to be preceded by a stressful episode. The most effective treatment for Bipolar I and II is **lithium**. Lithium reduces manic symptoms and eliminates mood swings for more than 50% of individuals. One major problem with lithium is that it works so well, many individuals consider themselves cured and stop taking it, causing a relapse. Pharmacotherapy is most effective when combined with psychotherapy. Individuals who do not respond to lithium treatment are given **anticonvulsants** like carbamazepine or divalproex sodium. Anticonvulsants are also used in lieu of lithium for individuals who have rapid cycling or dysphoric mania.

BIPOLAR I DISORDERS

The **criteria** for bipolar I disorder are as follows:

Criteria A	The individual must meet the criteria (listed below) for at least one manic episode. The manic episode is usually either proceeded or followed by an episode of major depression or hypomania.
Criteria B	The episode cannot be explained by schizophrenia spectrum and other psychotic disorders criteria.

The manic episode **criteria** are as follows:

Criteria A	An episode of significantly elevated, demonstrative, or irritable mood. There is significant goal-directed behaviors, activities, and an increase in the amount of energy the individual normally has. These symptoms are present for most of the day and last at least one week.
Criteria B	During the period described in criteria A, the individual will experience 3 of the following symptoms (if the individual presents with only an irritable mood, 4 of the following symptoms need to be present for diagnosis): • Less need for sleep • Excessive talking • Inflated self-esteem • Easily distracted • Flight of ideas • Engages in activities that have negative consequences • Engages in either goal directed activity or purposeless activity
Criteria C	The episode causes significant impairment socially.
Criteria D	The symptoms cannot be attributed to a substance.

BIPOLAR II DISORDERS

The **criteria** for bipolar II disorder are as follows:

Criteria A	The individual has had one or more major depressive episodes and one or more hypomanic episodes.
Criteria B	The individual has never experienced a manic episode.
Criteria C	The episode doesn't meet criteria for schizophrenia spectrum or other psychotic disorder.
Criteria D	The depressive episodes or alterations between the two moods cause significant impairment socially or functionally.

A **hypomanic episode** is severe enough to be a clear departure from normal mood and functioning, but not severe enough to cause a marked impairment in functioning, or to require hospitalization. The **criteria** for hypomania are as follows:

Criteria A	An episode of significantly elevated, demonstrative, or irritable mood. There are significant goal-directed behaviors, activities, and an increase in the amount of energy the individual normally has. These symptoms are present for most of the day and last at least 4 days.
Criteria B	During the period described in criteria A, the individual experiences 3 of the following symptoms (if the individual presents with only an irritable mood, 4 of the following symptoms need to be present for diagnosis): • Less need for sleep • Excessive talking • Inflated self-esteem • Easily distracted • Flight of ideas • Engages in activities that have negative consequences • Engages in goal directed activity or purposeless activity
Criteria C	The episode causes a change in the functioning of the individual.
Criteria D	The episode causes changes noticeable by others.
Criteria E	The episode does not cause social impairments.
Criteria F	The symptoms cannot be attributed to a substance.

CYCLOTHYMIC DISORDER

Cyclothymic disorder is characterized by chronic, fluctuating mood with many hypomanic and depressive symptoms, which are not as severe as either bipolar I or bipolar II. The **criteria** are as follows:

Criteria A	The individual experiences a considerable number of hypomania symptoms without meeting all the criteria for hypomanic episodes and experiences depressive symptoms that do not meet the criteria for major depressive episode for two years or more (can be for one year or more in <18 years of age).
Criteria B	During the above time period, the individual exhibits the symptoms more than half of the time and they are never symptom free for more than two months at a time.
Criteria C	The individual has not met the criteria for manic, hypomanic, or major depressive episodes.
Criteria D	The episode doesn't meet criteria for schizophrenia spectrum or other psychotic disorder.
Criteria E	The symptoms cannot be attributed to a substance.
Criteria F	The episodes cause significant impairment socially or functionally.

MAJOR DEPRESSIVE DISORDER
MAJOR DEPRESSIVE EPISODE

The **criteria** for a major depressive episode are as follows:

Criteria A	The individual experiences 5 or more of the following symptoms during 2 consecutive weeks. These symptoms are associated with a change in their normal functioning. (Note: Of the presenting symptoms, either depressed mood or loss of ability to feel pleasure must be included to make this diagnosis.): • Depressed mood • Loss of ability to feel pleasure or have interest in normal activities • Decreased aptitude for thinking • Thoughts of death • Fatigue (daily) • Inappropriate guilt or feelings of worthlessness • Observable motor agitation or psychomotor retardation • Weight loss or gain of more than 5% in one month • Hypersomnia or Insomnia (almost daily)
Criteria B	The episode causes distress or social or functional impairment.
Criteria C	The symptoms cannot be attributed to a substance or another condition or disease.
Criteria D	The episode does not meet the criteria for schizophrenia spectrum or other psychotic disorder.
Criteria E	The individual does not meet criteria for manic episode or a hypomanic episode.

DIAGNOSIS AND GENDER

Major depressive disorder is diagnosed when an individual has one or more major depressive episodes without having a history of manic, hypomanic, or mixed episodes. There are a few different **specifiers** (categories of associated features) for major depressive disorder issued by the DSM-5-TR:

- With anxious distress
- With melancholic features
- With peripartum onset
- With seasonal pattern
- With psychotic features (mood-congruent or mood-incongruent)
- With catatonia
- With atypical features
- With mixed features

Some studies estimate that 20% of women will have symptoms worthy of a diagnosis of major depressive disorder after giving birth.

From the beginning of adolescence on, the rate of major depressive disorder is about twice as great for females as for males. Before adolescence, the rates are about the same. Most major depressive disorders occur in the mid-twenties.

COGNITIVE-BEHAVIORAL ETIOLOGIES

Three major cognitive-behavioral etiologies have been offered for major depressive disorder:

- The **learned helplessness model** proposed by Seligman suggests afflicted individuals have been exposed to uncontrollable negative events in the past and have a tendency to attribute negative events to internal, stable, and global factors.
- **Rehm's self-control model** suggests depression occurs in individuals who obsess over negative outcomes, set extremely high standards for themselves, blame all of their problems on internal failures, and have low rates of self-reinforcement coupled with high rates of self-punishment.
- **Beck's cognitive theory** suggests depression is the result of negative and irrational thought and beliefs about the depressive cognitive triad (the self, the world, and the future).

PROGNOSIS AND CATECHOLAMINE HYPOTHESIS

The severity and duration of a major depressive episode varies from case to case, but symptoms usually last about six months before remission to full function. 20-30% of individuals have lingering symptoms for months or years. About 50% of individuals experience more than one episode of major depression. Oftentimes, multiple episodes are precipitated by some severe psychological trauma. The **catecholamine hypothesis** suggests major depressive episodes are due to a deficiency of the neurotransmitter norepinephrine. The **indolamine hypothesis** proposes that depression is caused by inferior levels of serotonin.

ETIOLOGY

Besides the catecholamine and indolamine hypotheses, there are a few other proposed ideas for the etiology of major depressive disorder. Some researchers speculate depression is caused by **hormonal disturbances**, like an increased level of cortisol. Cortisol is one of the stress hormones secreted by the adrenal cortex. Other researchers speculate there is a connection between depression and diminished new cell growth in certain regions of the brain, particularly the subgenual prefrontal cortex and hippocampus. The **subgenual prefrontal cortex** is the part of the brain associated with the formation of positive emotions. Many antidepressant drugs seem to stimulate new growth in the **hippocampus**.

SYMPTOMS

Symptoms of major depressive disorder vary with age. For **children**, common symptoms are:

- Somatic complaints
- Irritability
- Social withdrawal

Male preadolescents often display aggressive and destructive behavior. When **elderly** individuals develop a major depressive disorder, it manifests as memory loss, distractibility, disorientation, and other cognitive problems. Many major depressive episodes are misdiagnosed as major neurocognitive disorder (formerly dementia). It is very common in non-Anglo cultures for the symptoms of depression to be described solely in terms of their somatic content. Latinos, for instance, frequently complain of jitteriness or headaches, while Asians commonly complain of tiredness or weakness.

TREATMENT

The typical treatment program for major depressive disorder combines antidepressant drugs and psychotherapy. Three classes of **antidepressant medication** are commonly prescribed:

- **Selective serotonin reuptake inhibitors (SSRIs)** are prescribed for melancholic depressives; they have a lower incidence of serious adverse side effects than do tricyclics.
- **Tricyclics (TCAs)**, are prescribed for classic depression, involving vegetative bodily symptoms, a worsening of symptoms in the morning, acute onset, and short duration of moderate symptoms.

- **Monoamine oxidase inhibitors** are prescribed as a last resort for individuals who have an unorthodox depression that includes phobias, panic attacks, increased appetite, hypersomnia, and a mood that worsens as the day goes on.

> **Review Video: What is Major Depression?**
> Visit mometrix.com/academy and enter code: 632694

DEPRESSIVE DISORDER WITH SEASONAL PATTERN

Depressive disorder with seasonal pattern, formerly called seasonal affective disorder (SAD), is a depressive disorder that afflicts people in the Northern Hemisphere from October to April. Symptoms of this disorder are hypersomnia, increased appetite, weight gain, and an increased desire for carbohydrates. Research suggests this disorder is caused by circadian and seasonal increases in the level of melatonin production by the pineal gland from lack of sunlight. Affected individuals are treated with phototherapy (exposure to full-spectrum white light for several hours each day), aerobic exercise, and SSRIs.

PERSISTENT DEPRESSIVE DISORDER

The **criteria** for persistent depressive disorder are the following:

Criteria A	For at least two years, the individual experiences for most of a day, more days than they don't experience it, a depressed mood.
Criteria B	The individual experiences 2 or more of the following when depressed: • Low self-esteem • Decreased appetite or overeating • A feeling of hopelessness • Fatigue • Difficulty concentrating • Insomnia or hypersomnia
Criteria C	During the episode the individual has not had relief from symptoms for longer than 2 months at once.
Criteria D	The individual may have met the criteria for a major depressive disorder.
Criteria E	The individual does not meet criteria for cyclothymic disorder, manic episode, or hypomanic episode.
Criteria F	The episode does not meet the criteria for schizophrenia spectrum or other psychotic disorder.
Criteria G	The symptoms cannot be attributed to a substance.
Criteria H	The symptoms cause distress or impairment socially or functionally.

Of those with persistent depressive disorder, 25-50% of individuals show sleep EEG abnormalities. Women are 2-3 times more likely to suffer from persistent depressive disorder than men. Around 75% of individuals with persistent depressive disorder develop major depressive disorder within 5 years. First degree relatives are likely to also suffer major depression or persistent depressive disorder. Treatment programs for persistent depressive disorder usually include a combination of **antidepressant drugs** (especially fluoxetine) and either **cognitive-behavioral therapy or interpersonal therapy**.

> **Review Video: Persistent Depressive Disorder**
> Visit mometrix.com/academy and enter code: 361077

SUICIDE STATISTICS AND CORRELATES
GENDER, RACE, AND MARITAL STATUS

Statistics indicate that 4-5 times as many males as females successfully commit **suicide**. However, females attempt suicide about 3 times as often as males. The reason for this disparity is that men tend to employ more violent means of self-destruction, including guns, hanging, and carbon monoxide poisoning. Among racial and ethnic groups, the suicide rate is highest among whites. The exception is **American Indian** and **Alaskan Natives** aged 15-34, for whom suicide is the second leading cause of death. As for **marital status**, the highest rates of suicide are among divorced, separated, or widowed people. The suicide rate for single people trails that of those groups, but it remains higher than the suicide rate for married people.

HISTORY, AGE, AND DRUGS OF CHOICE

Suicide is the eighth leading cause of death for **males** in the United States, and sixteenth for **females**. Indicators that a person is at risk for a suicide attempt include:

- Previous suicide attempt in 60-80% of cases
- Warning issued by the prospective suicide in 80% of cases

Drug suicides are the most common (>70% annually). In order of preference, suicides use: Sedatives (especially benzodiazepines), antidepressants, opiates, prescription analgesics, and carbon monoxide from car exhaust. The most likely persona to commit a successful suicide is a male, Caucasian, 45-49 years of age. Women are more likely to be saved from an attempted suicide through treatment at an Emergency Department. The average age of those saved is 15-19. A sharp increase in suicides aged 10-19 may be due to the increased use of antidepressants, which now carry an FDA black box warning. Around 25% of suicide attempts by seniors over age 65 are successful.

PSYCHIATRIC DISORDERS AND BIOLOGICAL CORRELATES

Most of those who commit suicide are suffering from some mental disorder, most commonly **major depressive disorder** or **bipolar disorder**. Suicide associated with depression is most likely to occur within three months after the symptoms of depression have begun to improve. The risk of suicide among adolescents with depression increases greatly if the adolescent also has conduct disorder, ADHD, or is a substance abuser, particularly of inhaled solvents. As for biological correlates, people who commit suicide have been found to have low levels of **serotonin** and **5HIAA** (a serotonin metabolite). Individuals at risk for suicide need immediate psychological intervention and a 24-hour suicide watch.

COGNITIVE CORRELATES AND LIFE STRESS

Research into suicide has indicated that **hopelessness** is the most common predictor of an inclination to self-destruction. It is a more accurate predictor even than the intensity of depressive symptoms. **Self-assigned or society-assigned perfectionism** has also been blamed for suicide. Many suicides are preceded by some **traumatic life event**, like the end of a romantic relationship or the death of a loved one. For adolescents, the most common precipitant of suicide is an **argument with a parent or rejection by a boyfriend or girlfriend**. Among adolescents, the common warning signs of suicide are talking about death, giving away possessions, and talking about a reunion with a deceased individual.

FACTITIOUS DISORDER

An individual diagnosed with factitious disorder (FD) intentionally manifests physical or psychological symptoms to satisfy an intrapsychic need to fill the role of a sick person. The individual with FD presents the illness in an exaggerated manner and avoids interrogation that might expose the falsity. These individuals may undergo multiple surgeries and invasive medical procedures. They often hide insurance claims and hospital discharge forms. A disturbing variation of FD is **factitious disorder imposed on another** (sometimes referred to as Munchausen's syndrome by proxy), in which a caregiver intentionally produces symptoms in another individual. Usually, a mother makes her young child ill.

MALINGERING VS. FACTITIOUS DISORDER

Malingering is feigning physical symptoms to avoid something specific, like going to work, or to gain a specific reward. Consider malingering as a possibility when:

- A person obtains a medical evaluation for legal reasons or to apply for insurance compensation.
- There is marked inconsistency between the individual's complaint and the objective findings, or if the individual does not cooperate with a diagnostic evaluation or prescribed treatment.
- The individual has an antisocial personality disorder.

Malingering contrasts with factitious disorder because in FD the individual does not feign physical symptoms for personal gain or to avoid an adverse event, but does it with no obvious external rewards.

DISSOCIATIVE DISORDERS

Dissociative disorders are a disruption in consciousness, identity, memory, or perception of the environment that is not due to the effects of a substance or a general medical condition. These are all characterized by a disturbance in the normally integrative functions of identity, memory, consciousness, or environmental perception.

Dissociative identity disorder (previously multiple personality disorder)	Two or more personalities exist within one person, with each personality dominant at a particular time.
Dissociative amnesia	Inability to recall important personal data, more than forgetfulness. It is not due to organic causes and comes on suddenly.
Depersonalization/derealization disorder	Feeling detached from one's mental processes or body, as if one is an observer.

Cultural influences can cause or amplify some of the symptoms of dissociative disorders, so take these into account when making a diagnosis. For instance, many religious ceremonies try to foster a dissociative psychological experience; individuals participating in such a ceremony may display symptoms of dissociative disorder without requiring treatment.

DISSOCIATIVE AMNESIA

Individuals may be diagnosed with dissociative amnesia if they have more than one episode in which they are unable to remember important personal information, and this memory loss cannot be attributed to ordinary forgetfulness. The gaps in the individual's memory are likely to be related to a traumatic event. The three most common patterns of dissociative amnesia are:

- **Localized**, in which the individual is unable to remember all events around a defined period
- **Selective**, in which the individual cannot recall some events pertaining to a circumscribed period
- **Generalized**, in which memory loss spans the individual's entire life

It should be specified if this is with dissociative fugue, a subtype of dissociative amnesia, which is a purposeful travel that is associated with amnesia.

DISSOCIATIVE FUGUE AND DEPERSONALIZATION DISORDER

A **dissociative fugue** is a subtype of dissociative amnesia and is an abrupt, unexpected, purposeful flight from home, or another stressful location, coupled with an inability to remember the past. The individual is unable to remember their identity and assumes a new identity. Fugues are psychological protection against extreme stressors like bankruptcy, divorce, separation, suicidal or homicidal ideation, and rejection. Fugues happen in wars, natural disasters, and severe accidents. Fugues affect 2 in every 1,000 Americans. There will be no recollection of events that occur during the fugue. Individuals in a fugue state may seem normal to strangers. Dissociative fugue is a specifier that can be used with dissociative amnesia.

Depersonalization/derealization disorder is diagnosed when an individual has recurrent episodes in which they feel detached from their own mental processes or body or to their surroundings. In order to be diagnosed, this condition must be intense enough to cause significant distress or functional impairment.

SEXUAL DYSFUNCTIONS

A sexual dysfunction is any condition in which the sexual response cycle is disturbed or there is pain during sexual intercourse, and this causes distress or interpersonal difficulty. **Types** of sexual dysfunctions:

- Delayed ejaculation
- Erectile disorder
- Female orgasmic disorder
- Female sexual interest/arousal disorder
- Genito-pelvic pain/penetration disorder
- Male hypoactive sexual desire disorder
- Premature ejaculation
- Substance-induced sexual dysfunction

Male erectile disorder is the inability to attain or maintain an erection. This condition is linked to diabetes, liver and kidney disease, multiple sclerosis, and the use of antipsychotic, antidepressant, and hypertensive drugs. **Orgasmic disorders** are any delay or absence of orgasm after the normal sexual excitement phase. Premature ejaculation is orgasm that occurs with a minimum of stimulation and before the person desires it. Premature ejaculation may be in part due to deficiencies in serotonin.

PHYSICAL AND PSYCHOLOGICAL COMPONENTS AND TREATMENTS

Any individual with sexual dysfunction should be given a medical evaluation for diabetes, pelvic scars, kidney disease, hypertension, and drug interactions. Use sleep studies to determine if an impotent male gets an erection at night, and determine whether the cause of impotence is physical or psychological. **Psychological impotence** can be treated with cognitive-behavioral therapy. Sex therapy is most helpful in treating premature ejaculation. Sensate focus is used to reduce performance anxiety and increase sexual excitement. Kegel exercises, which strengthen the pubococcygeus muscle, can improve sexual pleasure. As for pharmacotherapy, Viagra is helpful in attaining and maintaining erections.

GENITO-PELVIC PAIN/PENETRATION DISORDER AND CATEGORIES OF SEXUAL DYSFUNCTIONS

Genito-pelvic pain/penetration disorder is persistent difficulty with genital pain associated with sexual intercourse or involuntary spasms in the pubococcygeus muscle in the vagina, which make it difficult to have sexual intercourse, or fear or anxiety related to anticipation of pain during intercourse. Sexual dysfunctions are categorized as lifelong or acquired, and generalized or situational, depending on their cause. **Generalized dysfunctions** occur with every sexual partner in all circumstances. **Situational dysfunctions** only occur under certain circumstances. The cause may be psychological, physical, or both.

PARAPHILIC DISORDERS

Paraphilic disorders are intense, recurrent sexual urges or behaviors involving either nonhuman objects, non-consenting partners (including children), or the suffering or humiliation of oneself or one's partner. **Common paraphilias** include:

- Fetishistic disorder
- Transvestic disorder
- Pedophilic disorder
- Exhibitionistic disorder
- Voyeuristic disorder
- Sexual masochism disorder
- Sexual sadism disorder
- Frotteuristic disorder (rubbing against a non-consenting person)

The most common **treatment** for paraphilia was previously in vivo aversion therapy, but now it is more common for treatment to include covert sensitization, in which the imagination is given aversion therapy. The medication Depo-Provera has been found to relieve paraphiliac symptoms for many men, although this relief ceases as soon as the man stops taking the drug.

GENDER DYSPHORIA

DSM-5-TR defines gender dysphoria (formerly gender identity disorder) as a marked incongruence between one's expressed gender and assigned gender that causes significant distress or impairment over a period of at least 6 months. Informally, gender dysphoria is used to describe a person's persistent discomfort and disagreement with their assigned gender. DSM-5-TR criteria for diagnosis in **children** include:

- Strong desire to be of the other gender or insistence that one is the other gender
- Strong preference for clothing typically associated with the other gender
- Strong preference for playing cross-gender roles
- Strong preference for activities stereotypical of the other gender and rejection of those activities stereotypical of one's assigned gender
- Strong preference for playmates of the other gender
- Strong dislike of one's own sexual anatomy
- Strong desire for the sex characteristics that match one's expressed gender

DSM-5-TR criteria for diagnosis in **adolescents and adults** include:

- Marked incongruence between expressed gender and one's existing primary and secondary sex characteristics
- Strong desire to rid oneself of these sex characteristics for this reason
- Strong desire for the sex characteristics of the other gender
- Strong desire to be of the other gender and to be treated as such
- Strong conviction that one's feelings and reactions are typical of the other gender

SLEEP-WAKE DISORDERS

Sleep-wake disorders include the following:

Insomnia disorders	Difficulty falling asleep, staying asleep, or early rising without being able to go back to sleep.
Hypersomnolence disorder	Sleepiness despite getting at least 7 hours with difficulty feeling awake when suddenly awoke, lapses of sleep in the day, feeling unrested after long periods of sleep.
Narcolepsy	Uncontrollable lapses into sleep, occurring at least three times each week for at least 3 months.
Obstructive sleep apnea hypopnea	Breathing related sleep disorder with obstructive apneas or hypopneas.
Central sleep apnea	Breathing related sleep disorder with central apnea.
Sleep-related hypoventilation	Breathing related sleep disorder with evidence of decreased respiratory rate and increased CO_2 level.
Circadian rhythm sleep-wake disorder	Sleep wake disorder caused by a mismatch between the circadian rhythm and sleep required by person.
Non-rapid eye movement sleep arousal disorder	Awakening during the first third of the night associated with sleep walking or sleep terrors.
Nightmare disorder	Recurring distressing dreams that are well remembered and cause distress.
Rapid eye movement sleep behavior disorder	Arousal during REM sleep associated with motor movements and vocalizing.
Restless legs syndrome	The need to move legs due to uncomfortable sensations, usually relieved by activity.

Review Video: Chronic Insomnia
Visit mometrix.com/academy and enter code: 293232

Review Video: Sedatives, Hypnotics, and Insomnia Management
Visit mometrix.com/academy and enter code: 666132

ADJUSTMENT DISORDERS

Adjustment disorders appear as maladaptive reactions to one or more identifiable psychosocial stressors. In order to make the diagnosis, the onset of symptoms must be within three months of the stressor, and the condition must cause impairments in social, occupational, or academic performance. The symptoms do not align with normal grief or bereavement. Symptoms remit within six months after the termination of the stressor or its consequences. The adjustment disorder should be specified with at least one of the following:

- Depressed mood
- Anxiety
- Mixed anxiety and depressed mood
- Disturbance of conduct
- Mixed disturbance of emotions and conduct

PERSONALITY DISORDERS

Personality disorders occur when an individual has developed personality traits so maladaptive and entrenched that they cause personal distress or interfere significantly with functioning.

124

There are five **traits** involved in personality disorders:

- Neuroticism
- Extraversion/introversion
- Openness to experience
- Agreeableness/antagonism
- Conscientiousness

The following are the **criteria** for personality disorders:

Criteria A	Long-term pattern of maladaptive personality traits and behaviors that do not align with the individual's culture. These traits and behaviors will be found in at least two areas: • Impulse control • Inappropriate emotional intensity or responses • Inappropriately interpreting people, events, and self • Inappropriate social functioning
Criteria B	The traits and behaviors are inflexible and exist despite changing social situations.
Criteria C	The traits and behaviors cause distress and impair functioning.
Criteria D	Onset was adolescence or early adulthood and has been enduring.
Criteria E	The behaviors and traits are not due to another mental disorder.
Criteria F	The behaviors and traits are not due to a substance.

CLUSTER A, B, AND C PERSONALITY DISORDERS

Personality disorders are **clustered** into three groups:

Cluster A (eccentric or odd disorders)	Cluster B (dramatic or excessively emotional disorders)	Cluster C (fear- or anxiety-based disorders)
Paranoid	Antisocial	Avoidant
Schizoid	Borderline	Dependent
Schizotypal	Histrionic	Obsessive-Compulsive
	Narcissistic	

PARANOID PERSONALITY DISORDER

Paranoid personality disorder is a pervasive pattern of distrust and suspiciousness that involves believing the actions and thoughts of other people to be directed antagonistically against oneself. In order to make the diagnosis, the individual must have at least four of the following **symptoms**:

- Suspects that others are somehow harming them
- Doubts the trustworthiness of others
- Reluctant to confide in others
- Suspicious without justification about fidelity of one's partner
- Reads hidden meaning into remarks or events
- Consistently has grudges
- Believes there are attacks on their character that others present do not perceive

SCHIZOID PERSONALITY DISORDER

Schizoid personality disorder is characterized by a pervasive lack of interest in relationships with others and limited range of emotional expression in contacts with others. Four of these **symptoms** must be present:

- Avoidance of or displeasure in close relationships
- Always chooses solitude
- Little interest in sexual relationships
- Takes pleasure in few activities
- Indifference to praise or criticism
- Emotional coldness or detachment
- Lacks close friends except first-degree relatives

SCHIZOTYPAL PERSONALITY DISORDER

Schizotypal personality disorder is characterized by pervasive social deficits, oddities of cognition, perception, or behavior. Diagnosis requires five of the following:

- Ideas of reference
- Odd beliefs or magical thinking
- Lack of close friends except first-degree relatives
- Bodily illusions
- Suspiciousness
- Social anxiety (excessive)
- Inappropriate or constricted affect
- Peculiarities in behavior or appearance

ANTISOCIAL PERSONALITY DISORDER

Antisocial personality disorder is a general lack of concern for the rights and feelings of others. In order to receive a diagnosis of antisocial personality disorder, the individual must:

- Be at least 18
- Have had a history of conduct disorder before age 15
- Have shown *at least three* of the following symptoms before the age of 15:
  o Failure to conform to social laws and norms
  o Deceitfulness
  o Impulsivity
  o Reckless disregard for the safety of self and others
  o Consistent irresponsibility
  o Lack of remorse
  o Irritability or aggressiveness

Antisocial personality disorder may also include an inflated opinion of self, superficial charm, and a lack of empathy for others.

BORDERLINE PERSONALITY DISORDER

Borderline personality disorder is a pervasive pattern of instability in social relationships, self-image, and affect, coupled with marked impulsivity. A diagnosis of borderline personality disorder requires five of the following **symptoms**:

- Frantic efforts to avoid being abandoned
- A pattern of unstable and intense personal relationships, in which there is alternation between idealization and devaluation

- Instability of self-image
- Potentially self-destructive impulsivity in at least two areas
- Recurrent suicide threats or gestures
- Affective instability
- Chronic feelings of emptiness
- Inappropriate anger
- Paranoid ideation or dissociative symptoms

The changes in self-identity may manifest as shifts in career goals and sexual identity; impulsivity may manifest as unsafe sex, reckless driving practices, and substance abuse.

Borderline personality disorder is most common in people between the ages of 19 and 34. Most individuals see substantial improvement over a period of 15 years. Impulsive symptoms are the first to recede.

> **Review Video: Borderline Personality Disorder**
> Visit mometrix.com/academy and enter code: 550801

Dialectical behavior therapy (DBT) is often used to treat borderline personality disorder; it combines cognitive-behavioral therapy with the assumption of Rogers that the individual must accept their problem before any progress can be made. There are three basic strategies associated with dialectical behavior therapy:

- Group skills training
- Individual outpatient therapy
- Telephone consultations

Regular DBT has reduced the number of suicides and violent acts committed by individuals with borderline personality disorder.

HISTRIONIC PERSONALITY DISORDER

Histrionic personality disorder is excessive emotionality and attention-seeking behavior. Five **symptoms** from the following list must be present:

- Annoyance or discomfort when not receiving attention
- Inappropriate sexual provocation
- Rapidly shifting and shallow emotions
- Vague and impressionistic speech
- Exaggerated expression of emotion
- Easily influenced by others
- Believes relationships are more intimate than they actually are
- Uses physical appearance to draw attention to self

NARCISSISTIC PERSONALITY DISORDER

Narcissistic personality disorder is grandiose behavior along with a lack of empathy and a need for admiration. The individual must exhibit five of these **symptoms** for diagnosis:

- Grandiose sense of self-importance
- Fantasies of own power and beauty
- Belief in personal uniqueness
- Need for excessive admiration
- Sense of entitlement
- Exploitation of others
- Lack of empathy

- Envious of others or believes others envy them
- Arrogant behaviors

AVOIDANT PERSONALITY DISORDER

Avoidant personality disorder is a pervasive pattern of social inhibition, feelings of inadequacy, and hypersensitivity to negative evaluation. A person with avoidant personality disorder exhibits at least four of these **symptoms**:

- Avoiding work or school activities that involve interpersonal contact
- Unwillingness to associate with any person who may withhold approval
- Preoccupation with concerns about being criticized or rejected
- Conception of self as socially inept, inferior, or unappealing to others
- General reluctance to take personal risks or engage in dangerous behavior
- Does not reveal self in intimate relationships, due to fear of shame
- Not able to excel in new situations due to fear of inadequacy

DEPENDENT PERSONALITY DISORDER

Dependent personality disorder is excessive reliance on others. A diagnosis of dependent personality disorder requires five of these **symptoms**:

- Difficulty making decisions without advice
- Need for others to assume responsibility for one's actions
- Fear of disagreeing with others
- Difficulty self-initiating projects
- Feelings of helplessness or discomfort when alone
- Goes to great lengths to get support from others
- Seeks new relationships when an old one ends
- Preoccupied with the thought of having to care for self

OBSESSIVE-COMPULSIVE PERSONALITY DISORDER

Obsessive-compulsive personality disorder is a persistent preoccupation with organization and mental or interpersonal control. Four of these **symptoms** are required for the diagnosis of obsessive-compulsive personality disorder:

- Preoccupation with rules and details
- Perfectionism that interferes with progress
- Excessive devotion to work
- Counterproductive rigidity about beliefs and morality
- Inability to throw away old objects
- Reluctance to delegate authority to others
- Rigid or stubborn
- Hoards money without spending

BEHAVIORAL PEDIATRICS

DISCLOSURE

Behavioral pediatrics, otherwise known as pediatric psychology, has become a more popular field because research revealed that many psychological disorders originate in childhood. For the most part, a pediatric mental health provider should be open with the child about their condition. Children may need some psychological help if they are to undergo any major medical procedures. Providers must relay any information related to the mental or medical condition in language the child can understand. **Multicomponent cognitive-**

behavioral interventions, in which the child is given information about their condition and armed with some coping strategies, are especially helpful.

HOSPITALIZATION, COMPLIANCE, AND SCHOOL ADJUSTMENT

Children who need to be **hospitalized** for a significant period of time are especially at risk of developing psychological problems, in large part because they have been separated from their families. Children and adolescents are generally less **compliant** with medical regimens. This may be because of poor communication, parent-child problems, or a general lack of skill. For adolescents, peer pressure and the desire for social acceptance may motivate noncompliance with potentially embarrassing medical programs. Children with serious medical conditions are more likely to have trouble **adjusting to school**. Problems may be caused by the illness itself, by the frequent absences it necessitates, or by the social stigma of illness. Some treatments, like chemotherapy, are associated with deficits in neurocognitive functioning and greater risk of learning disabilities.

Research

RESEARCH PROCESS

The key steps in the research process are as follows:

1. **Problem or issue identification**: Includes a literature review to further define the problem and to ensure that the problem has not already been studied
2. **Hypothesis formulation**: Creating a clear statement of the problem or concern, worded in a way that it can be operationalized and measured
3. **Operationalization**: Creating measurable variables that fully address the hypothesis
4. **Study design selection**: Choosing a study design that will allow for the proper analysis of the data to be collected

DATA

OBJECTIVE VS. SUBJECTIVE DATA

Both **subjective (qualitative)** and **objective (quantitative)** data are used for research and analysis, but the focus is quite different:

Subjective Data	Objective Data
Subjective data depend on the opinions of the observer or the subject. Data are described verbally or graphically, depending upon observers to provide information. Interviews may be used as a tool to gather information, and the researcher's interpretation of data is important. Gathering this type of data can be time-intensive, and it usually cannot be generalized to a larger population. This type of information gathering is often useful at the beginning of the design process for data collection.	Objective data are observable and can be tested and verified. Data are described in terms of numbers within a statistical format. This type of information gathering is done after the design of data collection is outlined, usually in later stages. Tools may include surveys, questionnaires, or other methods of obtaining numerical data.

DATA COLLECTION

Key points in data collection include the following:

- Data should ideally be collected close to the time of intervention (delays may result in variation from forgetfulness, rather than from the intervention process).
- Frequent data collection is ideal, but subject boredom or fatigue must be avoided as well. Thus, make the data collection process as easy as possible (electronic devices can sometimes help).
- Keep the data collection process short to increase subject responsiveness.
- Standardize recording procedures (collect data at the same time, place, and method to enhance ultimate data validity and reliability).
- Choose a collection method that fits the study well (observation, questionnaires, logs, diaries, surveys, rating scales, etc.) to optimize the data collection process and enhance the value of the data obtained.

STUDY DESIGNS

SELECTING A STUDY DESIGN

Key considerations that guide the selection of a study design include the following:

- **Standardization**: Whether or not data can be collected in an identical way from each participant (eliminating collection variation)
- **Level of certainty**: The study size needed to achieve statistical significance (determined via power calculations)

- **Resources**: The availability of funding and other resources needed
- The **time frame** required
- The capacity of subjects to provide **informed consent** and receiving **ethics approval** via Human Subjects Review Committees and Institutional Review Boards

COMMON STUDY DESIGNS

The three common study designs used in the research process include the following:

- An **exploratory research design** is common when little is known about a particular problem or issue. Its key feature is flexibility. The results comprise detailed descriptions of all observations made, arranged in some kind of order. Conclusions drawn include educated guesses or hypotheses.
- When the variables chosen have already been studied (e.g., in an exploratory study), further research requires a **descriptive survey design**. In this design, the variables are controlled partly by the situation and partly by the investigator, who chooses the sample. Proof of causality cannot be established, but the evidence may support causality.
- **Experimental studies** are highly controlled. Intervening and extraneous variables are eliminated, and independent variables are manipulated to measure effects in dependent variables (e.g., variables of interest)—either in the field or in a laboratory setting.

ETHICAL CONCERNS WITH STUDY DESIGN SELECTION

Ethical concerns involved with selecting a study design include the following:

- Research must not lead to harming clients.
- Denying an intervention may amount to harm.
- Informed consent is essential.
- Confidentiality is required.

SINGLE SYSTEM STUDY DESIGNS

Evaluation of the efficacy and functionality of a practice is an important aspect of quality control and practice improvement. The most common approach to such an evaluation is the **single system study approach**. Selecting one client per system ($n = 1$), observations are made prior to, during, and following an intervention.

The **research steps** are:

1. Selection of a problem for change (the target)
2. Operationalizing the target into measurable terms
3. Following the target during the baseline phase, prior to the application of any intervention
4. Observing the target and collecting data during the intervention phase, during which the intervention is carried out (There may be more than one phase of data collection.)

Data that are repeatedly collected constitute a single system study "time series design." Single system designs provide a flexible and efficient way to evaluate virtually any type of practice.

BASIC SINGLE SYSTEM DESIGN AND ADDITIONAL TYPES OF CASE STUDY OR PREDESIGNS

The most basic single system design is the **A-B design**. The baseline phase (A) has no intervention, followed by the intervention phase (B) with data collection. Typically, data are collected continuously through the intervention phase. Advantages of this design include the following:

- Versatility
- Adaptability to many settings, program styles, and problems
- Clear comparative information between phases

A significant limitation, however, is that causation cannot be demonstrated.

Three additional types of **case study or predesigns** are:

- **Design A**, an observational design with no intervention
- **Design B**, an intervention-only design without any baseline
- **Design B-C**, a "changes case study" design (where no baseline is recorded, a first intervention [B] is performed and then changed [C] and data are recorded)

COMMON SINGLE SYSTEM EXPERIMENTAL DESIGNS

Common single system experimental designs are described below:

- The **A-B-A design** begins with data collection in the pre-intervention phase (A) and then continuously during the intervention phases (B). The intervention is then removed (returning to "A") and data are again collected. In this way an experimental process is produced (testing without, with, and then again without intervention). Inferences regarding causality can be made, and two points of comparison are achieved. However, the ethics of removing a successful intervention leaves this study poorly recommended.
- The **A-B-A-B study** overcomes this failure by reintroducing the intervention ("B") at the close of the study. Greater causality inferences are obtained. However, even temporary removal of a successful intervention is problematic (especially if the client drops out at that time), and this design is fairly time-consuming.
- The **B-A-B design** (the "intervention repeat design") drops the baseline phase and starts and ends with the intervention (important in crisis situations and where treatment delays are problematic), saving time and reducing ethical concerns.

SAMPLING

TERMS USED IN SAMPLING

In sampling, the following concepts are considered:

- A **population** is the total set of subjects sought for measurement by a researcher.
- A **sample** is a subset of subjects drawn from a population (as total population testing is usually not possible).
- A **subject** is a single unit of a population.
- **Generalizability** refers to the degree to which specific findings obtained can be applied to the total population.

SAMPLING TECHNIQUES

The following are types of sampling techniques:

Simple random sampling	Any method of sampling wherein each subject selected from a population has an equal chance of being selected (e.g., drawing names from a hat).
Stratified random sampling	Dividing a population into desired groups (age, income, etc.) and then using a simple random sample from each stratified group.
Cluster sampling	A technique used when natural groups are readily evident in a population (e.g., residents within each county in a state). The natural groups are then subjected to random sampling to obtain random members from each county. The best results occur when elements within clusters are internally heterogeneous and externally (between clusters) homogeneous, as the formation of natural clusters may introduce error and bias.

Systematic sampling	A systematic method of random sampling (e.g., randomly choosing a number *n* between 1 and 10—perhaps drawing the number from a hat) and then selecting every *n*th name of a randomly generated or already existing list (such as the phone book) to obtain a study sample.

MEASUREMENTS

CATEGORIES OF MEASUREMENT

The four different categories of measurement are as follows:

Nominal	Used when two or more named variables exist (male/female, pass/fail, etc.)
Ordinal	Used when a hierarchy is present but when the distance between each value is not necessarily equal (e.g., first, second, third place)
Interval	Hierarchal values that are at equal distance from each other
Ratio	One value divided by another, providing a relative association of one quantity in terms of the other (e.g., 50 is one half of 100)

STATISTICS AND MEASURES OF CENTRAL TENDENCY

A statistic is a numerical representation of an identified characteristic of a subject.

- **Descriptive statistics** are mathematically derived values that represent characteristics identified in a group or population.
- **Inferential statistics** are mathematical calculations that produce generalizations about a group or population from the numerical values of known characteristics.

Measures of central tendency identify the relative degree to which certain characteristics in a population are grouped together. Such measures include:

- The **mean**, or the arithmetic average
- The **median**, or the numerical value above which 50% of the population is found and below which the other 50% is located
- The **mode**, or the most frequently appearing value (score) in a series of numerical values

> **Review Video: Mean, Median, and Mode**
> Visit mometrix.com/academy and enter code: 286207

MEASURES OF VARIABILITY AND CORRELATION

Measures of variability (or variation) include the following:

- The **range**, or the arithmetic difference between the largest and the smallest value (idiosyncratic "outliers" often excluded)
- The **interquartile range**, or the difference between the upper and lower quartiles (e.g., between the 75th and 25th percentiles)
- The **standard deviation,** or the average distance that numerical values are dispersed around the arithmetic mean

Correlation refers to the strength of relatedness when a relationship exists between two or more numerical values, which, when assigned a numerical value, is the **correlation coefficient** (r). A perfect (1:1) correlation has an r value of 1.0, with decimal values indicating a lesser correlation as the correlation coefficient moves away from 1.0. The correlation may be either positive (with the values increasing or decreasing together) or negative (if the values are inverse and move opposite to each other).

STATISTICAL SIGNIFICANCE

Statistical tests presume the null hypothesis to be true and use the values derived from a test to calculate the likelihood of getting the same or better results under the conditions of the null hypothesis (referred to as the "observed probability" or "empirical probability," as opposed to the "theoretical probability"). This likelihood is referred to as **statistical significance**. Where this likelihood is very small, the null hypothesis is rejected. Traditionally, experimenters have defined a "small chance" at the 0.05 level (sometimes called the 5% level) or the 0.01 level (1% level). The Greek letter alpha (α) is used to indicate the significance level chosen. Where the observed or empirical probability is less than or equal to the selected alpha, the findings are said to be "statistically significant," and the research hypothesis would be accepted.

TESTS

Three examples of tests of statistical significance are:

- The **chi square test** (a nonparametric test of significance), which assesses whether or not two samples are sufficiently different to conclude that the difference can be generalized to the larger population from which the samples were drawn. It provides the degree of confidence by which the research hypothesis can be accepted or rejected, measured on a scale from 0 (impossibility) to 1 (certainty).
- A **t-test** is used to compare the arithmetic means of a given characteristic in two samples and to determine whether they are sufficiently different from each other to be statistically significant.
- **Analysis of variance**, or **ANOVA** (also called the "**F test**"), which is similar to the *t*-test. However, rather than simply comparing the means of two populations, it is used to determine whether or not statistically significant differences exist in multiple groups or samples.

STATISTICAL ERROR

Types of statistical error include the following:

- **Type I error**: Rejecting the null hypothesis when it is true
- **Type II error**: Accepting the null hypothesis when it is false and the research hypothesis is true (concluding that a difference doesn't exist when it does)

DATA ANALYSIS

Data analysis involves the examination of testing results within their context, assessing for correlations, causality, reliability, and validity. In testing a hypothesis (the assertion that two variables are related), researchers look for correlations between variables (a change in one variable associated with a change in another, expressed in numerical values). The closer the correlation is to +1.0 or –1.0 (a perfect positive or negative correlation), the more meaningful the correlation. This, however, is not causality (change in one variable responsible for change in the other). Since all possible relationships between two variables cannot be tested (the variety approaches infinity), the "null hypothesis" is used (asserting that no relationship exists) with probability statistics that indicate the likelihood that the hypothesis is "null" (and must be rejected) or can be accepted. Indices of "reliability" and "validity" are also needed.

RELIABILITY AND VALIDITY

Reliability refers to consistency of results. This is measured via test–retest evaluations, split-half testing (random assignment into two subgroups given the same intervention and then comparison of findings), or in interrater situations, where separate subjects' rating scores are compared to see if the correlations persist.

Validity indicates the degree to which a study's results capture the actual characteristics of the features being measured. Reliable results may be consistent but invalid. However, valid results will always be reliable. **Methods for testing validity** include the following:

Concurrent validity	Comparing the results of studies that used different measurement instruments but targeted the same features
Construct validity	The degree of agreement between a theoretical concept and the measurements obtained (as seen via the subcategories of (a) convergent validity, the degree of actual agreement on measures that should be theoretically related, and (b) discriminant validity, the lack of a relationship among measures which are theoretically not related)
Content validity	Comprising logical validity (i.e., whether reasoning indicates it is valid) and face validity (i.e., whether those involved concur that it appears valid)
Predictive validity	Concerning whether the measurement can be used to accurately extrapolate (predict) future outcomes

Review Video: Testing Validity
Visit mometrix.com/academy and enter code: 315457

Chapter Quiz

Ready to see how well you retained what you just read? Scan the QR code to go directly to the chapter quiz interface for this study guide. If you're using a computer, simply visit the bonus page at **mometrix.com/bonus948/swclinical** and click the Chapter Quizzes link.

Psychotherapy, Clinical Interventions, and Case Management

Transform passive reading into active learning! After immersing yourself in this chapter, put your comprehension to the test by taking a quiz. The insights you gained will stay with you longer this way. Scan the QR code to go directly to the chapter quiz interface for this study guide. If you're using a computer, simply visit the bonus page at **mometrix.com/bonus948/swclinical** and click the Chapter Quizzes link.

Therapeutic Relationships and Communication

CONDITIONS REQUIRED FOR A POSITIVE THERAPEUTIC RELATIONSHIP

In order for a social worker to establish a **positive therapeutic relationship**, they must express non-possessive warmth and concern, genuineness, appropriate empathy, nonjudgmental acceptance, optimism regarding prospects for change, objectivity, professional competence, ability to communicate with a client, and self-awareness. Self-disclosure should be used only purposefully and for the client's benefit.

For clients to contribute to a positive therapeutic environment, they must have hope and courage to undertake change processes, be motivated to change, and trust in the worker's interest and skill. They must also be dealt with as an individual and not a case, personality type, or category. Clients must be able to express themselves, to make their own choices, and to change at their own pace.

PROFESSIONAL OBJECTIVITY IN SOCIAL WORKER-CLIENT RELATIONSHIP

Objectivity requires remaining neutral when making judgements. Because of the nature of social work, a large part of evaluation tends to be subjective and not easily quantified, but these evaluations can then reflect the social worker and the social worker's biases. The goal should be to make objective observations as much as possible—reporting what is seen and heard rather than the subjective opinion about those things. In order to ensure that opinions are objective, specific parameters should be developed for decision making. For example, when evaluating a client's socioeconomic status, judging by language and appearance may produce one opinion while judging according to occupation and income may produce another (and probably more accurate) opinion. The way a social worker measures may also reflect biases. For example, measuring gender by male and female only suggests a subjective rejection of other choices, such as non-binary or transgender.

PRINCIPLES OF COMMUNICATION

Communication involves the conveying of information, whether verbally or nonverbally, between individuals and has two key aspects: sending and receiving information. Each of these requires unique skills, and effective communication requires proficiency in both. **Essential principles of communication** include:

- All aspects of communication must be considered and interpreted in any exchange.
- Communication may be written, verbally spoken, or nonverbally delivered via body language, gestures, and expressions.
- Not all communication is intentional, as unintentional information may also be conveyed.
- All forms of communication have limits, further imposed by issues of perception, unique experiences, and interpretation.
- Quality communication accounts for issues of age, gender, ethnicity/culture, intellect, education, primary language, emotional state, and belief systems.

- Optimum communication is active (or reflective), using strategies such as furthering responses (nodding, etc.), paraphrasing, rephrasing, clarification, encouragement ("tell me more"), partialization (reducing long ideas into manageable parts), summarization, feelings reflection, exploring silence, and nonverbal support (eye contact, warm tone, neutral but warm expressions, etc.).

QUALITY COMMUNICATION WITH CLIENTS

The following are key rules for quality communication with clients:

- Don't speak for the client; instead allow the client to fully express themself.
- Listen carefully and try diligently to understand.
- Don't talk when the client is speaking.
- Don't embellish; digest what the client has actually said, not what was presumed to be said.
- Don't interrupt, even if the process is slow or interspersed with long pauses.
- Don't judge, criticize, or intimidate when communicating.
- Facilitate communication with open-ended questions and a responsive and receptive posture.
- Avoid asking "why" questions, which can be perceived as judgmental.
- Communicate using orderly, well-planned ideas, as opposed to rushed statements.
- Moderate the pace of speech and adjust expressions to fit the client's education, intellect, and other unique features.
- Ask clarifying questions to enhance understanding.
- Attend to nonverbal communication (expression, body language, gestures, etc.).
- Limit closed-ended and leading questions.
- Avoid "stacked" (multi-part) questions that can be confusing.

CONGRUENCE IN COMMUNICATION

Congruence in communication is consistently communicating the same message verbally and nonverbally. The individual's words, body language, and tone of voice should all convey the same message. If they do not, then the communication is incongruent, and the receiver cannot trust the communication. For example, if a person says, "I really want to help you," in a very harsh tone of voice and with an angry affect, the communication is incongruent, and the message may actually be perceived as the exact opposite of the words spoken. Communication is also incongruent if the individual gives a series of conflicting messages: "I'm going to get a job," "Why should I work?" "I know I need to work," "There's no point in taking a low-paying job." The social worker must be alert to the congruence of client communication in order to more accurately assess the client as well as be aware of personal congruence of communication when interacting with client. This helps to ensure that the social worker can cultivate a relationship built on trust.

ACTIVE LISTENING

Active listening techniques include the use of paraphrasing in response, clarification of what was said by the client, encouragement ("tell me more"), etc. Key **overarching guidelines** include the following:

- Don't become preoccupied with specific active listening strategies; rather, concentrate on reducing client resistance to sharing, building trust, aiding the client in expanding their thoughts, and ensuring mutual understanding.
- The greatest success occurs when a variety of active listening techniques are used during any given client meeting.
- Focus on listening and finding ways to help the client to keep talking. Active listening skills will aid the client in expanding and clarifying their thoughts.
- Remember that asking questions can often mean interrupting. Avoid questioning the client when they are midstream in thought and are sharing, unless the questions will further expand the sharing process.

ALLOWING CLIENTS UNINTERRUPTED OPPORTUNITIES TO SPEAK

There are many reasons to limit a client's opportunities to speak. Time may be inadequate, the workload may be impacted, the client may seem distracted or uninterested in sharing, etc. However, only by **allowing the client to divulge their true feelings** can the worker actually know and understand what the client believes, thinks, feels, and desires.

Barriers to client sharing include the following:

- **Frequent interruptions**: Instead, the social worker might jot a short note to prompt a question later.
- **Supplying client words**: A client may seem to have great difficulty finding words to express their feelings and the social worker may be tempted to assist. However, this may entirely circumvent true expression, as the client may simply say, "Yes, that's it," rather than working harder to find their true feelings.
- **Filling silence**: Long pauses can be awkward. The social worker may wish to fill the silence, but in so doing they may prevent the client from finding thoughts to share.

UTILIZING NONVERBAL COMMUNICATION

To facilitate the sharing process it is important for a social worker to present as warm, receptive, caring, and accepting of the client. However, the social worker should also endeavor not to bias, lead, or repress client expressions by an inappropriate use of **nonverbal** cues. Frowning, smiling, vigorous nodding, etc., may all lead clients to respond to the social workers' reactions rather than to disclose their genuine feelings and thoughts. To this end, a social worker will endeavor to make good eye contact, use a soft tone of voice, present as interested and engaged, etc., but without marked expressions that can influence the dialogue process. Sitting and facing the client (ideally without a desk or other obstruction in between), being professionally dressed and groomed, sitting close enough to be engaging without invading the client's space, and using an open posture (arms comfortable in the lap or by the sides, rather than crossed over the chest) can all facilitate the communication process.

LEADING QUESTIONS

Leading questions are those that predispose a particular response. For example, saying, "You know that it is okay to ask questions, don't you?" is a strongly leading question. While it may seem an innocuous way to ensure that someone feels free to ask questions, it may not succeed in actually eliciting questions. Instead, ask the client directly, "What questions do you have?" This way of asking not only reveals that questions are acceptable, but is much more likely to encourage the client to openly share any confusion they are having.

Even less forceful leading questions can induce a bias. For example, when a couple comes in for counseling, the social worker asking, "Would you like to sit over here?" could prevent the social worker from seeing how they elect to arrange themselves in relation to the social worker and each other (a very revealing element in the relationship). Instead, the worker might simply say, "Feel free to sit anywhere you'd like." Avoiding leading questions is an important skill in the communication process.

OBTAINING SENSITIVE INFORMATION FROM CLIENTS

Sensitive information includes that involving sexual activity, abuse, intimate partner violence, substance abuse, and mental health issues. Clients are more likely to answer questions truthfully if they have developed a relationship of trust with the questioner. **Methods of obtaining sensitive information** include the following:

- Embedding the questions in a series of questions in context: "Do you spend time with your friends?" "Are your friends sexually active?" "Do you think you are more or less sexually active than your friends?" "How many sexual partners have you had?"
- Asking for facts and not opinions
- Using familiar language and terminology

- Asking for permission to question, "Do you mind if I ask you about..." and explaining the reason for questioning, "In order to plan for your medical care, I need to ask you about..."
- Using a scale (1 to 10) rather than asking for detailed information
- Explaining what kinds of information can remain confidential and what kinds cannot (such as child abuse)

Interventions

PRINCIPLES OF TREATMENT PLANNING

GOALS AND OBJECTIVES

The treatment plan is used to set goals and objectives and to monitor progress. **Goals** are considered broad-based aims that are more general in nature (e.g., becoming less anxious, developing improved self-esteem), while **objectives** are the fundamental steps needed to accomplish the identified goals. Because objectives are used to operationalize goals, they must be written with considerable clarity and detail (questions of who, what, where, when, why, and how should be carefully answered). Properly constructed objectives must be based upon the client's perception of needs, as opposed to a clinician's bias, whenever possible. Finally, the treatment plan should be revised and updated as often as necessary to ensure that it remains an effective guiding and monitoring tool.

LENGTH OF TIME NEEDED TO ACCOMPLISH GOALS

While the length of time required to accomplish certain goals is largely dependent on the individual client, there are general expectations to time requirements based on the goals desired to be met:

- **Extended periods of time for treatment** are needed for those approaches that focus on personality change.
- **Shorter-term treatment** is called for in those approaches that focus on behavioral change, cognitive change, or problem solving. Examples are crisis intervention, task-centered treatment, cognitive therapy, and behavioral treatment.

CLINICAL PRACTICE IN SOCIAL WORK

Clinical practice in social work requires a master's degree to actively diagnose and treat clients, but must be understood at all levels of social work. Clinical practice has the following focuses:

- Seeks to **improve the internalized negative effects** of environmental factors including stress from health, vocation, family, and interpersonal problems.
- The worker assists individuals, couples, and families to **change** feelings, attitudes, and coping behaviors that hinder optimal social functioning.
- Practice is conducted in both **agencies and private practice**.
- Practice is differentiated from other practices by its **goal** of helping individuals change, facilitating personal adjustment, treating emotional disorders and mental illness, or enhancing intrapsychic or interpersonal functioning.
- Like all social work practice, **assessment** is psychosocial, focused on the person-in-environment, and has the goal of enhancing social functioning.

THEORETICAL BASES

The theoretical bases of clinical practice are as follows:

- The **psychosocial approach** focuses on intrapsychic and interpersonal change.
- The **problem-solving approach** seeks to solve distinct problems, based on psychosocial and functional approaches.
- The **behavior modification approach** seeks symptom reduction of problem behaviors, learning alternative positive behaviors.
- **Cognitive therapy** focuses on symptom reduction of negative thoughts, distorted thinking, and dysfunctional beliefs.
- The **crisis intervention approach** is the brief treatment of reactions to crisis in order to restore client's equilibrium.

140

- **Family therapy** treats an entire family system and sees the individual symptom bearer as indicative of a problem in the family as a whole.
- **Group therapy** is a model in which group members help and are helped by others with similar problems, receive validation for their own experiences, and test new social identities and roles.
- In the **narrative therapy** approach, the stories clients tell about their lives reveal how they construct perceptions of their experiences. The worker helps client construct alternative, more affirming stories.
- The **ecological or life model** focuses on life transitions, environmental pressures, and maladaptation between the individual and the family or environment. Focuses on interaction and interdependence of people and environments.
- The **task-centered approach** focuses on completing tasks to strengthen self-esteem and restore usual capacity for coping.

ASSUMPTIONS AND KNOWLEDGE BASE

Clinical practice assumes that individual behavior, growth, and development are brought about by a complex interaction of psychological and environmental factors.

The **required knowledge base** for the implementation of clinical practice in social work is as follows:

- An understanding of the theories of personality development
- An understanding of systems theory
- Knowledge of clinical diagnoses (DSM-5-TR)
- An understanding that significant influences on the individual are socio-cultural factors including ethnicity, immigration status, occupation, race, gender, sexual orientation, and socioeconomic class

ASSESSMENT PROCESS

The assessment process in clinical practice is as follows:

- Determine the **presenting problem**.
- Determine if there is a **match** between the problem and available services.
- Ongoing **data collection and reassessment** to enhance understanding of client's problems.
- The worker's role is to ask **questions** and ask for elaboration and description, observe client's behavior and affect, and organize data to create a meaningful psychosocial or diagnostic assessment.
- Sources of data other than client include **interviews** with family members, home visits, and contacts with teachers, clergy, doctors, social agencies, and friends.
- **Clinical diagnosis**: A product of the clinical social worker's understanding of the client's problems based on the data collected. It categorizes the client's functioning. Also includes relevant medical illnesses or physical conditions and their influence on client's emotional life and functioning.

KEY CONCEPTS

Key concepts used in clinical practice include the following:

Direct influence	The worker continually seeks to understand the client's view of self and situation.
Exploration	The worker offers advice and suggestions in order to influence the client.
Confrontation	The worker challenges the client to deal with inconsistencies between her or his words and actions, maladaptive behaviors, or resistance to treatment or change.
Clarification	The worker questions, repeats, or rephrases material the client discusses. The worker must be sensitive to the client's defensiveness.
Universalization	The normalization of problems. Problems are presented as a part of the human condition in order to help the client see them as less pathological.

Ventilation	The client's airing of feelings associated with the information presented about self and the situation. May alleviate the intensity of the client's feelings or feeling that they are alone in those feelings. The worker may need to help the client distinguish times when ventilation is useful and when it may increase intensity of feelings.
Catharsis	The release of tension or anxiety through reliving and intentionally examining early life, repressed, or traumatic experiences.

BEHAVIOR MODIFICATION APPROACH

THEORETICAL BASES

The theoretical bases of the behavior modification approach to social work practice are as follows:

- **Early classical conditioning research** (Pavlov)
- **Behavior modification theory**: Operant conditioning (Skinner, Thorndike, Watson, Dollard & Miller, Thomas)
- **Social learning theory**: Observing, imitating, modeling (Bandura)

ASSUMPTIONS ABOUT HUMAN BEHAVIOR

The following are assumptions this approach makes about human behavior:

- One can know a person only through the observable. Behavior can be explained by learning theory. Theory of the unconscious is unnecessary.
- A person has learned, dysfunctional behaviors rather than emotional illness. No presumptions about psychiatric illness.
- One expresses dysfunctional behavior in symptoms. Symptoms are defined as the observed individual behaviors that are labeled as deviant or problematic. Once the symptoms are removed, there are no remaining underlying problems.
- High priority goes to research and empirically based knowledge.

MOTIVATIONS FOR CHANGE AND THE MEANS THROUGH WHICH CHANGE OCCURS

The motivations for change in behavior modification include the following:

- Disequilibrium
- Anxiety
- Conscious desire to eliminate a symptom
- Agreement to follow a behavior modification program

The following are the means through which change occurs:

- **Operant or voluntary behavior** that is increased by positive or negative reinforcement and decreased by withholding reinforcement or punishing.
- **Involuntary behavior** that is increased or decreased by conditioning.
- Change depends upon environmental conditions or events that precede, are connected with, or follow the behavior.
- As a result of observing and imitating in a social context, modeling occurs; this is not learned by reward and punishment.

OPERANT BEHAVIOR AND RESPONDENT BEHAVIOR

Operant behavior is controlled by consequences of that behavior. Actions preceding or following the behavior need to be changed. **Respondent behavior** is behavior which is brought out by a specific stimulus. The individual must be desensitized to the stimuli, for example, in the case of phobias.

TREATMENT PLANNING

Treatment planning in the behavioral modification approach is as follows:

1. **Prioritize problems**. Identify maintaining conditions for selected problems.
2. Engage client in establishing goals for change.
3. **Establish baseline data** regarding the frequency of behavior.
4. Develop written or oral **contract**.

COGNITIVE THERAPY APPROACH

THEORETICAL BASE AND ASSUMPTIONS ABOUT HUMAN BEHAVIOR

The theoretical bases of the cognitive therapy approach are as follows:

- Albert Ellis' rational-emotive behavior therapy
- Aaron Beck's cognitive theory

Assumptions made by the cognitive therapy approach include:

- Mental distress is caused by the maladaptive and rigid ways we construe events, not by the events themselves.
- Negative automatic thoughts are generated by dysfunctional beliefs. These beliefs are set in motion by activating events, and they trigger emotional consequences. Future events are interpreted through the filter of these belief systems.
- Negative affect and symptoms of psychological disorders follow negative automatic thoughts, biases, and distortions.
- Irrational thinking carries the form of systematic distortions.

MOTIVATIONS FOR CHANGE AND MEANS THROUGH WHICH CHANGE OCCURS

The motivations for change in the cognitive therapy approach include:

- Disequilibrium
- Anxiety
- Desire to live without a symptom
- Agreement to work toward changing thought patterns

The following are means through which change occurs:

- Structured sessions
- Exploring and testing cognitive distortions and basic beliefs
- Homework between sessions, which allows the client to practice changes in thinking in a natural environment
- Changes in feelings and behaviors in the future come about through changes in the way the client interprets events

ASSESSMENT PROCESS AND ROLE OF THERAPEUTIC RELATIONSHIP

The following are conducted during the assessment in the cognitive therapy approach:

- List the client's cognitive distortions (e.g., catastrophizing, minimizing, negative predictions, mind-reading, overgeneralization, personalization)
- List the client's negative automatic thoughts and dysfunctional beliefs

The roles of the therapeutic relationship in cognitive therapy are as follows:

- The worker is a teacher, ally, and coach.
- The worker is active, directive, and didactic.

TREATMENT PLANNING PROCESS AND TREATMENT SKILLS AND TECHNIQUES

The treatment planning process is described below:

- Establish baseline data measuring client's negative automatic thoughts, distortions, and dysfunctional beliefs. How often do these thoughts occur and under what circumstances?
- Create target goals for change and alternative ways of thinking.
- Agree to contract for goals, homework, and time frame of treatment.

Treatment skills and techniques are as follows:

- Short term treatment
- A focus on symptom reduction
- Using a rational approach, focused on concrete tasks in sessions and for homework
- Per **Albert Ellis**: Be forcefully confrontive in order to reveal the client's thought system, get the client to see how that system defeats them, and work to change the thoughts that make up that system.
- Per **Aaron Beck**: A gentler, more collaborative approach. Help the client restructure their interpretations of events. "What is the evidence for this idea?" or "Is there another way to look at this situation?" Social skill building, group therapy, and milieu treatment are utilized.

TASK-CENTERED APPROACH

THEORETICAL BASES AND ASSUMPTIONS ABOUT HUMAN BEHAVIOR

The theoretical bases for the task-centered approach are as follows:

- Learning theory
- Cognitive and behavioral theory
- High priority on research-based practice knowledge

Assumptions of the task-centered approach include:

- An individual is not influenced solely by internal or unconscious drives, nor controlled solely by environmental forces.
- The client usually is able to identify her or his own problems and goals.
- The client is the primary agent of change and is a consumer of services.
- The worker's role is to help the client achieve the changes that they decide upon and are willing to work on.

MOTIVATIONS FOR CHANGE AND MEANS THROUGH WHICH CHANGE OCCURS

The following are motivations for change in the task-centered approach:

- A temporary breakdown in coping influences the client to seek help
- A conscious wish for change
- Strengthening of self-esteem through task completion

The following are means through which change occurs:

- Clarification of the problem or problems
- Steps taken to resolve or alleviate problems
- Changes in environment

PROCESS OF ASSESSMENT AND ROLE OF THERAPEUTIC RELATIONSHIP

The assessment process in the task-centered approach is described below:

- Examination and clarification of problems are primary. The problem must be one that concerns the client and is amenable to treatment.
- The worker and client create a rationale for resolution of the problem and note potential treatment benefits.

The role of therapeutic relationship in the task-centered approach to practice is described below:

- The relationship is not an objective in itself, but is a means of augmenting and supporting problem solving. Transference and countertransference aspects are minimized.
- The social worker expects that the client will work on agreed upon tasks and activities to resolve problems and provides acceptance, respect, and understanding.
- The social worker and the client have a collaborative relationship. The social worker seeks the client's input at all stages. The client is the consumer and the social worker is the authority with expertise who works on the client's behalf.

TREATMENT PLANNING AND CONTRAINDICATIONS

Treatment planning in the task-centered approach is described below:

- A **contract** must state an agreement upon what will be worked on, the social worker's and the client's willingness to engage in the work, and the limits of the treatment (time, etc.). The contract can be formal, oral, or written; it is dynamic and can be renegotiated.
- Both the worker and client agree on a specific **definition** of the problem(s) to be worked on and the changes sought in the process. This is expressed in both behavioral and measurable terms.

The task-centered approach is **inappropriate** for the following clients:

- Clients who are interested in existential issues, life goals, or discussion of stressful events.
- Clients who are unwilling or unable to use the structured approach to tasks.
- Clients who have problems that are not subject to resolution or improvement by problem-solving.
- Clients who are involuntary; some clients' treatment is mandated.

SYSTEMS THEORY APPROACH

THEORETICAL BASES

The theoretical bases to the systems theory approach are as follows:

- This approach is based on general system theory applied to social work treatment.
- Systems theory is a framework that a worker can use with any of the practice approaches in order to help the client establish and maintain a steady state.

KEY CONCEPTS IN SYSTEM THEORY

Boundary	Organizational means by which the parts of a system can be differentiated from their environment and which differentiates subsystems
Open and closed systems	Indicates whether boundary between a system and its environment is open or closed
Subsystem	Subset of the entire system
Entropy	Randomness, chaos, disorder in a system that causes a system to lose energy faster than it creates or imports it
Homeostasis	Changes a system makes in order to maintain an accustomed balance

ASSUMPTIONS ABOUT HUMAN BEHAVIOR AND MOTIVATIONS FOR CHANGE

Assumptions of the systems theory approach are as follows:

- Individuals have potential for **growth and adaptation** throughout life. They are active, problem solving and purposeful.
- Individuals can be understood as **open systems** which interact with other living systems and the nonliving environment.
- All systems are **interdependent**. Change in one system brings about changes in the others. Additionally, change in a subsystem brings about changes in other subsystems.
- Change occurs in the **individual**, in the **environment**, or in the **interaction** between the individual and the environment.

ASSESSMENT AND ROLE OF THE THERAPEUTIC RELATIONSHIP

A key assumption in the assessment process of the systems theory approach is that problems do not belong to the individual, but instead belong to the interaction of the behaviors or social conditions that create disequilibrium.

The role of therapeutic relationship in the systems theory approach is as follows:

- Depending on the problem and target of change, the relationship may be supportive, facilitative, collaborative, or adversarial. The worker may intervene on behalf of the client with individuals, the social support network, or the larger system.
- The relationship offers feedback to the client and to other systems.

TREATMENT PLANNING

Treatment planning in the systems theory approach is as follows:

- Planning begins with establishing specific goals, their practicability, and their priority.
- Target systems for intervention are identified in collaboration with the client.
- A specific contract is developed with the client or other systems that may be involved in the change process.

PSYCHOSOCIAL APPROACH

BASIC TENETS AND THEORETICAL BASES

The basic tenets of the psychosocial approach include the following:

- Problem-solving
- Crisis intervention
- Task-centered casework
- Planned short-term treatment

The following are the theoretical bases of this approach:

- **Psychoanalytic theory** (Sigmund Freud)
- **Ego Psychology**: Psychoanalytic base, with focus on ego functions and adaptation; defense mechanisms (Anna Freud); adaptations to an average expected environment (Hartmann); ego mastery and development through the life cycle (Erikson); separation or individuation (Margaret Mahler)
- **Social Science Theories**: Role, family and small group, impact of culture, communication theory, systems theory
- **Biological theories**: Ecological, homeostasis, behavioral genetics, medical model

> **Review Video: Psychoanalytic Approach**
> Visit mometrix.com/academy and enter code: 162594

ASSUMPTIONS ABOUT HUMAN BEHAVIOR

The following are assumptions about human behavior that the psychosocial approach to practice makes:

- The individual is always seen in the context of the environment, interacting with social systems (such as family), and influenced by earlier personal experiences.
- Conscious vs. unconscious and rational vs. irrational motivations govern individual behavior.
- Individuals can change and grow under fitting conditions throughout the life cycle.

MOTIVATIONS FOR CHANGE AND MEANS THROUGH WHICH CHANGE OCCURS

The following are motivations for change according to the psychosocial approach to practice:

- Disequilibrium, which induces anxiety and releases energy to change
- Conscious and unconscious needs and wishes
- Relationship with the worker (or group in group treatment)

The means through which change occurs include the following:

- Development of insight and resolution of emotional conflicts
- Corrective emotional experience in relationship with the worker
- Changes in affective, cognitive, or behavioral patterns that induce changes in interpersonal relationships
- Changes in the environment

ASSESSMENT

Assessment in the psychosocial approach has the following characteristics:

- Outlines the client's presenting problem and resources for addressing it.
- Determines if there is an appropriate match between the presenting problem and available services
- Begins in first interview and continues throughout treatment
- **Dynamic components**: Determining how different characteristics of the client and important relationships interact to influence their total functioning
- **Etiological components**: Determining the causative factors that produced the presenting problem and that influence the client's previous attempts to deal with it
- **Clinical components**: Articulation of the client's functioning (i.e., mental status, coping strategies and styles, a clinical diagnosis if pertinent)

ROLE OF THERAPEUTIC RELATIONSHIP

The role of the therapeutic relationship in the psychosocial approach is as follows:

- Mindful use of the relationship can **motivate** and create energy to change.
- Relationship should foster a **corrective** emotional experience.
- Client and **client's needs** are central. Self-disclosure by worker is used purposefully and only for client's benefit.
- Some **transference dynamics** may hamper treatment, but generally they should be seen and used as potential vehicles for promoting client self-understanding and changing problematic interpersonal patterns.
- To deal with possible **countertransference**, the worker should be self-aware, seek supervision and consultation to decrease countertransference reactions, and use her or his own therapy for dealing with countertransference.
- The worker should be aware that they may be perceived as more competent than the client and as the expert who is there to fix the client's problems. This can be **disempowering** to the client and works against a strengths perspective.

COMPONENTS AND PHASES OF TREATMENT PLANNING

The following are components of treatment planning:

- Development of a unique treatment plan based on the client's situation.
- Client goals and their practicality, given the client's abilities, strengths, and weaknesses, as well as availability of relevant services.
- Treatment plan is directed at changing the individual, the environment, or the interaction between the two.

The phases of treatment are as follows:

Phase	Focus
Engagement or assessment	Applicant becomes client; increasing motivation; initial resistance; establishing work relationship; assessment; informed consent re: confidentiality; roles, rights, and responsibilities of the client and worker
Contracting or goal setting	Mutual understanding between client and worker with regard to goals, treatment process, nature of roles and relationship, and intended time of treatment
Ongoing treatment and interventions	Working toward improving previously agreed upon problems; major focus is on current functioning and conscious experience; dealing with ongoing resistance, transference, and countertransference
Termination	Potential for growth, reiterate major themes of treatment, experience feelings about relationship ending

NARRATIVE THERAPY APPROACH

THEORETICAL BASES AND ASSUMPTIONS ABOUT HUMAN BEHAVIOR

The theoretical bases of the narrative therapy approach are as follows:

- Narrative therapy draws on the work of Michael White of the Dulwich Centre in Australia.
- It utilizes a variety of individual and personality theories, as well as social psychological approaches.

- It focuses on the stories people tell about their lives. These stories are interpreted through their subjective personal filters.
- Interventions are designed to reveal and reframe the ways clients structure their perceptions of their experiences.

Assumptions made about human behavior in the narrative therapy approach are as follows:

- Individuals' behaviors come from their interpretations of experiences.
- Subjective meanings influence actions. Meanings derived from interpretations of experience determine specifics of action.
- Narrative therapy is concerned with the telling and re-telling of the preferred stories of people's lives, as well as the performance and re-performance of these stories.

ASSESSMENT AND ROLE OF THERAPEUTIC RELATIONSHIP

Assessment in narrative therapy is characterized as the following:

- **Mapping how the problem influences the client's life and relationships**: How does the problem affect the client(s)?
- **Mapping the influence of the person or family in the life of the problem**: Clients start to see themselves as authors or co-authors of their own stories.
- This therapy builds on **strengths and abilities** of families and individuals rather than seeking weaknesses and deficits.

The role of the therapeutic relationship in the narrative therapy approach is as follows:

- The worker is co-constructor of new narratives.
- The relationship is a partnership; the authority of the therapist is minimized. Partnership does not use techniques that result in clients feeling coerced or manipulated.
- Relationship seeks and is an agent of client empowerment. The worker offers an optimistic, future-oriented perspective that builds on the client's abilities and strengths in moving toward change. Emphasizes client's possibilities, strengths, and resources.
- Worker guides therapeutic conversations to create new possibilities, fresh options, and opportunities to reframe the client's realities.

TREATMENT PLANNING

Treatment planning in narrative therapy includes the following:

- Together, the worker and client establish clear goals for their work.
- The worker and client divide out and work on small, specific, limited goals.
- The approach avoids a medical (disease) model that seeks explanations for problems or ascribes pathology to the family system.

PROBLEM-SOLVING APPROACH

THEORETICAL BASES

The theoretical bases for the problem-solving approach to social work practice are as follows:

- **Psychodynamic, with major influence from ego psychologists**: Erik Erikson (capacity for change throughout life), Robert White (coping, adaptation, mastery of environment), Heinz Hartmann (use of the conflict-free ego).
- **Social science theory**: Role theory, problem solving theory (John Dewey).

ASSUMPTIONS ABOUT HUMAN BEHAVIOR

Assumptions that the problem-solving approach to social work practice makes about human behavior include the following:

- Individuals are engaged in life-long problem-solving and adaptation to maintain, rebuild, or achieve stability, even as circumstances change.
- The individual is viewed as a whole person; the focus, however, is on the person in relation to a problem.
- Individuals have or can develop the motivation and ability to change.
- This perspective does not see the individual as sick or deficient, but instead as in need of help to resolve life problems.
- Each individual has a reachable moment at a time of disequilibrium, at which point they can most successfully mobilize motivation and capacity.
- An individual's cognitive processes can be engaged to solve problems, to achieve goals, and to grow emotionally.
- An individual has both rational/irrational and conscious/unconscious processes, but cognitive strengths can control irrationality.

MOTIVATIONS FOR CHANGE AND MEANS THROUGH WHICH CHANGE OCCURS

The following are motivations for change according to the problem-solving approach:

- Disequilibrium between reality and what the client wants
- Conscious desire to achieve change
- Positive expectations based on new life possibilities
- The strength of a supportive relationship and positive expectations of the worker

The means through which change occurs are as follows:

- Improved problem-solving skills. These may produce changes in personality or improved functioning, but these are secondary to problem resolution.
- Gratification, encouragement, and support that result from improvement in the problem situation. This and the worker's emotional support increase the possibility of change.
- Repetition and practice (drilling) of the problem-solving method increases possibility for replication of effective strategies in new situations.
- Insight, resolution of conflicts, and changes in feelings.
- Problem resolution concerning changes in the individual, the environment, and the interaction between the two.

ASSESSMENT

Assessment in the problem-solving approach is focused on the following:

- Focus first on **identifying the problem** and the aspects of the person or environment that can be involved in problem solving
- Assess **motivation, capacity, and opportunity (MCO)** of the client to resolve the problem
- Include a **statement of the problem** (objective facts and subjective responses to them), precipitating factors, and prior efforts to resolve it
- A **combined activity** of worker and client

ROLE OF THERAPEUTIC RELATIONSHIP

The role of the therapeutic relationship in the problem-solving approach is as follows:

- Mindful and continual use of **the supportive social work relationship** to motivate clients to engage in problem resolution.
- The worker is an expert in **problem-solving methodology** and guides clients through steps of problem resolution. The relationship grows as worker and client work on problems jointly.
- Work is focused on **practical problem solving**; therefore, transference and countertransference are less likely. These are only addressed if they are interfering with the work.

COMPONENTS AND ELEMENTS OF TREATMENT PLANNING

The following are components of treatment planning according to the problem-solving approach:

1. **Psychosocial**: Derived from an evaluation of the problem and the client's motivation, capacity, and opportunities (MCO).
2. **Functional**: The function of the agency serves as a boundary of service (i.e., adoption agency, mental health service)
3. **Interagency**: Using resources from other agencies in a network of services designed to help the client.

The **four P's** are the basic elements involved in treatment: A **person** has a **problem** and comes to a **place** for help given through a **process**:

1. Clearly identify the problem and the client's subjective response to it
2. Select a part of the problem that has possibility for resolution, identify possible solutions, and assess their achievability in light of MCO
3. Engage client's ego capacities
4. Determine steps or actions to be taken by the worker and client to resolve or alleviate the problem
5. Help the client carry out problem-solving activities and determine their effectiveness
6. Termination

ECOLOGICAL OR LIFE MODEL APPROACH
THEORETICAL BASES

The following are the theoretical bases of the ecological/life model approach:

- Ecology
- Systems theory
- Stress, coping, and adaptation theory
- Psychodynamic, behavioral, and cognitive theory

This approach follows a conceptual framework that has its focus on the **interaction and interdependence of people and environments**. It provides service to individuals, families, and groups within a community, organizational, and cultural environment.

ASSUMPTIONS ABOUT HUMAN BEHAVIOR AND THE MOTIVATION FOR CHANGE

Ecological/life model assumptions about human behavior are as follows:

- The individual is active, purposeful, and capable of problem solving. They have potential for growth and adaptation throughout life.
- There are three areas of life experience in which problems occur: life transitions, environmental pressures, and maladaptive lack of "fit" between the individual and a larger entity (the family, the community).
- Each individual client system depends upon or is interdependent with other systems.

151

The motivation for change in this approach stems from changes that the individual wants in relation to herself or himself, the environment, or the interplay between the two.

The worker's relationship with the client is based on mutuality, trust, and authenticity. Depending on the goal of the intervention, the worker and client relationship may be supportive, collaborative, or adversarial.

CRISIS INTERVENTION APPROACH

THEORETICAL BASE

The theoretical bases for the crisis intervention approach are as follows:

- **Psychodynamic therapy**, particularly ego psychology (Freud, Erikson, Rapoport) and Lindemann's work on loss and grief
- **Intellectual development** (Piaget)
- **Social science**: stress theory, family structure, role theory

SOURCES OF TRAUMA

Trauma can be introduced into an individual's life through various means:

- The trauma victim experiences a **threat** to her or his physical integrity or life. The trauma experience confronts a person with an extreme situation of fear and helplessness.
- Trauma may be **chronic** and repeated or may take the form of one event of short duration.
- Many of the symptoms related to PTSD and domestic violence are self-protective attempts at **coping** with **realistic threats**.

MOTIVATIONS FOR CHANGE AND MEANS THROUGH WHICH CHANGE OCCURS

The motivations for change in the crisis intervention approach are as follows:

- Disequilibrium caused by a stressful event or situation
- Energy, which is made available by anxiety about the situation
- A supportive relationship

The following are the means through which change occurs:

- Challenging old coping patterns and a reorganization of coping skills
- Growth, which occurs as the ego develops a larger repertoire of coping skills and organizes them into more complex patterns

ASSESSMENT AND MOTIVATIONS FOR CHANGE

The general assessment process in the crisis intervention approach is as follows:

- **Exploring the stress producing event or situation**, the individual's response to it, and responses to past crises
- Characteristic signs, phases, and patterns of adaptation and maladaptation to **crisis** (e.g., PTSD)
- Because of the need for quick action, a highly focused assessment that emphasizes **current state** of functioning and internal and environmental supports and deficits

Assessment in the crisis intervention approach also must be specific to the crisis experienced:

- **Assessment for PTSD**: Evaluate the nature of the trauma; the strengths and limitations that pre-date the trauma; the impact of trauma on the client's emotional life, self-esteem, and functioning; and whether the client remains at risk and the possible need for self-protective measures.

- **Assessment for domestic violence**: Evaluate if the client is still at risk and if practical protective measures are required. Legal reporting is not required for adult-adult domestic violence, however, if children are at risk as witnesses or victims the worker must make a report to child protective services.

Motivations for change in the crisis intervention approach are as follows:

- Reality-based fear and the need for protection
- Symptoms including depression, anxiety, dissociation, and low self-esteem

ROLE OF THERAPEUTIC RELATIONSHIP

The role of the therapeutic relationship in trauma-based social work is described below:

- For clients with PTSD, the worker is a protective presence. The worker guides the pace of treatment in order to avoid flooding the client with excessive traumatic memories that would promote regression. The worker creates an emotionally safe therapeutic space in which to remember and process the trauma.
- For clients who have experienced domestic violence, the worker may be a therapist, case manager, court-based victim's advocate, or broker to obtain services.

PHASES OF TREATMENT AND TREATMENT SKILLS AND TECHNIQUES

The phases of treatment in the crisis intervention approach are as follows:

1. Identify events that brought on the crisis.
2. Promote awareness of impact of crisis, both cognitive and emotional.
3. Manage affect leading to tension discharge and mastery.
4. Seek resources in networks (individual, family, social) and in community.
5. Identify specific tasks associated with healthy resolution of crisis.

The following are the treatment skills and techniques for this approach:

- **Brief treatment.** Like the crisis itself, treatment is time limited.
- **Present- and future-oriented.** Treatment can deal with the past, however, only to resolve old conflicts if they prevent work on the present crisis.
- Uses all **psychosocial and problem-solving techniques**, but reorders them; clinician is active, directive, and at times authoritative.

COPING MECHANISMS WHEN EXPERIENCING LOSS OR TRAUMA

Coping mechanisms available to assist clients after their experiencing loss or trauma include:

- **Emotion-focused strategies**: Used to reduce anxiety and help the individual avoid obsessing over problems. Strategies include progressive relaxation exercises, guided imagery, controlled breathing, and distractions (such as listening to music, playing a musical instrument, reading, and playing video games). Clients may use mindfulness to try to recognize unhealthy emotional responses and modify them. Exercise may help to distract the client from problems and increase sense of wellbeing. Rational coping, in which the client faces the problem directly rather than avoiding it, can lessen the long-term emotional effects.
- **Problem-focused strategies**: Used to resolve or ameliorate problems. Strategies include learning and applying various problem-solving methods, engaging in role playing, and learning organizational skills, such as more effective time management and making and adhering to schedules. Clients may change environments to one that is less stressful or dangerous, and may seek social support of friends or professionals.

PTSD TREATMENT

PTSD treatment consists of the following:

- Psychodynamic therapy
- Dialectical behavioral therapy (DBT): teaches skills to cope with intense feelings, reduce symptoms of PTSD, and enhance respect for self and quality of life
- EMDR (Eye Movement Desensitization and Reprocessing)
- Group therapy (support or DBT)

TREATING VICTIMS OF DOMESTIC VIOLENCE

Domestic violence treatment is as follows:

- Develop a safety plan for safe shelter, etc. to protect victim from perpetrator.
- Do not assess or treat domestic violence in marital or family therapy sessions as this may increase risk to the victim, inhibit revealing the violence history, and enrage the perpetrator.

> **Review Video: Domestic Abuse**
> Visit mometrix.com/academy and enter code: 530581

CLINICAL WORK WITH CHILDREN

Children are typically referred to treatment for symptoms or behavioral problems. The child's underlying conflicts reveal themselves through play and verbally in free expression. Play is the child's form of symbolic communication, an emulation of the real world, and the child's psychological reality.

THEORETICAL BASES

The theoretical base for the treatment of children is found in:

- Normal child development theory
- Psychosocial development theory (Sigmund Freud, Anna Freud, Erikson)
- Attachment theory
- Object relations theory

MOTIVATIONS FOR CHANGE

Motivations for change when treating children are as follows:

- If child is in alternative placement (foster care, etc.), the child's behavior may be seen as problematic by the agency or worker and treatment interventions may be sought
- The child is unhappy with peer relations or may be socially immature
- Unsatisfactory school adjustment (grades, problems with authority)
- Conflict with parents (struggle to cope with dysfunctional family or problems in parents' marriage)
- Feelings of anger, unhappiness
- Self-destructive behaviors such as cutting or eating disorders

ROLE OF THERAPEUTIC RELATIONSHIP

The role of the therapeutic relationship when treating children in social work practice is as follows:

- Worker as a therapist: provides a safe environment in which the worker can follow child's lead, show child acceptance, and create an environment for free expression
- Worker as advocate
- Worker as case manager and care coordinator
- Worker as protective service worker

- Worker as adoption and foster care specialist
- Worker as school guidance counselor

ASSESSMENT AND TREATMENT PLANNING

Assessment seeks to understand the child's inner feelings and conflicts, the parent-child interaction, the family dynamics and interactions, and practical difficulties and any environmental problems. Assessment will be sensitive to multi-problem families and will be culturally competent.

Treatment planning for children is as follows:

- Build on strengths, focus on areas where functioning is problematic (individual difficulties, family dysfunction, environmentally generated crises)
- Support adaptive behavior
- Set realistic goals and emphasize the issues that directly affect the care of the child
- Clarify the projected length of time of treatment; ongoing reevaluation
- Build relationship through management of concrete problems

MALTREATED OR TRAUMATIZED CHILDREN

TREATMENT PLANNING

Treatment planning for social work practice with a maltreated or traumatized child is discussed below:

- The principal goal is **protecting the child** from further harm and **halting** any further abuse, neglect, or sexual exploitation immediately and conclusively. This may require temporary or permanent removal of an offending caretaker or household member, or removal of the child from the home to a safe place.
- The secondary goal is creating conditions that **ensure that abuse or neglect does not recur** after supervision and treatment are terminated. This may include prosecution or incarceration of the offending party and evaluation of the non-offending parent's long-term capacity and motivation to protect the child.
- The official agency can and will use **legal authority** to ensure compliance with agency directives when necessary. The worker should be aware that the possibility of the child's removal may be the primary concern of the parent and may lead to panic, dissembling, or flight.
- Treatment's goal is to help parents learn **parenting and relational skills** that can change parental behavior and the child's responses.

ROLE OF THERAPEUTIC RELATIONSHIP

The role of the therapeutic relationship in social work practice with maltreated or traumatized children is discussed below:

- The worker is to establish trust and a working relationship with the family and build parental self-esteem.
- Treatment issues include the parents confusing the worker's clinical role with the role of child protective services and the parents viewing the clinician as a hostile part of the legal system, rather than as a trusted helper.
- Communication can be inhibited by the perception of coercion, which can also limit the treatment's effectiveness. Both parent and child may become unwilling to reveal potentially damaging facts.
- Worker should openly discuss mandated reporting obligations and responsibility to inform child protective services.

GERIATRIC SOCIAL WORK
THEORETICAL BASES

The theoretical bases of geriatric social work include the following:

- Psychodynamic theory
- Ego psychology
- Family systems theory
- Life-span development theory (Wieck)
- Continuity theory
- Normal aging and demographics of the aging population
- Impact of chronic illness and physical or cognitive limitations

ASSUMPTIONS ABOUT HUMAN BEHAVIOR

The following are assumptions geriatric social work makes about human behavior:

- Growth occurs throughout the life span, including during old age.
- Individuals are inherently adaptive and are capable of managing the disruptions, discontinuities, and losses that are characteristic of old age.
- Our culture demands and values independence. This can present a conflict with accepting the increasing need for help in old age.
- The younger generation's caring for the older may be seen as role reversal and may be challenging to both generations. Dependency in the aged, however, has a different meaning than dependency in childhood.
- Supportive services are preferable to institutional care whenever possible.
- Ageist assumptions or an individual's living in an institutional setting are not reasons to compromise self-determination or confidentiality.
- Individuals age in different ways.

MOTIVATIONS FOR CHANGE AND MEANS THROUGH WHICH CHANGE OCCURS

Motivations for change in geriatric social work include:

- The need for individuals to adapt to longer periods of old age and retirement as life expectancy increases. With a longer period of old age comes increased risk for chronic illness and physical or cognitive limitations.
- There is a greater need for multiple types of social services, supported housing, and care options.
- Adult children are also affected by their parents' aging and may need help dealing with the emotional impact or with care planning.

Change occurs through:

- Individual, couples, or family treatment
- Support groups or group therapy
- Recreational programs
- Education

ASSESSMENT AND TREATMENT PLANNING

Assessment in geriatric social work is concerned with:

- The presenting problem and the client's resources for resolving it
- When adult children are involved, the intergenerational dynamics and resources and the relevance and impact of family history on present functioning

- The presence and effect of chronic illness and physical or cognitive limitations
- Home safety
- Medications, their influence on functioning, and negative side effects
- The need for supportive services or institutional care
- ADLs (bathing, dressing, etc.) and IADLs (cooking, driving, etc.)

Treatment planning is concerned with:

- **Interventions**, solutions that offer choice and support the older adult's highest level of functioning.
- **Promoting independence** by planning home modifications through home-safety assessment and planning for assistive devices through assessing physical or cognitive limitations.

ROLE OF THERAPEUTIC RELATIONSHIP

The role of the therapeutic relationship is as follows:

- Individual, couple, or multi-generational family therapist
- Case manager
- Advocate
- Care planner (working with older adults and their children to determine level of care needed and options)
- Guardian (for the older adult who the court has declared mentally incompetent)
- Conservator (for the older adult who the court has declared incompetent to handle their own financial affairs)
- Educator
- Group therapist or leader
- Program planner

STRATEGIC CONSIDERATIONS

The following are strategic practice issues to be considered when working with older adults:

- Role reversal (worker often younger than client)
- Physiological changes
- Variation in physical and mental decline
- Clients often have experienced multiple losses
- Clients are often involuntary
- Respect and formality can be important to client
- Differences in generational perceptions: socialization around problems, values, and mores and attitudes toward receiving help, charity, and counseling
- Two categories of older adults: young-old (60-80) and old-old or frail-old (80+)

CLINICAL CONSIDERATIONS

The clinical considerations the worker should make in practice with older adults are as follows:

- Shorter interviews, possibly more frequent
- Varied questioning styles
- The worker is more active, directive, and demonstrative
- Home visits may be preferred to office visits
- Consider roles and attitudes of relatives and caretakers
- Awareness of possibility for abuse or exploitation
- Access to social services or other publicly funded programs

- Possible hearing impairment and need to make responses shorter, louder, and slower
- Reminiscence is an important style of communication

ADDITIONAL THERAPEUTIC INTERVENTIONS AND CONSIDERATIONS

PREVENTIVE MEASURES IN SOCIAL WORK

Gerald Caplan's (1964) **model for prevention** includes three types of preventive measures:

- **Primary**: The focus is on helping people to cope with stress and decreasing stressors in the environment, specifically targeting at-risk groups. Examples include teaching parenting skills to parents; providing support services to the unemployed; providing food, shelter, and other services to the homeless; and teaching about the harmful effects of drugs and alcohol to schoolchildren.
- **Secondary**: The focus is on identifying problems early and beginning treatment in order to shorten the duration of the disorder. Examples include follow-up for clients at risk for recurrence, staffing rape crisis centers, providing suicide hotlines, and referrals as needed.
- **Tertiary**: The focus is on preventing complications and promoting rehabilitation through teaching clients socially-appropriate behaviors. Examples include teaching the client to manage daily living skills, monitoring effectiveness of outpatient services, and referring clients to support services.

SYSTEMATIC DESENSITIZATION AND FLOODING

Systematic desensitization is a therapy used to treat anxiety disorders, typically those caused by a specific stimulus. The client is progressively exposed to anxiety-inducing objects, images, or situations, or is asked to imagine them, and is then encouraged to practice relaxation or other coping techniques to manage or eliminate the anxiety. Once the client learns to cope with a given level of exposure, the intensity of the exposure is increased and the process is repeated. This continues until the client is successfully desensitized to the stimulus.

Flooding is an extreme form of desensitization by exposure. While typical systematic desensitization gradually increases the intensity of the stimulus, flooding jumps directly to the final stage. The client is subjected to the full intensity of the anxiety-inducing stimulus for a prolonged period of time, sometimes several hours. Part of the reasoning for this method is that all of the physiology-based fear responses can only affect the person for limited time, and once the client is no longer affected, they will be better able to train themselves not to fear the stimulus.

CONTRACTING OR GOAL SETTING

The **contract** is compatible with various models of social work practice and is not limited to an initial working agreement, but is part of the total treatment process. The contract is helpful in facilitating the client's action in problem solving, maintaining focus, and continuing in therapy. The contract is an explicit **agreement** between the client and the worker concerning target problems, goals, strategies of social work intervention, and distinguishing the roles and tasks of the client and the worker. The contract includes mutual agreement, differentiated participation, reciprocal accountability, explicitness, realistic agreement, and flexibility. It is difficult to contract with **involuntary clients** who do not acknowledge or recognize problems, who see the worker as unhelpful, or who are severely disturbed or intellectually disabled. The worker should openly acknowledge the difficulty for both the client and worker in mandated treatment and negotiate a contract within those realities.

SUPPORTING/SUSTAINING, PARTIALIZATION, AND RESISTANCE

Supporting/sustaining, partialization, and resistance as they relate to clinical practice are as follows:

- **Supporting/sustaining**: The worker conveys confidence in, interest in, and acceptance of the client in order to decrease the client's feelings of anxiety, poor self-esteem, and low self-confidence. The worker uses interest, sympathetic listening, acceptance of the client, reassurance, and encouragement.

- **Partialization**: Helping the client to break down problems or goals into smaller, more manageable elements in order to decrease the client's sense of overwhelm and increase the client's empowerment. Discrete elements of the problem or goal can then be prioritized as more manageable or more important.
- **Resistance**: An unconscious defense against painful or repressed material. Resistance can be conveyed through silence, evasiveness, balking at worker's suggestions, or by wanting to end treatment prematurely. The worker should recognize and understand resistance as a chance to learn more about the client and work more deeply with the client to help them face resistance and use it effectively.

INTERPRETATION

Through interpretation, the social worker offers the psychodynamic meaning of the client's thoughts, feelings, and fantasies, particularly about the origins of problem behaviors. **Interpretation** seeks to improve the client's insight and work through difficult material by deepening and expanding the client's awareness. Interpretation may entail the following:

- Exposing **repressed** (unconscious) or **suppressed** (conscious) information
- Making connections between the **present** and the **past** to help the client see present distortions more clearly
- Integrating information from **different sources**, so that the client can gain a more realistic perspective

Interpretation should not be used with clients who are **emotionally fragile**.

COMPLEMENTARY THERAPEUTIC APPROACHES

Complementary therapeutic approaches involve interventions that differ from traditional social work practice and are adjunctive to primary interventions. Complementary therapies should be utilized with informed consent on the client's part and in the client's best interest, ensuring that professional boundaries are not breached. **Complementary therapeutic approaches** in social work generally focus on mind-body interventions to reduce stress as they are non-invasive and easily mastered:

- **Relaxation exercises**: Progressive muscle relaxation (Jacobson), tensing and relaxing muscles to bring about full-body relaxation.
- **Mindfulness**: Focusing on moment-to-moment state of awareness of self and mental activity to increase awareness of thoughts and feelings and to learn to refocus them.
- **Meditation**: Practicing to calm and clear the mind in order to reduce anxiety.
- **Cognitive reframing**: Replacing irrational thoughts with more rational ones to increase self-esteem.
- **Guided imagery**: Envisioning calming and relaxing images to reduce anxiety and discomfort.
- **Journaling**: Keeping a daily journal to help identify and modify daily stressors.
- **Controlled breathing (diaphragmatic)**: Using breath control to focus the mind and reduce anxiety.

MINDFULNESS

Mindfulness is a form of meditation based on Buddhist beliefs that focus on a constant moment-to-moment state of awareness of the self and mental activity. **Mindfulness** has been adapted from the spiritual to secular practice in the West. The purpose of mindfulness is to accept thoughts nonjudgmentally and to examine them as they pass through the mind, recognizing that thoughts are just thoughts and that the individual has the power to take negative thoughts (e.g., "I'm worthless") and replace them with positive ones (e.g., "I'm a hard worker"). The individual focuses not only on thoughts but on feelings and sensations (sounds, smells, sights, touch) in order to increase client awareness and to balance physical, spiritual, and mental health. Mindfulness-based therapy (Kabat-Zinn) utilizes Hatha Yoga and controlled breathing to help individuals concentrate without distractions. Mindfulness is helpful to reduce anxiety and stress and prevent recurrence of depression. Over time, individuals often develop a less negative internal dialog and a more positive attitude.

SELF-MANAGEMENT TECHNIQUES

Self-management techniques that clients can utilize include:

- **Harm reduction**: This strategy is used to reduce harmful behaviors, especially related to drug abuse and sexual behavior. The strategies that reduce the negative impact of the behaviors include providing clean needles to addicts, providing free condoms and other birth control, and using medications (such as methadone) to reduce cravings.
- **Limit setting**: This strategy is used to reduce risky behavior and avoid crises with the intent to teach and guide rather than to discipline. Limits are agreed upon, and when behavior escalates or limits exceeded, a positive choice is offered and the individual is reminded of the consequences of choices.
- **Anger management**: These strategies are used to help individuals control their tempers. Strategies include thinking before responding, utilizing time outs, using "I" statements, expressing anger when calm, exercising, suggesting resolutions to problems, avoiding holding grudges, and seeking help when needed.
- **Stress management**: These strategies help the individual relieve stress and anxiety. Strategies include meditating, deep breathing, focusing on the here-and-now, exercising (yoga is especially relaxing), utilizing self-hypnosis and relaxation exercises (including progressive muscle relaxation), utilizing acupressure (tapping meridian points) or aromatherapy, and engaging in hobbies or enjoyable activities.

SELF-MONITORING

Self-monitoring involves the awareness of emotions and actions in order to promote healthy behaviors. It is especially useful for clients who are disorganized, lack attention to details, exhibit repetitive behaviors, such as tapping of the foot or clearing the throat, or fail to carry out needed actions (such as class participation). Techniques include the following:

- Identifying those behaviors that the individual wants or needs to modify.
- Establishing an intervention system, such as responding to cues or indicators that require intervention.
- Helping the client to recognize triggers for behaviors and developing strategies to avoid them.
- Developing a method of keeping track of progress, such as a checklist or graph, to provide positive reinforcement.
- Assisting the client to plan ahead in order to avoid negative behaviors. For example, if a client needs to avoid drinking, the client may need to leave a party and arrange for transportation early to avoid temptation.

TRANSFERENCE AND COUNTERTRANSFERENCE

Transference is the client's unconscious redirection of feelings for another person toward the worker in an attempt to resolve conflicts attached with that relationship or relationships. The worker should help the client understand transference, how it relates to relationships in her or his past, and how it may be contributing to present difficulties in relationships.

Countertransference is the worker's unconscious redirection of feelings for another person or relationship toward the client. The worker should understand her or his own countertransference reactions, be aware of their presence and consequences, and use supervision or therapy to gain greater understanding of them and not impose them on the client.

TERMINATION OF TREATMENT

Termination offers an opportunity to rework previously unfinished issues. Frequently, earlier symptoms of the presenting problem resurface at this time. This reemergence is not necessarily a reason to continue treatment, but the client should continue to work during the termination period to strengthen earlier gains. Termination offers an opportunity for growth in dealing with loss and endings. The client should acknowledge, verbalize, and manage feelings about endings (such as anger, abandonment, sadness, etc.). Termination can be an opportunity to reassess the meaning of previous losses in the client's life. Termination provides a chance to evaluate the treatment and the treatment relationship. What goals were met or unmet? What was effective or ineffective? Which client resources outside of treatment may continue after termination?

FACTORS AFFECTING HOW CLIENT APPROACHES TERMINATION

Factors affecting how the client will approach termination include the following:

- The degree of the **client's participation** in the treatment process.
- The degree of the **client's success and satisfaction**.
- **Earlier losses** the client may have experienced.
- Mastery of the **separation-individuation stage** of development in early life.
- The **reason** treatment is ending: if the ending is seen as against client's wishes or as a rejection, termination may be more intense.
- The **timing** of termination—is it occurring at a difficult or favorable moment in the client's life?
- Is termination part of a plan to **transfer** the client? If so, this time should be used to put together ideas about focus and goals for next treatment relationship.

WORKER'S ROLE IN TERMINATION PROCESS

The role of the leader in the termination process is as follows:

- Plan sufficient **time** for termination. In long-term treatment this would be four to eight sessions.
- **Inform the client** if the work is ending prematurely.
- Be aware of one's own **countertransference** attitudes and behaviors about termination.
- Continue to be **sensitive, observant, empathic, and responsive** to the client's response to termination.
- Encourage the client's **dealing** with the experience of termination. **Confront** client's inappropriate and dysfunctional coping with the experience.
- Promote the client's **belief** in their ability to care for themself and direct their own life.
- Present the possibility for **future contact** at times of difficulty.
- Go over the **client's resources** (internal and environmental) that the client can draw on before making the decision to reenter treatment.

Family Therapy

GOALS OF FAMILY THERAPY

Family therapy is a therapeutic modality theorizing that a client's psychiatric symptoms are a result of **pathology within the client's family unit**. This dysfunction is due to problems within the system, usually arising from conflict between marital partners. Psychiatric problems result from these behaviors. This conflict is expressed by:

- **Triangulation**, which manifests itself by the attempt of using another family member to stabilize the emotional process
- **Scapegoating**, which occurs when blaming is used to shift focus to another family member

The **goals** of family therapy are:

- To allow family members to recognize and **communicate their feelings**
- To determine the **reasons for problems** between marital partners and to **resolve** them
- To assist parents in **working together** and to strengthen their **parental authority**
- To help define and clarify **family expectations and roles**
- To learn more and different **positive techniques for interacting**
- To achieve **positive homeostasis** within the family
  - Homeostasis means remaining the same, or maintaining a functional balance. Homeostasis can occur to maintain a dysfunctional status as well.
- To enhance the family's **adaptability**
  - Adaptability is maintaining a balanced, positive stability in the family. A prerequisite for balanced stability, and a basic goal of family therapy, is to help the client family develop strategies for dealing with life's inevitable changes. Morphogenesis is the medical term often applied to a family's ability to react functionally and appropriately to changes.

THEORETICAL APPROACHES TO FAMILY THERAPY

Four theoretical approaches to family therapy are **strategic, behavioral, psychodynamic,** and **object relations** theories:

- A **strategic approach** to family therapy was proposed by Jay Haley. Haley tried to map out a different strategic plan for each type of psychological issue addressed. With this approach, there is a special treatment strategy for each malady.
- A **behavioral approach** uses traditional behavior-modification techniques to address issues. This approach relies heavily on reinforcement strategies. B.F. Skinner is perhaps the most famous behaviorist. This approach relies on conditioning and often desensitizing as well.
- The **psychodynamic approach** attempts to create understanding and insight on the part of the client. Strategies may be diverse, but in all of them the therapist acts as an emotional guide, leading the client to a better understanding of mental and emotional mechanisms. One common example is Gestalt therapy.
- **Object relations theory** asserts that the ego develops attachment relationships with external and internal objects. A person's early relationships to objects (which can include people) may result in frustration or rejection, which forms the basis of personality.

STRATEGIC FAMILY THERAPY

Strategic family therapy (Haley, 1976) is based on the following concepts:

- This therapy seeks to learn what **function** the symptom serves in the family (i.e., what payoff is there for the system in allowing the symptom to continue?).
- **Focuses**: Problem-focused behavioral change, emphasis of parental power and hierarchical family relationships, and the role of symptoms as an attribute of the family's organization.
- Helplessness, incompetence, and illness all provide **power positions** within the family. The child uses symptoms to change the behavior of parents.

Jay Haley tried to develop a strategy for each issue faced by a client. Problems are isolated and treated in different ways. A family plagued by alcoholism might require a different treatment strategy than a family undermined by sexual infidelity. Haley was unusual in that he held degrees in the arts and communication rather than in psychology. Haley's strategies involved the use of directives (direct instructions). After outlining a problem, Haley would tell the family members exactly what to do. If John would bang his head against the wall when he was made to do his homework, Haley might tell a parent to work with him and to be there while he did his homework.

VIRGINIA SATIR AND THE ESALEN INSTITUTE'S EXPERIENTIAL FAMILY THERAPY

Virginia Satir and the Esalen Institute's experiential family therapy draws on sociology, ego concepts, and communication theory to form **role theory concepts**. Satir examined the roles that constrain relationships and interactions in families. This perspective seeks to increase intimacy in the family and improve the self-esteem of family members by using awareness and the communication of feelings. Emphasis is on individual growth in order to change family members and deal with developmental delays. Particular importance is given to marital partners and on changing verbal and nonverbal communication patterns that lower self-esteem.

SATIR'S COMMUNICATION IMPEDIMENTS

Satir described four issues that impede communication between family members under stress. Placating, blaming, being overly reasonable, and being irrelevant are the **four issues which blocked family communication**, according to Virginia Satir:

- **Placating** is the role played by some people in reaction to threat or stress in the family. The placating person reacts to internal stresses by trying to please others, often in irrational ways. A mother might try to placate her disobedient and rude child by offering food, candy, or other presents on the condition that he stop a certain behavior.
- **Blaming** is the act of pointing outwards when an issue creates stress. The blamer thinks, "I'm very angry, but it's your fault. If I've wrecked the car, it's because you made me upset when I left home this morning."
- **Irrelevance** is a behavior wherein a person displaces the potential problem and substitutes another unrelated activity. A mother who engages in too much social drinking frequently discusses her split ends whenever the topic of alcoholism is brought up by her spouse.
- Being overly reasonable, also known as being a **responsible analyzer** is when a person keeps their emotions in check and functions with the precision and monotony of a machine.

MURRAY BOWEN'S FAMILY SYSTEMS THEORY

Bowen's family systems theory focuses on the following concepts:

- The role of **thinking versus feeling/reactivity** in relationship/family systems.
- Role of **emotional triangles**: The three-person system or triangle is viewed as the smallest stable relationship system and forms when a two-person system experiences tension.

Mometrix

- **Generationally repeating family issues**: Parents transmit emotional problems to a child. (Example: The parents fear something is wrong with a child and treat the child as if something is wrong, interpreting the child's behavior as confirmation.)
- **Undifferentiated family ego mass**: This refers to a family's lack of separateness. There is a fixed cluster of egos of individual family members as if all have a common ego boundary.
- **Emotional cutoff**: A way of managing emotional issues with family members (cutting off emotional contact).
- Consideration of thoughts and feelings of **each individual family member** as well as seeking to understand the family network.

> **Review Video: Bowen Family Systems**
> Visit mometrix.com/academy and enter code: 591496

FAMILY SYSTEM THEORY ASSUMPTIONS ABOUT HUMAN BEHAVIOR

Family systems theory makes several basic assumptions:

- Change in one part of the family system brings about change in other parts of the system.
- The family provides the following to its members: unity, individuation, security, comfort, nurturance, warmth, affection, and reciprocal need satisfaction.
- Where family pathology is present, the individual is socially and individually disadvantaged.
- Behavioral problems are a reflection of communication problems in the family system.
- Treatment focuses on the family unity; changing family interactions is the key to behavioral change.

MOTIVATIONS FOR CHANGE AND MEANS THROUGH WHICH CHANGE OCCURS

The **motivations for change** according to Bowen's family systems theory are as follows:

- **Disequilibrium** of the normal family homeostasis is the primary motivation for change according to this perspective.
- The family system is made up of three subsystems: the marital relationship, the parent-child relationship, and the sibling relationship. **Dysfunction** that occurs in any of these subsystems will likely cause dysfunction in the others.

The **means for change** in the family systems theory approach is the family as an interactional system.

CONTRIBUTIONS TO FAMILY SYSTEMS THEORY

The **psychodynamic theory** emphasizes multi-generational family history. Earlier family relations and patterns determine current ones. Distorted relations in childhood lead to patterns of miscommunication and behavioral problems. Interpersonal and intrapersonal conflict beneath apparent family unity results in psychopathology. Social role functioning is influenced by heredity and environment.

Don Jackson, a major contributor to family therapy, focuses on **power relationships**. He developed a theory of double-bind communication in families. Double-bind communication occurs when two conflicting messages communicated simultaneously create or maintain a no-win pathological symptom.

ASSESSMENT AND TREATMENT PLANNING IN THE FAMILY SYSTEMS THEORY

Assessment in family systems theory includes the following:

- Acknowledgement of **dysfunction** in the family system
- **Family hierarchy**: Who is in charge? Who has responsibility? Who has authority? Who has power?
- Evaluation of **boundaries** (around subsystems, between family and larger environment): Are they permeable or impermeable? Flexible or rigid?
- How does the **symptom** function in the family system?

164

Treatment planning is as follows:

- The therapist creates a mutually satisfactory contract with the family to establish service boundaries.
- Bowenian family therapy's goal is the differentiation of the individual from the strong influence of the family.

SAL MINUCHIN'S STRUCTURAL FAMILY THERAPY

Sal Minuchin's structural family therapy seeks to strengthen boundaries when family subsystems are enmeshed, or seeks to increase flexibility when these systems are overly rigid. Minuchin emphasizes that the family structure should be hierarchical and that the parents should be at the top of the hierarchy.

Joining, enactment, boundary making, and mimesis are four techniques used by Salvador Minuchin in structural family therapy:

- **Joining** is the therapist's attempt at greeting and bonding with members of the family. Bonding is important when obtaining cooperation and input.
- Minuchin often had his clients enact the various scenarios which led to disagreements and conflicts within families. The **enactment** of an unhealthy family dynamic would allow the therapist to better understand the behavior and allow the family members to gain insight.
- **Boundary making** is important to structural family therapies administered by Salvador Minuchin, because many family conflicts arise from confusion about each person's role. Minuchin believed that family harmony was best achieved when people were free to be themselves yet knew that they must not invade the areas of other family members.
- **Mimesis** is a process in which the therapist mimics the positive and negative behavior patterns of different family members.

THERAPEUTIC METHODS EMPLOYED BY CARL WHITAKER

Carl Whitaker, known as the dean of family therapy, developed **experiential symbolic family therapy**. Whitaker would freely interact with other family members and often played the part of family members who were important to the dynamic. He felt that experience, not information and education, had the power to change family dynamics.

Whitaker believed that in family therapy, theory was also less important than experience and that co-therapists were a great aid to successful counseling. Co-therapists freed one of the counselors to participate more fully in the counseling sessions. One counselor might direct the flow of activity while the other participated in role playing. The "psychotherapy of the absurd" is a Whitaker innovation which was influenced by the "theatre of the absurd," a popular existential art form at the time. In this context, the absurd is the unreasonable exaggeration of an idea, to the point of underscoring the underlying meaninglessness of much of human interaction. A person who repeated a neurotic or destructive behavior, for example, was being absurd. The **psychotherapy of the absurd**, as Whitaker saw it, was a method for bringing out repeated and meaningless absurdities. A person pushing against an immovable brick wall, for example, might eventually understand the psychological analogy to some problem behavior.

THEORIES OF CAUSALITY

Multiple theories of causality exist in the interpretation of family dynamics, which are then applied to the selection of therapeutic interventions. While linear causality (the concept that one cause equals one effect) uses a direct line of reasoning and is commonly used in individual counseling, **circular/reciprocal causality** is often used in family therapy and refers to the dynamic interactions between family members. Think of a situation in which one member of a family (a father, perhaps) has a severe emotional problem accompanied by violent and angry outbursts. The father periodically assaults his teenage son. Reciprocal or circular causality would apply in this family situation, since the father's angry behavior resonates throughout the family, causing different problems for each person. The spouse might feel inadequate to protect her son and sink into a depression. The other children would suffer, too, from anxiety and fear that the same treatment would befall them. Owing to circular causality, a single cause can have many effects.

PARADOXICAL INTERVENTION STRATEGIES

Paradoxical intervention strategies involve the use of the client's disruptive behavior as a treatment itself, requiring the client to put the behavior in the spotlight to then motivate change. This technique tries to accomplish the opposite of what it suggests on the surface. Interventions include the following:

- **Restraining** is advising that a negative behavior not be changed or be changed only slightly or slowly. This can be effectively used in the context of couples therapy when a couple is struggling with intimacy issues. The therapist may challenge the couple to refrain from sexual intimacy for a period of time, thus removing certain stressors from that dynamic, possibly resulting in a positive intimate experience that occurs naturally and spontaneously.
- **Positioning** is characterizing a negative behavior in an even more negative light through the use of exaggeration. "David, do you feel you are not terrifying your family enough with your reckless driving or that you ought to drive faster in order to make them worry more about your wellbeing? Perhaps that way you will know that they care about you," says the therapist using positioning as a technique. It is important that this technique be used only with great care, as it can be harmful to clients with a negative self-image. It is generally used in situations where the client is behaving in a certain negative way in order to seek affirmation or attention.
- **Prescribing the symptom** is another paradoxical technique used by therapists to obtain an enlightened reaction from a client. A therapist using this technique directs the client to activate the negative behavior in terms that are absurd and clearly objectionable. 'John, I want you to go out to that sidewalk overpass above the freeway and yell as loud as you can at the cars passing below you. Do it for at least four hours." The therapist prescribes this activity to cure his client's dangerous tendency toward road rage.
- **Relabeling** is recasting a negative behavior in a positive light in order to get an emotional response from the client. "Perhaps your wife yells at you when you drink because she finds this behavior attractive and wants your attention," the therapist might say. The therapist might even support that obviously illogical and paradoxical argument by pointing out invented statistics, which support the ridiculous assertion.

EXTINCTION, TIME OUT, AND THOUGHT STOPPING

Behavior modification is a term used in facilities like schools and jails to bring behavior into line with societal or family rules:

- **Extinction** is the process of causing a behavior to disappear by providing little or no reinforcement. It is different from punishment, which is negative reinforcement rather than no reinforcement at all. Very often, a student will be removed from the general population and made to sit alone in a quiet room. In schools, this goes by various names, but is often called in-school suspension (ISS). It is hoped that, through lack of reinforcement and response from outside, the offensive behavior will become extinct.
- **Time out** is another extinction technique, generally applied to very young children. A disobedient child will be isolated for a specified, usually short time whenever they misbehave. The method's operant mechanism assumes that we are all social animals and require the reinforcement of the outside world. Deprived of this, we adapt by altering our behavior.
- **Thought stopping** is a learned response which requires the participation and cooperation of the client to change a negative behavior. When it is successful, the client actively forbids negative thoughts from entering their mind.

SPECIFIC FAMILY THERAPY INTERVENTIONS

FAMILY THERAPY INTERVENTIONS USED WITH OCD

Family therapy interventions used to treat individuals with **obsessive-compulsive disorder (OCD)** include therapy oriented to develop expression of thoughts and impulses in a manner that is appropriate. This approach assumes that family members often:

- Attempt to avoid situations that trigger OCD responses
- Constantly reassure the individual (which often enables the obsession)

Family therapy to address these issues involves:

- Remaining neutral and not reinforcing through encouragement
- Avoiding attempts to reason logically with individual

FAMILY THERAPY INTERVENTIONS FOR PANIC DISORDERS

Family dynamics and therapy interventions for **panic disorders** include:

- Individuals with agoraphobia may require the presence of family members to be constantly in close proximity, resulting in marital stress and over-reliance on the children.
- Altered role performance of the afflicted member results in family and social situations that increase the responsibility of other family members.
- The family must be educated about the source and treatment of the disorder.
- The goal of family therapy is to reorganize responsibilities to support family change.

FUNCTIONAL FAMILY THERAPY FOR ADOLESCENTS WITH ANTISOCIAL BEHAVIOR

Functional family therapy (FFT) is designed for adolescents (11–17 years of age) with **antisocial behavior**. FFT uses the principles of family systems theory and cognitive-behavioral therapy and provides intervention and prevention services. While the therapy has changed somewhat over the past 30 years, current FTT usually includes three phases:

1. **Engagement/motivation**: The therapist works with the family to identify maladaptive beliefs to increase expectations for change, reduce negativity and blaming, and increase respect for differences. Goals are to reduce dropout rates and establish alliances.
2. **Behavior change**: The therapist guides the parents in using behavioral interventions to improve family functioning, parenting, and conflict management. Goals are to prevent delinquent behavior and build better communication and interpersonal skills.
3. **Generalization**: The family learns to use new skills to influence the systems in which they are involved, such as school, church, or the juvenile justice system. Community resources are mobilized to prevent relapses.

MULTISYSTEMIC THERAPY FOR ADOLESCENTS WITH ANTISOCIAL BEHAVIOR

Multisystemic therapy (MST) is a **family-focused program** designed for adolescents (11–17 years of age) with antisocial and delinquent behaviors. The primary goal is **collaboration** with the family to develop strategies for dealing with the child's behavioral problems. Services are delivered in the family's natural environment rather than at a clinic or office with frequent home visits, usually totaling 40–60 hours over the course of treatment. Sessions are daily initially and then decrease in frequency. A variety of different therapies may be used, including family therapy, parent training, and individual therapy. Therapists use different approaches but adhere to basic principles, including focusing on the strength of the systems, delivering appropriate treatment for developmental level, and improving family functioning. The goals of therapy are to improve family relations and parenting skills, to engage the child in activities with nondelinquent peers, and to improve the child's grades and participation in activities, such as sports.

THERAPEUTIC METHODS FOR COUNSELING AN ADOLESCENT WITH BEHAVIORAL PROBLEMS

When an **adolescent's behavior** is a problem, some parents have them sign an agreement to perform in a specified manner. The agreement may state that a reward will be provided to the adolescent so long as the contract is upheld. The therapist can help parents and children write an effective contract. Another time-honored method of behavior conditioning is the withholding of leisure activity until chores are done. In a family therapy session, the therapist might advise stating the case like this: "Your television has a parental guide lock which will not be turned on unless you can demonstrate that all your homework is complete."

ROLE OF THE THERAPIST

The role of the therapist in family therapy is to interact in the here and now with the family in relation to current problems. The therapist is a consultant to the family. Some aspects of the therapist's role differ according to school of thought:

- **Structural**: The therapist actively challenges dysfunctional interaction.
- **Strategic and Systemic**: The therapist is very active.
- **Milan School**: Male/female clinicians are co-therapists; a team observes from behind a one-way mirror and consults and directs the co-therapists with the clients.
- **Psychodynamic**: The therapist facilitates self-reflection and understanding of multi-generational dynamics and conflicts.
- **Satir**: The therapist models caring, acceptance, love, compassion, nurturance in order to help clients face fears and increase openness.

KEY CONCEPTS OF FAMILY THERAPY

Key **concepts of family therapy** include the following:

Behavior modeling	The manner in which a child bases their own behavior on the behavior of their parents and other people. In other words, a child will usually learn to identify acceptable behaviors by mimicking the behavior of others. Some children may have more difficulty with behavior modeling than others.
Boundaries	The means of organization through which system parts can be differentiated both from their environment and from each other. They protect and improve the differentiation and integrity of the family, subsystems, and individual family members.
Collaborative therapy	Therapy in which a different therapist sees each spouse or member of the family.
Complementary family interaction	A type of family relationship in which members present opposite behaviors that supply needs or lacks in the other family member.
Complementarity of needs	Circular support system of a family, in which reciprocity is found in meeting needs; can be adaptive or maladaptive.
Double-bind communication	Communication in which two contradictory messages are conveyed concurrently, leading to a no-win situation.
Family of origin	The family into which one is born.
Family of procreation	The family which one forms with a mate and one's own children.
Enmeshment	Obscuring of boundaries in which differentiation of family subsystems and individual autonomy are lost. Similar to Bowen's "undifferentiated family ego mass." Characterized by "mind reading" (partners speak for each other, complete each other's sentences).
Heritage	The set of customs, traditions, physical characteristics, and other cultural artifacts that a person inherits from their ancestors.
Homeostasis	A state of systemic balance (of relationships, alliances, power, authority).
Identified patient	The "symptom bearer" in the family.
Multiple family therapy	Therapy in which three or more families form a group with one or more clinicians to discuss common problems. Group support is given and problems are universalized.
Scapegoating	Unconscious, irrational election of one family member for a negative, demeaned, or outsider role.

Group Work

SOCIAL WORK VALUES IN GROUP PRACTICE

The underlying values of social work practice with groups include:

- Every individual has dignity and worth.
- All people have a right and a need to realize their full potential.
- Every individual has basic rights and responsibilities.
- The social work group acts out democratic values and promotes shared decision making.
- Every individual has the right of self-determination in both setting and achieving goals.
- Positive change is made possible by honest, open, and meaningful interaction.

PURPOSES AND GOALS OF GROUP PRACTICE

Group practice takes a multiple-goal perspective to solving individual and social problems and is based on the recognition that group experiences have many important functions and can be designed to achieve any or all of the following:

- Provide restorative, remedial, or rehabilitative experiences
- Help prevent personal and social distress or breakdown
- Facilitate normal growth and development, especially during stressful times in the life cycle
- Achieve a greater degree of self-fulfillment and personal enhancement
- Help individuals become active, responsible participants in society through group associations

ADVANTAGES OF GROUP WORK

Advantages of group work include the following:

- Members can help and identify with others dealing with similar issues and situations.
- Sometimes people can more easily accept help from peers than from professionals.
- Through consensual validation, members feel less violated and more reassured as they discover that their problems are similar to those of others.
- Groups give opportunities to members to experiment with and test new social identities and roles.
- Group practice is not a replacement for individual treatment. Group work is an essential tool for many workers and can be the method of choice for some problems.
- Group practice can complement other practice techniques.

> **Review Video: Group Work and its Benefits**
> Visit mometrix.com/academy and enter code: 375134

IMPORTANCE OF RELATIONSHIPS IN GROUP WORK

Establishing meaningful, effective relationships in group work is essential, and its importance cannot be overemphasized. The worker will form multiple changing relationships with individual group members, with sub-groups, and with the group as a whole. There are multiple other parties who have a stake in members' experiences, such as colleagues of the worker, agency representatives, relatives, friends, and others. The worker will relate differentially to all of those individuals.

TYPES OF SOCIAL WORK GROUPS

The different types of social work groups are as follows:

- **Educational groups**, which focus on helping members learn new information and skills.
- **Growth groups**, which provide opportunities for members to develop a deeper awareness of their own thoughts, feelings, and behavior, as well as develop their individual potentialities (i.e., values clarification, consciousness-raising, etc.).
- **Therapy groups**, which are designed to help members change their behavior by learning to cope with and improve personal problems and to deal with physical, psychological, or social trauma.
- **Socialization groups**, which help members learn social skills and socially acceptable behaviors and help members function more effectively in the community.
- **Task groups**, which are formed to meet organizational, client, and community needs and functions.

GROUP STRUCTURE AND GROUP PROPERTIES

Group structure refers to the patterned interactions, network of roles and statuses, communications, leadership, and power relationships that distinguish a group at any point in time.

Group properties are attributes that characterize a group at any point in time. They include:

- Formal vs. informal structure
- Primary group (tight-knit family, friends, neighbor)
- Secondary relationships (task centered)
- Open vs. closed
- Duration of membership
- Autonomy
- Acceptance-rejection ties
- Social differentiation and degrees of stratification
- Morale, conformity, cohesion, contagion, etc.

CLOSED GROUPS VS. OPEN GROUPS

Groups can be either closed or open, serving different functions and purposes:

Closed Groups	Open Groups
• Convened by social workers. • Members begin the experience together, navigate it together, and end it together at a predetermined time (set number of sessions). • Closed groups afford better opportunities than open groups for members to identify with each other. • Closed groups provide greater stability to the helping situation, and they allow the stages of group development progress more powerfully. • Closed groups provide a greater amount and intensity of commitment due to the same participants being counted on for their presence.	• Open groups allow participants to enter and leave according to their choice. • A continuous group can exist, depending on the frequency and rate of membership changes. • The focus shifts somewhat from the whole group process to individual members' processes. • With membership shifts, opportunities to use the group's social forces to help individuals may be reduced. The group will be less cohesive, and therefore less available as a therapeutic instrument. • The social worker is kept in a highly central position throughout the life of the group, as they provide continuity in an open structure.

SHORT-TERM GROUPS AND FORMED GROUPS

Some circumstances call for the formation of short-term and/or formed groups:

Short-Term Groups	Formed Groups
• Short-term groups are formed around a particular theme or in order to deal with a crisis. • Limitations of time preclude working through complex needs or adapting to a variety of themes or issues. • The worker is in the central position in a short-term group.	• Deliberately developed to support mutually agreed-upon purposes. • Organization of the group begins with the realization of a need for group services. • The purpose is established by an identification of common needs among individuals in an agency or worker caseload. • The group is worker-guided in interventions and timing by an understanding of individual and interpersonal behavior related to the group's purpose. • It is advisable to have screening, assessment, and preparation of group members in formed groups. • Different practice requirements for voluntary and non-voluntary groups exist, as members will respond differently to each.

SMALL GROUP THEORY

SYSTEM ANALYSIS AND INTERACTIONAL THEORY OF SMALL GROUPS

The system analysis and interactional theory of small groups is a broadly used framework for understanding small groups. In this framework, small groups are living systems that consist of interacting elements that function as a whole. In this framework, a social system is a structure of relationships or a set of patterned interactions. System concepts help maintain a focus on the whole group, and explain how a group and its sub-groups relate functionally to larger environments. This framework describes how interaction affects status, roles, group emotions, power, and values.

SOCIAL SYSTEM CONCEPTS AND GENERAL SYSTEMS CONCEPTS

The following are **social system concepts** used in the system analysis and interactional theory of small group work:

- **Boundary maintenance**: Maintaining group identities and separateness
- **System linkages**: Two or more elements combine to act as one
- **Equilibrium**: Maintaining a balance of forces within the group

General systems concepts used in the system analysis and interactional theory of small group work are as follows:

- **Steady state**: The tendency of an open system to remain constant but in continuous exchange
- **Equifinality**: The final state of a system that can be reached from different initial conditions
- **Entropy**: The tendency of a system to wear down and move toward disorder

SYMBOLIC INTERACTIONISM

Symbolic interactionism is characterized by the following:

- Emphasizes the **symbolic nature** of people's relationships with others and the external world versus a social system analysis that emphasizes form, structures, and functions.
- Group members play a part in determining their own actions by recognizing symbols and **interpreting meaning**.

172

- Human action is accomplished mainly through the process of **defining and interpreting situations** in which people act. The worker uses such concepts to explain how individuals interact with others, and to understand the following:
  - The role of the individual as the primary resource in causing change
  - The significance of social relationships
  - The importance of self-concept, identification, and role identity in group behavior
  - The meanings and symbols attributed to group interactions

GESTALT ORIENTATIONS AND FIELD THEORY

Gestalt psychology played a major part in the development of group dynamics. Contrasting with earlier psychologies that stressed elementary sensations and associations, Gestalt theorists viewed experiences not in isolation, but as perpetually organized and part of a **field** comprised of a system of co-existing, interdependent factors. Group dynamics produced a plethora of concepts and variables:

- Goal formation
- Cohesion
- Group identification and uniformity
- Mutual dependency
- Influences and power
- Cooperation and competition
- Productivity

Group dynamics (or group processes) provide a helpful framework of carefully defined and operationalized relevant group concepts.

SOCIOMETRY

Sociometry, inspired by the work of J. L. Moreno, is both a general theory of human relations and a specific set of practice techniques (psychodrama, sociodrama, role playing).

- Sociometric tests are devised to measure the affectivity factor in groups.
- Quality of interpersonal attraction in groups is a powerful force in rallying group members, creating feelings of belonging, and making groups sensitive to member needs.

COGNITIVE CONSISTENCY THEORY AND BALANCE THEORY

The basic assumption of **cognitive consistency theory** is that individuals need to organize their perceptions in ways that are consistent and comfortable. Beliefs and attitudes are not randomly distributed but rather reflect an underlying coherent system within the individual that governs conscious processes and maintains internal and psychosocial consistency.

According to the balance theory, processes are balanced when they are consistent with the individual's beliefs and perceptions. Inconsistency causes imbalance, tension, and stress, and leads to changing perceptions and judgments which restore consistency and balance. The group worker incorporates varying ideas from these orientations. Some stress the need for the group to be self-conscious and to study its own processes, emphasizing that cognition is apparent in contracting, building group consciousness, pinpointing or eliminating obstacles, and sharing data.

SOCIAL REINFORCEMENT AND EXCHANGE THEORY

The **social reinforcement and exchange theory** in regard to group work is summarized as follows:

- Social exchange theorists propose that members of groups are motivated to seek **profit** in their interactions with others (i.e., to maximize rewards and minimize costs).
- Analysis of interactions within groups is done in terms of a series of **exchanges or tradeoffs** group members make with each other.
- The individual member is the **primary unit of analysis**. Many of the core concepts of this theory are merely transferred to the group situation and do not further the understanding of group processes.

GROUP FORMATION

ELEMENTS IN THE GROUP FORMATION PROCESS

The key elements in the group formation process include the following:

- The worker makes a clear and uncomplicated statement of purpose that includes both the members' stakes in coming together and the agency's (and others') stakes in serving them.
- The worker's part should be described in as simple terms as possible.
- Identify the members' reactions to the worker's statement of purpose and how the worker's statement connects to the members' expectations.
- The worker helps members do the work necessary to develop a working consensus about the contract.
- Recognize goals and motivations, both manifested and latent, stated and unstated.
- Recontract as needed.

WORKER'S ROLE IN GROUP MEMBER SELECTION

The worker's process of selecting members for a group is as follows:

- The worker explains **reasons** for meeting with group applicants.
- The worker elicits applicants' **reactions** to group participation.
- The worker assesses applicants' **situations** by engaging them in expressing their views of the situation and goals in joining the group.
- The worker determines **appropriateness** of applicants for the group, accepts their rights to refuse membership, and provides orientation upon acceptance into the group.

HETEROGENEITY VS. HOMOGENEITY IN GROUP FORMATION

Issues of heterogeneous vs. homogenous group formation include the following:

- A group ought to have sufficient homogeneity to provide stability and generate vitality.
- Groups that focus on socialization and developmental issues or on learning new tasks are more likely to be homogeneous.
- Groups that focus on disciplinary issues or deviance are more likely to be heterogeneous.
- The composition and purposes of groups are ultimately influenced or determined by agency goals.

BEGINNING PHASE OF GROUP PROCESS

INTERVENTION SKILLS

Intervention skills of the social worker that are used in the **beginning phase** of group process include the following:

- The worker must tune into the needs and concerns of the members. Member cues may be subtle and difficult to detect.
- The worker must seek members' commitment to participate through engagement with members.

- The worker must continually assess the following:
  - Members' needs/concerns
  - Any ambivalence/resistance to work
  - Group processes
  - Emerging group structures
  - Individual patterns of interaction
- The worker must facilitate the group's work.

FACILITATING THE GROUP'S WORK

The social worker's role in facilitating group process is as follows:

- Promote **member participation and interaction**.
- Bring up **real concerns** in order to begin the work.
- Help the group keep its **focus**.
- Reinforce observance of **rules** of the group.
- Facilitate **cohesiveness** and focus the work by **identifying emerging themes**.
- Establish worker **identity** in relation to group's readiness.
- **Listen** empathically, **support** initial structure and rules of the group, and **evaluate** initial group achievements.
- Suggest **ongoing tasks or themes** for the subsequent meeting.

STRESSORS

The following are stressors that the worker might experience in the beginning phase of group process:

- Anxiety regarding gaining acceptance by the group
- Integrating group self-determination with an active leadership role
- Fear of creating dependency and self-consciousness in group members which would deter spontaneity
- Difficulty observing and relating to multiple interactions
- Uncertainty about the worker's own role

MIDDLE PHASE OF GROUP PROCESS

Intervention skills of the social worker used in the **middle phase** of group process include the following:

- Judge when work is being avoided
- Reach for opposites, ambiguities, and what is happening in the group when good and bad feelings are expressed
- Support different ways in which members help each other
- Partialize larger problems into more manageable parts
- Generalize and find connections between small pieces of group expression and experience
- Facilitate purposeful communication that is invested with feelings
- Identify and communicate the need to work and recognize when work is being accomplished by the group

ONGOING GROUP DEVELOPMENT

Group development refers to the ongoing group processes that influence the progress of a group, or any of its sub-groups, over time. Group development typically involves changing structures and group properties that alter the quality of relationships as groups achieve their goals. Understanding group development gives social workers a blueprint for interventions that aid the group's progression toward attaining goals. A danger in using development models is in the worker forcing the group to fit the model, rather than adapting interventions for what is occurring in the group. A complex set of properties, structures, and ongoing processes influence group development. Through processes that are repeated, fused with others, modified, and reinforced, movement occurs.

MODELS OF GROUP PRACTICE

LINEAR STAGE MODELS OF GROUP DEVELOPMENT

There are many models of group development, often describing the group's process through a series of **linear stages** in which the group progresses predictably from one to another.

Tuckman's five stages of group development are as follows:

1. **Form**: Group comes together, rules are established and agreed upon, and members are relatively subdued and hesitant.
2. **Storm**: Expression of feelings begins by the members who still feel individual versus members of the group; there may be resistance to cues by the social worker or signs of cynicism.
3. **Norm**: A sense of unity and teamwork prevails; members begin to interact with and encourage one another.
4. **Perform**: A sense of hierarchy dissipates as the member take control of the group process and feel empowered in an open and trusting team environment.
5. **Adjourn**: The team recognizes time for closure, some members may mourn the loss of the group and need guidance and support for next steps, and reflection on progress and celebration of accomplishments occur.

The **Boston Model** (Garland, Jones, & Kolodny) of group development is as follows:

1. **Preaffiliation stage**: Consists of regulation by the worker, expressions of concern or anxiety, heavy dependence on the worker, hesitant disclosure of personal goals, clarification of purpose, timeline, and roles
2. **Power and control stage**: Consists of limit setting, clarification, and the use of the program
3. **Intimacy stage**: Consists of handling transference, rivalries, and a degree of uncovering
4. **Differentiation stages**: Consist of clarification of differential and cohesive processes, and group autonomy
5. **Separation**: Consists of a focus on evaluation, handling ambivalence, and incorporating new resources

The **Relational Model**, developed by Schiller, in regard to group development in groups of women, is as follows:

- Preaffiliation
- Establishing a relational base
- Mutuality and interpersonal empathy
- Challenge and change
- Separation and termination

SOCIAL GOALS MODEL

The social goals model of group practice is as follows:

- The primary focus is to influence a wide range of small group experiences, to facilitate members' identifying and achieving of their own goals, and to increase social consciousness and social responsibility.
- It assumes a rough unity between involvement in social action and the psychological health of the individual. Early group work was concerned with immigrant socialization and emphasized principles of democratic decision making, in addition to tolerance for difference.

- The methodology is focused on establishing positive relationships with groups and members, using group processes in doing with the group rather than for the group, identification of common needs and group goals, stimulation of democratic group participation, and providing authentic group programs stemming from natural types of group living.

REMEDIAL/REHABILITATIVE MODEL

The remedial/rehabilitative model of group practice is as follows:

- It uses a medical model and the worker is focused primarily on **individual change**.
- This model includes **structured** program activities and exercises.
- It is more commonly found in organizations concerned with **socialization**, such as schools, and in those concerned with treatment and social control (inpatient mental health treatment, etc.).
- Practice techniques in this model focus on **stages** of treatment.
  - **Beginning**: Intake, group selection, diagnosis of each member, and setting specific goals.
  - **Middle**: Planned interventions. Worker is central figure and uses direct means to influence group and members. Worker is spokesperson for group values and emotions. Worker motivates and stimulates members to achieve goals.
  - **Ending**: Group members have achieved maximum gains. Worker helps clients deal with feelings about ending. Evaluation of work, possible renegotiation of contract.

RECIPROCAL INTERACTIONAL OR MEDIATING MODEL

The reciprocal interactional or mediating model of group practice can be summarized as follows:

- The social worker is referred to as a **mediator** and participates in a network of reciprocal relationships. Goals are developed mutually through contracting process. The interaction and insight of group members is the primary force for change in what is seen as a "mutual aid" society.
- **Worker's task**: Help search for common ground between group members and the social demands they experience, help clients in their relationships with their own social systems, detect and challenge obstacles to clients' work, and contribute data.
- **Phases** of intervention:
  - **Tuning in or preparation for entry**: The worker helps the group envision future work, but makes no diagnosis. The worker is also sensitive to members' feelings.
  - **Beginning**: The worker engages group in contracting process, and the group establishes clear expectations.
  - **Middle**: The middle phase consists of searching for common ground, discovering/challenging obstacles, data contribution, sharing work visions, and defining limits/requirements
  - **Ending**: Finally, the worker is sensitive to their own reactions and members' reactions and helps members evaluate the experience and consider new beginnings.

FREUDIAN/NEO-FREUDIAN APPROACH

The Freudian/Neo-Freudian approach to group practice is as follows:

- Groups consist of 8-10 members.
- Interaction is mainly through discussion.
- Group members explore feelings and behavior, and interpret unconscious processes.
- The worker uses interpretation, dream analysis, free association, transference relations, and working through.
- This approach aims to help group members re-experience early family relationships, uncover deep-rooted feelings, and gain insight into the origins of faulty psychological development.

TAVISTOCK GROUP-CENTERED MODELS

The Tavistock "group as a whole" group-centered model for group practice is as follows:

- This approach derives from Wilfred Bion's work with leaderless groups. Bion developed analytic approaches that focused on the **group as a whole**.
- Latent group feelings are represented through the group's prevailing emotional states or **basic assumption cultures**.
- The therapist is referred to as a **consultant**. The consultant does not suggest an agenda, establishes no rules and procedures, but instead acts as an observer. A major role of the consultant is to alert members to ongoing group processes and to encourage study of these processes.
- The consultant encourages members to explore their experiences as group members through **interaction**.

GROUP THERAPY METHODS

PROCESS GROUPS

Irvin Yalom's "here-and-now" or process groups are characterized by the following:

- Yalom stressed using clients' **immediate reactions** and discussing members' **affective experiences** in the group.
- Process groups have relatively unstructured and spontaneous sessions.
- Process groups emphasize **therapeutic activities**, like imparting information, or instilling hope, universality, and altruism.
- The group can provide a **rehabilitative narrative** of primary family group development, offer socializing techniques, provide behavior models to imitate, offer interpersonal learning, and offer an example of group cohesiveness and catharsis.

MORENO'S PSYCHODRAMA GROUP THERAPY

Moreno's psychodrama group therapy is summarized as follows:

- **Spontaneous drama techniques** contribute to powerful therapy to aid in the release of pent-up feelings and to provide insight and catharsis to help participants develop new and more effective behaviors.
- The five **primary instruments** used are the stage, the client or protagonist, the director or therapist, the staff of therapeutic aides or auxiliary egos, and the audience.
- Psychodrama group therapy can begin with a **warm-up**. The warm-up uses an assortment of techniques such as self-presentations, interviews, interaction in the role of the self and others, soliloquies, role reversals, doubling techniques, auxiliary egos, mirroring, multiple doubles, life rehearsals, and exercises.

BEHAVIORAL GROUP THERAPIES

Behavioral group therapies are characterized by the following:

- The **main goals** are to help group members eliminate maladaptive behaviors and learn new behaviors that are more effective. Behavioral groups are not focused on gaining insight into the past, but rather on current interactions with the environment.
- It is one of the few research-based approaches.
- The worker utilizes **directive techniques**, provides information, and teaches coping skills and methods of changing behavior.

- The worker arranges **structured activities**. The primary techniques used include restructuring, systematic desensitization, implosive therapies, assertion training, aversion techniques, operant-conditioning, self-help reinforcement and support, behavioral research, coaching, modeling, feedback, and procedures for challenging and changing conditions.

INFLUENCING THE GROUP PROCESS

Influencing group process in group work methodology can be done through the following:

- The worker's ability to recognize, analyze, understand, and influence group process is necessary and vital. The group is a system of relationships rather than a collection of individuals. This system is formed through associations with a unique and changing quality and character (this is known as group structures and processes).
- Processes that the worker will be dealing with include understanding group structures, value systems, group emotions, decision-making, communication/interaction, and group development (formation, movement, termination).

EXTERNALIZING

The worker must be prepared to help individual members profit from their experiences in and through the group. Ultimately, what happens to group members and how they are influenced by the group's processes determines the success of any group experience, not how the group itself functions as an entity. The worker should give attention to helping members relate beyond the group (**externalizing**), to encouraging active participation and involvement with others in increasingly wider spheres of social living. This should occur even when the group is relatively autonomous.

PROGRAMMING

The importance of programming in group work methodology is as follows:

- The worker uses activities, discussion topics, task-centered activities, exercises, and games as a part of a planned, conscious process to address individual and group needs while achieving group purposes and goals.
- Programming should build on the needs, interests, and abilities of group members and should not necessitate a search for the unusual, esoteric, or melodramatic.
- Social work skills used in implementing programs include the following: initiating and modifying program plans to respond to group interests, self-direction, responsibility, drawing creatively upon program resources in the agency and environment, and developing sequences of activities with specific long-range goals.
- Using program activities is an important feature of group practice.

CONTRACTING WORKING AGREEMENTS IN GROUP WORK

Only if group members are involved in clarifying and setting their own personal and common group goals can they be expected to be active participants on their own behalf. **Working agreements** consider not only worker-member relationships, but also others with a direct or indirect stake in the group's process. Examples would be agency sponsorship, collaborating staff, referral and funding sources, families, caretakers, and other interested parties in the public at large.

The following are the **social worker's role in contracting**:

- Setting goals
- Determining membership
- Establishing initial group structures and formats

All three of these elements require skillful management by the worker.

ANALYZING GROUP PROCESSES

The following are categories for analyzing group work:

- Communication processes
- Power and influence
- Leadership
- Group norms and values
- Group emotion
- Group deliberation and problem solving

GROUP PRACTICE WITH SPECIAL POPULATIONS

GROUPS FOR SERIOUS MENTAL ILLNESS

Group work with clients who have serious mental illness should include the following elements:

- **Clearly defined programs** that use psychosocial rehabilitation approaches (not psychotherapeutic).
- Focus on making each group session **productive and rewarding** for group members.
- **Themes** addressed include dealing with stigma, coping with symptoms, adjusting to medication side effects, dealing with problems (family, relationships, housing, employment, education, etc.), and real and imagined complaints about mental health treatment organizations.
- Many groups in community-based settings focus on helping members learn **social skills** for individuals with limited or ineffective coping strategies.
- Mandated groups in **forensic settings** are highly structured and focus on basic topics such as respect for others, responsibility for one's behavior, or staying focused.

CHEMICAL DEPENDENCY GROUPS

Group work for chemical dependency focuses on the following:

- Group work is the treatment of choice for **substance use disorder**.
- Guidelines for these groups include maintaining confidentiality, using "I" statements, speaking directly to others, never speaking for others, awareness of one's own thoughts and feelings, honesty about thoughts and feelings, and taking responsibility for one's own behavior.
- Types of groups used include:
  - **Orientation groups** that give information regarding treatment philosophy/protocols.
  - **Spiritual groups** that incorporate spirituality into recovery.
  - **Relapse prevention groups** that focus on understanding and dealing with behaviors and situations that trigger relapse.
  - **AA and NA self-help groups** utilize the principles and philosophies of 12-step programs. For family and friends, **Nar-Anon** and **Al-Anon groups** provide support.

PARENT EDUCATION GROUPS

Parent education groups are used in social agencies, hospitals, and clinics. They are often labeled as psycho-ed groups or parent training groups and use a cognitive-behavioral approach to improve the parent-child relationship. Parent education groups are often structured to follow manuals or curricula. Their main focus is helping parents improve parent-child interactions, parent attitudes, and child behaviors.

ABUSED WOMEN'S GROUPS

Abused women's groups can be described as follows:

- Provide a warm, accepting, and caring environment in which members can feel secure.
- Structured for consciousness raising, dispelling false perceptions, and resource information.

- Common themes these groups explore include the use of power which derives from the freedom to choose, the need for safety, the exploration of resources, the right to protection under the law, and the need for mutual aid.
- Basic principles of these groups include respect for women, active listening and validation of members' stories, ensuring self-determination and individualization, and promoting group programs that members can use to demonstrate their own strength and achieve empowerment.
- For post-group support, groups typically seek to utilize natural supports in the community.

GROUPS FOR SPOUSE ABUSERS

Groups for spouse abusers (perpetrators of domestic violence) are explained below:

- Work with this population is typified by resistance and denial.
- Clients have difficulty processing guilt, shame, or abandonment anxiety and tend to convert these feelings into anger.
- These clients have difficulties with intimacy, trust, mutuality, and struggle with fear of abandonment and diminished self-worth.
- Mandatory group treatment is structured. It is designed to challenge male bonding that often occurs in such groups.
- Including spouses/victims in these groups is quite controversial in clinical literature.

GROUPS FOR SEX OFFENDERS

Groups for sex offenders are summarized below:

- Typically, membership in these groups is ordered by the court. There is no assurance of confidentiality, as workers may have to provide reports to the courts, parole officers, or other officials.
- Clients typically deny wrongdoing, test workers, and are often resistant.
- In groups with voluntary membership, confidentiality is extremely important, as group members often express extreme fear of exposure.
- Prominent themes include denial, victim-blaming, blaming behavior on substances, blaming behavior on uncontrollable sex drives/needs.
- Treatment emphasizes the importance of conscious control over drives/needs, regardless of their strength or if they are natural.
- A culture of victimization is strongly discouraged.

GROUPS FOR CHILDREN OF ALCOHOLICS

Groups for children of alcoholics are discussed below:

- Individuals who grow up with parents who abuse alcohol and/or drugs often learn to distrust others as a survival strategy. They become used to living with chaos and uncertainty and with shame and hopelessness.
- These individuals commonly experience denial, secrecy, and embarrassment.
- They may have a general sense of fearfulness, especially if they faced threats of violence, and tend to have rigid role attachment.
- Treatment in these groups requires careful planning, programming, and mutual aid in the form of alliances with parental figures and other related parties in order to create a healthy environment that increases the individual's safety and ability to rely on self and others.

GROUPS FOR SEXUALLY ABUSED CHILDREN

Groups for sexually abused children are summarized below:

- The worker must pay particular attention to her or his own attitudes toward sexuality and the sexual abuse of children.
- Important in these groups are contracting, consistent attendance, and clearly defined rules and expectations.
- Clients may display control issues and may challenge the worker's authority.
- Confidentiality is not guaranteed.
- Termination can be a particularly difficult process.
- Common themes that come up include fear, anger, guilt, depression, anxiety, inability to trust, and delayed developmental/socialization skills.
- Programming can include ice breaking games, art, body drawings, letter writing, and role playing.

TERMINATION OF GROUP PROCESS

Group members' experience of termination and the worker's role in helping group members to cope with the ending of the group are discussed below:

- Group members may have feelings of loss and may desire to minimize the painful feelings they are experiencing.
- Members may experience ambivalence about ending.
- The social worker will:
  - Examine her or his own feelings about termination
  - Focus the group on discussing ending
  - Help individuals express their feelings of loss, relief, ambivalence, etc.
  - Review achievements of the group and members
  - Help members prepare to cope with next steps
  - Assess members' and group's needs for continued services
  - Help members with transition to other services

METHODS OF FORESTALLING OR DEALING WITH TERMINATION

The following are group members' methods of forestalling or dealing with termination:

- **Simple denial**: A member may forget ending, act surprised, or feel "tricked" by termination.
- **Clustering**: Members may physically draw together, also called super-cohesion.
- **Regression**: Reaction can be simple-to-complex. Earlier responses reemerge, outbursts of anger, recurrence of previous conflicts, fantasies of wanting to begin again, attempts to coerce the leader to remain, etc.
- **Nihilistic flight**: Members may reject and perform rejection-provoking behavior.
- **Reenactment and review**: Members begin recounting or reviewing earlier experiences in detail or actually repeating those experiences.
- **Evaluation**: Members assess meaning and worth of former experiences.
- **Positive flight**: There is a constructive movement toward self-weaning. Members find new groups, etc.

Community Organization and Social Planning

SOCIAL PLANNING AND PROGRAM DEVELOPMENT
COMMUNITY PRACTICE MODEL OF SOCIAL PLANNING

The community practice model of social planning as discussed by Weil and Gamble states that social planning is for the purpose of coordinating, developing, and growing social services and policies. Often considered highly technical, the process has moved over time from being in the hands of experts to being community driven, with concomitant increases in community participation, cohesion, proactive activity, empowerment, and sustainability.

Social planning can be participatory and community led, or it may take place in fundraising organizations such as the United Way. It may involve making physical changes to the environment, such as the revitalization of buildings, and it may involve increasing quality of life for members of particular sectors, such as the aged or the mentally ill.

COMMUNITY RESOURCES, OUTREACH, AND ADVOCACY

Social planning encompasses a range of activities that may serve to connect people with established **resources** or increase their access to those resources. Establishing or increasing accessibility may require social workers to first get community members to buy into the project, which may prove difficult when members have been let down by projects or agencies before.

When a would-be **advocate** finds their potential sector to be apathetic, angry, and mistrustful, the frustration the advocate experiences is rational but not helpful. Fostering participation first requires a connection that establishes enough hope, trust, and motivation to get community members in on the ground floor. Without this initial participation, it's highly unlikely that members will feel empowered by the process or willing to take part in it. Thus, **community outreach** becomes a vital, ongoing strategy for social planning agendas.

IMPORTANCE OF NETWORKING IN THE COMMUNITY

Creating a program usually requires coordination among various groups. Establishing and maintaining **networks** among agencies and community leaders is important in not only identifying community needs, but also eliciting ideas for solutions and motivating community members to participate. Community leaders are an important resource because they know the problems and potentials of their communities while maintaining their own connections to individuals in those communities. With a finger on the pulse of a neighborhood, they can advise social workers in program development and delivery, preventing problems that would be unanticipated by service providers from outside that community. Connecting active community leaders to external resources may create a situation in which the social worker's role is primarily that of supporter and liaison to other agencies, while the community does the work of the program.

INVOLVEMENT OF COMMUNITY MEMBERS AND PARTICIPANTS IN PROGRAM DEVELOPMENT

Community or sector members can be involved at the earliest stages of program development by being part of the needs assessments and by providing information about the environment in which the program is to take place, two important elements of program development. Participants can also be active in recruiting others to the program, monitoring and reporting obstacles and possible solutions, and providing regular feedback. Feeling an ownership in a program gives participants the chance to create real, positive changes. In this way, what may start as a small community program may evolve over time into more comprehensive community organization.

INVOLVEMENT OF BENEFICIARIES IN PROGRAM DEVELOPMENT

Modern social work practice includes the recruitment and involvement of potential **beneficiaries**, ideally as experts in regard to identifying problems, suggesting solutions, and being involved in the process not only as beneficiaries but as important sources of monitoring, feedback, and evaluation. In this process, social workers may act as advocates and solution-focused advisors, problem-solvers, and connectors, while participants share

183

the challenges and excitement of full participation. The larger the project, the greater the need for social workers' expertise in mediation and negotiation as many groups with conflicting agendas, values, and needs come together in one program.

STEPS OF PROMOTING COMMUNITY CHANGE

Mark Homan's *Promoting Community Change: Making it Happen in the Real World, 6th Edition* (2016) examines community-based planning as a process with multiple levels of consideration. According to Homan, the social worker must consider the following when attempting to **promote community change**:

- **Know the community**: Understand perspectives about the community, assess the community's needs and currently available resources, and conduct community-based participatory research.
- **Utilize powerful planning**: Identify one's own discomforts and opportunities, identify one's vision and goals based on potentiality, identify current obstacles and resources, identify time frames and people who can handle specific tasks, create indicators to show task completion, and measure both effectiveness and indicators of trouble.
- **Raise other resources**: Create a budget and ask for what is needed, fundraise, gain contributions from others, utilize the internet in fundraising, receive funding from private and public organizations, and utilize grant writing.
- **Get the word out**: Identify the populations that need to be reached, send messages that are controlled (but be aware of messages that others can control), and utilize e-organizing.
- **Build an organized effort**: Understand that organizations are built around issues, develop the organization, understand structural limitations, utilize small group processes, understand the steps of incorporation, and sustain the organization.
- **Take action**: Utilize action strategies and tactics (confrontation, negotiation, collaboration, co-optation, and advocacy), know the strategies and tactics that an opponent may use, and understand the commandments of change.

APPROACHES FOR WORKING WITH COMMUNITIES AND LARGER SYSTEMS

Social workers may be called upon to work for **change and progress in large systems**, such as in school districts, in multi-site agencies, and with governmental entities. In such situations, there are two key approaches:

- The **horizontal approach** is used in working with centralized agencies and in communities. It involves bringing key participants (stakeholders) into the process of problem identification, consensus building, goal setting, and implementation and monitoring of an improvement process.
- The **vertical approach** is used when there is a need to reach outside or beyond the community or centralized entity environment. This approach involves learning about hierarchical levels of leadership in government, charitable organizations, grant-funding institutions, etc., and then collaborating with key leaders in problem identification, consensus building, goal setting, and program implementation and monitoring to achieve the necessary goals. An understanding of systems theory and eco-systems (or life model) theory can aid in this process.

THE SOCIAL-PSYCHOLOGICAL AREA OF COMMUNITY

There are several interpretations of the social-psychological area of community.

- One is the belief that people of a community are bound together by an existing **area of interest**. They feel connected based on goals they share, needs, values, and activities that makeup the feeling of community.
- Another is the belief that there is a **personal-psychological community** within each individual. This is the view from one person that reflects what the community is like. Children and lower-class individuals tend to view community as having more narrow boundaries than middle- and upper-class adults do.

- Another view is the **cultural-anthropological view of community**, which looks at community as a form of social living that is defined by attitudes, norms, customs, and behaviors of those living in the community.

COMMUNITY ORGANIZATION PRACTICE

TASKS/GOALS

The following are **tasks and goals** of community organization practice:

- Change public or private **priorities** in order to give attention to problems of inequality and social injustice
- Promote **legislative change** or public funding allocation
- Influence **public opinions** of social issues and problems
- Improve **community agencies/institutions** in order to satisfy needs of the community better
- Develop **new ways** to address community problems
- Develop **new services** and coordinate existing ones
- Improve community **access** to services
- Set up new **programs** and services in response to new or changing needs
- Develop the capacity of **grassroots citizen groups** to solve community problems and make claims on public resources for under-served communities
- Seek justice for oppressed **minorities**

VALUES

The following are **values** of community organization practice:

- Working with, not for, clients to enhance their participatory skills
- Developing leadership, particularly the ability to foresee and act on problems
- Strengthening communities so that they are better able to deal with future problems
- Redistributing resources in order to enhance the resources of the disadvantaged
- Planning changes in systematic and scientific ways
- Rational problem-solving process: studying the problem, defining it, considering possible solutions, creating a plan, then implementing and evaluating the plan
- Advancing the interests of the disadvantaged in order for them to have a voice in the process of distribution of social resources

DIFFERENCES FROM OTHER FORMS OF SOCIAL WORK PRACTICE

Differences between community organization practice (COP) and other forms of social work practice include the following:

- COP highlights knowledge about social power, social structure, social change, and social environments.
- COP acknowledges the reciprocal process between the individual and the social environment. It seeks to influence and change the social environment as it is seen as the source and likely solution for many problems.
- In the view of COP, social problems result from structural arrangements rather than from personal inadequacies. Consequently, the reallocation of resources and social power leads to changes in the community and eventually in individuals.

UNDERLYING ASSUMPTIONS

Assumptions that underlie community organization practice include the following:

- Members of the community want to improve their situation.
- Members of the community are able to develop the ability to resolve communal and social problems.

- Community members must participate in change efforts rather than have changes imposed on them.
- A systems approach which considers the total community is more effective than imposing programs on the community.
- One goal of participation in community organization initiatives involving social workers is education in democratic decision-making and promoting skills for democratic participation.
- The organizer enables members to address community problems independently, in part through their learning, analytic, strategic, and interpersonal skills.

UTILIZATION OF TACTICS IN COMMUNITY ORGANIZATION

Various tactics should be utilized when approaching community organization and community program development:

- **Collaborative tactics** include problem solving, joint action, education, and mild persuasion. They require a perceived consensus in goals, power equality, relatively close relationships, and cooperation/sharing.
- **Campaign tactics** include hard persuasion, political maneuvering, bargaining/negotiation, and mild coercion. They require perceived differences in goals, inequality in power, and intermediate relationships.
- **Contest tactics** include public conflict and pressure. They require public conflict, disagreement concerning goals, uncertain power, distant or hostile relationships.

To determine the best tactics to use in community organization, consider the following **factors**:

- The degree of differences or commonality in the goals between the community group and the target system.
- The relative power of the target system and the community group.
- The relationship of the community group to the target system.

MEETING NEEDS OF COMMUNITIES THROUGH COMMUNITY PRACTICE

The conception of a community program should begin with the observation of **a need in the community**, something that may be obvious and publicly discussed or covert and difficult to define. The type of program then determines the level of intervention, its length, cost, participants, and desired goals and outcomes. Weil (1994) identified four **vital processes in community practice**:

- Development
- Organization
- Planning
- Action for progressive social change

The development process can encompass a range of activities affecting small neighborhood groups or may entail major, international efforts. The social or economic development of a particular community may empower members to make changes in the way they work along with their housing, health, safety, and economic future.

COMMUNITY ORGANIZATION PRACTICE MODELS

Model	Foundations
Locality development model	• Involves working in a neighborhood with the goal of improving the quality of community life through broad-spectrum participation at the local level. • Process-oriented with the purpose of helping diverse elements of the community come together to resolve common problems and improve the community. • Tactics include consensus and capacity building. As the organization resolves smaller problems, it facilitates the solving of more complex and difficult problems. • The worker's roles include enabler, coordinator, educator, and broker.
Social planning model	• Involves careful, rational study of a community's social, political, economic, and population characteristics in order to provide a basis for identifying agreed-upon problems and deciding on a range of solutions. Government organizations can be sponsors, participants, and recipients of information from social planners. • Focuses on problem solving through fact gathering, rational action, and needs assessment. • Tactics may be consensus or conflict. • The worker's roles include researcher, reporter, data analyst, program planner, program implementer, and facilitator.
Social action model	• This model requires an easily identifiable target and relatively clear, explainable goals. Typically, the target is a community institution that controls and allocates funds, community resources, and power, and clients are those who lack social and economic power. • Assumption in this model is that different groups in the community have interests that are conflicting and are irreconcilable. In many cases, direct action is the only way to convince those with power to relinquish resources and power. • Tactics include conflict, confrontation, contest, and direct action. • The worker's roles include that of advocate, activist, and negotiator.
Social reform model	• In collaborating with other organizations for the disadvantaged, the worker's role is to develop coalitions of various groups to pressure for change. • This model is a mixture of social action and social planning. • Strategies include fact gathering, publicity, lobbying, and political pressure. • Typically, this approach is pursued by elites on behalf of disadvantaged groups.

CITIZEN PARTICIPATION

With American culture becoming more private and individualistic over the past decades, **citizen participation** in social change diminished as racial and multicultural tensions rose. Civic clubs tend to attract or recruit people of similar social backgrounds: however, community study circles, created by Everyday Democracy (formerly the Study Circle Resource Center) have focused on bringing people of diverse cultures together in a deliberative democratic process to discuss and take action on community problems. A community organizing in this fashion meets not only the most pressing community needs, but also builds connections among community members who might not otherwise encounter each other in the course of their daily lives.

Program Development and Service Delivery

PROGRAM PLANNING

METHODS OF STRATEGIC PLANNING

Strategic planning involves the overall guidance of an organization in accordance with its stated vision. It includes decision-making, activities, and resource allocation of the organization and is administered by higher-echelon managers. **Four methods of strategic planning** include the following:

1. **Alignment of strategies and outcomes** is used to fine-tune what is working and change what is not working.
2. **Issues-based planning,** which is often used when resources are low, looks at the most important current issues and brainstorms alternatives.
3. **Organic planning** in real time uses a dialogue model to strategize for change.
4. **Vision and goals-based planning** uses the vision, mission, and goals to create an action plan.

GOAL-SETTING IN PROGRAM PLANNING

Goal-setting needs to be part of the planning process, and some goals may also be referred to the clients for their input. The larger the program, the greater the variety of goals, which may range from setting staff training benchmarks to meeting funding application dates as well as marking particular milestones in the program itself. Goals need to be precisely delineated, measurable, and as objective as possible. Goal setting has a recursive element: for example, setting a deadline helps with focus and achievement, whereas having no deadline can cause projects to languish.

PLANNING SERVICE DELIVERY

Service delivery is another factor to consider in the planning process. In a community where public transportation is limited, holding a first-aid class necessary for employment in food service at a center on the edge of town may prevent people from participating. Anticipating and resolving such basic and important problems ideally begins in the program planning stage, but when unanticipated issues arise, having the flexibility to create spontaneous solutions can mean the difference between the success and failure of a program.

PROCESS AND PROGRAM EVALUATION

PROCESS EVALUATION

The process of a program may evolve as feedback systems return information about how individual elements of the program are faring. Outcomes, identified at the beginning planning stages, can be assessed only at the end of the program. Goals are intermediary steps in the process and may be used as milestones marking progress toward the ultimate desirable outcomes. The purpose of a **process evaluation** is to catch errors or omissions in planning and to provide for changes that occur either in the program environment or due to the program itself.

Process evaluation takes place throughout the program as it runs, ideally identifying and correcting problems. Methods of process evaluation are necessarily primary, including interviews, focus groups, and observation. Outcome, or summative evaluations, will often include posttest measures providing quantitative data as well as qualitative measures.

PROGRAM EVALUATION

Program evaluation is important for several reasons:

- It demonstrates a **belief in and accountability for the program** on the part of the agency and establishes credibility.
- Documenting the progress and changes due to the program enables the administrators to **pass along their findings to communities** seeking to solve similar problems.
- **Funders** are interested in demonstrable success, and the only way to produce such evidence to those outside the program is in documentation. Even a successful program can lose its funding if it fails to demonstrate its success in measurable ways.

STEPS TO PROGRAM EVALUATION

The proper steps to program evaluation are as follows:

1. Determine what will be evaluated
2. Identify who will be the consumer of the research
3. Request the staff's cooperation
4. Indicate what specific program objectives are
5. Outline objectives of evaluation
6. Choose variables
7. Develop design of evaluation
8. Apply evaluation design (conduct the evaluation)
9. Analyze and interpret findings
10. Report results and put them into practice

OUTCOME ASSESSMENT

Different programs will be assessed differently, with some being a fairly straightforward matter of gathering statistics and others a more elaborate process of surveys, interviewing, tracking participants across time, and gathering information from a variety of agencies. **Outcome measures** should be identified early on and assessed for reliability and validity, appropriateness to the program, fitness to the particular outcome to be measured, practicality of use, and cost.

As outcomes are used to justify continuing or enlarging a program and are important measures in requesting additional funding, rigorous and professional reporting becomes even more crucial. Even when there are failures, careful cataloging can assist in later program development efforts. A project may have unintended outcomes, helpful or harmful, which should also be noted, for further research or to provide warnings and prevent those errors from occurring in later work.

OUTCOME EVALUATIONS

Outcome evaluations may be more than a single measure administered once, as programs are often planned to have a reach extending over a long period of time. For example, to see if an after-school program for girls reduces teen pregnancies and increases their educational achievement, outcomes may be measured over years. Ideally, there is also a way to identify and measure unintended outcomes because programs may have more global effects than initially understood. Process evaluations may show up surprise effects along the way, allowing for changes to ameliorate or eradicate the negative or enhance and document the positive. In outcome evaluations, feedback from interviewed participants may also help pinpoint unexpected results.

FORMATIVE/SUMMATIVE EVALUATIONS

Formative evaluations, which are done while the program is in progress, must be considered as part of the design process, and the degree to which the formative evaluations will be utilized to guide or assess the process must be determined. Formative evaluations that are appropriate should be developed for each stage. For example, a policy change may be followed by a brief questionnaire asking about the effectiveness of the policy. If the evaluations are used to guide development of the rest of a program, then strict timelines for completing the evaluations and assessing results should be part of the plan.

Summative evaluations, which are done at the completion of the program, should be planned to assess outcomes. As part of the design process, it's important to determine what exactly needs to be evaluated and how best to carry out the assessment to render the needed data.

COST-BENEFIT AND COST-EFFECTIVE ANALYSIS

A **cost-benefit analysis** uses the average cost of an event and the cost of intervention to demonstrate savings. For example, if an agency pays for 40 hours of overtime costs weekly (1.5 X hourly salary of $27 = $40 per hour), the cost would be $1620 per week or $84,240 per year. If a new hire would cost $56,160 plus benefits of $19,656 the total cost of the new hire would be $75,816 (1.35 X base salary). Cost-benefit analysis reveals the current event cost of $84,240 minus the intervention cost of $75,816 renders a cost benefit of $8424.

A **cost-effective analysis** measures the effectiveness of an intervention rather than the monetary savings. For example, if the rate of pregnancies among female adolescents in a county averages 75 per 1000 and an aggressive program of education and access to birth control decreases the rate to 55 per 1000, the program resulted in 20 fewer adolescent pregnancies per 1000.

INTERORGANIZATIONAL RELATIONSHIPS AND SOCIAL NETWORK ANALYSIS

Healthcare and social welfare fields often remain poorly integrated into larger community networks and systems. Social work agencies need to better coordinate and build partnerships to more fully meet the needs of their individual clients and the community at large. One **barrier to interorganizational relationships** is the allocation of resources, as funds for both healthcare and social services are limited. A related concern is the interpenetration of organizational boundaries, often established to preserve resources and each organization's client base. Consequently, there is often conflict within and between agencies on how best to proceed to the next level of service and who will be primarily responsible. One way to overcome past divisiveness is to have shared memberships in key planning processes, by which to map the flow of care from one level to the next. Always central to this process is the need to enhance how different agencies communicate with one another to provide cohesiveness and continuity.

BASIC FISCAL MANAGEMENT PRINCIPLES

Understanding basic fiscal management principles is critical in the social work environment, where the work is almost always budget driven.

- The **operating budget** may include various private, local, state, or federal grants or donations and each of those may have specific requirements for use and/or separate budgets.
- **Expenses** must not exceed income, and interventions must be paid for out of the correct budget or budget category, so appropriate record keeping and coding of services are essential.
- **Return-on-investment** must be considered and calculated for any new proposals, such as hiring of staff.
- With **fee-for-service contracts**, services and payments are usually outlined in detail and the social workers must comply with directives.
- With **performance-based contracts**, in which reimbursement is based on meeting performance measures, measures to cut expenses and improve outcomes are generally central concerns. Every intervention must be assessed accordingly, but there is more freedom in prescribing interventions.

Case Management

LINKING AND MONITORING IN CASE MANAGEMENT

At times, the social worker may take the role of case manager for certain clients or populations. Case managers must **link** clients with the service providers and resources needed, to the extent appropriate resources are available. Case managers are also responsible for helping clients overcome any obstacles in using the resources they are provided. When a client is unable to articulate their own needs, case managers must advocate and speak for them to get the assistance required. If necessary, help from an agency's administrative staff may be needed to fully address the services required.

High-quality continuous **monitoring** is a key case management function. Good working relationships between case managers, clients, and direct service providers are essential to ensure a successful monitoring and accommodation process. Changes in plans and linkages may at times become necessary, as the client and/or available services may change and evolve.

BALANCING CASES AMONG SOCIAL WORKERS

Cases should be balanced in the equitable distribution of time requirements and the proportional distribution of the social workers' experience or expertise. Variables to take into consideration in assigning caseloads include the amount of risk to clients (and the self-care required by social workers in high-intensity cases), the complexity of cases, the nature of the problem being addressed, and factors such as paperwork and travel time of the social worker. Highly intense cases should be assigned to staff workers with the experience to handle them, but concentrating such emotionally-draining work on a few members of staff will also increase burnout and put these valuable team members at increased risk. Increasing training opportunities and providing consistent supervision for staff members can help create a stronger, more highly functioning team.

CONNECTING THE CLIENT TO DIRECT SERVICE PROVIDERS

The goal of case management is to ensure that clients with multiple issues receive the comprehensive services and aid they need in a timely and effective manner. In the role of case manager, the social worker does not provide direct services; instead, they connect the client to direct service providers. The social worker is responsible for all the services provided by the direct service agency engaged. Thus, the social worker and the agency staff need a close working relationship, to ensure that all client needs are being met. While all areas of health and human services use case managers, they are especially utilized for the mentally ill, the elderly, and the disabled, as well as in matters of child welfare. Having one case manager responsible for all the needs of a client provides clients with the one-on-one attention they need and prevents them from falling between the cracks because too many direct service people are involved.

CASE PRESENTATION

The case presentation is the primary way the social worker can communicate their knowledge of the client to others. The challenge is to create a comprehensive, factual document that's also manageably brief and to the point. The **elements of a case presentation** include the following:

- Identifying information such as age, gender, culture, and economic status
- Family history
- Personal and social history
- Medical and psychological diagnoses
- The presenting problem(s) in terms of assessments, diagnoses, and current mental status
- A summary of the social worker's impression of the client
- Theories about potential ways of helping the client, treatment plans, and goals

Consultation and Collaboration

SOCIAL WORKERS ROLE IN THE HEALTHCARE TEAM
COMPONENTS, GOALS AND ATTRIBUTES

Social workers may be involved on hospital units and play a critical role in the healthcare team, working amongst other disciplines to care for a client. Key components, goals, and attributes of the **interdisciplinary treatment and healthcare team** include:

- **Components**: Interdisciplinary treatment employs the talents of multiple professionals to design a comprehensive treatment plan, with each team member having input based on their specialty. The client is included as a member of this team.
- **Goals**: The intention is to develop appropriate interventions for each client, which are to be consistently implemented and assessed on a regular basis by everyone involved in the client's care.
- **Attributes**: Dedication to the team, collective accountability, common goals and intervention viewpoints, egalitarian leadership, decision making by consensus, open communication, and open and free examination of roles and relationships.

TYPICAL MEMBERS

Typical members of a healthcare team may include:

- **Dietitian**: Provides ethnically relevant dietary recommendations, is aware of the psychological importance of food, understands the psychology of eating disorders, and is aware of food-drug interactions (such as MAOI's and grapefruit juice, etc.).
- **Nurse**: Responsible for around-the-clock care, activities of daily living (ADLs), and security of client and staff. Clinical nurse specialists may perform individual, family, or group psychotherapy.
- **Ministry**: Aids and supports the spiritual beliefs of the client and family and may provide marital or personal counseling.
- **Psychiatry**: Diagnoses and treats mental health conditions using counseling and/or medication, responsible for admission and discharge, and may provide individual, group, or family therapy.
- **Psychology**: Performs diagnostic testing, provides treatment plans, and may provide individual, family, or group therapy.
- **Social Work**: Evaluates how family, social, and environmental factors contribute to the client's problems, and collaborates with internal and external agencies to set up a support system for the client's goals.
- **Volunteer Agencies**: Organizations that provide ancillary support to individuals with mental health problems.

TEAM MEETINGS

Interdisciplinary team meetings occur as a gathering of several disciplines to coordinate care and services for the client. During these meetings, the client's diagnosis, current issues, family support, medication, and progress are all discussed, as well as any other issues that may arise. Additionally, many team meetings collectively gather information that will be used in the future for when the client is eventually discharged to other services or home. The disciplines that may be present at meetings in addition to the social worker include the physician or psychiatrist, nurse, pharmacist, occupational or physical therapist, nutritionist, and case manager. Each team member presents on the topics of their expertise as they relate to the client in order to produce a full picture of the client, and therefore create a holistic approach to the client's care.

PROMOTING COLLABORATION

Promoting collaboration and assisting others to understand and use the resources and expertise of others requires a commitment both of time and effort. Examples of promoting collaboration include the following:

- Coaching others on methods of collaboration, which can include providing information in the form of **handouts** about effective communication strategies and **modeling** this type of communication with the staff being coached.
- **Team meetings** are commonly held on hospital units and provide an opportunity to model collaboration and suggest the need for outside expertise to help with planning client care plans.
- Selecting a **diverse group** for teams or inviting those with expertise in various areas to join the team when needed can help team members to appreciate and understand how to use the input of other resources.

COLLABORATION WITH EXTERNAL AGENCIES

The social worker must initiate and facilitate collaboration with external agencies because many have direct impacts on client care and needs:

- **Industry** can include other facilities sharing interests in the client's care or pharmaceutical companies. The social worker may have a dialog with drug companies about their products and how they are used in specific populations because many medications are prescribed to women, children, or the aged without validating studies for dose or efficacy.
- **Payors** have a vested interest in containing healthcare costs, so providing information and representing the interests of the client is important.
- **Community groups** may provide resources for clients and families, both in terms of information and financial or other assistance.
- **Political agencies** are increasingly important as new laws are considered about social work case load and infection control in many states.
- **Public health agencies** are partners in healthcare with other facilities and must be included, especially in issues related to communicable disease.

CONFLICT RESOLUTION

Conflict is an almost inevitable product of collaboration with the client and other team members, and the social worker must assume responsibility for **conflict resolution**. While conflicts can be disruptive, they can produce positive outcomes by forcing people to listen to different perspectives and opening dialogue. The social worker should make a plan for dealing with conflict resolution. The best time for conflict resolution is when differences emerge but before open conflict and hardening of positions occur. The social worker must pay close attention to the people and problems involved, listen carefully, and reassure those involved that their points of view are understood. Steps to conflict resolution are as follows:

1. Allow both sides to present their side of the conflict without bias, maintaining a focus on opinions rather than individuals
2. Encourage cooperation through negotiation and compromise
3. Maintain the focus, providing guidance to keep the discussions on track, and avoid arguments
4. Evaluate the need for renegotiation, formal resolution process, or a third party
5. Utilize humor and empathy to diffuse escalating tensions
6. Summarize the issues, outlining key arguments
7. Avoid forcing resolution if possible

Managing a Consultation

Consultation is a natural part of working in human services, as clients often present with multiple needs that call on different specialties. Managing a consultation prevents complications when the following steps are taken:

1. The **client's permission** should be obtained for the social worker to share relevant information with the consultant.
2. The consultation should have a **clearly defined purpose**: The nature of the problem should be identified as completely as possible.
3. The **role of the consultant** should also be defined and understood by all parties.
4. The **process should be outlined**, with understanding reached as to its time considerations and the limits of the consulting role.

Issues of Communication That Influence Case Consultation

Case consultation involves communication between a social worker and a direct service provider. The client could be an individual, family, or community. To be successful, consultation must have a purpose, a problem, and a process. The person requesting the consultation has the right to decline help, so the consultant must have high-value ideas to gain the trust of the consultee. An effective consultation process requires that the consultee determine the need for consultation and initiate the request for consultation, then the consultant and consultee must collaborate in assessing the problem, determine a plan for help, negotiate contracts, have a mutual list of objectives, determine the action to be taken, implement the plan, and measure and report the outcomes in a clear and concise manner. Communication is at the core of the process, so the consultant must have quality communication and problem-solving skills to be successful.

Networking and Consultation

Networking and consultation can help the social worker get the best help for the client while also reducing stress on the social worker. Building a network of professionals whose expertise overlaps and complements one's own will save time and effort when it becomes necessary to locate services and information outside one's own sphere of expertise. Establishing a personal-professional relationship allows one to partner with others, possibly sidestepping red tape and wait times, to get assistance for clients. Perhaps just as important is that the social worker has a group of outside experts whose advice they can trust, just as those experts can trust the social worker.

Social Policy and Social Change

SOCIAL POLICY

Social policy refers to the collection of laws, regulations, customs, traditions, mores, folkways, values, beliefs, ideologies, roles, role expectations, occupations, organizations, and history that all focus on the fulfillment of critical social functions.

ADVOCATING FOR POLICY CHANGE

In advocating for policy change, the social worker engages with institutions, groups, and individuals to bring about changes in procedures, practices, or policies that will benefit clients. The process of advocacy is a combination of education and persuasion, beginning with the assumption that policy makers are unaware of or do not understand the negative effects of their current policies. In such a case, educating and informing policy makers as well as raising their awareness of the problems are the first steps in advocacy.

ASPECTS OF PERSUASION

The aspects of persuasion involve using influence to convince policy makers and then the public that the issue is important and needs to be addressed. Networking and coalition building make the best use of resources and get a critical mass behind the push for change. Acquiring funding from private funders and legislators may require grant writing, high-level networking, or social media campaigns as well as carefully documented research on the problem and its possible solutions. Once the change is in effect, evaluation sets the stage for ongoing advocacy efforts.

SOCIAL POLICY ANALYSIS

Social policy analysis is the research supporting the process of solving problems through policy making or change. Like many other aspects of macro practice, it involves a step-by-step procedure that identifies the problem; creates alternatives focused on efficiency, equity, and liberty; assesses the benefits of alternatives (such as comparing costs and benefits for each); and chooses the best alternative. Designing and implementing the policy is followed by evaluating the outcomes of the change.

Analysis is often both the starting point and the ending point in policy advocacy. Gathering and interpreting the data on conditions is fundamental in convincing people that a particular problem exists (and having a mutual understanding of its scope and duration and the harm it causes) and that the problem stems from particular sources, which can be addressed by the means identified by the research.

THEORIES OF SOCIAL CHANGE
MODERNIZATION THEORY OF SOCIAL CHANGE

Modernization theory, developed after World War II, focused on the democratization of the Global South, where new countries were emerging after many years of colonialism. More recently, modernization provided the basis for the Republican Party under President Reagan and the UK's Conservatives' Prime Minister Thatcher to come to power. With conservative economic policies in effect, the rich were accorded more benefits (such as lower taxes) under the idea that assets would begin to trickle down to the poor. This strategy has been called the neoliberal development model.

MARXISM

Marxism sought to change society by rejecting the concept of market capitalism and by creating a paternalistic father state where, in theory, all people were equal. As social change focused on collectivization, individual freedoms were abolished, creating a system of oppression and tyranny. The Marxist belief that societal change would and should occur not in increments but in revolution threatened not only Western ideals of market capitalism but the ideal of personal freedom, a combination that proved intolerable and caused immeasurable suffering by way of wars, political reactivity, and the Cold War. Countries once part of the USSR are still finding their way out of the web of economic and social isolation and poverty that trapped them for decades.

DEPENDENCY THEORY

Dependency theory (or international structuralism) arose in the 1960s and 1970s, combining criticism of modernization with Marxist ideals. Adopting the stance that modernization was Western countries' attempt to economically exploit Latin American countries in an updated version of colonialism, populist leaders attempted to restrain the economic takeover of their countries. Third-world solidarity through economic and social justice would be the means of improving the lives of the people.

SUSTAINABLE DEVELOPMENT THEORY

The sustainable development theory is a recent and popular developmental theory that denies that increased industrialism is the only necessary component of economic growth and that materialism is responsible for many of the world's ills, both socially and environmentally. The fair-trade movement is one expression of sustainability, replacing gigantic corporate interests with small, often family-run local enterprises. Sustainability embraces the importance of community as an extension of the family, work practices that support individual workers, and the belief that education pays off in more than creating a knowledgeable workforce but in developing an empowered community.

Support Programs

SOCIAL SERVICES AND SOCIAL WELFARE SERVICES IN THE US

Social services endeavor to maintain quality of life in society and include social welfare (poverty and poor health prevention via entitlements), along with other government and privately operated programs, services, and resources. **Types of social services** include the following:

- Education
- Employment
- Health and medical services
- Housing
- Minimum income grants
- Nutrition
- Retirement
- Welfare (for children and the elderly)

Benefits include cash grants (e.g., unemployment and supplemental income) and in-kind benefits (e.g., food stamps). **Delivery systems** include the following:

- **Employment-based**, obtained by or through employment, such as health insurance, retirement, and disability (both short- and long-term, including maternity and family leave)
- **Government-based**, consisting of tax relief, such as deductions (e.g., dependents, medical costs) at the local, state, or federal level
- **Philanthropy-based**, comprising programs for needy families, at-risk youth, etc.
- **Personal contributions**, such as child care, private healthcare, etc.
- **Public-based**, whereby not-for-profit agencies and public agencies provide services, such as shelters, adoption services, and disaster relief, free or at a reduced rate (sliding scale, etc.)

ELIGIBILITY CRITERIA FOR SOCIAL SERVICE PROGRAMS

Eligibility for social services can be determined in many different ways. Three common methods include:

- **Universal eligibility**: Open to all applicants
- **Selective eligibility**: Criteria are specified (e.g., age, dependent children) and often means-tested (for income and resources) with sliding scale costs
- **Exceptional eligibility**: Open only to individuals or groups with special needs (e.g., veterans, people with specific disabilities) and usually not means-tested

SOCIAL SECURITY ACT OF 1935

The Social Security Act (SSA) of 1935 provided old-age-survivor benefits, with full coverage beginning at age 65. Full eligibility gradually increases to age 67 for those born in or after 1960. To be fully vested, one must have 40 lifetime credits (earned at 4 credits per year). Reduced compensation may be available for those retiring earlier. Today, the program covers not only retirees, but those with certain permanent disabilities and the minor children of deceased beneficiaries, in certain situations. As an insurance trust fund, the program was intended to be self-sustaining by all those who pay in.

SOCIAL SECURITY DISABILITY, WORKER'S COMPENSATION, AND SUPPLEMENTAL SECURITY INCOME

Individuals with a permanent disability severe enough to prevent them from becoming gainfully employed may qualify for **Social Security Disability (SSD)**. The disabling condition must be expected to last for at least one year or to result in the individual's demise.

Individuals who contract a job-related illness or who are injured in the course of their work are covered by the social insurance program known as **worker's compensation**. Injuries resulting from intoxication, gross negligence, or deliberate misconduct are not covered. Coverage varies from state to state for this federally mandated, state-administered program. Funding is primarily employer based, though some states may supplement operation costs.

Supplemental Security Income (SSI) is a federally funded program supplemented by the state. It ensures baseline cash income to bring means-tested recipients above the poverty line. Poor elderly, disabled, and blind persons are the primary recipients.

UNEMPLOYMENT INSURANCE AND CHILD WELFARE PROGRAMS

Unemployment insurance is a benefit to prevent undue economic hardship, providing for individuals who become involuntarily and temporarily unemployed. To be eligible, an individual must be actively seeking gainful employment. Benefits include job-seeking assistance and cash payments in reduced proportion to the lost income. The benefits are time limited and once exhausted they cannot be obtained again unless a new episode of employment and job loss occurs. Originating with the Social Security Act of 1935, the program is federally mandated and state administered. Funding comes from employer taxes, distributed by the states to those needing assistance.

A variety of child welfare services and programs have been created for the safety, care, and support of abused, disabled, homeless, and otherwise vulnerable children. Services include adoption and foster care. Agencies investigating abuse and securing out-of-home placement, if necessary, also exist, along with programs for family maintenance and reunification.

GOVERNMENT FUNDING AND OVERSIGHT OF SOCIAL SERVICE PROGRAMS

Government programs are **funded** by income taxes and Social Security taxes. Income taxes are termed "progressive" because they increase as income increases. Taxes such as sales taxes and Social Security taxes are termed "regressive" because they are flat-rate taxes that offer non-proportional relief to those in low-income situations. Flat-rate tax reform efforts have continued to fall short primarily because of the loss of available deductions, in spite of proposals for tax elimination for the very poor. Dependent deductions can be crucial to low-income families, and home mortgage deductions are crucial for some homebuyers. A trend to privatization of government programs has increased in recent years (e.g., government oversight and funding of privately operated agencies). However, concerns about adequacy, availability, and accountability remain.

AVAILABLE FOOD AND NUTRITION ASSISTANCE PROGRAMS IN THE US

Available food and nutrition assistance programs in the US include:

- **Supplemental Nutrition Assistance Program (SNAP)**, previously food stamps: SNAP provides funds to purchase approved groceries, issued according to family size and income (selective eligibility, means-tested), state-administered and federally funded.
- **WIC (Women, Infants, and Children)**: WIC is a means-tested, selective eligibility program providing assistance to pregnant women, mothers of infants up to 5 months old, breastfeeding mothers of infants up to 12 months old, and children under 5 years old. Subsidies are provided for specific nutritious foods (infant formula, eggs, etc.). The program is state-administered and federally funded.
- **School lunch programs**: These programs provide federally funded assistance to children in means-tested families.
- **Elderly Nutrition Program**: This program provides food assistance for needy persons over age 60 via local churches and community centers.
- **Meals on Wheels**: This locally funded and administered program delivers meals to means-tested individuals and families.

PUBLIC HOUSING PROGRAMS

Public housing consists of government-built residential facilities that provide low-cost to no-cost rent for means-tested poor individuals and families. The **Subsidized Housing Program** offers federal funds to reduce

rental costs for the means-tested poor and to aid in maintaining public residential facilities. Additional public housing assistance programs include home loan assistance programs, home maintenance assistance programs, and Section 8 low-income reduced rent programs (rental vouchers).

TANF PROGRAM AND GENERAL ASSISTANCE

The **Temporary Assistance for Needy Families (TANF) program** replaced the Aid to Families with Dependent Children (AFDC) program. TANF was created by the 1996 Personal Responsibility and Work Opportunity Reconciliation Act (also known as welfare reform) and is a federally funded, state-administered block grant program. The focus is on moving recipients into the workforce and returning welfare to its intended temporary and transitional role.

General Assistance (GA) refers to a variety of social welfare programs developed by state and local government to aid those unable to meet eligibility for federal assistance programs. Eligibility criteria vary from state to state (even region to region, in some areas). Because there is no mandate for GA programs, they do not exist in all states, though most states have created some form of safety net of this kind.

MEDICARE

Medicare was established in 1965 and is now run by the Centers for Medicare and Medicaid Services. Coverage was initially instituted solely for those over age 65 but was expanded in 1973 to include the disabled. **Eligibility criteria** include an individual or spouse having worked for at least 10 years in Medicare-covered employment and US citizenship. Coverage options include up to four sections:

Medicare Part	Coverage Offered
Part A	Hospital insurance (hospital care, skilled nursing home care, hospice, and home healthcare)
Part B	Medical insurance (doctor's services and outpatient hospital services, diagnostic tests, ambulance transport, some preventive care including mammography and Pap tests, and durable medical equipment and supplies)
Part C	Medicare Advantage (MA), run by private companies to provide Part A and Part B benefits and often additional benefits such as vision, hearing, and health and wellness programs
Part D	Medicare Advantage-Prescription Drug plans (MA-PD) that include prescription drug coverage

MEDICAID

1965 Title XIX Social Security Act introduced **Medicaid** as a federal-state matching plan for low-income individuals supervised by the federal government. Funding comes from federal and state taxes, with no less than 50%, but no more than 83%, being funded federally. Each state is able to add optional eligibility criteria on the list, and they may also put restrictions (to a point) on federally directed aid. Patients who receive Medicaid cannot get a bill for the aid, but states are able to require small copayments or deductibles for particular types of help.

Federal regulations require that states support certain individuals or groups of individuals through Medicaid, although not everyone who falls below the federal poverty rate is eligible. **Mandatory eligibility groups** include the following:

- Patients deemed categorically needy by their state and who receive financial support from various federal assistance programs
- Individuals receiving Federal Supplemental Security income (SSI)
- Patients that are older than 65 that are blind or have complete disability

- Pregnant women and children younger than 6 years of age who live in families that are up to 133% of the federal poverty level (some states allow for a higher income to meet eligibility in this class)
- Adults under the age of 65 that make less than or equal to 133% of the federal poverty level and are not receiving Medicare

Review Video: <u>Medicare and Medicaid</u>
Visit mometrix.com/academy and enter code: 507454

FINANCIAL AND ORGANIZATIONAL STATUS OF NOT-FOR-PROFIT AGENCIES

In many ways, not-for-profit (nonprofit) entities operate similarly to for-profit entities. However, there are some key differences:

- Not-for-profit organizations must not be structured to pursue commercial purposes (i.e., profiteering on goods and services sold to the public).
- Members of a not-for-profit organization may not personally benefit as shareholders or investors.
- Certain tax benefits can accrue to not-for-profit organizations, within parameters defined by the Internal Revenue Service, which are not available to for-profit entities.
- Finally, the goals of these organizations tend to be charitable in nature (e.g., caring for vulnerable populations), and they seek and receive funding primarily via government and philanthropic grants, as well as from gifts, donations, and fundraising events.

Leadership

LEADERSHIP VS. MANAGEMENT

The definition of various roles and responsibilities differ from leader to manager.

Factor	Leader	Manager
Role	Encourages change and values achievements of self and others	Maintains stability and values end-results
Problem-solving	Facilitates decision-making and encourages innovative approaches	Makes decisions and decides on the course of action, generally with tried-and-true approaches
Power	Derives from personal charisma and the trust of others	Derives from position and authority granted by the organization
Actions	Proactive, anticipating problems and taking action to prevent them	Reactive, looking for solutions to problems after they occur
Risk taking	Willing to take risks to achieve results	Avoids risk taking as a threat to stability
Organizational culture	Shapes the current culture and seeks modifications	Supports and endorses the current culture
Resources (human)	People who follow and provide support	Employees who are hired to serve in subordinate positions
Focus (work)	Leading people to work more effectively	Managing the flow of work and personnel effectively
Goals	Focuses on long-term goals	Focuses on short-term goals

LEADERSHIP STYLES

Leadership styles often influence the perception of leadership values and commitment to collaboration.

Charismatic	This style depends upon personal charisma to influence people and may be very persuasive, but this type of leader may engage "followers" and relate to one group rather than the organization at large, limiting effectiveness.
Bureaucratic	This leader follows the organization's rules exactly and expects everyone else to do so. This is most effective in handling cash flow or managing work in dangerous work environments. This type of leadership may engender respect but may not be conducive to change.
Autocratic	An autocratic leader makes decisions independently and strictly enforces rules, but team members often feel left out of the process and may not be supportive. This type of leader is most effective in crisis situations, but may have difficulty gaining the commitment of staff
Consultative	A consultative leader presents a decision and welcomes input and questions although decisions rarely change. This type of leadership is most effective when gaining the support of staff is critical to the success of proposed changes.
Participatory	This leader presents a potential decision and then makes a final decision based on input from staff or teams. This type of leadership is time-consuming and may result in compromises that are not wholly satisfactory to management or staff, but this process is motivating to staff who feel their expertise is valued.
Democratic	A democratic leader presents a problem and asks staff or teams to arrive at a solution, although the leader usually makes the final decision. This type of leadership may delay decision-making, but staff and teams are often more committed to the solutions because of their input.

201

Laissez-faire (free rein)	This leader exerts little direct control but allows employees/teams to make decisions with little interference. This may be effective leadership if teams are highly skilled and motivated, but in many cases, this type of leadership is the product of poor management skills and little is accomplished because of this lack of leadership.

POWER

Power is defined as the ability to influence others in intended ways. **Sources of power** depend on the following:

- Control of resources
- Numbers of people
- Degree of social organization

Power exists in several forms, some conducive in motivating and inspiring long-term change, others effective only in the short term.

- **Coercive power** uses one's ability to instill fear and enforce negative consequences to motivate specific actions or steer away from other actions.
- **Reward power** uses one's ability to provide incentives (bonuses, recognition) to motivate specific actions.
- **Legitimate power** is power resulting from stature, title, or position and is only effective when the position of power is universally respected by those who are subordinate to the position of power.
- **Expert power** comes from having a unique and specific skill set that is essential for growth and change.
- **Referent power** results from gaining the trust and respect of one's followers by leading by example and putting the greater good above the self. This is the most effective power in motivating change.

Supervision and Administration

ADMINISTRATION

Administration can be described as follows:

- Managing organizations and all of their parts in order to maximize goals and have the organization succeed and grow
- Directing all the activities of an agency
- Organizing and bringing together all human and technical resources in order to meet the agency's goals
- Motivating and supervising work performed by individuals and groups in order to meet agency goals

AGENCY POLICIES AND PROCEDURES

Agencies usually have written statements of values and a mission, and new employees are given copies of the statements in their orientations or induction periods. Mission and value statements disseminate the general goals and attitudes of the agency. **Policies** are more specific documents outlining important **procedures** for areas such as informed consent, documentation, confidentiality, and antidiscrimination. In agencies that value the autonomy of staff, there are policies enabling employees to provide feedback about organizational customs or policies operating contrary to the best interests of clients or employees.

IMPACT OF AGENCY POLICY AND PROCEDURES ON SOCIAL WORK PRACTICE

The work environment for social workers is as important as for any professionals. The **agency's policies and culture** should be in alignment with the ethics and values of the profession, supporting the wellbeing and development of the staff. Workload management, appropriate supervision, ongoing professional development opportunities, and fair pay and benefits provide a supportive structure for social workers. Formal or informal policies should never compel social workers to engage in risky behaviors in regard to client confidentiality, informed consent, or health and safety of clients or workers. As in any job, employees should be given access to training and recognition if they are to experience job satisfaction and quality of life.

AGENCY ADMINISTRATION, STRUCTURE, AND BUREAUCRACY

All organizations should have a **mission statement** that sets forth the purpose, goals, and target service population of the organization. An **organizational structure** is then needed to pursue the delivery of services and achievement of the identified goals. An agency typically has three levels of **bureaucratic staff**: institution-wide leaders, management-level staff, and direct service providers. Typical social service agencies follow a classic Weberian bureaucratic model of organization. In a bureaucracy, leadership flows from the "top down," and tasks are rationally delegated to employees and departments best suited to achieve administrative and agency goals.

Key **characteristics of a bureaucracy** (according to Max Weber) include the following:

- Labor is divided by functions and tasks according to specialized skills or a specific focus needed.
- A hierarchical structure of authority is in place.
- Recruitment and hiring are based upon an initial review of key qualifications and technical skills.
- Rigid rules and procedures are generally applied impartially throughout the organization and specify employee benefits, duties, and rights.
- Activities and responsibilities are rationally planned to achieve overarching agency goals.

ADMINISTRATIVE FUNCTIONS IN AN AGENCY/ORGANIZATION

Basic administrative functions include the following:

- **Human resource management**: Recruiting, interviewing, hiring, and firing, as well as orienting and reassigning employees within the organization.
- **Planning and delegation**: Ensuring that the organization's mission, goals, objectives, and policies are in place, appropriate, and effective, and delegating necessary tasks to achieve these ends.
- **Employee evaluations, reviews, and monitoring** to ensure competency and efficiency.
- **Advocacy**: Horizontal interventions (between staff or across a department) and vertical interventions (between departments and hierarchical staff relationships) to resolve conflicts and complaints.
- **Conflict resolution**: Acting as a mediator and a protector of the various parties involved, ensuring equitable outcomes that remain within the scope of the organization and its goals.

RELATIONSHIPS BETWEEN ADMINISTRATORS, SUPERVISORS, AND SUPERVISEES

While all agency staff are concerned with providing quality services, **administrators** have a more external focus, while supervisors and direct service staff are focused internally. Administrators are charged with broad program planning, policy development, and ensuring agency funding, along with managing the agency's public image and community perceptions. By contrast, **supervisors** are more responsible for the implementation of policy and programs and ensuring staff adherence to those guidelines provided. New employees (during a probationary period) and those seeking licensure may engage in more formal supervision experiences as **supervisees**. In the case of supervision for licensure, a written agreement will outline the goals, purpose, and scope of the supervision, along with meeting frequency and duration (to accrue required licensure hours), evaluations, whether or not sessions will be recorded (videotaped, etc.), and how feedback will be provided. Consultation and supervision differ, as consultation is an episodic, voluntary problem-solving process with someone having special expertise, in contrast to continuous and mandatory oversight with administrative authority.

BOARDS OF DIRECTORS
FUNCTIONS

The power and authority vested in a **board of directors** depends upon whether they are overseeing a private or public agency. Public agencies have board members that are largely advisory or administrative, with less direct authority than those overseeing private entities. In private agencies or voluntary organizations, the board is empowered to define the general path of the agency and to control all systems and programs operating under its auspices. The board is responsible to any sources that provide monetary contributions, to the community, to the government, and to all consumers that use the agency's programs. To be successful, members of a social service agency's board must have knowledge of all operations. The function of the board is to oversee the design of policies, develop short- and long-term planning, confirm the hiring of personnel, oversee general finances and financial expenditures, deal with the public, and be accountable for the actions of the agency.

SELECTION AND COMPOSITION

The agency's mission and overall goals must be kept paramount when **choosing board members**. Members must be committed, honest, and able to invest their time and energy in the agency. Responsibilities must be discharged with personal expertise and through meaningful relationships within the community. Interpersonal skills are essential, as board members deal directly with the other members of the board, professionals at the agency, and the general public. Some boards require the representation of certain professions within the community (e.g., a banker), but all members must bring a particular expertise to the board. The agency's mission and the personal responsibilities of each board member should be understood, and a specific orientation experience should be provided to ensure this understanding. Terms are typically limited to three years, with the possibility of a second term for those making unique contributions. The terms should rotate to ensure that seasoned board members are always available.

RELATIONSHIP OF AGENCY STAFF WITH BOARD MEMBERS

The board of directors oversees the development of policies by agency administrators, and the staff of the agency carries out the policies as approved. The board must hold the staff accountable for the implementation of the policies, because policy operationalization may utilize a variety of potential pathways. Administration evaluates the staff, and the performance of the staff ultimately reflects on the agency, which in turn reflects on the board. Representative staff members have the right to communicate with the board about any problems they face in implementing the policies. Open lines of communication between the board and the staff ensure success in the agency. The board, administration, and staff should have a triangular relationship based on clear job descriptions that state the responsibilities of each party.

SUPERVISION

ASPECTS OF SUPERVISION

There are three aspects of supervision:

- **Supportive supervision** assists the social worker in handling stress and in learning self-care. Both activities are needed to provide the best service to clients.
- **Educational activities** identify needs and teach new skills.
- **Administrative aspects** of supervision are concerned with accountability to the public; for example, numbers of documented supervision hours are required to meet licensing requirements.

GROUP SUPERVISION

Group supervision has been described as a blending of mediation and mutual aid as supervisor-led and peer groups can provide workers with the four Cs of supervision: confidence, competence, compassion, and creativity. The need for information, balanced with the need for self-care, make supervision a multipurpose activity designed to support the effectiveness and efficiency of workers in their capacity to help clients.

Two primary structures of group supervision are the supervisor-led group and the peer group. In a supervisor-led group, the supervisor holds the group as any group therapist would, creating a safe, nonjudgmental environment and mediating among group members.

SOCIAL WORK SUPERVISORY ROLES

As a middle manager, supervisors oversee direct service staff and report to administrative directors; they provide indirect client services (via direct service staff) and primarily serve the agency.

Supervisory roles include the following:

- **Recruitment and orientation**
- **Management**: Delegating duties, overseeing staff work, and resolving conflicts
- **Education, training, and staff development**: Instructing staff regarding policies and procedures, and ensuring that training is available or pursued via in-service meetings, workshops, and continuing education courses
- **Assessment and review**: Evaluating and providing feedback regarding staff performance
- **Support**: Helping staff resolve issues and cope with stress and promoting a healthy work environment
- **Advocacy**: Resolving complaints and pursuing necessary support for staff
- **Role modeling** of quality practice, values, and ethics
- **Program evaluator**: Ensuring that policies and procedures are effective and that staff adhere to guidelines

SUPERVISION GROUPS

Supervision groups may be theme-centered, case-centered, or worker-centered, with many groups addressing all three as relevant issues arise. Many supervision groups move between an educational stance and a focus on self-reflective practice, allowing for teaching and growth of self-understanding as necessary components of professional development. In group supervision as in individual supervision, the supervisor may be held accountable for the actions of their supervisees (*respondeat superior*) in ethical situations that may come to legal action.

PEER SUPERVISION

Supervision should be regularly scheduled, transparent, and open and nonjudgmental, whatever the model used. Three models of peer supervision include the **developmental**, **role-centered**, and the **psychodynamic models**, and peer groups will vary within those models based on the group focus and whether or not case presentation is part of the process.

SOCIAL WORKER'S RESPONSIBILITY TO SEEK OUT AND RECEIVE SUPERVISION

Supervision is important in the care of clients, in continuing learning for social workers, and in ethical competence. If a social worker finds herself or himself in a situation in which supervision is not provided in the workplace, it is that person's ethical duty to find appropriate supervision. With technologic advances, even remotely based social workers can arrange virtual supervision, provided that they take precautions for clients' confidentiality. Social workers have the right to privacy in their supervision sessions.

IDENTIFYING AND FILLING LEARNING NEEDS

Identifying learning needs and developing objectives are important in supervision because client care depends on the skills and understanding of the social worker as well as their attentiveness to ethics. Supervision is a vital part of professional development, and the knowledgeable supervisor notes and matches the learning style (visual, auditory, or kinesthetic) of the supervisee to methods of teaching, can explain the reasons for the assigned interventions, and is able to give constructive feedback and evaluate the learning process. With the social worker's value on empowering the individual, the ideal supervision process includes the participation of the supervisee in identifying learning needs and working in concert with the supervisor to meet them.

POSITIVE WORK ENVIRONMENT

Creating a positive work environment includes policies and procedures that support employees (good supervision and professional development opportunities), good terms of employment (e.g., salaries and benefits, chances for recognition and advancement), autonomy instead of micromanagement, and good physical working conditions. The culture of the workplace should uphold the values of the social work profession, provide for the health and safety of employees, and have strategies in place to prevent burnout and employee turnover.

TRANSFERENCE AND COUNTERTRANSFERENCE IN SUPERVISORY RELATIONSHIPS

Transference can be as overt and disturbing as an attempt to create a romantic or sexual relationship with a supervisor or as subtle as wanting to please or compete with a supervisor who reminds the social worker of someone in their life outside the profession.

Countertransference is the set of irrational feelings, thoughts, or ideas of the supervisor toward the supervisee that may be acted out, repressed, or addressed in supervision, depending on the appropriateness of the situation. In a parallel process, transferential issues between the social worker and client may arise, as can similar issues between social worker and supervisor. Working with the powerful and sometimes confusing conflicts generated by the various forms of transference bring history, personal feelings, and ethical considerations together, making supervision a rich, challenging, and interesting process.

Chapter Quiz

Ready to see how well you retained what you just read? Scan the QR code to go directly to the chapter quiz interface for this study guide. If you're using a computer, simply visit the bonus page at **mometrix.com/bonus948/swclinical** and click the Chapter Quizzes link.

Professional Relationships, Values, and Ethics

Transform passive reading into active learning! After immersing yourself in this chapter, put your comprehension to the test by taking a quiz. The insights you gained will stay with you longer this way. Scan the QR code to go directly to the chapter quiz interface for this study guide. If you're using a computer, simply visit the bonus page at **mometrix.com/bonus948/swclinical** and click the Chapter Quizzes link.

Legal Issues and Client Rights

LIABILITY FOR SOCIAL WORKERS

Concepts relating to liability for social workers are as follows:

- Clients can sue social workers for malpractice.
- The chain of liability extends from the individual worker to supervisory personnel to the director and then to the board of directors of a nonprofit agency.
- Most agencies carry malpractice insurance, which usually protects individual workers; however, workers may also carry personal liability and malpractice insurance.
- Supervisors can be named as parties in a malpractice suit as they share vicarious liability for the activities of their supervisees.

GENERAL RIGHTS FOR SOCIAL WORK CLIENTS

General rights for social worker clients include:

- Confidentiality and privacy
- Informed consent
- Access to services (if service requirements cannot be met, a referral should be offered)
- Access to records (adequately protective but not onerously burdensome policies for client access to services should be developed and put in place)
- Participation in the development of treatment plans (client cooperation in the treatment process is essential to success)
- Options for alternative services/referrals (clients should always be offered options whenever they are available)
- Right to refuse services (clients have a right to refuse services that are not court ordered; ethical issues exist when involuntary treatment is provided, but mandates do not allow options other than referrals to other sources of the mandated service)
- Termination by the client (clients have a right to terminate services at any time and for any reason they deem adequate, except in certain court-ordered situations)

RIGHT TO PRIVACY

Every individual has a right to expect that personal information disclosed in a clinical setting, including data such as their address, telephone number, social security number, financial information, and health information

will not be disclosed to others, and no preconditions need be fulfilled to claim this right. The 1974 Federal Privacy Act (PL 93-579) also stipulates that clients be informed of the following:

- When records about them are being maintained
- That they can access, correct, and copy these records
- That the records are to be used only for the purpose of obtaining absent written consent otherwise

Exceptions include:

- Need-to-know sharing with other agency employees
- Use for research if identifying information is omitted
- Release to the government for law enforcement purposes
- Responding to a subpoena
- In emergencies, where the health and safety of an individual is at risk

While the law applies only to agencies receiving federal funds, many state and local entities have adopted these standards.

CLIENT'S RIGHT TO REFUSE SERVICES

The right to refuse services rests with adults, so ordinarily an adult (or an emancipated minor who has been granted the rights of adulthood) can refuse any medication, treatment, counseling, or placement, although this is not always true in social work. Court orders override these rights, and if the court has declared a person is incompetent, this person's guardian makes the decisions. Additionally, if the court has ordered specific treatment, therapy, or placement, then the client must comply even against the client's wishes. Children, including adolescents, have no rights to refusal, but they should be consulted as much as possible, and their wishes should be respected and incorporated into the plan of care. For example, if a child does not want to be placed into a group home, then other living arrangements should be explored because forcing a child to do something often results in poor outcomes.

CONFIDENTIALITY
HIPAA

In 1996 the federal government passed legislation providing privacy protection for personal health information. Known as **HIPAA** (Health Insurance Portability and Accountability Act), this act:

- Places privacy protections on personal health information and specifically limits the purposes for its use and the circumstances for its disclosure.
- Provides individuals with specific rights to access their records.
- Ensures that individuals will be notified about privacy practices. The act applies only to "covered entities," which are defined as healthcare providers (physicians and allied healthcare providers), clearinghouses for healthcare services, and health plans.

> **Review Video: HIPAA**
> Visit mometrix.com/academy and enter code: 412009
>
> **Review Video: Ethics and Confidentiality in Counseling**
> Visit mometrix.com/academy and enter code: 250384

POLICIES REFLECTING EXPECTATION OF CONFIDENTIALITY

Organizational policies can reflect the **expectation of confidentiality** through the following:

- Records must be secured and locked.
- Policies should be in place that ensure that records are not left where unauthorized persons are able to read them.
- Computerized records should be secured with the same attention given to written records (hard copies).
- Agencies must provide spaces that permit private conversations so that conversations about clients can be held where they cannot be overheard.

UTILIZATION OF INFORMED CONSENT

Through **informed consent**, a client may provide consent for the worker to share information with family members, or with other professionals or agencies for purposes of referral. When the client provides this consent, they have reason to expect that shared information is in their best interest and designed to improve their situation.

CONFIDENTIALITY FOR SOCIAL WORKERS VS. LAWYERS OR CLERGY

Social work privilege does not have the same force as that of attorneys and clergy. Unlike clergy and attorneys, social workers may be compelled to testify in court under certain circumstances.

A social worker who is sued for malpractice may reveal information discussed by clients. The worker should aim to limit the discussion of the content of clinical discussions to those statements needed to support an effective defense.

NASW Code of Ethics

ETHICAL PRINCIPLES

- **Service**: Social workers are responsible for providing help to individuals; finding solutions to social problems; and using their professional knowledge and skills in service of others, including unpaid volunteer efforts.
- **Social justice**: Social workers seek social change and access to information, services, and resources that improve the lives of those who are poor, unemployed, discriminated against, or suffering other social injustices. Social workers seek to provide these individuals with access to opportunities and decision-making, and to promote knowledge about social inequities and ethnic diversity within their profession and to the public.
- **Dignity and worth of the person**: Social workers remain aware of their responsibility to the individual and society as a whole. Social workers comprehend the need to resolve conflicts that arise between the individual and the society, and encourage autonomy in addressing needs and making changes.
- **Importance of human relationships**: Social workers recognize the importance of partnerships in serving others and strengthening relationships in the community.
- **Integrity**: Social workers always strive to maintain ethical standards and practice accordingly, and to apply these same ethical standards to the organizations that they serve.
- **Competence**: Social workers work within their area of competence and continually strive to improve their knowledge and skills and to contribute to the growth of the profession.

SOCIAL WORKERS' ETHICAL RESPONSIBILITIES TO CLIENTS

1.01 COMMITMENT TO CLIENTS

While a social worker's primary responsibility is to the welfare of the client, clients should be advised that the greater needs of society and legal requirements (such as reporting abuse or risks for harm to the self or others) may at times supersede the needs of any single client.

1.02 SELF-DETERMINATION

Social workers recognize that clients have the right to self-determination and should actively support them as they identify their goals. This right to autonomy is limited only when it presents a risk to the client or others.

1.03 INFORMED CONSENT

- Social workers serve clients only in a professional capacity and provide informed consent with language understandable to the clients so that they clearly understand the risks, benefits, costs, durations, limits of service, and their right to ask questions and even refuse consent.
- Social workers provide information in a manner that is comprehensible to the client, using appropriate language and an interpreter/translator if necessary.
- Social workers protect the interests of those unable to provide informed consent and seek consent from appropriate third parties, ensuring that the third parties respect the interests of the clients and that all efforts are made to enhance the clients' abilities to consent.
- Social workers should provide detailed information about involuntary services, including the type of service and any rights the clients have regarding refusal of service.
- Social workers should inform clients about policies regarding the use of technology while providing services.
- Social workers using technology during the provision of services (such as intake screening or interviews) should obtain informed consent at the initial contact and should request identifiers (e.g., name and location) when using technology to communicate.

- Social workers should assess clients' intellectual, emotional, and physical suitability for technology that allows for electronic/remote services and their ability to give informed consent for such use. Social workers should ensure clients understand the right to refuse the use of technology and should be prepared to provide alternative forms of service.
- Social workers must ensure that informed consent is obtained for audio recordings, video recordings, or observations by a third party.
- Social workers should obtain informed consent from a client before carrying out an electronic search for information about the client unless the purpose is to protect the client or others from harm or for other critical professional reasons.

1.04 COMPETENCE

- Social workers should provide services only within the limits of their education and level of competence.
- Social workers should only utilize techniques and interventions for which they received training and adequate preparation.
- Social workers should ensure that emerging practices are safe for the client and exercise diligence through research and training even when standards for such practices are not yet established.
- Social workers must be competent in the use of technology and aware of potential challenges.
- Social workers must comply with all applicable laws and regulations regarding technology.

1.05 CULTURAL COMPETENCE

- Social workers should appreciate diverse cultures and understand their effects on behavior and society.
- Social workers must utilize knowledge of diverse cultures to guide practice, empower those who are marginalized, act against racial injustice and discrimination, and recognize personal privilege.
- Social workers must reflect on their own biases, recognize the knowledge clients have about their own cultures, and commit to continuous learning. Social workers must ensure that institutions exhibit cultural humility.
- Social workers must educate themselves about issues of social and cultural diversity and oppression related to race, ethnicity, national origin, color of skin, sexual identification and expression, age, marital status, political and religious affiliations, immigration status, and differences in abilities.
- Social workers must recognize potential cultural and socioeconomic barriers to the use of electronic technology and should assess issues that may impact delivery or access to services.

1.06 CONFLICTS OF INTEREST

- Social workers must avoid conflicts of interest by remaining alert and exercising impartial judgement; informing clients of the possibility or existence of conflicts of interest; and taking steps to resolve any issues in the best interests of the clients, including terminating a professional relationship if necessary.
- Social workers must not exploit professional relationships for personal gain or interests of any kind.
- Social workers should avoid dual or multiple relationships with current or former clients that could pose a risk of client exploitation or harm, and should make efforts to protect clients and set appropriate boundaries if dual or multiple relationships are unavoidable.
- Social workers must clarify professional obligations when providing services to two or more individuals in a relationship, try to avoid or minimize conflicts of interest, and make the clients aware of any possible conflicts of interest and the role the social worker will take in those instances.
- Social workers should avoid communicating with clients for personal or non-work-related reasons using electronic media (social media, email, telephone, video, text messaging).
- Social workers must remain alert to the possible negative effects (boundary violations, dual relationships, client harm) that can result from posting personal information on social media.

- Social workers must understand that posting information about personal affiliations (race, ethnicity, national origin, color of skin, sexual identification and expression, age, marital status, political and religious affiliations, immigration status, and differences in abilities) on social media may negatively impact their ability to work with some clients.
- Social workers should not establish or accept social media relationships with clients because they could lead to boundary violations, dual relationships, and client harm.

1.07 PRIVACY AND CONFIDENTIALITY

- Social workers should respect clients' rights to privacy by not asking for unnecessary personal information and not sharing clients' personal information with others.
- Social workers may only divulge confidential information with the consent of the client or someone legally authorized to represent the client.
- Social workers must maintain the confidentiality of information obtained in a professional capacity unless disclosure is necessary to prevent harm to the client or others, and any such disclosure should be the minimum necessary and only that which is directly relevant.
- Social workers should advise clients of any necessary disclosure of confidential information in advance (if possible), whether with or without client consent.
- Social workers should discuss issues related to confidentiality, including limits and legally required disclosures, early in the relationship and as necessary.
- Social workers providing counseling services to families or groups of clients should discuss issues related to confidentiality, including agreements to respect confidentiality and avoid disclosure on social media without consent. Social workers must also advise clients that there is a risk that someone in the family or group may break these agreements and disclose confidential information.
- Social workers providing counseling services should advise clients of any relevant policies concerning the social worker's disclosure of confidential information among the members of the group.
- Social workers must avoid disclosure of confidential information to a third-party payer without consent of the client.
- Social workers should avoid any discussion of confidential information, electronically or personally, in any setting (elevator, hallway, restaurant, etc.) or situation in which privacy is not absolutely ensured.
- Social workers must try to lawfully protect the confidentiality of clients during legal proceedings. If ordered by the courts to disclose confidential information without client consent, and if that information may be harmful to the client, then the social worker should ask the court to withdraw the request for information, limit the order, or keep the records under seal to avoid public exposure.
- Social workers responding to media requests for information should protect the confidentiality of clients.
- Social workers should ensure the confidentiality of written and electronic records, ensure that records are stored securely, and ensure that the records are protected from unauthorized access.
- Social workers should ensure that electronic communications (email, texts, social media, cellphones) to clients or third parties are appropriately safeguarded (encryption, firewalls, and/or passwords).
- Social workers must have policies and procedures in place to notify clients of any breach of confidential information.
- Social workers must follow applicable laws and standards when notifying clients of unauthorized access to clients' records, electronic communication, or storage systems.
- Social workers must communicate to clients the policies regarding the use of electronic technology, including the use of search engines to obtain information about clients.
- Social workers should avoid searching electronically for information about clients unless professionally necessary and should, whenever possible, do so only with client consent.
- Social workers should not post any confidential or identifying information about clients on professional websites or social media.
- Social workers must dispose of client records in accordance with applicable laws and licensure, ensuring that clients' confidentiality is protected.

- Social workers must ensure that clients' confidentiality is protected in the event that a social worker terminates practice, becomes incapacitated, or dies.
- Social workers should avoid sharing any identifying information about clients in the course of teaching or training others.
- Social workers should avoid providing identifying information of clients to consultants unless the clients have given consent.
- Social workers should maintain the confidentiality of clients even after the clients have died.

1.08 ACCESS TO RECORDS

- Social workers should allow clients reasonable access to their records, interpret for or consult with the client regarding records that may result in misunderstanding or harm, and limit access only if access may result in serious harm to the clients. If a client requests access to their records, then this request must be documented. If access to the records is not granted, then the rationale for withholding them must also be noted.
- Social workers should disclose policies regarding the use of technology to allow clients to access their records.
- Social workers must protect the confidentiality of individuals who are identified or discussed in clients' records when allowing clients access to those records.

1.09 SEXUAL RELATIONSHIPS

- Social workers must not engage in sexual activities of any kind with current clients, and they are also prohibited from maintaining sexual communications in person or through technology (consensual or forced) with them.
- Social workers should not engage in any type of sexual activity or sexual contact with relatives of clients or those with whom the clients have close relationships. Such conduct could pose potential harm to the client and negatively affect the social worker-client relationship. Also, the burden for setting appropriate boundaries lies with the social worker, not with the client or anyone else.
- Social workers should avoid engaging in any type of sexual activity or sexual contact with former clients. If the social worker feels that an exception is warranted, it is the social worker's responsibility to demonstrate that the former client has not been intentionally or unintentionally exploited, coerced, or harmed.
- Social workers should avoid providing clinical services to individuals with whom they have previously had a sexual relationship because of the potential for harm to the individuals and the difficulty in maintaining appropriate professional boundaries.

1.10 PHYSICAL CONTACT

Social workers should avoid physical contact with clients that may be misconstrued and/or cause harm to the clients (e.g., cradling, caressing). Social workers must ensure that all physical contact with clients is appropriate and that clear and socially sensitive boundaries are established.

1.11 SEXUAL HARASSMENT

Social workers should not sexually harass clients by making sexual advances, solicitations, requests for sexual favors, or other forms of contact of a sexual nature (whether physical, electronic, verbal, or written).

1.12 DEROGATORY LANGUAGE

Social workers should always communicate with respectful language and avoid any type of communication with derogatory language.

1.13 PAYMENT FOR SERVICES

- Social workers should set fair and reasonable fees that reflect the services provided and the clients' ability to pay.
- Social workers should avoid accepting bartering in lieu of fees for professional services because it may result in conflicts of interests, exploitation, or other inappropriate boundaries. Bartering is only appropriate if it is an accepted practice in the local community, is at the request of the client, and involves no coercion. The social worker must be able to demonstrate that agreeing to bartering is not detrimental to the clients and does not negatively affect the professional relationship.
- Social workers should not request payment of a private fee for services for which the client is already entitled.

1.14 CLIENTS WHO LACK DECISION-MAKING CAPACITY

Social workers must ensure that the rights and interests of clients are safeguarded, especially with clients who are unable to make informed decisions.

1.15 INTERRUPTION OF SERVICES

Social workers should ensure that clients will have continuity of services in the event that the social worker becomes unavailable because of an inability to communicate electronically, relocation, disability, or death.

1.16 REFERRAL FOR SERVICES

- Social workers should refer clients to other professionals if they believe the knowledge and expertise of those professionals will better serve the needs of the clients.
- Social workers referring clients to other professionals should ensure that transfer is orderly and that all pertinent information is disclosed with clients' permission.
- Social workers may not give or receive payment for referring clients to other professionals if the social worker provided no professional services.

1.17 TERMINATION OF SERVICES

- Social workers should end services to clients who are no longer in need of such services.
- Social workers should avoid abandoning clients and minimize the effects of doing so if it becomes necessary, ensuring that the clients will continue to receive needed services.
- Social workers who see clients on a fee-for-service basis may end services for nonpayment as long as the clients are not at risk of harm to self or others and the clients are aware of clinical and other consequences of nonpayment.
- Social workers should not end services with a client in order to pursue a different type of relationship with the client (sexual, social, financial).
- Social workers should make clients promptly aware of any future termination or interruption of services and assist them with transfers or referrals so that services can be continued.
- Social workers leaving employment should advise clients of the options for continuing services and discuss the risks and benefits of those options.

SOCIAL WORKERS' ETHICAL RESPONSIBILITIES TO COLLEAGUES

2.01 RESPECT

- Social workers must treat colleagues with respect and fairly represent their qualifications, views, and obligations.
- Social workers should avoid unwarranted criticism of colleagues to clients or other professionals in any form, such as by making negative comments about their professional ability, race, ethnicity, national origin, color of skin, sexual identification and expression, age, marital status, political and religious affiliations, or immigration status.
- Social workers should strive to serve clients by cooperating with social work colleagues and other professionals.

2.02 CONFIDENTIALITY

Social workers must recognize and protect the confidentiality of colleagues regarding information shared during a professional relationship, and should ensure that colleagues understand the social workers' role in safeguarding confidentiality and any possible exceptions.

2.03 INTERDISCIPLINARY COLLABORATION

- Social workers participating in interdisciplinary teams with established ethical obligations should draw on their viewpoints and experience to help make decisions that affect clients' wellbeing.
- Social workers who have ethical concerns about team decisions should try to resolve the conflicts or pursue other means to assure the clients' wellbeing.

2.04 DISPUTES INVOLVING COLLEAGUES

- Social workers must avoid exploiting the disputes of others, such as those between a colleague and their employer, to further their own careers.
- Social workers should avoid taking advantage of clients during any conflicts with colleagues or discussing such conflicts with clients.

2.05 CONSULTATION

- Social workers should consult with and ask for advice from colleagues when doing so is beneficial to clients.
- Social workers should be knowledgeable about the expertise and competence of colleagues and consult only with those who are qualified to deal with the issue at hand.
- Social workers should avoid disclosing any unnecessary information about clients when consulting with colleagues.

2.06 SEXUAL RELATIONSHIPS

- Social workers in a position of authority should not engage in sexual activities or sexual contact of any kind with subordinates.
- Social workers who engage in sexual relationships with colleagues should ensure that there are no conflicts of interest and should transfer professional responsibilities as necessary to avoid conflicts of interest.

2.07 SEXUAL HARASSMENT

Social workers must not sexually harass subordinates by making sexual advances; solicitations; requests for sexual favors; or physical, electronic, verbal, or written communications of a sexual nature.

2.08 IMPAIRMENT OF COLLEAGUES

- Social workers who are aware of the impairment of a colleague related to personal, psychosocial, mental health, or substance abuse problems, and who recognize that the impairment is affecting the colleague's professional practice, should address those concerns directly with the colleague and help them to develop a plan of correction.
- Social workers should take the necessary steps to report a colleague's impairment through the appropriate channels (employer, NASW, licensing bodies, regulatory bodies, professional organizations) if the colleague has failed to address their impairment.

2.09 INCOMPETENCE OF COLLEAGUES

- Social workers who are aware of incompetence on the part of colleagues should address those concerns directly with the colleagues and assist them in developing a plan of correction.
- Social workers should take the appropriate steps to report a colleague's incompetence through the appropriate channels (employer, NASW, licensing bodies, regulatory bodies, professional organizations) if the colleague has failed to address their impairment.

2.10 UNETHICAL CONDUCT OF COLLEAGUES

- Social workers should take necessary actions to prevent, expose, or correct any type of unethical conduct by colleagues, including technological misconduct.
- Social workers must be aware of policies and procedures (national, state, and local) established to deal with colleagues' unethical behavior, including those of an employer, the NASW, licensing bodies, regulatory bodies, and professional organizations.
- Social workers who are aware of the unethical behavior of colleagues should address this with the colleagues directly (if possible) if doing so may resolve the issue.
- Social workers should take the necessary and appropriate steps to report colleagues that have acted unethically through the appropriate channels (licensing bodies, regulatory bodies, NASW National Ethic Committee, and other professional ethics committees).
- Social workers should defend and help colleagues charged with unethical conduct if the colleagues are innocent.

SOCIAL WORKERS' ETHICAL RESPONSIBILITIES IN PRACTICE SETTINGS

3.01 SUPERVISION AND CONSULTATION

- Social workers who serve as supervisors or consultants should have the necessary knowledge, skills, and competence to do so.
- Social workers who serve as supervisors or consultants should establish clear boundaries that are appropriate and culturally sensitive.
- Social workers who serve as supervisors should avoid dual or multiple relationships (including those involving social media) with those being supervised in order to avoid exploitation or possible harm.
- Social workers who serve as supervisors should evaluate supervisees fairly and respectfully.

3.02 EDUCATION AND TRAINING

- Social workers, in their roles as educators, field instructors, or trainers, should provide the most current professional information within their own areas of knowledge and competence.
- Social workers, in their roles as educators, field instructors, or trainers, should evaluate students fairly and respectfully.
- Social workers, in their roles as educators, field instructors, or trainers, should ensure clients are aware that services are provided by students.
- Social workers, in their roles as educators, field instructors, or trainers, should avoid dual or multiple relationships (including those involving social media) with students in order to avoid exploitation or possible harm, and should establish clear boundaries that are appropriate and culturally sensitive.

3.03 PERFORMANCE EVALUATION

Social workers responsible for the supervision of others should evaluate their performance fairly based on established, stated criteria.

3.04 CLIENT RECORDS

- Social workers should ensure that all documentation (paper and electronic) accurately describes the services provided.
- Social workers should ensure that documentation is timely and sufficient so that clients receive necessary current and future services.
- Social workers should document events in a manner that protects clients' privacy while providing information that is necessary for the delivery of services.
- Social workers should store records after services are terminated in the manner and for the time period required by laws, agency policies, or contractual agreements.

3.05 BILLING

Social workers should have accurate billing practices that identify who provide the services being charged and the extent of those services.

3.06 CLIENT TRANSFER

- Social workers should carefully consider whether to accept clients who request services but are already receiving services from other providers. They should ascertain the nature of the clients' current relationship with other providers and assess the risks and benefits of changing service providers.
- Social workers providing services to clients who had previous service providers should discuss with the clients whether consultation with the previous provider(s) is warranted.

3.07 ADMINISTRATION

- Social workers should advocate for adequate internal and external resources to best serve the needs of their clients.
- Social workers should advocate for fair and nondiscriminatory resource allocation procedures, applying appropriate and consistent principles even when all clients' needs cannot be met.
- Social workers in administrative positions should develop policies to ensure there are adequate resources for supervision of staff.
- Social workers in administrative positions should develop policies to ensure their working environment is in compliance with the NASW Code of Ethics and should eliminate any conditions that may negatively impact compliance with the Code.

3.08 CONTINUING EDUCATION AND STAFF DEVELOPMENT

Social worker supervisors and administrators should ensure continuing education and staff development to address current and emerging knowledge pertaining to social work and ethics for all of the staff working under them.

3.09 COMMITMENTS TO EMPLOYERS

- Social workers should honor the commitments they have made to their employers and employing agencies.
- Social workers should take steps to improve policies and procedures of employing agencies.
- Social workers should make an effort to ensure that employers are aware of the ethical obligations that the social workers have to the NASW Code of Ethics and the implications these obligations have for practice.
- Social workers should not allow any policy, regulation, or orders from an employing organization interfere with their ethical practice of social work. They should ensure that the employing agencies' practices are consistent with the Code of Ethics.
- Social workers should ensure that employing organizations practice nondiscriminatory work assignments, policies, and procedures.
- Social workers should only work or assign students to employing organizations that treat personnel fairly.
- Social workers should exercise care with employing organizations' resources, save funds when possible, and avoid any misuse or misappropriation of funds.

3.10 LABOR-MANAGEMENT DISPUTES

- Social workers may participate in labor unions, including organizing and forming unions, in order to better provide for clients.
- Social workers who are involved in labor-management disputes must ensure their actions are guided by the values, principles, and ethics of the profession and should consider the impact their actions may have on clients.

SOCIAL WORKERS' ETHICAL RESPONSIBILITIES AS PROFESSIONALS

4.01 COMPETENCE

- Social workers should accept assignment or employment only in areas for which they have competence or plan to acquire competence.
- Social workers should always plan to be proficient in all practice, remain current in emerging knowledge, critically review professional literature, and participate in continuing education regarding social work practice and ethics.
- Social workers should utilize recognized knowledge and ethics in the field of social work as the basis for practice.

4.02 DISCRIMINATION

Social workers must not support or practice any type of discrimination based on race, ethnicity, national origin, sexual identification and expression, political and religious affiliations, immigration status, and differences in abilities.

4.03 PRIVATE CONDUCT

Social workers' private conduct should not interfere with their ability to carry out their professional duties.

4.04 DISHONESTY, FRAUD, AND DECEPTION

Social workers should not engage in or condone any dishonest, fraudulent, or deceptive practices.

4.05 IMPAIRMENT

- Social workers should avoid letting their personal, legal, psychosocial, mental health, or substance abuse problems interfere with their fulfillment of professional responsibilities.
- Social workers whose personal, legal, psychosocial, mental health, or substance abuse problems interfere with their fulfillment of professional responsibilities should seek professional help and take corrective action (reduce workload, terminate their practice, or take any necessary actions) to protect the interests of clients and other interested parties.

4.06 MISREPRESENTATION

- Social workers should keep statements and actions carried out as private individuals separate from what they do as social workers representing the profession, professional organization, or place of employment.
- Social workers should take care when representing a professional social work organization to reflect the official and authorized positions of the organization.
- Social workers should ensure that any representations to others (clients, agencies, public) regarding professional qualifications, accomplishments, credentials, and services are accurate. Social workers should claim only those professional credentials to which they are entitled and should correct any misunderstandings related to their credentials.

4.07 SOLICITATIONS

- Social workers should not attempt to solicit potential clients who may be vulnerable and easily influenced, manipulated, or coerced.
- Social workers should not attempt to solicit testimonials or endorsements from current clients or others who may be vulnerable and easily influenced.

4.08 ACKNOWLEDGING CREDIT

- Social workers should take credit (including authorship) only for work they are personally responsible for or that they contributed to.
- Social workers should be open about the work and contributions of others.

219

SOCIAL WORKERS' ETHICAL RESPONSIBILITIES TO THE PROFESSION

5.01 INTEGRITY OF THE PROFESSION

- Social workers should strive to maintain, refine, and advocate for high practice standards.
- Social workers should take steps to advance and spread the social work profession and its values, ethics, and knowledge through study, research, discussion, and appropriate criticism.
- Social workers should lend their time and expertise to support activities, such as teaching, researching, consulting, providing testimony, giving presentations, and participating in professional organizations that promote respect for the social work profession.
- Social workers should freely share their knowledge and contribute to social work literature to broaden and spread the knowledge base of the profession.
- Social workers should actively prevent social work practice that is unauthorized or unqualified.

5.02 EVALUATION AND RESEARCH

- Social workers should oversee and evaluate policies, programs, and interventions.
- Social workers should further efforts to contribute to knowledge.
- Social workers should carefully evaluate emerging knowledge and apply evidence derived from evaluation and research to their practice.
- Social workers must consider the ramifications of their evaluation and research, and should ensure guidelines are followed to consult with institutional review boards and protect participants in research.
- Social workers should obtain voluntary and written informed consent that covers specific details about a project, including risk and benefits, from participants for their evaluation and research. They should also avoid any type of coercion or implied penalty for declining to participate.
- Social workers should ensure that participants utilizing technology in evaluation and research give informed consent from any such use, are able to use the technology, and have an alternative available.
- Social workers who engage in evaluation and research with participants who are unable to give informed consent should provide explanations proportional to their understanding and seek informed consent from an appropriate proxy.
- Social workers should avoid carrying out evaluation and research that does not include consent, such as through observations or archival research, unless no acceptable alternative is available and the research can be justified through diligent review.
- Social workers should ensure that any participants in evaluation and research are aware of their right to withdraw at any time without suffering any negative consequences.
- Social workers should ensure that any participants in evaluation and research are provided with appropriate supportive service.
- Social workers should ensure that any participants in evaluation and research have protection from any type of distress or danger.
- Social workers who are evaluating services should share collected information only with those who have a legitimate professional interest.
- Social workers should ensure that the anonymity and confidentiality of any participants in evaluation and research are protected and that participants are aware of limits to confidentiality, measures taken to ensure confidentiality, and plans for destruction of records with research data.
- Social workers should ensure that the identification of participants in evaluation and research is omitted from records unless participants have consented to disclosure.
- Social workers should ensure that all evaluation and research findings are accurately reported in published data, should correct any errors, and should avoid any falsifications or fabrications.
- Social workers who engage in evaluation and research should avoid any conflicts or dual relationships with participants and should alert participants to the possibility of conflicts of interest and strive to resolve any such issues.
- Social workers should strive to educate themselves and others about responsible research practices.

Social Workers' Ethical Responsibilities to the Broader Society

6.01 Social Welfare

Social workers should advocate for society's general welfare through betterment efforts ranging from community to international levels and by encouraging the development of all individuals and environments. Social workers should promote the improvement of living conditions so that people have access to basic needs; values (socioeconomic, political, and cultural); and institutions that support social justice.

6.02 Public Participation

Social workers should encourage public participation in the development of social policies and institutions.

6.03 Public Emergencies

Social workers should, during public emergencies, be prepared to provide any appropriate professional services needed.

6.04 Social and Political Action

- Social workers should actively engage in social and political actions to spread the access that people have to the elements of society that allow them to meet basic needs (resources, jobs, services, opportunities). Social workers should be cognizant of how politics affect practice and should actively promote policies that improve the lives of people, allowing them to meet basic needs and promoting social justice.
- Social workers should take actions to ensure that all people have access to expanded choices and opportunities, especially those who are vulnerable or otherwise disadvantaged or oppressed and easily exploited.
- Social workers should highlight the importance of social and cultural diversity and promote policies and practices that increase respect for this diversity and expand knowledge about culture. Social workers should support policies and programs that demonstrate cultural competence and equality and protect social justice.
- Social workers should take steps to fight against the discrimination and exploitation of any person, group, or class because of personal, legal, psychosocial, mental health, or substance abuse problems.

Record-Keeping and Documentation

PRINCIPLES OF DOCUMENTATION AND RECORD MANAGEMENT

All records of social work should be considered legal documents and stored in locked cabinets (if paper) or secured electronically (if digital). Records should never be placed so that unauthorized individuals can gain access. Records should be organized according to established guidelines so that information is easily accessible. **Principles of documentation** include the following:

- Avoid the use of jargon and slang
- Ensure that each page of the record contains the client's name to ensure it is in the correct record
- Document all important information so that other case workers could assume care of the client
- Leave no lines blank in documents and mark errors by drawing one line through the text and initialing the entry (in paper documenting)
- Report the source of all information
- Avoid abbreviations that are not approved
- Spell check electronic entries
- Describe observations (flat affect, lethargic, monotone) and avoid judgment and diagnoses (depressed)
- Use appropriate coding and descriptions for billing and reporting purposes

ELEMENTS OF SOCIAL WORKER'S CLIENT RECORDS

The elements of a social worker's client records include:

- **Face page**: Demographic information
- **Family tree**: Information about members, such as profession and history of drug abuse
- **Eco map**: Diagram of resources, such as neighbors, community, friends, extended family
- **Psychological report**
- **Court orders**: Such as termination of parental rights (TPR)
- **Education records**: Schools attended, grades, disciplinary actions, attendance
- List of **goals** and **plan of care**
- **Monthly progress reports**: From meetings with child and foster parent or caregiver
- **Family support team (FST) reports**: From meeting with interested parties to evaluate child's progress in meeting goals (usually submitted to the court)
- **Permanency plan review team reports**: From meeting (usually every 6 months) with all interested parties (parents, foster parents, CASA workers, social workers, supervisor etc.) to determine progress and the need for any modification in the plan (usually submitted to court)
- Additional reports, such as **CASA (court appointed special advocate) reports**
- **Financial records**: Such as social security or death benefits
- **Discharge summary**

FORMAL RECORDS

Formal records created by social workers may include the following:

Type of Record	Details Included
Proposals	A proposal is a formal request to develop a project, buy equipment, or suggest a course of action, such as a solution to a problem. An informal proposal may be in the form of a letter. A grant proposal usually requires a specific format explaining the need and the plan for use of the grant and may be quite detailed.
Letters	A letter is a formal written or typed form of communication that is sent by mail to another individual, such as letters requesting information or letters of recommendation.
Brochures and pamphlets	Social workers may develop educational brochures and pamphlets about services or areas of concern (such as drug abuse).
Reports	Social workers may do various types of reports, including the assessment report, reports to the court, summary reports, and discharge reports. The reports often follow a prescribed format.
Evaluations	Social workers may carry out evaluations as part of progress reports for clients and may evaluate programs for effectiveness. Social workers may also carry out supervisory evaluations of other staff members.

CASE RECORDING AND DOCUMENTATION PRACTICES

Different agencies have different requirements and processes for **case recordings** used in supervision and evaluation. The traditional method was audio recordings, but with technological advances, video recording has become completely accessible. Clients should sign informed consent and confidentiality forms allowing supervisors to view their sessions for training purposes, and there should be policies in place for video storage methods, the length of time videos are kept, how and when they will be destroyed, and other considerations affecting confidentiality.

IMPORTANCE OF FILING IN RECORD-KEEPING

Keeping correspondence in paper or digital files is another important part of record-keeping and can impact clients' lives as well as the credibility of the agency. **Files** also serve an important purpose in the current employment environment where social workers may change agencies and need to come rapidly to a general overview of a client's past, perhaps receiving service through several social workers over a period of years. Letters communicating with other agencies can help the new social worker on the scene form an impression of the kind of help clients have received from that agency, even when case workers have come and gone.

RECORD-KEEPING REQUIREMENTS

Each agency has its own particular **reporting and record-keeping requirements**, which will vary by location, population served, funding bodies, governmental oversight, boards of committees, and even technological considerations. In general, issues of confidentiality and informed consent will be similar across agencies, and the age and intellectual capacity of clients will also influence reporting requirements. Social workers whose schedules take them out into communities may keep a work journal during the day, reporting their activities to their agency upon returning to the office. In the case of journaling, the social worker should protect the client's confidentiality by omitting identifying information.

Professional Development and the Use of Self

CORE SOCIAL WORK VALUES

According to the NASW, the core social work values are as follows:

- Service
- Social justice
- Dignity and worth of the person
- Importance of human relationships
- Integrity
- Competence

CORE SOCIAL WORK GOALS

Core social work goals held by the major social work theorists are to help clients:

- Improve social functioning
- Resolve problems
- Achieve desired change
- Meet self-defined goals

SOCIAL WORK ROLES

Social workers may serve in many roles, including the following:

Role	Responsibilities
Administrator	Evaluating and developing policies and managing programs
Advocate	Defending, representing, and supporting vulnerable clients
Broker	Providing resource and service linkages to individuals in need
Case manager	Connecting, coordinating, and monitoring client services
Counselor	Exploring, treating, and resolving client, family, or group issues and problems
Educator and teacher	Researching and providing educational information, organizing and leading classes, teaching knowledge, skills, and behaviors that facilitate successful coping, growth, and relationships
Policy maker or lobbyist	Working to identify, understand, and resolve problems in local communities or in society as a whole by garnering support from key interest groups to marshal and wield influence for positive and necessary change

STAGES OF PROFESSIONAL DEVELOPMENT

Professional development is supported by education, conferences, and practice that help increase and refine skills and knowledge of the field. Activities of professional development include mentoring and coaching, supervision, consultation, assistance with technical matters, and interdisciplinary collaboration with other communities of care.

The **steps of professional development** begin with the orientation process. Social workers tend to work autonomously but with regular supervision. Teamwork follows, with workers moving from independent operations to working as part of a group. Later career development includes specialization and then acting as a mentor or supervisor oneself.

PERFORMANCE APPRAISAL OF PROFESSIONAL SOCIAL WORKERS

Performance appraisals may vary from self-assessment, to narrative assessment, to checklists, and assessments based on outcomes related to a list of goals. Despite the varied forms of appraisal, basic skills are almost always evaluated:

Skill Evaluated	Focuses of Evaluation
Work-associated skills	The ability to carry out the processes and procedures of social work, including applying appropriate interventions and dealing effectively with client problems and concerns.
Organizational skills	The ability to manage time effectively and carry out job responsibilities in a timely and efficient manner.
Leadership and management skills	The ability to serve as a model for others, to influence other professionals, and to lead and supervise effectively.
Cultural competence	An awareness of different cultures (including customs and religions) and understanding of cultural sensitivity when dealing with others.
Communication skills	The ability to document and code correctly, and to communicate effectively with co-workers and clients. Ability to use conflict resolution strategies and to accommodate various points of view.

TIME MANAGEMENT APPROACHES

Approaches that the social worker can utilize for time management include the following:

- **Planning ahead**: Maintaining a master schedule that lists visits and meetings
- Keeping **schedule** up to date on a daily basis
- **Utilizing color coding**: Using colored stickers or pens to indicate different needs, such as red stickers for those things that require urgent attention
- **Scheduling a time to return calls**: Making calls first thing in the morning so that any alterations needed in the schedule can be made promptly
- Utilizing time management or case management **software**
- Making appropriate **referrals**
- Preparing **reports** (such as those submitted to the court) in advance, avoiding last minute rush
- Making **to-do lists** or **action plans**
- Creating **templates** for frequently used forms and letters
- **Filing** immediately and throwing out unnecessary paperwork
- Utilizing **GPS and mapping software** to plan routes of visits
- **Prioritizing** work
- Avoiding all **procrastination**

SOCIAL WORKER SELF-CARE
BURNOUT AND SECONDARY TRAUMA

Burnout, a response to ongoing stress, is a problem pervasive in social work. Social workers often have excessive workloads and work long hours, often including unwanted overtime because of inadequate staffing. Social workers may feel that they have little control over their work and do not receive sufficient reward or support. They may also feel that social workers are often treated unfairly or are victims of bullying in the workplace. Stress tends to build up over time, interfering with the individual's ability to concentrate and to carry out duties effectively. Additionally, dealing with clients' trauma may lead to **secondary trauma** with signs similar to PTSD: nightmares, insomnia, or anxiety, which increase the risk of burnout. Stages of stress leading to burnout include:

1. Fight or flight response: Withdrawal, discord
2. Emotional reaction: Anger, shock, surprise

3. Negative thinking: Despair, anger, depression, anxiety
4. Physical reaction: Headaches, GI upset, backache
5. No change in stressor or person: Increased stress
6. Burnout

Social workers may need to negotiate a smaller workload, utilize time management strategies, take small periodic breaks, and participate in stress management programs.

COMPASSION FATIGUE

Compassion fatigue can occur when people overly identify with the pain and suffering of others and begin to exhibit signs of stress as a result. These people are often empathetic, tend to place the needs of others above their own, and are motivated by the need to help others. Indications include:

- Blaming others and complaining excessively
- Isolating oneself from others and having trouble concentrating
- Exhibiting compulsive activities (gambling, drinking)
- Having nightmares, sleeping poorly, and exhibiting a change in appetite
- Exhibiting sadness or apathy
- Denying any problems and having high expectations of self and others
- Having trouble concentrating
- Questioning spiritual beliefs, losing faith
- Exhibiting stress disorders: tachycardia, headaches, insomnia, pain

Social workers who exhibit compassion fatigue may need to take a break from work in order to recover some sense of self and may benefit from stress management programs, cognitive behavioral therapy, relaxation and visualization exercises, and physical exercise.

Chapter Quiz

Ready to see how well you retained what you just read? Scan the QR code to go directly to the chapter quiz interface for this study guide. If you're using a computer, simply visit the bonus page at **mometrix.com/bonus948/swclinical** and click the Chapter Quizzes link.

LCSW Practice Test #1

1. Which of the following population groups BEST fits the following description?

Many within this population are able to fully function with little support, whereas some need extensive support and care. Approximately 30% or more of individuals in this population suffer from a mental health disorder. They commonly live with relatives. Chronic health problems often go undiagnosed for these individuals.

   a. Youth in foster care
   b. People with intellectual and developmental disabilities (IDD)
   c. The elderly population
   d. Immigrants

2. When comparing the experience of male and female individuals within the criminal justice system, which of the following statements is NOT true?

   a. Women are more likely than men to be incarcerated in jail rather than prison.
   b. The female offender population is increasing at a faster rate.
   c. Males have higher rates of mental illness than females.
   d. Women are more likely to meet drug dependence or abuse disorder criteria.

3. A school social worker is scheduled to see a 9-year-old boy regarding disruptive behavior in the classroom. Rather than begin with an office visit, the counselor directly observes his behavior in the classroom. There the social worker noted the following: he seemed to constantly fidget and squirm in his seat; he talked nonstop; he was frequently out of his seat, running, touching, and playing with anything and everything he could reach. The teacher's efforts to quiet him appeared to be forgotten almost instantly. When an art period was begun, which engaged most children, he still had difficulty as he was easily distracted and seemed to switch constantly from one activity to another. He appeared unable to slow down long enough to receive even simple and clear instructions. The few moments he was quiet, he seemed lost in daydreaming, staring out the classroom windows. The most likely diagnosis for this child is:

   a. Attention-deficit/hyperactivity disorder (ADHD)
   b. Conduct disorder
   c. Obsessive-compulsive disorder
   d. Oppositional defiant disorder

4. Which of the following is NOT predictive of the mental health status of LGBTQ individuals in midlife?

   a. Self-transcendence
   b. The degree to which they have disclosed their LGBTQ identity
   c. Finance-related anxiety
   d. Body shame

227

5. A social worker is seeing a client who has previously been diagnosed with heroin use disorder. He has not met the criteria for substance use disorder, except for craving, for 5 months. He lives at his mother's home and is using a methadone treatment program. He would be classified as:

    a. Early remission
    b. Sustained remission
    c. Not in remission
    d. Early remission, controlled environment

6. Which of the following is NOT true of the task-centered practice model?

    a. Task-centered practice can be used as a stand-alone treatment or in conjunction with other treatment approaches.
    b. The client and social worker first develop a shared understanding of the problem and its root causes.
    c. By the end of each session, the client must explicitly agree to complete the planned tasks.
    d. Tasks may be developed for the social worker or others to complete, in addition to the client.

7. The following definition is the MOST accurate when describing interventions based on which theory? "The client's past experiences are used to understand and effect change upon their current thoughts and behaviors."

    a. Psychodynamic theory
    b. Cognitive theories
    c. Family systems theory
    d. Strengths-based practice theories

8. George, a middle-aged male, informs his social worker that he has begun using marijuana frequently with his coworkers after hours. He reports having occasionally used this drug when he was younger, but he had stopped use until recently. George started a new job 3 months ago, after being laid off from his previous position, which he had kept for 10 years. He denies any physical ailments. George's mother abused substances when he was a child, but he no longer has any contact with her. George says that his new job has been stressful but he has been finding ways to cope. What approach should the social worker use to understand the many factors involved in his situation?

    a. Cognitive behavioral therapy
    b. Biopsychosocial approach
    c. Psychodynamic therapy
    d. Biomedical approach

9. Which of the following statements is TRUE regarding co-occurring disorders?

    a. Approximately 40% of adolescents with substance use disorders also have a mental health disorder.
    b. With co-occurring substance use and mental health disorders, the mental health disorder occurs first in approximately two-thirds of individuals.
    c. Only 25% of adults with co-occurring mental illness and substance use disorders receive treatment for both disorders.
    d. One in four individuals with a mental disorder causing serious impairment also has a substance use disorder.

10. The MOST important protective factor for lesbian, gay, bisexual, transgender, and queer or questioning (LGBTQ) youth is:

    a. Family understanding
    b. Family acceptance
    c. Family education
    d. Family cohesion

11. A single mother and a teenage son present for relationship problems. The son is actively defiant of instructions, argues regularly over minor requests, and can be spiteful and resentful over normal parenting efforts. School performance is marginal, but only one unexcused absence has occurred during the current school year, which is nearing its end. The most appropriate diagnosis would be:

    a. Oppositional defiant disorder
    b. Conduct disorder
    c. Intermittent explosive disorder
    d. Parent-child relational problem

12. Which of the following BEST describes the role of the social worker in solution-focused brief therapy (SFBT)?

    a. To ask questions that reflect the client's language and values in order to point the client in the direction of the solution
    b. To notice evidence of client values and skills and use reflective statements and questions to explore them with the client
    c. To identify what has worked in the past and to help the client apply that solution to the current problem
    d. To provide feedback and suggestions to strengthen the client's ideas

13. An adolescent client has been referred to a social worker for mental health support. To understand the client's history before the appointment, the social worker should:

    a. Schedule a phone call with the parents to get their views on the issue.
    b. Review documentation provided by the family, which may include medical, school, or legal records.
    c. Call the referring professional for further information on why the client requires additional support.
    d. Choose not to review any documentation so as not to influence their professional opinion on the issue.

14. A lesbian couple has decided to start couples therapy to better their 4-year marriage. They met in college and dated for 3 years before deciding to get married. They have some family support but have experienced most of their extended family members excluding them because of their sexual orientation. When asked what they would like to improve during therapy, the couple begins to show visible signs of frustration with each other. The social worker cannot get either person to agree on a treatment goal. What is the NEXT step in beginning therapy with this couple?

    a. Provide examples of common goals that other couples have used in their therapy to help the clients choose what feels right for them.
    b. Support the couple in determining what their long-term goals are in their marriage.
    c. Offer individual therapy to each person so they each can feel heard and supported in their own ways.
    d. Let each person choose a treatment goal that she would like her spouse to work on.

15. A social worker wants to gather data demonstrating the efficient use of funding for a homelessness prevention program. Which of the following is the BEST set of data to gather for this purpose?

    a. Total number of households with eviction prevented and average cost per household
    b. Total number of individuals on the homeless shelter waiting list who were established in new housing without a shelter stay, and the average cost per individual
    c. Total number of households maintained in own housing or established in new housing without a shelter stay, and the average cost per household
    d. Average cost per household served compared with the estimated cost per day of the homeless shelter (to demonstrate the cost savings)

16. Which of the following is a primary difference between a biopsychosocial assessment and a mental status exam?

  a. The mental status exam includes objective and subjective information, whereas the biopsychosocial assessment only includes information obtained from the client or from other appropriate sources.

  b. The components of a biopsychosocial assessment are documented in clearly described sections, with the results of the mental status exam included but not in a specific section.

  c. The biopsychosocial assessment is focused on the development of the client's presenting problems, whereas the mental status exam provides an account of the client's current functioning.

  d. Much of the mental status exam can be completed by observation, whereas the biopsychosocial assessment requires the social worker to ask specific questions.

17. Brad, a 40-year-old, has recently left the military and returned to civilian life. Brad is struggling to reconnect with his wife and two children since returning home. He feels unprepared for the emotional needs of his children and states that keeping up with the day-to-day tasks of family life is difficult. He is unsure of how to fit back into his previous roles outside of the military. The social worker should begin by:

  a. Assuring the client that these feelings are normal and that no therapy is required

  b. Explaining to the client what the symptoms of depression include

  c. Exploring the client's accomplishments in the military

  d. Asking the client to determine the goal of therapy

18. During an initial assessment with a child regarding a report of possible parental neglect, a social worker receives the following answer: "My mom's name is Joan Smith. She is a good mom. She takes care of me. She is a good mom. I like to spend time with her." As the assessment continues, the child continues to repeat this answer in varying ways. What can the social worker conclude from this type of response?

  a. The child is giving a scripted response, and there are underlying concerns of abuse or neglect.

  b. Nothing can be assumed from this information.

  c. The child loves and cares for his mother, and his mother loves and cares for him.

  d. The child is afraid of his mother but is unsure if he can trust the social worker.

19. A social worker is seeing a 16-year-old youth who has, for the past year, been losing his temper frequently, is regularly argumentative with adults, often refuses to follow direct requests, is easily annoyed, and routinely uses blaming to escape responsibility. Approximately four months ago he was caught in a single episode of shoplifting. The most appropriate diagnosis for this youth is:

  a. Oppositional defiant disorder

  b. Conduct disorder

  c. Intermittent explosive disorder

  d. Antisocial personality disorder

20. When completing a comprehensive geriatric assessment, which variable is the MOST important to assess in order to understand the full scope of an individual's functional ability?

  a. Instrumental activities of daily living (IADLs)

  b. Mental health diagnosis

  c. The home and community environment

  d. Availability of family and/or caregiver support

21. Which treatment is MOST effective for obsessive compulsive-disorder (OCD) in adults?

  a. A combination of psychotherapy and medication

  b. A twice-daily medication regime of 5 mg of Zoloft

  c. Thought-stopping techniques through cognitive behavioral therapy

  d. Brain mapping and neurofeedback

22. SCM and TLM emphasize many social work values. The more recently developed Social Action, Leadership, and Transformation (SALT) model applies which social work ethical principle more explicitly than either SCM or TLM?

   a. Social workers push for social justice.
   b. Social workers' primary goal is to help people in need and to address social problems.
   c. Social workers recognize the central importance of human relationships.
   d. Social workers advocate for the rights and needs of marginalized people groups.

23. At a transitional family shelter, a newly arrived mother and her three children are being reviewed during an interdisciplinary team consultation. The team consists of the social worker, a housing specialist, and an education and employment specialist. The mother lost her job in another city and was attempting to find work in a larger city. They were living in her car when it was burgled of all possessions. All seem unwell and congested. The oldest child, a 4-year-old boy, has severe asthma and needs a sheltered setting. The 3-year-old girl seems expressively vacant and emotionally detached. The 9-month-old female infant is clearly hungry and lacks diapers and other basic necessities. Food is being obtained for them all. Prior to presenting to the agency director, the FIRST social work step should be to:

   a. Complete a psychosocial assessment for mental health issues.
   b. Inquire about the availability of extended family support.
   c. Obtain clean, warmer clothing from a local clothes closet.
   d. Promptly refer the asthmatic boy to a medical doctor.

24. As part of a pending disability application, a social worker meets with the client. The client voices complaints about significant chronic back and shoulder pain, which is the basis of the claim. During the course of the in-home assessment, the social worker notes that the individual is able to bend down to move and pick things up, and is able to reach over her head into an upper cabinet—all without apparent difficulty or complaints of pain. The most appropriate determination would be:

   a. Illness anxiety disorder
   b. Malingering
   c. Factitious disorder
   d. Somatic symptom disorder

25. A middle-aged female is attending her biweekly therapy appointment with a social worker. She is struggling with social anxiety disorder, but she has made a goal to meet with one friend once a month. She has a date set with a friend for this weekend and is experiencing increased anxiety as the date gets closer. Which of the following interventions would be the BEST option to provide the client?

   a. Provide the client with two articles about social anxiety disorder to read and learn more about her disorder as a means to manage anxiety through client education.
   b. Provide the client with a handout to complete at home when feeling increased anxiety as a means to manage her anxiety.
   c. Provide the client with time within the current session to practice reducing negative thoughts about the upcoming meeting with her friend.
   d. Provide the client with a list of different coping skills for her to try on her own when she faces anxiety prior to meeting with her friend.

26. A social worker receives a mental health referral for a client that speaks Nepali. The Nepali community is very small in the social worker's service area. The social worker's supervisor mentioned at the last team meeting to be very careful with scheduling interpreters because they are very costly. What is MOST important for the social worker to do when planning interpretation services for the intake session?

    a. Explain to the client the importance of keeping his scheduled appointment or calling the social worker to cancel because an interpreter has been arranged.

    b. Ask the client if he has a family member or friend that could interpret because this may be more comfortable for the client than a stranger.

    c. Find out if the interpreters all live locally or if some live in other cities.

    d. Set a reminder to confirm the appointment with the client 48 hours ahead of time, so the interpreter can be canceled if the client cannot keep the appointment.

27. A social worker's agency intake paperwork does not provide space for a client to specify their preferred pronouns. Which is the BEST microlevel intervention for the social worker to give clients the opportunity to provide this important information?

    a. The social worker should work with the intake supervisor to update the intake forms.

    b. When introducing oneself to a new client, the social worker should share their pronouns, and then ask what the client's pronouns are.

    c. The social worker should make their own intake form that provides space for the client to share their pronouns.

    d. The social worker should submit feedback to the human resources department that agency policy needs to be updated so that space for pronouns is included on agency forms.

28. An 18-year-old client presents with an aloof manner that is indifferent and withdrawn. He has no friends and spends most of his time outside of school building model airplanes. He does not fit the criteria for autism disorders. His mother tells the social worker that he's always been "different; impossible to talk to; not a bad boy, just not really there, somehow." What is the most likely DSM-5-TR diagnosis for this young man?

    a. Schizotypal personality disorder

    b. Schizophreniform disorder

    c. Schizoid personality disorder

    d. Highly introverted personality

29. A 52-year-old man has been referred to see a social worker for "family and work problems." Two months ago, he lost his job as an executive in a major corporation, and has not found new work. On intake, the social worker discovers his drinking has increased, and he reports feeling depressed most days. He can't seem to enjoy doing anything, not even golf, which he used to love. Rather, all he can seem to do is sleep and "sit around the house." He feels useless, empty, and helpless to change his situation. He has tried reading the want ads, but he just can't seem to focus. He's gained over 18 pounds. He then adds, "Sometimes I seem to hear voices, telling me I'm just 'no good,' and that things will never get better. When that happens, I try to plug my ears, but it doesn't help. Only booze seems to get the voices to stop. Do you think I'm going crazy?" What is the client's probable primary diagnosis?

    a. Major depressive disorder

    b. Major depressive disorder with psychotic features

    c. Alcohol use disorder

    d. Alcohol-induced depressive disorder

30. An elderly man has been living in a low-income apartment complex for 10 years. His landlord has just increased his rent with less than 30 days' notice and has refused to fix the faulty heating. The tenant will not be able to afford his new rent and his medications. What is the BEST course of action?

   a. Set him up with an elder advocate to ensure that the landlord is properly managing the apartment units and tenant needs, per his lease agreement.
   b. Talk with the landlord to request a pause on the increase in rent.
   c. Find discounted or generic versions of the same medications that the client is taking now.
   d. Connect with financial resources that can assist him with a one-time payment toward his rent.

31. The update to the *Diagnostic and Statistical Manual of Mental Disorders, Fifth Edition* (DSM-5) included major changes to categories and classifications. Which of the following is NOT a DSM-5 category?

   a. Sleep-wake disorders
   b. Sexual dysfunctions
   c. Pervasive developmental disorders
   d. Gender dysphoria

32. Which of the following skills are the MOST important for community social workers?

   a. Facilitation and participatory planning
   b. Communication and agenda setting
   c. Building consensus and research
   d. Facilitation and research

33. A social worker has been called to evaluate a 23-year-old man in a hospital emergency room. He presented with fear that he was having a heart attack, but medical staff have ruled this out following laboratory and clinical testing. He notes that his symptoms have subsided, but that when he arrived, his heart was pounding, and he was tremulous, gasping for breath, and had significant tightness in his chest. He recognized the symptoms as being cardiac in nature, as his father died recently from a heart attack when similar symptoms were present. After lengthy discussion, he revealed that the symptoms had been coming and going rapidly over the last month, and that he had actually been sleeping in his car outside the hospital for the last several days to ensure he could get help when needed. The symptoms struck and peaked quickly (within minutes), leaving him fearful that help would not be available if he didn't remain close. These symptoms MOST closely resemble:

   a. Anxiety disorder due to a medical condition
   b. Generalized anxiety disorder
   c. Acute stress disorder
   d. Panic disorder

34. A couple presenting for counseling evaluation reveals that the wife comes from a dysfunctional, neglectful, alcoholic home and has little trust or tolerance for relationships. Consequently, their marriage is marred by constant arguing and distrust, frequent demands that he leave, episodes of impulsive violence, alternating with brief periods of excessive over-valuation (stating that he is the "best thing that ever happened" to her, "too good" for her, etc.). Which is the most likely diagnosis?

   a. Antisocial personality disorder
   b. Histrionic personality disorder
   c. Borderline personality disorder
   d. Narcissistic personality disorder

35. The below definition describes the coping strategies used in which of the following settings?

> A unique set of psychological adaptations that result in a chronic biopsychosocial state characterized by anxiety, depression, hypervigilance, muted affect, social withdrawal, and dependence on external controls.

    a. An intimate relationship with a violent partner
    b. A correctional facility
    c. A home with a violent parent
    d. A school in which chronic bullying occurs

36. A social worker is working with a couple to address concerns with their relationship. One partner says, "I am so tired of him misunderstanding me. He doesn't listen!" The other reports frustration that he cannot trust his partner. The social worker notices something during the first session that could be contributing to both of these concerns. What has the social worker most likely observed?

    a. Multitasking during the conversation
    b. Changes in tone of voice
    c. Lack of congruence
    d. Limited vocabulary

37. Which of the following strategies would NOT be used by community social workers guided by conflict theory?

    a. Consensus building during a meeting with city leaders and residents
    b. Supporting efforts to pass citywide caps on annual rent increases
    c. Organizing a protest at the city hall
    d. Inviting city leaders to participate in a poverty simulation

38. A study attempts to measure the efficacy of a new antidepressant medication. A "control" group of depression sufferers will receive only a placebo, while an "intervention" group will receive the new medication. In this study, the "null hypothesis" would state the following:

    a. The intervention group will report fewer symptoms of depression than the control group.
    b. The control group will report fewer symptoms of depression than the intervention group.
    c. Both the control group and the intervention group will report fewer depressive symptoms.
    d. There shall be no measurable difference in depression symptom reporting between the control group and the intervention group.

39. A client is brought into a county mental health clinic by law enforcement. He has no personal identification, and cannot recall any personally identifying information. This forgetfulness appears to be genuine, not due to any threat or allegation of any kind. He does have receipts and other papers on his person that indicate he was recently many hundreds of miles away, but he cannot confirm or deny this. There is no history of head trauma, substance abuse, or prior mental illness that can be ascertained. The MOST appropriate initial working diagnosis would be:

    a. Dissociative identity disorder
    b. Dissociative amnesia with dissociative fugue
    c. Depersonalization/derealization disorder
    d. Dissociative trance

40. A director of a case management agency has noticed that the case managers directly supporting clients have had feelings of being isolated from their coworkers during the COVID-19 pandemic. Many of the recently onboarded case managers are unsure of how to problem-solve common situations. What type of supervision would be BEST for those case managers?

   a. Individual supervision would provide the opportunity to address each unique situation according to each case manager's strengths.
   b. Peer supervision would allow all case managers to benefit from each other's questions and problem-solving skills.
   c. Interdisciplinary supervision would provide the case managers with different professional insight regarding their concerns.
   d. Dual supervision would permit the case managers to have more than one supervisor to give constant access to a higher-ranking professional to help problem-solve.

41. At all stages of social work practice, supervision is needed in order to accomplish which one of the following goals?

   a. Prevent social worker burnout.
   b. Improve the quality of clinical practice.
   c. Reduce the social worker's liability.
   d. Maintain the social worker's license.

42. Which one of the following variables has the greatest impact on the development of children who are separated from their parents?

   a. Trauma
   b. Attachment
   c. Brain chemistry
   d. Mental health

43. While reviewing the client documentation for a staff member, a social work supervisor notices that the counseling sessions completed with Stacey, a 17-year-old female, are longer and more frequent when compared with the rest of the supervisee's cases. When asked to describe the counseling sessions with Stacey, the supervisee says, "Stacey is great. She reminds me of what I was like at her age and loves to talk with me. It's great to give her the support I wish I would have had at age 17!" If the supervisor wants to better understand the length and frequency of Stacey's sessions, which of the following questions would be the MOST helpful to ask next?

   a. How have you provided Stacey with support?
   b. What has Stacey been learning and doing to achieve the goals on her individual service plan?
   c. What strategies have you used to maintain appropriate boundaries with Stacey?
   d. Why are you meeting with Stacey more than with your other clients?

44. A client wishes to make it a goal to be reunited with his children after a history of addiction. Which one of the following options BEST embodies a specific, measurable, attainable, relevant, and time-based (SMART) goal for this client?

   a. I will schedule visits with my children on a regular basis to increase our connection.
   b. I will call my children more often over the next 3 months.
   c. I want to be reunited with my children by December 25.
   d. I will visit my children twice per week over the next 3 months.

45. In a neonatal unit, a prematurely born infant boy has been receiving support until ready for discharge home. The hospital social worker meets with the parents to discuss discharge planning. The parents are excited and nervous to bring him home. During a follow-up call 2 weeks later, the parents report issues with the infant's sleep and constant crying. The pediatrician has been consulted, and no medical issues have been identified. How can the hospital social worker help at this time?

    a. The hospital social worker cannot assist with additional support due to the infant being discharged.
    b. The hospital social worker can provide a therapeutic relationship to help the parents discuss their concerns and problems.
    c. The hospital social worker can assist with making referrals to appropriate providers, such as mental health and occupational therapists.
    d. The hospital social worker cannot assist with support because this situation is outside of the scope of practice.

46. A 5-year-old kindergartener who was recently diagnosed with autism spectrum disorder has been enrolled in intellectual/developmental disability support through his local community mental health organization. During the intake process, the boy's father laments over the loss of a "normal" future for his son and relates the major anxiety that he has experienced since his son's diagnosis. The intellectual/developmental disability social worker sees that the father is struggling with accepting his son's diagnosis. The father should be referred for:

    a. Cognitive behavioral therapy
    b. Educational handouts to increase his understanding of autism spectrum disorder
    c. Family counseling to help process his emotions regarding his son's diagnosis
    d. Grief counseling

47. Simon is 66 years old and was recently ordered by the court to attend counseling for an outburst in a grocery store, where he threw a can of beans at the clerk for being too slow in ringing up his purchases. His wife attends the first session as well, and although he insists his memory is "as good as it ever was," she shakes her head. He seems distracted and angry; she placates him, but he lashes out verbally. When the caseworker asks her if anything has changed recently, she tells him that Simon has always been a good-natured, easygoing man, but that lately he has been "difficult." As they are leaving, Simon, looking puzzled, says, "I don't even know why we're here."

What is the FIRST possible diagnosis a caseworker would consider in this case?

    a. Alcoholism
    b. Alzheimer's disease
    c. Bipolar disorder
    d. Impulse-control disorder

48. A client reports having increased racing thoughts, less sleep, and increased motivation to complete short-term goals over the past week and a half. The client denies any substance use. Based on the client's likely diagnosis, what medication would assist with mood stabilization?

    a. Depakote
    b. Xanax
    c. Klonopin
    d. Zoloft

49. A medical social worker sees a copy of the client's karyotype test in the medical record. What will the social worker be able to learn from this report?

    a. Whether monosomy or trisomy has occurred
    b. The reason for the client's chromosomal abnormality
    c. The client's blood type
    d. The type of genetic mutation that the client has

50. When writing a clinical case presentation, a social worker should:

    a. Avoid using a case that is close to termination of services because there will not be time to incorporate colleagues' feedback into future treatment sessions.

    b. Only include identifying information when it is necessary to accurately understand the case.

    c. Describe successful and unsuccessful treatment strategies.

    d. Provide only a few details in each section so that colleagues have practice asking clarifying questions.

51. Which of the following is a primary prevention strategy to support healthy aging?

    a. Coordinating volunteer opportunities for elders at local schools

    b. Increasing uninsured adults' access to mental health services with a sliding scale fee

    c. Offering career change workshops and resources for employed middle-aged adults

    d. Facilitating the donation of farmers market produce to the local senior center for cooking demonstrations

52. A social worker at a mental health agency is working with an adolescent client who has had aggressive outbursts. During a regular meeting with the family, the client becomes upset and flips over his chair. What should the social worker do FIRST?

    a. The social worker should use de-escalation tactics.

    b. The social worker should leave the room and call 911.

    c. The social worker should call for help from coworkers.

    d. The social worker should request that the mother remove the adolescent from the office.

53. In addition to the digestive system, what other body systems are involved with processing and delivering nutrients throughout the body?

    a. Circulatory and lymphatic

    b. Lymphatic and endocrine

    c. Endocrine and circulatory

    d. Respiratory, endocrine, and circulatory

54. Which of the following is the MOST necessary consideration to demonstrate the impact of a community-based project?

    a. Include community members at all phases of the project.

    b. Set measurable objectives and benchmarks for the project.

    c. Research the community conditions and target problem(s).

    d. Engage local political and civic institutions.

55. In motivational interviewing, strategies that highlight a discrepancy are used to:

    a. Help the client make a decision.

    b. Build the client's confidence that they are able to make a change.

    c. Make the client aware of what they want.

    d. Increase the client's hope for change.

56. A new social worker has been working in the field for 3 months. She feels overwhelming stress from her long to-do list, which often results in her working late into the night; items are added to the list daily. She is wondering if she has chosen the wrong career path. What would be the BEST way for the social worker to manage her stress?

    a. Set boundaries that include time limits for responding to work-related requests.

    b. Self-medicate to manage her stress.

    c. Speak with her loved ones to vent her frustrations.

    d. Look for other jobs that could be a better fit.

57. Which of the following are evidence-based strategies used to reduce criminal recidivism?

   a. Cognitive behavioral therapy (CBT), post-incarceration supervision, individualized assessment, and job training programs

   b. Solution-focused therapy, housing assistance, individualized assessment, and drug courts

   c. CBT, housing assistance, drug courts, and individualized assessment

   d. Acceptance and commitment therapy (ACT), drug courts, halfway houses, and high-intensity programs for all prisoners

58. To meet criteria for diagnosis of schizophrenia, a client must have at least two out of three major symptoms for a significant amount of time during a one-month interval. Which of the following is NOT one of the three major symptoms necessary to diagnose schizophrenia?

   a. Delusions

   b. Hallucinations

   c. Disorganized speech

   d. Blunted affect

59. A medical social worker gets a call from a community social worker regarding a mutual client. The medical social worker does not have a consent on file to speak with the community social worker. What should the medical social worker do?

   a. The medical social worker should explain to the community social worker that no information can be provided without a signed consent form.

   b. The medical social worker should ask if the client gave verbal permission to communicate with the office.

   c. The medical social worker should attempt to call the client to obtain consent to speak with the community social worker.

   d. The medical social worker should answer the community social worker's questions without revealing any protected health information.

60. An elderly male who is readying himself to be placed in hospice care has invited his family to attend the intake meeting with the hospice agency. The hospice social worker visits the client at his home for the appointment. When the client decides to sign the do-not-resuscitate (DNR) form, the client's family becomes outraged. What is the MOST appropriate response from the social worker?

   a. "You do not have to decide at this time. Why don't you take the form and think it over? You can let me know how you are feeling in a few days."

   b. "I hear that your family loves you very much and is struggling to cope with your terminal diagnosis."

   c. "I understand that this is a difficult topic. You have the right to choose your medical care and create advance directives for how that care should be carried out. We will respect your wishes."

   d. "It sounds like it may be helpful to schedule a meeting with your doctor in which you could discuss which advance directives are the right choices for you."

61. A new social worker has been hired to provide telehealth services through a local community agency. The social worker is provided a laptop loaded with the electronic medical system, a computer mouse, and an Internet hot spot. The social worker enjoys visiting a local coffee shop to work during the day. During a typical day at the coffee shop, the social worker decides to leave her laptop to grab a napkin. She minimizes the electronic medical system on the laptop so she doesn't have to log back in. When she returns, her electronic medical system is open to a different chart than when she left. The social worker should:

   a. Assume that she forgot what chart she was working on before getting out of her seat.

   b. Check the browsing history on her laptop.

   c. Immediately report the Health Insurance Portability and Accountability Act of 1996 (HIPAA) violation to her supervisor.

   d. Call the client to be on the safe side because their information may have been stolen.

62. While completing an initial assessment, a social worker learns that a new client has 10 years of sobriety from drug use. The client has initiated work with the social worker to address the intense anxiety that she has experienced in the past 4 months. In order to support the client's continued sobriety and understand the interaction between her past substance use and her current symptoms of anxiety, which is the MOST important follow-up question?

    a.   Were you experiencing anxiety symptoms before you started using drugs?
    b.   How did you respond to feelings of anxiety once you were using drugs?
    c.   When you completed your drug treatment program, what new strategies did you learn to recognize and avoid anxiety triggers?
    d.   What, specifically, were the drugs(s) that you used?

63. A newly married 23-year-old woman has been referred for counseling due to her experiences of painful intercourse. She was not sexually active prior to marriage, and so there is no history to draw upon for past experiences. The problem is painful penetration, not involving spasms of the vagina but characterized by marked vaginal dryness. The proper term for her condition is:

    a.   Female sexual interest/arousal disorder
    b.   Genito-pelvic pain disorder
    c.   Substance/medication-induced sexual dysfunction
    d.   Female orgasmic disorder

64. A supervisor who oversees ten case managers is getting ready for the agency's annual audit. In order to prepare, the supervisor schedules peer reviews between coworkers. One case of each social worker is given to a coworker to review for accuracy of documentation deadlines, consent forms, and updated demographic information. The data from this peer review will inform the supervisor of all of the following EXCEPT:

    a.   The need for additional training in certain areas of service delivery in which multiple case managers lacked the appropriate documentation
    b.   The customer service ratings of each case manager
    c.   Which case managers are struggling to meet the documentation deadlines
    d.   The frequency at which consent forms are signed and returned by individuals and families

65. A social work intern is training under an experienced domestic violence social worker who is also her field instructor. The intern is helping to facilitate a women's support group. The field instructor notices the intern using incorrect language when she speaks with the support group members (e.g., calling members victims, asking why they were abused). The intern is pulled aside after the meeting to review the principles of trauma-informed care. What is the response that BEST educates and supports the intern?

    a.   "The language you were using is harmful to the recovery of the individuals who we support. We use empowering language, such as using the term *survivor* instead of the term *victim*."
    b.   "Unfortunately, due to the language that I witnessed you using today, I will need to put you on a 2-week probation from facilitating the support group. During this time, we will review the appropriate language and approaches to use when working with domestic violence survivors."
    c.   "I would like for you to spend the remainder of your shift today researching appropriate ways to interact with domestic violence survivors, including the language to use when discussing their situations."
    d.   "Let's reflect on the terms that you used today during the support group when referring to and communicating with the women. Do you feel that these terms are empowering? What other terms might be more appropriate?"

66. In a county psychiatric emergency clinic, a social worker is asked to evaluate a 19-year-old woman for unspecified psychotic behavior. She is accompanied by her parents, who brought her to the clinic. Upon contact it is noted that she is disheveled and unkempt in grooming and hygiene. In talking with the social worker, she often pauses inexplicably, rambles about something unrelated, laughs to herself, and then turns her face away. Episodically attending to the social worker, she spontaneously claims that the worker is controlling her mind, and indicates that she sees odd objects floating around the social worker. There is no recent history of substance abuse (though remotely positive for amphetamines), and her symptoms have been prominent for most of the past year, though particularly acute this evening when she attacked her mother, claiming that she was a clone and trying to pull her "real mom" out of the clone's body. The most likely diagnosis for this presentation is:

a. Bipolar disorder
b. Schizoaffective disorder
c. Schizophrenia
d. Substance-induced psychosis

67. Infant mental health services are able to provide a parent with what type of support for the child?

a. Diagnoses for early-onset mental health conditions
b. Access to psychiatric doctors who are contracted with Medicaid for psychiatric evaluations
c. Specialized childcare facilities that are trained in working with young children who have a mental health diagnosis
d. Early intervention for mental health conditions that may present at a young age

68. Rose often becomes frustrated in school, makes loud noises in public, and doesn't understand what people are saying to her. She often seems rude. To her trusted teacher, she fluently describes a life of loneliness and confusion, but even in her family, no one understands her. She cannot read as well as most adolescents in her age group, but her IQ is quite high. However, she is considering not going to college because she thinks it would be too difficult. What is MOST likely Rose's problem?

a. Rose has elective mutism
b. Rose has autism
c. Rose is hearing impaired
d. Rose is visually impaired

69. After working for 8 years with survivors of interpersonal violence, a social worker has developed a new set of strategies to help survivors prevent revictimization. When applying for a grant to fund this new program, the social worker should include which of the following?

a. A logic model
b. A strategic plan
c. A statement of impact
d. A theory of change

70. A mother schedules a new-client appointment for her preteen daughter with a social worker. The mother reports recent behavioral changes of the daughter that are difficult to manage. During the intake appointment, the client discloses that she has developed feelings for a girl in her science class. She has never dealt with feelings like this before. The social worker should:

a. Disclose the reported feelings to the client's parents because the client is a minor and the parents are paying for therapy.
b. Validate the client's feelings and explain that this is something they can explore in ongoing sessions.
c. Encourage the client by stating that the feelings will fade away as she goes through hormonal changes.
d. Explore these feelings more deeply by asking the client why she thinks they have arisen.

71. A 72-year-old widow comes to see a social worker for help with feelings of bereavement. Her spouse died of a sudden heart attack just over a year ago. There was no prior history of a heart condition, so the loss came as a substantial shock and without forewarning. Since that time, the client feels she has been unable to recover emotionally. She notes remaining intensely preoccupied with thinking about her husband, cries more days than not, feels estranged from others in many ways without him (e.g., other friends and couples seem distant), and describes her emotions as generally numb, when not overwhelming. Sometimes she yearns to die so that she can "be with him" again. There is no overt suicidality, but there is a feeling that life without him is meaningless in many ways. The MOST appropriate early diagnostic impression would be:

   a. Major depressive disorder
   b. Post-traumatic stress
   c. Uncomplicated bereavement
   d. Prolonged grief disorder

72. Which of the following is a core function of the social worker when implementing the task-centered practice model?

   a. To identify and resolve anticipated obstacles to task completion
   b. To build client insight regarding factors contributing to the problem so they can be addressed or avoided
   c. To complete tasks to address environmental or systemic obstacles to the client's success
   d. To assess client confidence and motivation using scaling questions

73. A social worker has been asked to evaluate program effectiveness at multiple community senior day care centers. The most effective approach to take would be:

   a. Action research
   b. Self evaluation
   c. Point-specific research
   d. Cluster evaluation

74. A 26-year-old woman is seeing a social worker regarding her persistent desire to leave her bedroom window blinds open so that she might be seen disrobing by her male neighbor, who participates voyeuristically in an open way. She is aware that the activity is fraught with problems—he is a married man, and potentially other passersby might see in her window from the street. To this point, however, she finds these risks somewhat exciting and stimulating. She also finds herself compulsively thinking about the activity and planning ways to be "caught" by the man in compromising moments. Diagnostically, her behavior is best described as:

   a. Frotteurism
   b. Voyeurism
   c. Exhibitionism
   d. Other specified paraphilia

75. A child's genetic test shows that a small number of genes have mutated. Which of the following is TRUE?

   a. The chromosomes are also abnormal in some way.
   b. Environmental factors caused the genes to mutate.
   c. The mutations will impact the genotype.
   d. The child's phenotype will be no different than if the genes had not mutated.

241

76. A therapist receives a subpoena from the courthouse to release all assessments and progress notes for her client. The therapist worries that the information within the documentation is sensitive to the therapeutic healing of her client. Which one of the following options BEST reflects what the therapist should do?

a. The therapist should first meet with her client to discuss the sensitive information documented in the reports and obtain consent to release the information.
b. The therapist should provide all documentation to the judge immediately.
c. The therapist should speak with a lawyer first to determine if the subpoena is legally valid.
d. The therapist should only send the documentation that would not be harmful to her client.

77. Approximately how many children are diagnosed with attention-deficit/hyperactivity disorder in the United States?

a. 23%
b. 11.7%
c. 9.4%
d. 5%

78. A new child protective services case manager has been assigned his first case, which involves a family of Native American heritage. The social worker has not worked with a family of this ethnicity before. To properly assess for risk factors, he should FIRST:

a. Research proper social work methods to support this family in a manner that is appropriate to their culture.
b. Complete a home visit and take note of all the risk factors present in the home.
c. Use a standardized assessment for new child protective services cases to maintain a consistent approach across all cases.
d. Consult with his coworkers on how to appropriately approach this case.

79. Which of the following is the FIRST step of evidence-based practice (EBP)?

a. Identify the problem(s) to be addressed by the intervention.
b. Collaborate with the client to make a list of questions regarding the identified problem(s).
c. Identify reputable, reliable sources of information and data pertaining to social work interventions.
d. Specify the problem and the desired outcome, and select two intervention options to compare.

80. A social worker's first priority for working with a client in a heightened state of stress is to:

a. Refer the client to a doctor or psychiatrist for emergency stress-relieving medication.
b. Help the client return to the previous level of functioning.
c. Offer resources for mitigating the immediate needs brought on by the crisis.
d. Teach the client new skills to manage stress.

81. A 34-year-old man makes an appointment to see a social worker for help coping with a difficult relationship in his life. At intake, the social worker learns that he feels a famous movie actress has hidden affection for him. He has written her many times through her fan club, and has received letters from club personnel—never from the actress herself. But, he explains, this is just because she's "not currently free to express her feelings openly" due to a waning relationship with a wealthy businessman. When talking about the businessman, there are clear feelings of competition. When asked for greater detail or information to buttress his beliefs, he avoids the questions. The MOST appropriate early diagnostic impression would be delusional disorder, with the following subtype:

a. Grandiose type
b. Jealous type
c. Persecutory type
d. Erotomanic type

82. An adult female arrives to therapy with a social worker, presenting with generalized anxiety disorder. The client has immense anxiety surrounding the fear that someone will break into her home in the middle of the night. She says, "Actually, this sounds ridiculous. Never mind." The social worker can use which therapeutic concept to increase genuine trust with her client?

   a. Congruence in communication
   b. Open body language
   c. Collaboration in treatment plan development
   d. Constricted affect

83. In a large metropolitan area, three agencies focus on the needs of the homeless population. The agencies' leaders were frustrated with the city's lack of investment in affordable housing. A social work consultant helped the three agencies create a structure of collaboration and a plan of action to address this issue. Their collective work resulted in two formerly homeless individuals joining the city council's homelessness prevention task force and new citywide caps on annual rent increases. Which strategy is the MOST likely to have influenced the council's creation of rent increase caps?

   a. The formation of a coalition
   b. Research gathering
   c. Personal testimony of the two new task force members
   d. Community organizing

84. Children are most likely to experience negative effects from which parental characteristic?

   a. Their mother is incarcerated.
   b. Either parent has a mental health disorder.
   c. Their father is incarcerated.
   d. Either parent has a substance abuse disorder.

85. A therapist has received a referral for a legally mandated client through the local child protective services office. The client remains silent during the first two sessions. The therapist would like to decrease the power imbalance within the therapeutic relationship. The following are all examples of ways to decrease the power imbalance, EXCEPT:

   a. Use the client's last name when speaking.
   b. Speak in simple language during sessions.
   c. Articulate the limits of the therapist's role.
   d. Maintain respect for the client's dignity and autonomy, even if she chooses to remain silent during sessions.

86. In working with an 11-year-old girl, it is noted that she seems to have limited verbal skills, including problems in word selection and use. Intelligence testing indicates normal cognitive capacity. Other testing has not shown any sensory impairments or other medical conditions. These early indicators are BEST suggestive of which of the following tentative diagnoses?

   a. Speech sound disorder
   b. Childhood-onset fluency disorder
   c. Autism spectrum disorder
   d. Language disorder

87. A client presents with his wife, who is complaining that he has had a change in cognitive function, including language and memory. The client denies loss of pleasure in normal activities and denies feeling sad. The client is able to manage his medications but requires someone to set up his medication box and set a timer for him. The worker suspects:

a. Neurocognitive disorder
b. Delirium
c. Depression
d. Schizophrenia

88. Of those with either a mental health diagnosis or a substance use disorder, roughly how many will experience the other at some point in their lives?

a. One-third
b. One-quarter
c. One-half
d. Two-thirds

89. A social worker at a foster care agency is responsible for providing weekly counseling to children placed in foster homes and for supporting their foster parents. The social worker knows that children who have experienced maltreatment or abuse are quite vulnerable to future abuse. Which of the following strategies should she use to MOST effectively protect those children from the effects of further abuse?

a. Work closely with the foster family to prevent additional abuse or neglect from occurring during the children's placement.
b. Support the children's ability to express their feelings and needs.
c. Provide the children's parents coaching and support to build positive parenting strategies.
d. Before they return home, provide the children with a work phone number so the social worker can intervene as soon as another incidence of abuse occurs.

90. During a weekly supervision meeting, the supervisor describes a new case that is being transferred to the social worker. This case was previously managed by the supervisor before he took his promotion. The supervisor describes the case with casual language, noting that he "got a lot of billing hours with this case" because conversations were easy and lasted longer with this family. When looking in past case notes and authorizations, the social worker sees increased authorizations for services that were not justifiable for the family's need. What should happen next?

a. The social worker should decline to take the case.
b. The social worker should meet with the family to complete case notes and authorizations as directed by the supervisor.
c. The social worker should report the concerning, unethical behaviors to the director of the program.
d. The social worker should take the case but adjust the family's expectations for ongoing services and authorizations.

91. "Single system" research designs involve observing one client or system only ($n = 1$) before, during, and after an intervention. Because of their flexibility and capacity to measure change over time, single-system designs are frequently used by practitioners to evaluate:

a. Their practice
b. Difficult clients
c. Conformation to policy
d. Regulation adherence

92. The results of a program evaluation have been finalized and sent to the program director for review. This evaluation shows that the current program's service delivery is not performing to the standards laid out by the board of directors. The program director should decide to:
    a. Meet with the board of directors and provide an explanation of the services offered and how they are currently being delivered.
    b. Work with agency leadership to reevaluate how services are delivered.
    c. Identify the top reason for service delivery issues and create a task force to determine how to implement a positive change in the program.
    d. Ask the board of directors to change the standards for service delivery.

93. A husband and wife are working with a social worker to address the husband's job loss and lack of initiative in finding employment. The husband reports that he and his wife do not communicate, and the wife "constantly vents about our troubles" to her mother. This is an example of:
    a. Subjugated narratives
    b. Triangulation
    c. Unbalancing
    d. Covert change

94. A social worker has been asked to see a 15-year-old girl for problems with body image and eating. After speaking with her, the social worker discovers that she suffers with an intense desire to lose weight, feeling that this will help her be more attractive to the opposite sex and more popular in her social circle. She is by no means obese, although she is not overly slender. Her parents recently noted an increase in grocery costs, and that food seemed to be disappearing around the house inordinately quickly—often "junk" food and other quick snacks. Finally, late one night, her mother passed the bathroom and heard the daughter "purge" her food. She confronted her and discovered that the daughter had been "binge" eating and inducing vomiting for some months. She estimates that she purges about 10 times per week. Some modest weight loss had occurred. The most appropriate diagnosis would be:
    a. Anorexia nervosa, purging type
    b. Bulimia nervosa, severe
    c. Bulimia nervosa, moderate
    d. Eating disorder, not otherwise specified

95. A social worker is assigned the case of an 18-year-old male with an intellectual disability. He has aged out of foster care and is in need of safe, affordable housing. The individual has experienced child abuse, neglect, and sexual abuse through his biological family. The social worker is able to find a new home for him that includes two roommates and staffing to assist with his activities of daily living. After the second night, the social worker receives a call from the staff stating that the individual was violently raped by his roommate. He is now in the emergency room. The social worker has consequently become unable to sleep or perform other casework. She is requesting to be removed from any cases requiring housing placements. The social worker is experiencing:
    a. Post-traumatic stress disorder
    b. Burnout
    c. Verbalized, secondhand trauma
    d. Secondary trauma

96. A couple brings their 3-year-old child to an outpatient therapy center for his first therapy session. They report his symptoms as follows: refusing to follow directions, bullying others, and a persistent angry mood. The child is MOST LIKELY diagnosed with:

- a. Conduct disorder
- b. Bipolar disorder, type I
- c. Oppositional defiant disorder
- d. Major depressive disorder

97. Which of the following is NOT influenced by a community's incarceration rate?

- a. The policies within the local school district
- b. The local incidence rate of homelessness
- c. The average cost of living within the community
- d. The mental health of community residents

98. A social worker brings a difficult case (described below) to the attention of their supervisor. After considering the details of the case, the social work supervisor suggests that the client's unique life experience has a significant influence on their current functioning. The client is most likely to be part of which of the following populations?

> The client will not readily reveal their thoughts or feelings, instead maintaining a stoic demeanor. The client struggles to make decisions and defers to others whenever possible. The client appears much older than their reported age and is obese.

- a. They have an intellectual disability.
- b. They served time in prison.
- c. They have a history of homelessness.
- d. They have a chronic illness.

99. A male social worker is receiving a new case from a female coworker. During the case transfer meeting, the client reports feeling unsafe around men that are "larger" than him. The client is elderly and slim in size. The male social worker happens to be taller and bigger than the client. The male social worker should:

- a. Ignore this and work with the client as best as he can.
- b. Discuss the option of the female coworker maintaining the case.
- c. Ask the client if he thinks that his size will impede the development of their therapeutic relationship.
- d. Ask the client to describe the origination of these feelings of unsafety.

100. A social worker is called to a medical clinic to evaluate a 56-year-old woman who presents with persistent fears of a new diagnosis of melanoma. She had a small skin lesion removed from her nose approximately 2 years ago, which had precancerous tissue changes upon evaluation by pathology. Since that time, she has become intensely preoccupied with the status of her skin, and tends to check and recheck every blemish that occurs. Frequent visits to her dermatologist have not resulted in the identification of any new dermatological problems, and despite reassurances her worries continue unabated. The problem has grown to the point that she regularly asks her spouse to help her monitor her skin and examine her back to ensure there are no new problems. He has grown increasingly frustrated. She also refuses to go outdoors unless overly swathed to ward off any exposure to the sun. This has resulted in her increasingly avoiding the outdoors altogether. The MOST likely diagnosis for her presentation is:

- a. Malingering
- b. Factitious disorder
- c. Illness anxiety disorder
- d. Somatic symptom disorder

101. A supervisor notices that one of her supervisees struggles to complete documentation on time but receives great reviews from client-satisfaction surveys. The supervisor has reason to believe that the social worker may leave the agency if given a poor performance review. The supervisor should:

    a. Record the social worker's performance accurately, including strengths and weaknesses, without regard to the social worker possibly terminating employment.

    b. Record the great reviews that the social worker receives from clients because client satisfaction is most important.

    c. Report the data that reflect the late and missing documentation because county and state audits will file a corrective action plan against the agency.

    d. Document the late documentation and the great client reviews—not overemphasizing either—to keep a good working relationship with the supervisee.

102. Which one of the following health issues is NOT disproportionately experienced by prison inmates?

    a. Arthritis

    b. Heart disease

    c. Asthma

    d. Diabetes

103. A social work supervisor wants to prevent her staff from experiencing burnout. Which of the following strategies would be the MOST effective?

    a. Provide a lunch-and-learn training on professional self-care strategies.

    b. Promote the use of vacation time.

    c. Ensure that the caseload size and difficulty reflect the staff's experience level.

    d. Provide flexible scheduling and co-created job expectations.

104. Which of the following activities is NOT a shared responsibility of the social work supervisor and supervisee?

    a. The documentation of the supervision session

    b. The selection of tools for supervision evaluation

    c. The development of the agenda for supervision

    d. The maintenance of liability insurance

105. MOST trauma responses are NOT:

    a. Distressing

    b. Psychologically effective

    c. Able to resolve without clinical intervention

    d. Indicative of mental illness

106. Which of the following variables is MOST likely to reduce professional objectivity in the social worker–client relationship?

    a. The social worker has vicarious trauma.

    b. The social worker and client live in the same rural area and see one another regularly at community locations such as the store and gas station.

    c. The client reminds the social worker of someone in their personal life with whom they have a great deal of conflict.

    d. The social worker and client are friends on social media.

107. A social work supervisor is informed by the program administrative assistant that client intake documentation completed by the social work staff is consistently missing several required details. This prevents the timely submission of billing and creates a backlog of administrative tasks. What is the MOST effective strategy to use first to address this issue?

a. At the next team meeting, the supervisor will remind the staff to provide all of the required information on intake documents.

b. At the next team meeting, the supervisor will role-play an intake appointment with one of the staff members while the others complete the intake paperwork. The supervisor will then lead the team in a review of their documentation.

c. The supervisor will implement a new procedure in which the supervisor will fully review all client intake documents before they are turned in to the administrative assistant.

d. The administrative assistant will reformat the intake documents so that all required details are highlighted in bold.

108. A social worker is completing the initial assessment for a new client that identifies as gay and has sought support as they contemplate coming out. Consideration of which variable will BEST help the social worker understand the client's sociohistorical context and the impact it may have on the client's approach to coming out?

a. Race
b. Gender
c. Age
d. Geographic location

109. What is the primary goal of family life education programs?

a. Prevention
b. Self-efficacy
c. Education
d. Reflection

110. An elderly female client has been attending her first two sessions at the dialysis clinic where a social worker works. Her son is listed as her medical power of attorney. Prior to her third session, she is temporarily hospitalized with pneumonia and discharged to an assisted living center. The dialysis clinic is notified that her mentation has changed and she is currently demonstrating signs of delirium and unable to speak coherently. Her son calls the day of her third session to say that his mother will forgo any further dialysis treatment. The social worker explains the risks of such a decision to the son, and later calls to speak with the client directly about her thoughts and concerns, but the client does not answer and does not call back. Knowing that without this consistent treatment the patient will deteriorate rapidly, the social worker MUST do which of the following?

a. Continue to call the client and offer to help her resolve any concerns that she has regarding treatment or resources.

b. Respect the client's decision regarding treatment per the son's report.

c. Send the client a letter through certified mail reminding her of the risks of not remaining in treatment.

d. Report the decision to the nephrologist for outreach to the client's son to help change the client's mind.

111. A social worker has two different clients with an overdue balance for services following loss of employment. Both clients have been making progress toward their treatment goals. One client is working with a job coach and has some promising job leads, whereas the other client does not seem to be proactively seeking employment and may be developing symptoms of depression. Which of the following MUST the social worker do before terminating services?

a. Continue to provide short-term services while completing the referral process to another service provider with a more accessible sliding scale fee.
b. Have detailed discussions with both clients regarding the fee-for-service agreement and the consequences of the current nonpayment.
c. Immediately refer the clients to another service provider.
d. Assess if either client poses a risk to self or others; if so, the social worker must refer to a service provider with an immediate opening for service.

112. Which of the following information resources is the MOST comprehensive source of information on a given topic?

a. A systematic review
b. A meta-analysis
c. A critical appraisal
d. A research summary

113. A social worker receives a call from an upset client, who begins to use profanity. How should the social worker respond?

a. The social worker should answer the client's questions politely in order to de-escalate the situation.
b. The social worker should say, "I am here to help you, but I must adhere to the agency's policy. If profanity continues to be used on this call, I will need to disconnect and speak with you at another time."
c. The social worker should apologize for any responsibility he had in making the client upset in order to maintain a positive therapeutic relationship with the client.
d. The social worker should alert his supervisor to determine if a case transfer is needed.

114. After a nationally publicized incident involving substance use, state lawmakers are now creating a policy that will decrease funding for substance use centers and use the newly obtained funds to increase support in state-run prisons. Choose the answer that BEST reflects the responsibilities that social workers have through the National Association of Social Workers (NASW) Code of Ethics in this scenario.

a. Social workers are responsible for advocating and educating lawmakers about why substance use centers are necessary to the health of the community.
b. Social workers who specifically support those with substance use disorders are best equipped to advocate against the policy change.
c. Social workers are responsible for organizing protests, marches, and lobbying efforts to keep current funding levels for substance use centers.
d. Social workers are responsible for engaging the individuals and families that will be affected by this policy to collaborate in advocacy efforts against this policy change.

115. Which of the following definitions MOST accurately describes EBP?

a. An intervention model that has been proven to effectively address a specific problem
b. A process of inquiry combining research, clinical expertise, and client values
c. A model of research that originated in the field of medicine and has been modified for use in the social work profession
d. A prescriptive decision-making model to identify the best psychosocial intervention for a client's problem

116. Which is the MOST likely way in which the content of a social work case presentation will differ if solution-focused treatment approaches are being used as compared with narrative therapy?

    a.   The demographics presented when using narrative therapy will be more detailed.

    b.   The background information will not be as detailed with solution-focused treatment, because with this modality, the past does not matter as much as the present and future.

    c.   With solution-focused treatment, more solution-focused interventions will be planned.

    d.   The client is more likely to be an adult with narrative therapy.

117. Which of the following is a strength of the newer developmental theories, which include the developmental experiences of LGBTQ individuals?

    a.   They focus on the coming-out process, with attention to the gradual process that this is for many individuals.

    b.   Several of them reflect the specific experiences of transgender individuals.

    c.   The coming-out process is described as having internal (personal) and external (social) processes.

    d.   They have replaced the older developmental theories that perpetuate heteronormative views.

118. A case manager gets a new assignment. The child referred for services speaks fluent English and some Polish, whereas the parents speak Polish and can understand some English. Unfortunately, the Polish interpreter did not show up to the scheduled meeting today. The social worker should:

    a.   Speak directly to the child in English because that is the client who is referred for services.

    b.   Send the family home and speak with the interpretation agency about the issue.

    c.   Ask the parents if they feel comfortable moving forward without an interpreter.

    d.   Do not hold the meeting; use the interpretation service over the phone to reschedule with the family for another time.

119. What is the difference between the social work values of service and social justice?

    a.   The values of service and social justice are the same because they both involve addressing social problems.

    b.   The value of service involves serving local communities to improve the lives of vulnerable and oppressed individuals, whereas social justice involves challenging social injustices.

    c.   The value of service involves serving those in need, whereas social justice involves pursuing social change for oppressed and vulnerable populations.

    d.   The value of social justice involves raising up minority populations through systemic change, whereas service involves meeting a required number of volunteer hours each year to maintain licensure.

120. A new agency will begin providing local services to community members in 5 months. The agency would like to have a variety of contract service providers ready and a list of local resources for clients. The director of the program has been assigned to connect with other agencies in the community. What is the BEST next step for the director to start networking professionally?

    a.   The director should plan to attend an upcoming conference that all the local providers will be attending, 3 months from now.

    b.   The director should schedule a time to meet with other program directors in the community to introduce the new agency and share how they would like to partner with the community.

    c.   The director should send an email to local providers introducing the new agency and sharing how the agency would like to partner with them.

    d.   The director should connect with others through LinkedIn (a social media platform for professionals) to increase the effectiveness and efficiency of the director's networking project.

121. A geriatric client has been awaiting discharge from her short-term rehabilitation center after recovering from recent surgery. During her final social work visit, the client informed the social worker that she is concerned about returning home to her verbally abusive spouse. The social worker feels pressured by the center's administration to discharge the client because her spouse is not physically abusive and her in-home therapies are scheduled to begin. The social worker should:

a. Discharge the client home with her spouse, per administration request.
b. Schedule ongoing, home-based visits in order to discharge the client safely.
c. Obtain detailed information from the client and complete an adult protective services report before completing the day shift at the center.
d. Invite the spouse to have a counseling session at the center before determining if the client is safe to discharge.

122. Sam and Chrissy have been married for 7 years and have started therapy as a "last-ditch effort" before getting a divorce. They will commit to only six therapy sessions before making a final decision. During the first session, the couple identifies a weekend trip 2 years ago as a time they last felt connected and had fun together. What should the social worker help them explore about this weekend trip?

a. Their actions and responses to one another, including the wording, tone, and attitude
b. Unclear; the scenario does not specify what their current problems are
c. The assumptions and perspective that they had about one another at that time
d. The specific activities or experiences that they engaged in

123. What social work core value do family life education intervention programs MOST exemplify?

a. The dignity and worth of a person
b. The importance of human relationships
c. Social justice
d. Self-determination

124. A dualistic view of the connection between mind and body is one of the primary barriers to treatment acceptance for individuals with:

a. Somatic symptom disorder
b. Bipolar disease
c. Substance use disorder
d. Factitious disorder

125. A social worker at a domestic violence shelter has become increasingly cynical about his client's ability to develop new relationship patterns and cannot seem to muster the energy to prepare for the group skill-building sessions. He has recently begun looking for a new job, hoping that a new supervisor will notice all of his hard work and help him regain the passion for social work that he once had. What type of professional distress is this social worker experiencing?

a. Compassion fatigue
b. Occupational stress
c. Burnout
d. Vicarious trauma

126. A social work supervisor observes a newly hired social worker as they complete their first intake appointment. The newly hired social worker becomes visibly upset during the session as the client shares details of a recent traumatic event. The social worker moves on to another topic of the assessment as soon as the client pauses to take a sip of water, missing the opportunity to ask follow-up questions to understand the impact of this event on the client. Which of the following is the BEST strategy to use in the next supervision session?

    a. Provide training on mindfulness strategies to help staff remain centered during client sessions.
    b. Use reflective questions to build the social worker's awareness of how the client's disclosure impacted their completion of the initial assessment.
    c. Ask if the social worker has had counseling to address their own experiences of trauma.
    d. Explain the importance of gathering sufficient information about client problems during the intake session.

127. During the termination phase of treatment, which of the following interventions should the social worker do FIRST?

    a. Help the client consider future challenges and identify cognitive and behavioral indications that indicate that the client may need additional support.
    b. Help the client understand how their new skills and cognitive strategies can apply to other areas of their life.
    c. Begin to decrease the intensity of services to ease the client's transition from the services and the supportive relationship with the social worker.
    d. Review the treatment process with the client.

128. A female junior-year college student is newly diagnosed with bipolar disorder and is referred to the campus social worker for ongoing support. The student is struggling to maintain her classwork and good relationships with her housemates. The student assumes that she should be able to "get back to normal" because she has started taking medication. The social worker should:

    a. Spend time with the student to discuss how bipolar disorder can affect her functioning.
    b. Agree that the student should be getting back to normal once she has received 12 weeks of individual therapy.
    c. Explain that the student will get back to normal once the medication has time to take effect—at least a few weeks.
    d. Inquire about how well the student has adhered to the medication regimen as prescribed.

129. The rate of nonsuicidal self-injury (NSSI) within a school is BEST understood by examining which student variable?

    a. Age
    b. Traumatic experience
    c. Gender
    d. Social connections

130. A diverse group of professionals within a city have come together to discuss the health of their community. A social worker is facilitating a discussion to develop consensus around three issues to focus on in the coming year. The group has narrowed the priority list to three; however, several group members remain hesitant to finalize them as the annual priorities. What should the social worker do NEXT to help the group reach consensus?

a. Facilitate a debate regarding the pros and cons of each of the three issues.
b. Ask those with concerns what the priority issues would need to include in order for them to be in support.
c. Schedule an additional meeting to have another discussion because unanimous agreement on the three priority issues selected does not seem likely.
d. Ask each member to express their opinion about the three issues and how they could positively impact the community.

131. A social worker has submitted a notice of resignation and is making plans for the final few visits with her clients. Another social worker at the agency will assume responsibility for the cases; however, he will not be available to meet with the clients in a joint visit like the departing social worker would prefer. Which approach should the departing social worker use to BEST help the clients to remain enrolled and be willing to work with a different social worker?

a. Document what techniques have helped the clients, so the new social worker can use them, too.
b. Share as much information as possible about the new social worker with the clients, so the clients know what to expect.
c. Ask the clients to describe their progress since their enrollment and identify what they would like to work on next. Take notes and provide the clients with the document, encouraging them to share this information with the new social worker.
d. Remind the clients of how important it is for their mental health to continue in services with the new social worker.

132. Which of the following statements is NOT accurate regarding the similarities between motivational interviewing (MI) and psychoeducation?

a. Both techniques use a didactic approach to increase the client's sense of empowerment and confidence.
b. Both techniques are effective across many formats, including individual, family, and group.
c. Both techniques can be used to support family engagement with a child welfare caseworker.
d. Both techniques are characterized by a nonhierarchical relationship between the client and the social worker.

133. A social worker at a rural nonprofit agency receives a referral for a family that has recently learned that their infant has a multifactorial condition. The mother reports feelings of distress and guilt. Which one of the mother's concerns is the social worker UNABLE to confidently address?

a. "If I had gotten the prenatal testing, I could have prevented the issue."
b. "I drank some alcohol before I knew that I was pregnant, and that is to blame."
c. "This occurred because I did not take a multivitamin during or before pregnancy."
d. "I cannot have any more children because they will all have this condition."

134. A therapist is working with a new client over telehealth. The therapist has begun to connect with the client on a personal level because they are similar in age, interests, and fears. The therapist has begun to share personal information with the client that is not beneficial to the client's needs. This type of situation is called:

a. Countertransference
b. A dual relationship
c. Transference
d. A boundary violation

135. Which of the following demographic groups is the MOST overrepresented among suicide victims?

a. The elderly population (ages 65+)
b. Native Americans
c. Hispanic/Latino ethnicity
d. Veterans

136. A college student studying social work is struggling to maintain her self-care practices while attempting to succeed in her classes, social work field placement, and part-time job. She is beginning to feel that a social work degree may not be right for her due to the increased stress levels. When speaking with her professor, she is encouraged to focus on consistently implementing self-care strategies. Which one of the following options would be the MOST appropriate self-care choice for the student?

a. The student chooses to study more in order to decrease stress with schoolwork.
b. The student chooses to increase the hours spent at her part-time job to decrease financial stress.
c. The student chooses to schedule a consistent time to meditate each day.
d. The student chooses to eat a salad on days that she is the most stressed.

137. When comparing neglect and physical abuse of children, which of the following is NOT true?

a. Victims of neglect have more difficulty returning home following discharge from residential treatment compared to victims of physical abuse.
b. Neglect is associated with a wider range of damage than physical abuse.
c. Children under the age of 1 experience higher rates of neglect than physical abuse.
d. Victims of neglect are less likely to be identified and receive support compared to victims of physical abuse.

138. For the past 4 weeks, a private-practice social worker has been working with a client who has anger management issues. The individual has not been consistent with payment and currently has an overdue bill of $100. At the initial intake session, the social worker verbally reviewed the financial expectations with the client but did not obtain a signed document reflecting the payment policy. What is the social worker's ethical responsibility in terms of terminating services for nonpayment?

a. The client is not meeting the expectations of the payment policy and should be terminated.
b. The social worker cannot terminate because the client presented with anger management issues, which should be made the priority at this time.
c. Before the next session, the social worker should inform the client that all future appointments will be canceled if payment is not made within 72 hours.
d. At the next session, the social worker should review the payment policy and obtain the client's signature.

139. For which of the following groups is the collaboration of family or caregivers MOST needed for the successful implementation of mental health treatment strategies?

a. Teenagers
b. Recently adopted children
c. Young adults with severe intellectual disabilities
d. Youth recently discharged from a residential facility

140. Which one of the following individuals is most at risk when reentering society following a period of imprisonment?

a. A 40-year-old who served 11 years, now has family support, and is living with a friend
b. A 48-year-old who served 9 years, now has limited social support, and has unstable housing
c. A 24-year-old who served 6 years and now lives with their grandmother
d. A 29-year-old who served 4 years, has a mild physical disability, and is now living with an older sibling's family

141. Which of the following statements correctly matches a teaching strategy with the desired educational outcome?

   a. Learners develop insight while listening to a lecture.
   b. Case discussions support comprehension of complex material.
   c. Simulations provide the opportunity for problem solving and critical thinking.
   d. A lecture helps learners build new skills.

142. A thorough trauma assessment should be completed:

   a. For anyone experiencing symptoms of anxiety or depression
   b. For anyone experiencing symptoms of post-traumatic stress disorder
   c. If a trauma screening has been completed
   d. For every child in foster care

143. There is only one social worker at an oncology office in a small community. The social worker is assigned to all clients. The social worker chooses to join a book club that meets regularly. During the first book club meeting, the social worker recognizes one of the other members as a client at the oncology office. What should the social worker do NEXT?

   a. The social worker should wait to acknowledge the client in this social setting and allow the client to lead the interaction.
   b. The social worker should no longer attend this book club to avoid a dual relationship.
   c. The social worker should request that the human resources department hire another social worker in order to transfer this client case, along with obtaining more help in the oncology office.
   d. The social worker should speak to the client one-on-one at the book club meeting to agree upon how to interact and acknowledge each other in the book club.

144. How can a feedback loop impact the first stage of a community-led structural intervention (CLSI)?

   a. Modifying goals of the community intervention
   b. Generating new strategies to gather research more effectively
   c. Guiding the development of programs to meet community needs
   d. Compelling civic leaders to address the identified problem

145. Which of the following is a mezzo-level, primary prevention strategy for child maltreatment?

   a. Parenting classes at a community center for parents of children with disabilities
   b. A parent coaching program that requires referral from a doctor or a mental health professional
   c. Free, family-friendly, community-wide events with recreational activities, food, and access to local resources
   d. A weekly educational program for pregnant teen mothers

146. A social worker is working with an adult client experiencing gender dysphoria. The client has requested a referral for surgical treatment. Which of the following is NOT a required component of this referral process?

   a. The social worker must complete a psychosocial assessment.
   b. The social worker must produce documentation that outlines support of the client's request for surgery.
   c. The social worker must provide psychotherapy to prepare the client for the implications of surgery.
   d. The social worker must consider whether or not they have competence in working with adults experiencing gender dysphoria.

147. When using cognitive interventions to prevent substance use, it is MOST important to help the client identify:

   a. The reasons that the client uses substances
   b. The impact of the substance use on the client's life
   c. What the client thinks about their substance use
   d. What the client thinks about when presented with an opportunity to use

148. A social worker is the director of counseling services for the employee assistance program at a large insurance company. It is noticed that women report higher rates of discrimination from coworkers than men. This is best understood using which theoretical framework?

   a. Minority stress theory
   b. Intersectionality theory
   c. Human dynamics theory
   d. Selective incivility theory

149. Which of the following outcomes of a social worker's personal disclosure does NOT reflect social work best practice?

   a. It brings the social worker a sense of personal satisfaction.
   b. It causes the social worker–client relationship to be less formal.
   c. The client feels concern for the social worker.
   d. The client shares expert advice with the social worker.

150. Which of these components of social work practice has the MOST impact on a social worker's ability to establish and maintain appropriate professional boundaries?

   a. The social worker's communication with the client
   b. The frequency and quality of the social work supervision
   c. The social worker's mental health status
   d. The accuracy and depth of training related to social work professional boundaries

151. When planning treatment, a social worker must choose treatment strategies that reflect all of the following EXCEPT:

   a. The information provided to the client during the consent process
   b. The client's presenting problem
   c. The social worker's areas of competence
   d. Research related to the client's characteristics

152. Which of the following caregiver characteristics is a reliable predictor of child maltreatment?

   a. Misattribution
   b. Caregiver dissatisfaction with the child
   c. Inconsistent engagement of needed mental health treatment
   d. Alcoholism

153. The prevalence of direct social work practice has impeded the integration of which theory into social work practice?

   a. Psychodynamic theory
   b. Person-in-environment theory
   c. Constructivist theory
   d. Psychoanalytic theory

154. The niece of an elderly man reaches out to the local senior services agency to ask for assistance. She checks in on her uncle twice a week because he lives alone. Today, she found her uncle in the same clothes that she had left him in a few days prior. She found piles of trash around the home. Her uncle refused to see his doctor to discuss health and safety concerns. The niece is unable to provide any more support to him. The geriatric social worker should FIRST:

    a. Write down the elderly man's demographic information to perform a check-in visit to determine his level of health and safety.

    b. Ask if the man has a power of attorney and describe how the niece can obtain it for her uncle.

    c. Explain that as long as her uncle remains competent, there is no support that she can force her uncle to use.

    d. Provide the niece with resources on how to obtain services for her uncle.

155. A middle school student meets with the school social worker due to concerns about isolating behaviors and declining grades. This student has been on the school's honor roll for the past 2 years. Upon further discussion, the school social worker becomes aware that the student's parents are separating. The student is struggling with the changes in her home environment. To increase positive connections using the person-in-environment theory, the school social worker should:

    a. Schedule a meeting with the student and her parents to discuss the behaviors and identify positive connections that can be made through the school or the community.

    b. Disclose this information to the student's teachers so they can take this stress into account when grading the student's work.

    c. Encourage the student to spend more time with her classmates during her free periods as a means to lift spirits and distract her during these times.

    d. Assign the student to the classroom of her favorite teacher from childhood to assist with activities for the younger students.

156. Which of the following factors can reduce the likelihood of a client experiencing emotional difficulty during the termination phase of treatment?

    a. If the social worker and client process the treatment experience

    b. If the client has a strong therapeutic relationship with the social worker

    c. If treatment has resulted in positive changes for the client

    d. If treatment ends according to the timeline established at the beginning of treatment

157. A client is describing an upsetting experience and abruptly changes the topic. The social worker notices that the client had become increasingly agitated immediately before changing the topic, does not respond when asked to further discuss the upsetting experience, and had continued on by discussing a different topic. Using a psychoanalytic approach, the social worker recognizes this as:

    a. Avoidance

    b. Distraction

    c. Resistance

    d. Discomfort

158. Which of the following gives the correct order in which the social work licensing requirements must be completed?

    a. Register with the Association of Social Work Boards (ASWB), meet state requirements for the license, pass the licensing test, and apply to the licensing board for approval.

    b. Pass the licensing test, meet state requirements for the license, apply to the licensing board for approval, and register with ASWB.

    c. Apply to the licensing board for approval, register with ASWB, pass the licensing test, and meet state requirements for the license.

    d. Meet state requirements for the license, apply to the licensing board for approval, register with ASWB, and pass the licensing test.

159. A social worker is practicing in a hospital setting. The social worker realizes that a personal friend has been admitted when seeing their name and date of birth on the list of patients. Although the social worker is not assigned to the client, he opens up the client's chart in the electronic medical record to see what is going on. The social worker:

    a. Did not violate any ethics because nothing was changed in the chart
    b. Violated the Health Insurance Portability and Accountability Act (HIPAA) by opening up the chart when the client was not assigned to him
    c. Should walk over to the client's room in person to check in with his friend
    d. Should ask his supervisor to be assigned to the client because he would be the best advocate for his friend

160. A social worker has completed the initial assessment for a young adult with a moderate intellectual disability who has limited verbal communication. Using careful observation and caregiver input, the social worker has identified several symptoms of anxiety and depression. The social worker would like to collaborate with another professional to identify and implement an effective treatment approach. Which of the following should the social worker collaborate with FIRST?

    a. An occupational therapist
    b. A psychiatrist
    c. A speech-language pathologist
    d. An intervention specialist

161. Client-centered theory emphasizes the importance of which three practice behaviors?

    a. Unconditional positive regard, genuineness, and openness
    b. Empowerment, authenticity, and professional use of self
    c. Empathy, unconditional positive regard, and congruence
    d. Openness, empathy, and reflective questioning

162. Which is the BEST definition of a feedback loop?

    a. The process of gathering feedback from community members
    b. The process of reflecting on intervention results to determine the next step
    c. Using products of reflection to inform the current and next steps at each stage of an intervention
    d. A process in which a multidisciplinary team reviews client feedback and provides a response

163. An independently licensed social worker with 3.5 years of practice experience has recently moved to a new city. The social worker primarily uses SFBT and cognitive behavioral intervention strategies in their practice. Which of the following supervision models will be the MOST likely to provide the type of support and oversight that this social worker needs?

    a. One-on-one consultation with a child psychologist
    b. A social work supervision group led by an experienced, independently licensed social worker
    c. One-on-one supervision with an independently licensed social worker with a supervision/training credential
    d. A peer consultation group focused on SFBT

164. Which of the following does NOT contribute to treatment engagement for children?

    a. The use of frequent assessment throughout treatment, in addition to the initial assessment
    b. The provision of services in an integrated service environment
    c. Ensuring that the client understands the intervention's purpose
    d. The age of the social worker

165. The supervisor at a hospice agency has asked the social worker to become more effective with prioritizing his tasks. The social worker has the following items to prioritize today:

1. Create a report of all completed home visits, which is past due by 1 day.
2. Call to schedule a new-client appointment, which is due in 24 hours.
3. Make a home visit with a client that must be completed by the end of the week.
4. Return a missed call to a respite facility regarding some required discharge paperwork.
5. Attend a meeting this morning with a client and her children about concerns of possible neglect from her in-home staff.

The social worker is only able to complete four tasks today. Which one of the following choices prioritizes the tasks that MUST be completed today, in order of importance?

    a. 1, 2, 5, 4
    b. 4, 1, 5, 3
    c. 2, 5, 3, 4
    d. 5, 4, 2, 1

166. When completing a trauma assessment, a social worker will:

    a. Use standardized measures.
    b. Be relatively brief, leaving many details intentionally unexplored.
    c. Assess every experience of trauma that the client can remember.
    d. Assess the type of trauma, when the trauma (or multiple traumas) occurred, the chronicity and severity of the trauma, and the level of risk for future trauma.

167. An experienced social worker wants to develop a new youth program to support his community. Which one of the following choices correctly orders the steps to plan and develop a new program?

    a. Create a planning team, complete a needs assessment, decide on a time line for the start of services, identify program goals, and implement those program goals.
    b. Decide on a time line for the start of services, identify program goals, complete a needs assessment, create a planning team, and implement those program goals.
    c. Complete a needs assessment, identify program goals, create a planning team, decide on a time line for the start of services, and implement those program goals.
    d. Create a planning team, identify program goals, decide on a time line for the start of services, complete a needs assessment, and implement those program goals.

168. At an agency that provides mental health services funded by managed care networks, staff are required to only use brief modalities of treatment and provide services to all clients referred within their assigned zip code area. Which core value may these practices be in the MOST conflict with?

    a. Social justice
    b. Dignity and worth of the person
    c. Integrity
    d. Competence

169. Which of the following demographic characteristics is the MOST related to an increased vulnerability to biopsychosocial problems?

    a. Age
    b. Race
    c. Gender
    d. Zip code

170. A rural social services agency is applying for grant funding to provide monthly health and wellness events. Nurses from the local hospital will provide health screenings and engaging presentations on preventive health topics. What primary role does a memorandum of understanding (MOU) have as part of the grant application?

    a.   To verify the legal agreement between the social service agency and the hospital because their collaboration is necessary for the grant-funded services

    b.   To describe the rationale for the specific health screening and presentation topics

    c.   To outline the role and responsibilities of the nursing staff participating in the events because they are not the primary grant applicant

    d.   To demonstrate that the social service agency and hospital have discussed and agreed upon each of their roles, responsibilities, and shared resources, and have committed to collaborate

Answer Key and Explanations for Test #1

1. B: All of the statements in this description are true of the IDD population. Most statements are at least somewhat true for the elderly population, although closer to 20% of this group have mental health disorders, and chronic health problems are not as likely to be undiagnosed. Some immigrants also share these characteristics, with multigenerational households being more common and access to healthcare being complicated by language diversity and access to care providers. They experience mental health disorders at rates of approximately 20% for first-generation immigrants up to more than 50% for third-generation immigrants. Youth in foster care do face challenges with consistent healthcare, but not so much that undiagnosed, chronic issues are a distinctive characteristic. Youth in foster care live with foster parents typically unrelated to them.

2. C: Incarcerated females consistently have higher rates of mental illness compared to incarcerated males. Although studies indicate that the prevalence of mental illness varies by year and by prison system, female prisoners have a higher rate of mental illness in nearly every study. The same is true for substance use disorders. Although the overall incarceration rate has been declining in recent years, the number of incarcerated women has been increasing steadily for more than a decade. Women are more likely to be in jail compared to prison and are often held in jail prior to trial due to their inability to post bail.

3. A: The most likely diagnosis for the young boy is attention-deficit/hyperactivity disorder (ADHD). Conduct disorder would not be appropriate, as this child is not deliberately cruel or violent toward others. Obsessive-compulsive disorder does not fit, as the child is not fixated on either ritualistic behavior or things, per se, but is simply chaotically busy. Oppositional defiant disorder is not an appropriate diagnosis, as this child is not deliberately uncooperative or argumentative. Caution is needed, however, in making the diagnosis. The behavior must not be situationally due to problems at home, and it must have persisted for six months or longer. Further, and most importantly, it must not be simple youthful exuberance or even a "high-energy" personality. Rather, the diagnosis is properly made when the behaviors are extreme, and well out of step with other peers. Having multiple involved adults complete the Connor Rating Scales (i.e., parents, grandparents, the teacher, a pediatrician, etc.) can reduce the chance of inappropriately applying this burdensome diagnosis.

4. B: It is now understood that being out, or being out in only limited ways, is not predictive of poor mental health. The other characteristics listed (self-transcendence, financial anxiety, and body shame) have been found to be predictive of the mental health status of LGBTQ adults in midlife. Self-transcendence is about the process of extending beyond (transcending) the self and relating to that which is greater than the self. For some, this may be a spiritual entity or the universe at large. In addition to the anxieties related to money that might be experienced by any individual, LGBTQ individuals' financial anxieties may be compounded by increased discrimination in the workplace that negatively impacts career prospects and earning potential. LGBTQ individuals experience body shame/body image issues at twice the rate (40%) of the non-LGBTQ population (18%), often contributing to the formation of eating disorders and/or body dysmorphic disorder.

5. A: In early remission, the criteria for a substance use disorder have previously been met, but none of those criteria have been fulfilled (except for the criteria for craving) for a period of between 3 months and 1 year. In sustained remission, none of those criteria are fulfilled (except for the criteria for craving) for 1 year or longer. If the client is in remission in a controlled environment, this should be specified. Some clients may be on maintenance therapy, which is a replacement medication that can be taken to avoid withdrawal symptoms. The client could still be considered in remission from a substance use disorder if, while using maintenance therapy, they do not meet any criteria for that substance use disorder except for craving. This client does not live in a controlled environment, such as a sober house, and can be considered in remission despite being in maintenance therapy as long as he has not met criteria for use disorder except craving.

261

6. B: Although the social worker does need to understand the client's identified problem, identifying the root causes or precipitating events/context is not a prerequisite of the task-centered practice model. The social worker may ask questions to help the client develop clarity regarding specific facets of the problem, but this is based on objective data/information from the client rather than the result of theorizing. For instance, if the client's problem is related to finances, the social worker might ask questions to better understand the client's income, expenses, and needs. The deeply rooted values and norms related to money—such as the client's issues with money stemming from parents' financial challenges—are not explored. The other answer choices are all true statements regarding the task-centered practice model.

7. A: Psychodynamic theory is specifically concerned with a person's past experiences that form the foundation of their current psychological processes. Interventions based upon this theory support the client to identify, understand, and process past experiences that are influencing current thought and behavior patterns on a conscious and/or subconscious level. With cognitive theory strategies, the client's current thoughts are the focus. Interventions based upon family systems theory may also include some exploration of past family interactions; however, the primary focus is on the present relationship dynamics. Strengths-based approaches use the client's past to identify strengths, rather than understand current behavior. Past experiences are explored in order to identify strategies, skills, and attributes that were used to navigate difficulty and overcome adversity.

8. B: The biopsychosocial approach is a way for the social worker to assess biological factors (e.g., genetics, diet, exercise, sleep, drug use), psychological factors (e.g., behaviors, beliefs, coping skills), and social factors (e.g., family, friends, culture, traumas). The biomedical approach, which was previously used by psychiatrists and doctors, only assesses the biological and medical factors involved. Cognitive behavioral therapy is a therapeutic way to help clients change unhelpful thought processes or intrusive thoughts associated with anxiety and depression. Psychodynamic therapy is an in-depth approach to uncover the unconscious processes of the client's thinking.

9. D: One in four individuals with a mental disorder causing serious impairment also has a substance use disorder. Approximately 70% of adolescents with substance use disorders also have a mental health disorder. Although mental health disorders were once thought to occur first more often, there is actually great variance in which one comes first. Fewer than 10% of adults with serious mental health disorders with a co-occurring substance use disorder receive treatment for both disorders.

10. B: Family acceptance has been found to be a critical protective factor for LGBTQ youth, protecting against depression, suicidal ideation, and substance use. Access to educational resources that provide accurate information can support a family's increased understanding of their LGBTQ family member. This could, in turn, influence the development of empathy and acceptance. Family cohesion is a general family strength.

11. A: The degree of discord is substantial, and the level of verbal conflict is high, thus oppositional defiant disorder would be the most appropriate diagnosis. A parent-child relational problem tends to be less severe in nature, while conduct disorder is much more severe (i.e., involves violations of the rights of others, physical aggression, or property damage, persistent truancy, etc.). Intermittent explosive disorder addresses impulsive acts of aggression or violence (as opposed to premeditated or planned behaviors). Persistent conduct disorder carried into adulthood may meet criteria for antisocial personality disorder.

12. B: A primary focus of a social worker when using SFBT is the exploration of the client's strengths and life experiences, particularly "exceptions." In SFBT, exceptions are moments or experiences in which the problem was not present. The social worker crafts reflective statements and questions to help the client explore these exceptions and then bring attention to elements that might contribute to a solution. The social worker does not believe that they know the solution, but rather engages in a co-construction of a solution with the client. Answer A, "point the client in the direction of the solution," suggests that the social worker knows the solution and is trying to get the client to see it. Answer C is technically true, but answer B is a better description of how the social worker would do this. Answer D does not reflect the values or focus of SFBT.

13. B: The social worker should review any provided documentation, including demographics, trauma history, medical history, current school records, or legal paperwork, that was provided by the parents/guardians at intake. Understanding the client's history can assist the social worker in providing the best treatment for the individual.

14. B: The social worker should support the couple in identifying goals or skills that would benefit and improve their marriage. Social workers should not influence the type of goals that couples would like to work on because it is not the social worker's place to decide. Allowing each spouse to decide on a goal for the other person would not support the couple as a whole but instead would give the opportunity to create even more division.

15. C: Data should reflect households served, rather than individuals. Households facing eviction are a significant portion of program recipients, but those on the verge of homelessness should also be included. Staying with a friend or family is considered homelessness when the person cannot stay there for more than 14 days, which is typically the requirement to get on the homeless shelter waiting list. Comparing the cost per household with a shelter stay is a helpful statistic; however, it is less helpful than the data in answer C.

16. D: The information needed to complete a mental status exam is often gathered during the completion of the biopsychosocial assessment. Any portions of the mental status exam that were not observed or learned about during the biopsychosocial assessment can then be specifically addressed. The mental status exam and the biopsychosocial assessment may include objective and subjective information (answer A). The mental status exam should be documented as such with a clear heading (answer B). Both portions of answer C are true and do not describe a difference between the biopsychosocial assessment and the mental status exam.

17. D: The social worker should begin by asking the client to determine the goal of therapy. This will help the social worker and client work together toward a common goal. The social worker should not dismiss the client's feelings. Based on the information provided, depression is not an appropriate diagnosis. The client's specific military history does not have a bearing on the direction of therapy at this time, although this may be explored during a later session if it is a root of the client's difficulties.

18. A: The social worker can assume that the child was provided a script to use when being asked about his home life and the care he receives. The social worker should continue to assess and intervene to ensure the safety and well-being of the child.

19. A: The most appropriate diagnosis for this youth is oppositional defiant disorder. Intermittent explosive disorder is only appropriate when a behavior is compulsive in nature. While anger may be a part of that picture, it tends to be an overreaction to a provocation; other relevant compulsions include gambling, skin-picking, kleptomania, etc. The hallmark of conduct disorder is deliberate cruelty and wanton disregard for others' rights and property. This client lacks any pervasive and long-standing evidence in this regard. Antisocial personality disorder is only diagnosed after the age of 18 when there was a history of conduct disorder prior to the age of 15.

20. C: An individual's level of functional ability reflects the interaction between their intrinsic capacity and the environment in which they live. For example, the functional ability of an individual with poor respiratory functioning (an intrinsic quality) will be significantly impacted by living in a poorly ventilated apartment above a restaurant (environmental quality). Understanding why their functional ability is low (poor environment) will lead to the needed intervention (moving) to maximize their functional ability. IADLs are tasks that enable an individual to live independently. Although important to assess, the environment is most critical to assess because it may prevent an individual from completing an IADL that they could successfully do in another setting. Mental health diagnosis (an intrinsic quality) and the availability of caregiver support are important aspects to assess, but they are not as critical for understanding functional ability.

21. A: The most effective treatment for obsessive-compulsive disorder (OCD) is a combination of psychotherapy and medication. The dosage and type of medication must be determined by a psychiatrist. Brain mapping can assist in identifying psychiatric conditions, including OCD, but it is not a form of treatment for this diagnosis. Cognitive behavioral therapy often includes an intervention called thought stopping. Thought stopping is used to block negative thoughts and replace them with neutral or positive thoughts. This is found to be an ineffective treatment in the context of OCD because this is a common ritual that individuals with OCD use, so it increases their symptoms. Effective treatment would include helping the individual experience their thoughts and use increasing exposure to the object of their fear and changing the response to that stimulus.

22. A: The SALT model more explicitly focuses on leadership that is socially conscious and focused on issues of social justice. All three models focus on helping people in need, addressing social problems, and recognizing the importance of human relationships (answers B and C). Answer D is not one of the social work ethical principles.

23. D: The first step should be to promptly refer the asthmatic boy to a medical doctor. Asthma can be life-threatening, and the child is also described as congested and unwell. Given that "all" possessions were lost, it is reasonable to conclude that the child has little or no remaining inhaler medicines for an asthma crisis. While all may attend the medical visit, the boy needs to be seen urgently. Following or concurrently, a complete psychosocial evaluation needs to be completed. After further evaluation, the key elements of a case presentation for the director should include: 1) psychosocial history: mental health issues and social history such as living situation, finances, education, etc.; 2) individual issues: substance abuse history, legal history, physical abuse and neglect history, as well as resources, strengths, and resiliency, etc.; 3) family history, family dynamics, and extended family resources; 4) potential community resources and supports; 5) diversity issues: culture, language, race/ethnicity, orientation, etc.; 6) potential ethical issues and presenting issues in self-determination; and 7) intervention recommendations, including requisite resources.

24. B: Malingering is a V code (which indicates other conditions that may be a focus of clinical attention), not a diagnosis. Malingering involves feigning symptoms primarily to derive an external reward (lawsuit settlement, disability benefits, etc.). Illness anxiety disorder involves a misapprehension or misinterpretation of bodily symptoms. Factitious disorder involves a feigning of symptoms primarily in order to receive the attention offered when one assumes a sick role, even in the absence of external reward. Somatic symptom disorder is characterized by complaints regarding several organ systems involving different body sites and functions rather than a single body organ or situation.

25. C: Although using additional resources such as articles, handouts, and coping skills might be helpful to the client, allowing time in the session to practice coping skills is the most beneficial option. Allowing the client to try using these skills on her own for the first time without practice may decrease the chance that she will attempt them when needed. Showing her how a skill can be successfully used during the session gives the client the opportunity to ask questions or adjust the coping skill to what works best for her.

26. C: Whenever possible, the social worker should arrange interpretation services that will support the client to be honest and feel confident that confidentiality will be maintained. It is best practice to not have friends or family members serve as interpreters. If the Nepali community in the social worker's location is very small, it is likely that the client will know the interpreters if they live locally. If an interpreter from another locale is available, this may provide the best chance of the interpreter and client not having a close relationship. If only local interpreters are available, it is important for the social worker to explain this to the family and confirm their comfort using the interpretation services to complete the mental health assessment and services. Answers A and D are helpful strategies for using the funding for interpretation services judiciously. The social worker should use these or similar strategies whenever using interpretation services.

27. B: Microlevel interventions are used directly between the social worker and client, such as directly asking the client what their pronouns are. Although using the social worker's own intake forms with new clients is a microlevel intervention, it is not best practice to do so. Rather than making their own form, the social worker could engage in mezzo-level interventions to impact the procedures and policies of their agency.

28. C: Because this young man's withdrawn behavior has been persistent throughout his lifespan, he would most likely be considered to have a schizoid personality. Schizotypal personality disorder shares the elements of discomfort in social environments but also includes evidence of illusions and magical thinking which are not evident in this individual's description. Schizophreniform disorder is much less adaptive and contains features of schizophrenia, and although someone might be considered to have a highly introverted personality, introversion is not a diagnosable condition.

29. B: The probable primary diagnosis is major depressive disorder with psychotic features. The precipitating event was his job loss, which led to depression. When the depression deepened, he started "hearing voices," and he drank to cope with the negative messages (and to cope with his depression). Therefore, while the alcohol use must be included in his diagnostic formulation, it would not be his primary diagnosis. Of note, the diagnosis of major depression with psychotic features is missed about 25% of the time in an emergency room, with only the depression typically identified.

30. A: Because the landlord seeks to obtain as much financial compensation as possible for the apartment unit with zero responsibility for maintenance, an elder advocate can assist the tenant in retaining his rights. The lease agreement must be followed; otherwise, the landlord will obtain too much power over the tenant. This is reflective of conflict theory, which discusses the power struggles between different roles (e.g., chief executive officer vs. employees, landlord vs. tenant). Although considering discounted or generic versions of the individual's medications may help him financially, this likely will not address the discrepancy in rent, nor does it address the unfair treatment of the elderly man.

31. C: Pervasive developmental disorders is NOT a DSM category. The DSM-5-TR classifications are:

- Neurodevelopmental disorders:
- Schizophrenia spectrum and other psychotic disorders
- Bipolar and related disorders
- Depressive disorders
- Anxiety disorders
- Obsessive-compulsive and related disorders
- Trauma- and stressor-related disorders
- Dissociative disorders
- Somatic symptom and related disorders
- Feeding and eating disorders
- Elimination disorders
- Sleep-wake disorders
- Sexual dysfunctions
- Gender dysphoria
- Disruptive, impulse-control, and conduct disorders
- Substance-related and addictive disorders
- Neurocognitive disorders
- Personality disorders
- Paraphilic disorders
- Other mental disorders and additional codes
- Medication-induced movement disorders and other adverse effects of medications
- Other conditions that may be a focus of clinical attention

Most disorders that were classified as pervasive developmental disorders under DSM-IV will now fall under the classification of neurodevelopmental disorders, and more specifically, communication disorders or autism spectrum disorder.

32. A: Research and experience have proven the immense value that community members, and/or those directly impacted by the target problem(s), can bring to all stages of a community assessment, planning, intervention, and evaluation. Involvement of the community in these ways is called participatory planning. Effective community practice requires the participation and cooperation of a wide variety of people and/or organizations. It is therefore critical that community social workers develop strong facilitation skills to gather input, build shared vision and goals, navigate conflict and disagreement, and incorporate information from feedback loops. Although communication is arguably a critical social work skill for community practice, agenda setting is not at this level of importance. Research is also a critical skill for community social work practice, but without participatory planning skills, the social worker is more likely to lead the research efforts rather than to build community capacity by training community members to gather research (a research approach called action research).

33. D: These symptoms most closely resemble panic disorder. The symptoms of a panic attack appear very quickly and generally peak within 10 minutes. Typical symptoms include rapid heart rate, shortness of breath, light-headedness, trembling, derealization and depersonalization (feeling surreal and detached from self), nausea, dizziness, numbness, and tingling feelings. These are typically accompanied by feelings of impending doom and/or death. Many of the symptoms are a direct result of hyperventilation during the acute panic phase. Anxiety disorder due to a medical condition is not correct, as there is no underlying medical condition. Generalized anxiety disorder is not correct, as it does not have sudden onset but rather is an accumulation of worry and anxiety that persists for 6 or more months (without an underlying medical condition or substance use precipitant). Acute stress disorder is not correct, as it involves a precipitating PTSD-like traumatic event that induces the symptoms of stress.

34. C: The most likely diagnosis is borderline personality disorder. The key features of BPD involve instability in relationships and affect, poor self-image, and high impulsivity. Violations of personal rights and apathy common to antisocial personality disorder are insufficiently pronounced. While evidence of histrionic behavior exists, the devaluation/over-valuation pattern common to BPD is not accounted for via histrionic personality disorder. Likewise, the need for admiration, pervasive with narcissism, is not mentioned here.

35. B: This definition describes some of the biopsychosocial indicators of institutionalization, a process by which prisoners cope with the myriad stressors, norms, and demands of prison life by adapting their thoughts, emotions, and behaviors. Some individuals embody these characteristics in the other settings listed, particularly hypervigilance, anxiety, depression, and social withdrawal. However, muted affect and a dependence on external controls are most unique to the prison population. Muted affect develops over time as prisoners learn to control and suppress their emotional reactions. Dependence on external control is required of prisoners because nearly all personal responsibility and initiative are prohibited. Over time, many individuals in prison become completely dependent on external control structures and are personally unable to cope with making decisions.

36. C: Congruence in communication refers to the alignment of the communication content (words), tone of voice, and nonverbal communication. For instance, if someone says "I hate you" in a kind voice while smiling, their communication lacks congruence. Incongruent communication between partners in a couple is associated with increased misunderstanding and diminished trust. Changes in tone of voice or having a limited vocabulary may influence misunderstanding, but they are not likely to impact trust. Multitasking may influence misunderstanding and trust, to a degree, but it is not as likely to occur during a counseling session.

37. A: Although conflict theories vary in many ways, most agree that those with power shape the structures of society to maintain their power, resulting in inequality and oppression. According to some conflict theorists, consensus building within a group of leaders and residents can only result in maintenance of the status quo because those with power compel the residents to agree to their priorities. The high cost of rent, with dramatic annual increases, perpetuates poverty for renters and prosperity for property owners. Many conflict theorists believe that conflict, such as protests and strikes, create necessary upheaval in order to bring about change. Many conflicts occur due to conflicting values and lack of insight regarding the "other." A poverty simulation is

Mometrix

one strategy used to help city leaders gain insight and empathy about the realities of those in poverty, which could influence them to develop policies and laws to reduce poverty and its impact in the community.

38. D: The null hypothesis for this study would state that there shall be no measurable difference in depression symptom reporting between the control group and the intervention group. The null hypothesis (often designated H_0) proposes that no relationship exists between two variables (often designated X and Y) other than that arising from random chance alone. If a study's results demonstrate a significant difference, then the null hypothesis is "rejected." If no significant differences emerge, then the study "failed to reject the null hypothesis." Statistical testing does not prove any hypotheses, but instead disproves them via rejection.

39. B: Key features of dissociative amnesia with dissociative fugue are localized or selective amnesia surrounding certain events, or generalized amnesia involving identity and life history, along with some sort of purposeful travel or simply aimless wandering. The amnesia must produce significant distress, and/or impairment in social, occupational, or other significant areas of personal function. It must not be a result of substance ingestion or a medical (especially neurological) condition. Dissociative identity disorder (known in the past as multiple personality disorder) would not be correct, as it involves the development of one or more separate identities.

40. B: Peer supervision will increase connectivity, decrease feelings of isolation, and create effective communication and relationships between coworkers. Through peer supervision, case managers can also learn from one another with regard to their shared experience during the COVID-19 pandemic. Interdisciplinary and dual supervision would not increase the connection among the case managers, nor would it help increase problem-solving skills in the staff.

41. C: In order for a social worker to reduce their professional liability, they must obtain supervision from another licensed social worker. The social work supervisor will provide additional credibility and support regarding the competency and ethical standing of the social worker and their practice decisions. In the event of litigation, supervision documentation can be used in court to demonstrate that the social worker's practice decisions were reviewed by another professional and were in line with NASW standards and social work ethics. There are numerous ways that a social worker of any stage can prevent burnout and improve their clinical practice, including but not limited to supervision. Supervision is not needed to maintain an independent social work license.

42. C: When children endure trauma and other adverse experiences, their brains secrete high levels of the stress hormone cortisol. This has been shown to negatively impact brain structure and functioning, contributing to higher rates of depression, anxiety, poor emotional regulation, and acting-out behaviors. Furthermore, the impaired brain structures may continue to adversely impact functioning throughout their lifespan. Changes in brain chemistry are a primary mechanism through which the other variables impact children's development.

43. B: An open-ended question focused on the client's goal will invite the social worker to discuss the clinical services, rather than how the supervised social worker feels about providing services or what they have done. It will also provide information related to the service plan and about whether the frequency and length of sessions reflect the client's needs and goals identified in the individual service plan. If the supervisee has overidentified with Stacey, she may find it difficult to focus on the client's progress or goals. Option C is an effective, open-ended question that is better to ask once the supervisor has more information. Questions that start with "why" often feel more confrontational and can encourage defensiveness. It is best for the supervisor to learn more before using such a direct question.

44. D: The goal of visiting his children twice per week over the next 3 months is the only choice that is specific, measurable, attainable, relevant, and time-based. Using the SMART goal model will assist the client in measuring progress over the specified time period. The other options did not provide specifics or measurable markers to check progress toward goal attainment.

45. C: The social worker can continue to assist the family in making referrals to appropriate providers because this situation relates to discharge planning. It would not be appropriate for the social worker to act as a long-term therapist for the family because that is out of their scope of practice.

46. A: With this statement, the father may be assuming that his child will not be able to function in society and will rely on his support into adulthood. The social worker recognizes that the child is eligible for many forms of support to increase his skills throughout his lifetime. The father should be referred for cognitive behavioral therapy, which will help him determine whether his concerns are realistic and find ways to approach the situation; it is an evidence-based approach to anxiety management. Educational handouts can assist in increasing knowledge, but they will not help the father process difficult emotions. Family counseling would be inappropriate because the diagnosis is not a conflict that needs resolving; rather, the father needs coping skills to work through his emotions. Grief counseling would be beneficial during a loss of a family member or friend, but not to cope with a new diagnosis.

47. B: Simon's age, change of personality, aggressive behavior, and confusion point to senile dementia and possibly Alzheimer's disease.

48. A: The client's symptoms are congruent with bipolar I disorder criteria. Depakote is the first-line drug recommended as pharmacotherapy for bipolar I disorder. Although it is an antiseizure medication, it also has mood-stabilizing effects in the context of bipolar I disorder. Zoloft (sertraline) is an antidepressant that can also be prescribed to assist with symptoms of bipolar I disorder, but it should not be taken without a mood-stabilizing medication. Klonopin (clonazepam) is used to treat seizures or panic disorders, and it is not indicated for bipolar disorder. Xanax (alprazolam) is prescribed for anxiety or panic disorders.

49. A: A karyotype is a picture of an individual's chromosomes, arranged into 23 pairs. This visual display of the chromosomes provides a clear view of any pairs that are missing a chromosome (monosomy) or that have an extra chromosome (trisomy). This is the only feature of the chromosomes that is clearly understood from this report. Other tests are needed to determine the type of genetic mutation, the reason for the abnormality (if it can be conclusively known), and the client's blood type.

50. C: Many social workers may not wish to share unsuccessful strategies, especially if they were, in hindsight, poorly chosen or implemented. It is valuable to share successful and unsuccessful treatment strategies because each may provide valuable information regarding the client's needs and what an effective treatment might be. Case selection for presentation is influenced by a variety of factors that could indicate the use of a case close to termination, or even a past client no longer receiving services. No identifying information should be included in the presentation, unless a release of information was completed by the client for this purpose (which occurs rarely, if ever). Although any case presenter must choose some details to omit for the sake of time, sparse information should only be used if the express intention of the case presentation is to be a learning exercise. Otherwise, all pertinent information should be included to ensure accurate understanding of the case.

51. C: Primary prevention strategies that support healthy aging include those targeting younger individuals who are not yet at risk for symptoms or conditions associated with aging. Research has identified self-esteem and self-achievement as the psychological factors that strongly influence healthy aging. Supporting middle-aged adults seeking a career change could have a positive impact on both of these psychological factors. Answers A and D are focused on the elderly population, making them secondary if not tertiary strategies. Answer B targets adults of all ages; however, it is a secondary prevention strategy for healthy aging because the adults have mental health concerns, a risk factor for decreased health.

52. A: The social worker can use de-escalation tactics before resorting to the remaining options and before the situation becomes dangerous. The individual has not threatened to harm himself or others, so 911 does not need to be contacted at this time. The mother would likely have difficulty removing the client from the room when he is already upset.

53. A: The lymphatic system, although perhaps more commonly known for partnering with the immune system to protect the body from disease, also distributes fluid and nutrients in the body. The circulatory system transports oxygen and nutrients within the blood throughout the body. The endocrine system produces hormones. The respiratory system brings air into the body and removes carbon dioxide.

54. C: Postintervention data cannot adequately communicate a project's impact without having the preintervention data for comparison. Measurable objectives and benchmarks are critical to secure funding and focus resources intentionally, and they allow specific accomplishments to be communicated regarding the project's impact. However, the quantitative and qualitative impact of each objective is best demonstrated with the baseline conditions for comparison. Engagement of local political and civic institutions is a key part of addressing problems and maintaining long-term impacts in the community.

55. C: When highlighting a discrepancy, the social worker draws the client's attention to two of their desires, values, or goals that are in contradiction to or compete with one another. This can encourage the client to reflect on which is more important or preferable, because they are not both possible at the same time. Highlighting a discrepancy is not an effective strategy for building confidence in the ability to change or increasing the hope for change.

56. A: One form of effective self-care includes setting boundaries. Social workers can become compassion-fatigued or burnt out by the stress and trauma that they help to manage daily. This social worker is struggling to manage these new emotions while meeting the needs of her job. Self-medicating is not appropriate because it does not directly address the stress in order to create healthy coping skills. Speaking with her loved ones or looking into other positions may help in the meantime, but setting boundaries to provide herself with self-care is the best option to manage her stress in the long term.

57. C: CBT, provided during and/or after incarceration, has consistently been found to decrease recidivism. ACT and solution-focused therapy are not evidence-based strategies for this purpose. Post-incarceration supervision, although widely used, has not been found to decrease recidivism. More intensive supervision has actually been found to increase the likelihood of further criminal activity. Similarly, high-intensity programs for prisoners negatively impact the recidivism rate for lower-risk individuals. Individualized assessment is therefore critical to identify the unique needs and strengths of each prisoner to determine the type and level of support needed during and after their incarceration. Such assessment also increases the identification and treatment of persons with mental health and substance abuse disorders, which is critical to reducing recidivism. Housing assistance has been found to reduce recidivism more effectively than job training programs, although halfway houses specifically do not tend to be effective. Job training does not guarantee that the individual will find and maintain a job, and failing to do so often leads to homelessness. Those with housing assistance have the time and resources to build job stability in the months and years following incarceration.

58. D: While a client with schizophrenia may present with a blunted affect, it is not necessary to make a diagnosis of schizophrenia. According to DSM-5-TR, Criterion A of diagnosing schizophrenia states that the client must present with at least two of the five following symptoms: delusions, hallucinations, disorganized speech, grossly disorganized or catatonic behavior, and negative symptoms (i.e., diminished emotional expression or avolition). However, at least one of the symptoms must be delusions, hallucinations, or disorganized speech.

59. A: The medical social worker should not assume that the community social worker obtained verbal consent. Rather, the medical social worker should request that a signed consent form be sent to the office. The social worker should not provide any information regarding the client without consent being provided first.

60. C: In order to maintain the client's self-determination, the social worker should remind the client and family that the decision of care remains with the client. The social worker should approach the subject with compassion and understanding because the family is struggling emotionally with the client's decision. A DNR form is an advance directive. The client has the right to determine how he would like to receive care in case he is unable to communicate his wishes later on. Although commenting on the family's love for the client is appropriate, it does not advocate for the client's right to self-determination.

61. C: The social worker has violated HIPAA regulations regarding the security of the information included in the electronic medical record system. The social worker must report this breach of security as quickly as possible to her supervisor. The remaining options are insufficient and do not adhere to HIPAA regulations regarding breaches of privacy.

62. D: The key phrase in this question is "in order to support the client's continued sobriety." Knowing the drug(s) used is the most important factor to inform the social worker's specific goal of preventing relapse, because drugs vary in the amount of time that physical and/or mental cravings persist. The use of certain drugs can result in the potential of mental cravings for many years, long after physical cravings have subsided. If continued cravings are suspected, this will influence which strategies and skills are a focus of the client's treatment to ensure that the potential of cravings is adequately addressed.

63. B: Genito-pelvic pain disorder refers to any form of pain during sexual intercourse that persistently recurs. Causes can include involuntary contractions of the outer third of the vagina (involving the pubococcygeus muscles), vaginal dryness, inflammation, infection, skin conditions, sexually transmitted infections (STIs), or any other underlying medical condition. Female sexual interest/arousal disorder would not be correct because it involves a psychological aversion to or avoidance of sexual activity, rather than physical pain. Female orgasmic disorder is incorrect because it involves a failure to reach orgasm, even with appropriate stimulation, excluding an underlying medical condition.

64. B: Although customer service is important, the peer review audit will provide insight for the supervisor to understand who on their team is struggling to meet document deadlines, the amount of signed consent forms that the agency receives back from clients, and if there are areas in which case managers need additional training. Customer service ratings are not included in the peer review auditing process.

65. D: Although the other responses appropriately identify the problems with the intern's language, they do not show support for the intern in her learning journey. The intern has been assigned to the domestic violence agency to learn and to be guided in correctly working with this population. By responding with open-ended questions, the field instructor is able to gain insight on why the intern thought that the language she used was appropriate and to reframe her thinking through education.

66. C: The client is clearly displaying both hallucinations (seeing things not there, e.g., objects floating) and delusions (believing things that are not true, e.g., thought control), as well as the rambling and disorganized speech characteristic of schizophrenia. The condition has existed longer than 6 months, though it is currently in an acute phase. No subtype specifier is required, as with the advent of DSM-5, prior specifiers (e.g., paranoid, disorganized, undifferentiated), with the exception of catatonic type, are no longer used. A diagnosis of bipolar disorder would not be correct, as there is no evidence of mood cycling and this is not an exacerbated manic phase with psychotic features. Schizoaffective disorder would not be correct, as it requires the presence of a clear affective component (mania or depression), which is not in evidence either by history or presentation. Substance-induced psychosis requires the proximate use of a mind-altering substance (such as methamphetamine), which is also not in evidence. While there is a remote history (and one cannot entirely rule out more recent ingestion), the parents indicate the symptoms have been consistently present for the greater part of a year, which precludes the episodic presentation of substance-induced psychosis.

67. D: Infant mental health services are funded by insurance to support families with young children (ages 0–6) who are at risk of developing a mental health condition at a young age. These trained professionals will provide in-home support to help parents understand how to respond to behaviors and will encourage the strengthening of the parent–child relationship.

68. C: Difficulty learning to read is a particular problem for hearing-impaired students, and many hearing-impaired people grow up in families in which other members do not learn sign language, and attend schools in which there are limited opportunities to interact with teachers and students who know how to use sign language. Frustration with not being able to communicate and with not catching verbal cues can make deaf people seem rude to others. Because Rose communicates fluently with her teacher, elective mutism and autistic disorders would be ruled out in this example.

69. D: A theory of change is an explanatory description of the cause and effect that a proposed set of strategies will have on the desired outcome. In contrast to a logic model, which describes what the inputs, actions, and desired outcomes of a program are, a theory of change explains the cause-and-effect logic of why the inputs/actions will lead to the desired outcomes. When presenting a new, untested program, a theory of change will be the most persuasive information to provide to potential funders. A statement of impact describes the impact that a program has already had. A strategic plan is used by an organization's leaders to communicate to employees the goals, action steps, and planned impact for the plan's time period.

70. B: The social worker should validate the feelings expressed by her client as a means of building rapport and should let the client know that she is here to help navigate these feelings. The social worker must let the client know that this is a safe place to discuss these feelings and that there is room to unpack them in future sessions. Because this is a new-patient appointment, the social worker must also spend time gathering additional information for intake purposes. For that reason, exploring the client's feelings deeper may not be appropriate or most opportune at this time. Further, the social worker should avoid asking "why" because this can be interpreted as being judgmental and may become a barrier in the therapeutic relationship. It is inappropriate to disclose this information to the client's parents because this would break client-counselor confidentiality. Encouraging the client by stating that these feelings will fade with hormonal changes is misleading, discounts the client's feelings in the moment, and will not foster a therapeutic relationship.

71. D: Prolonged grief disorder is diagnosed when intense and compromising grief extends at least beyond the first year. Key features with the client are her sense of meaninglessness without her spouse, estrangement from others, emotional numbness, and preoccupying thoughts about dying to be with him again. The diagnosis of major depression would not be correct because the focus is on the loss, rather than a generalized meaninglessness, hopelessness, and helplessness. Post-traumatic stress would not be correct because it centers on key features associated with experiencing an overwhelming and traumatic event (such as combat), with flashbacks and other emotions tied directly to the event itself, rather than to a loss. Uncomplicated bereavement would not be correct, as the intensity and compromising features of the loss are not resolving over time, but rather becoming overly protracted. Of note, DSM-5 removed the "bereavement exclusion." It is possible to be diagnosed with both bereavement and major depression if the circumstances warrant.

72. A: The task-centered practice model shares many characteristics with problem solving and SFBT, but it has a unique and structured focus on the identification and resolution of obstacles to task completion. This may include obstacles at a micro, mezzo, or even macro level. The client, social worker, or others may have tasks developed and "assigned" to them to address these obstacles. The completion of tasks, however, is not a core function of the social worker in this practice model, but is an intervention used at appropriate times. Task-centered practice intentionally does not include work to build client insight regarding the problem's origins; instead, it uses the problem as defined and understood by the client at that time. Scaling questions are not used in task-centered practice.

73. D: Cluster evaluations are optimum where multiple sites, programs, and interests are involved. The evaluative steps involve visiting each site, collecting records, orienting to each site, and identifying unique service plans. Next, a networking conference is held to identify commonalities and uniqueness among the programs. Cluster-level questions focus on information from early data collection and initial program analyses. Later conferences focus on findings and outcomes, with recommendations for change. Cluster evaluation involves many participants, and thus offers considerable certainty about the conclusions reached. Its primary limitations include the potential for bias and groupthink to occur.

74. D: The most likely diagnosis to describe this behavior would be other specified paraphilia. Exhibitionism involves a minimum of 6 months of recurrent urges, fantasies, and/or behaviors involving the exposure of one's genitals to an unsuspecting person, or where clinically significant distress or impairment in social, occupational, or other meaningful areas of functioning occurs. In this case, however, the recipient of the client's disrobing behaviors is not an unsuspecting stranger, nor does the vignette specify that she exposes her genitals or if she fully or only partially disrobes. Thus, this is more an act of consensual sex-play, rather than exhibitionism. Voyeurism is not correct, as it involves watching an unsuspecting person disrobing. Frotteurism is inaccurate, as it involves intense sexual arousal from the urge, fantasy, or act of touching or rubbing against a nonconsenting person.

75. C: The genotype is an individual's collection of genes. Any mutations would impact the individual's genotype. This will in turn affect their phenotype—the physical expression of their genetic makeup. Gene mutations do not always impact chromosomes' structure or number, especially when the number of mutated genes is small. Although environmental factors (such as toxins or trauma) can impact the genetic makeup of offspring, this is not always the case.

76. C: The therapist should first determine if the subpoena is legally valid by consulting with a lawyer. If the subpoena is deemed legally valid, the social worker can request that the court limit the order of the subpoena and/or seal the records. The therapist cannot decide which documents to send on her own without direction from the court order. If the court refuses to limit the order of the subpoena, the therapist must send all of the requested documentation.

77. C: In the United States, 9.4% of children have been diagnosed with attention-deficit/hyperactivity disorder. Boys are twice as likely as girls to have this diagnosis. Preteens and teenagers are more likely to have this diagnosis than are preschool-aged children.

78. A: The social worker should first research the proper methods used to work with a Native American family in a manner that is culturally appropriate. The social worker must keep in mind the cultural differences in raising children and consider how risk factors may present differently across different cultures. After completing this research, the social worker may then complete a home visit and use a standardized assessment while keeping those cultural differences in mind.

79. D: The first step of EBP is the formulation of a question that includes four components: the specific client problem, two possible interventions (one can be to "do nothing"), and the desired outcome. This question will guide the identification of relevant research (step 2 of EBP). Answer A includes only a portion of the first step. Answer B is not part of the EBP process, although it could be a helpful exercise. Answer C is an activity that is necessary in order to implement the EBP process.

80. B: In a crisis, the social worker's first priority is to help the client to manage stress in a way that allows the client to return to the previous level of functioning. Once the client has returned to a baseline status, the social worker can assist with connecting the client to referrals and resources, along with identifying new coping skills.

81. D: The most appropriate early diagnosis would be delusional disorder, erotomanic type. The client openly indicates that this famous person has loving feelings for him, in spite of the fact they've never met or directly communicated in any way. Classic features of erotomania (sometimes also called de Clérambault syndrome) include identification with someone in higher status (famous, wealthy, etc.), and it is more common among women than men. The symptoms are not infrequently manifest in either schizophrenia or bipolar mania, at which point either would be the proper primary diagnosis (e.g., bipolar, acute manic phase, with erotomanic features). Grandiose type is not correct, as it focuses on a client's belief that they have special talents, unique understandings, or an unrecognized or unreported extraordinary accomplishment. Jealous type is not correct, as the inordinate jealousy must be centered in faulty perceptions of infidelity in a real relationship. Persecutory type is not correct, as it focuses on a fear of a conspiracy by others to do the client harm.

82. A: Congruence in communication uses the therapeutic concept of reflecting one's inner experience as a therapist to the outward expressions shown to the client. This genuine reaction helps build strong rapport and trust with the client. Constricted affect is the sense that emotions are being muted as they relate to the information being communicated; this would not make the client feel supported and understood. Collaborating on treatment plan development is part of the therapeutic process, but it would not help the client feel like she could trust the social worker to be vulnerable. Open body language is a method of therapeutic communication, but it would be less impactful in making the client feel she is in a safe, nonjudgmental environment than congruence in communication would.

83. B: Research gathering is the most likely strategy to have resulted in the creation of rent increase caps because it could be used to provide the council with information regarding rent increases, average family incomes, the amount of financial aid available, eviction rates, homeless shelter waiting lists, and other details of the community's housing context. These data are likely to be more compelling than personal testimony. Community organizing focuses on building the skills of community members to help them develop capacity and power to influence community well-being. Although the personal experiences of homeless or formerly homeless individuals may have been insightful to the council, they are not likely to have been persuasive enough to influence a policy change. The vignette does not clearly state that a coalition was formed. The three agencies may have formed a coalition, and, if so, this would have helped them maximize their collective resources and influence.

84. A: Incarceration of a parent, particularly of the primary caregiving parent, is uniquely disruptive for children. These children are at a high risk for homelessness, disrupted education, child welfare placement, poverty, criminal activity, and antisocial behavior. Incarcerated mothers are more likely to have been the primary caregiving parent compared to incarcerated fathers. Incarcerated adults are disproportionately from populations already at risk for poverty, mental illness, and substance use, often resulting in negative effects for their children even before the incarceration takes place. Although children of parents with mental health and/or substance abuse disorders often experience negative effects, the severity of the disorders and related effects vary greatly. Many of these children experience few negative effects, due to the illness being less severe and a range of resiliency factors.

85. A: Using a client's first name (rather than last) would be a way to decrease the power imbalance, but it would be considered too formal to use her last name during each interaction. The therapist holds power in this relationship, especially because they are legally mandated sessions. The client has not come to therapy of her own accord. The therapist should use the remaining options as ways to connect and create a safe place for the client.

86. D: Language disorder is characterized by substantial impairment in speaking, as seen in lower scores on standardized tests of language use in the presence of otherwise normal cognitive capacity. Speech sound disorder (formerly called phonological disorder) presents as substantial impairment in making appropriate speech sounds, sufficient to impede success in academic, occupational, or interpersonal communication. Childhood-onset fluency disorder (stuttering) involves a disturbance in the timing and fluency of speech, unrelated to age and normal development.

87. A: The client is exhibiting symptoms of a neurocognitive disorder. He is having cognitive changes without depressive symptoms. His cognitive symptoms have mildly diminished his activities of daily living, but he is able to complete them with modifications, indicating a mild neurocognitive disorder.

88. C: Roughly half of individuals with either a mental health diagnosis or a substance use disorder will develop the other at some point in their life. These commonly co-occur, and the social worker should be acutely aware of the possibility of a mental health disorder underlying substance use and vice versa.

89. B: Helping children build protective factors is the most effective way to increase their resiliency in the event of future abuse. Children's social and emotional competence is one protective factor, which answer B would support. Working to prevent abuse or neglect while in the foster home is an important part of the social worker's responsibilities. Increasing the parents' knowledge of parenting skills is an important protective factor; however, doing so is not within the social worker's current job responsibilities. It is not appropriate for the social worker to encourage children to contact her if abuse occurs. She should instead help the children make a plan to tell a teacher, police officer, or other "helper" in the child's community that is a mandated reporter.

90. C: The social worker must recognize the unethical behavior on the part of the supervisor. With the boundaries being crossed regarding authorizations and support, the social worker must report this behavior to the director, who will investigate the situation. It is not sufficient to simply decline the case or continue with managing the case without first addressing this breach.

91. A: Single-system designs are commonly used by practitioners to evaluate their practice. The evaluation process involves: 1) problem identification (called the "target" of the research); 2) operationalization (selecting measurable indices that represent the problem); and 3) determining the "phase" (the time over which measurement will occur), including a "baseline phase" (without intervention) and an "intervention phase." This may also include a "time series design," where data is collected at discrete intervals over the course of the study.

92. C: The program director should identify the top reason for service delivery issues and create a task force to determine how to implement a positive change in the program. Meeting with the board of directors to explain how supports are currently delivered would not provide a solution or any improvement to the program. Connecting with agency leadership to reevaluate service delivery would be appropriate but would not address the findings of the evaluation. The program director should not ask that standards be adjusted due to poor performance. It is up to the program director to make sure that the services are delivered in a manner consistent with the board of directors' vision and mission statement.

93. B: Triangulation occurs when there is tension and conflict within a subsystem. A third person (in this case, the mother-in-law) is brought into the subsystem to reduce anxiety and stabilize the subsystem. Members of subsystems and triangles often engage in fluctuating patterns of communication based on the degree of tension and communication among participants. A subjugated narrative is a concept used in narrative therapy to describe a person's narrative being suppressed by dominant stories, which are those defined by one's cultural beliefs, values, and norms. Unbalancing is a structural family therapy technique used to briefly join with another subgroup or family member to change the relationship dynamics. Strategic family therapy uses covert change when providing hints, suggestions, or indirect messages to encourage change in a family (e.g., positively reinforcing certain behaviors).

94. B: The most appropriate diagnosis would be bulimia nervosa, severe. The diagnosis could not be anorexia nervosa, as she has not lost substantial weight, and although of post-menarchal age, there is no indication that she has experienced amenorrhea (much less for three consecutive cycles). The diagnosis is bulimia nervosa, as her behavior has persisted for 3 or more months. The degrees of severity are as follows: Mild: purging 1-3 times/week. Moderate: purging 4-7 times/week. Severe: purging 8-13 times/week. Extreme: purging 14 or more times/week.

95. D: The social worker is experiencing symptoms of secondary trauma from the description of the violent sexual abuse. Secondary trauma is the appropriate term to describe the emotional stress of hearing firsthand accounts of trauma. The social worker should work with her supervisor to identify counseling resources for herself and coping skills that she can practice. Post-traumatic stress disorder results when an individual struggles to recover from experiencing a traumatic event. Burnout comes from being physically, mentally, and emotionally exhausted from long-lasting stress events.

96. C: Oppositional defiant disorder includes irritable or angry mood, arguing with adults/authority figures, defying rules, actively annoying others, and blaming others for mistakes. For this age range (5 years old or younger), this behavior must occur at least once per week. Conduct disorder is characterized by physical violence, lying, elopement, stealing, and vandalism. To be diagnosed, the child must show one of these symptoms prior to the age of 10. Although bipolar disorder is typically diagnosed during teenage years, these symptoms can occur at any age. In children, DSM-5-TR has listed it as disruptive mood dysregulation disorder. Temper outbursts must occur at least three times per week for 1 year. Irritability must be persistent. These symptoms must be present in two settings. Major depressive disorder can be diagnosed at any age, but it is typically diagnosed during puberty; its symptoms include feeling sad, loss of motivation, insomnia, fatigue, decreased ability to think, and often thinking about death.

97. C: Communities with high incarceration rates tend to be poorer compared to those with lower incarceration rates. However, the rate of incarceration has not been specifically found to influence the cost of living, which reflects the cost of necessities such as food, housing, and healthcare in a particular place. Schools in communities with high incarceration rates are much more likely to have zero-tolerance policies compared to communities without these policies. Families with one or more members in jail or prison are at increased risk of homelessness. These community members, including those without any connection to the criminal justice system, have been found to have a higher incidence of depression and anxiety.

98. B: The client characteristics listed are all common for individuals having spent time in state or federal prison. Although members of all of the populations listed may demonstrate some of these characteristics, their prevalence among the prison population is far higher. In order to maintain personal safety in a highly controlled, high-risk, low-care environment, inmates learn to suppress their thoughts and feelings. Stripped of all personal responsibility and autonomy, they learn to defer in all ways to those in authority, potentially even losing the ability to think for themselves. Approximately 74% of inmates are overweight or obese, a much higher prevalence compared to the other populations listed, and they age physiologically more quickly compared to non-inmates. Individuals that have served prolonged prison sentences are physiologically equivalent to being approximately 10 years older than their chronological age.

99. C: The male social worker should ask the client during the case transfer meeting if he thinks that his size will impede the development of their therapeutic relationship. This offers the client the opportunity to discuss his fears and concerns before being officially assigned to the male social worker. It is also an opportunity for the male social worker to begin developing good rapport with the client through active listening and establishing trust that the social worker is prioritizing the client's best interests.

100. C: The key features of illness anxiety disorder (care-seeking type) include an intense preoccupation with the acquisition of a serious health problem, an absence of actual somatic symptoms (or only very mild symptoms), an honest belief and fear of an illness (i.e., not manipulative in any way), a high level of health anxiety, and excessive health-preoccupied behaviors that have continued for more than 6 months. Care-seeking type can be specified, as the client continues to seek help and support from a medical provider on a regular basis, even after adequate reassurances have been provided. Malingering is not correct, as it involves exaggerating or falsely claiming symptoms for secondary gain (e.g., insurance claims, to be relieved of unpleasant work). Factitious disorder is not correct, as it involves the deliberate fabrication of symptoms without the intent to receive tangible or concrete rewards, but rather for the nurturance or attention thereby derived. Somatic symptom disorder is not correct, as it requires the presence of actual somatic (physical) symptoms. Note: somatization disorder, hypochondriasis, pain disorder, and undifferentiated somatoform disorder was removed from DSM-5 and replaced with somatic symptom disorder.

101. A: The supervisor cannot adjust performance reviews based on how the social worker may react. The supervisor's documentation should be accurate, providing data reflecting the strengths and weaknesses of the supervisees.

102. B: Heart disease is not disproportionately diagnosed in the prison population compared to the general population. Arthritis, asthma, and diabetes are consistently identified in the research as disproportionately impacting the prison population.

103. D: Research has shown that social workers are less likely to feel distress (which leads to burnout) if they have the ability to influence how their job is performed and what the expectations are. Training on self-care strategies is helpful, but too often the information is not applied. At best, the training will increase staff awareness regarding self-care. The use of vacation time can support a healthy work/life balance and provide a necessary break to recuperate from work stress. However, the strategies suggested by the correct answer would help prevent work stress while supporting work/life balance. Assessing the caseload size and client difficulty for each social worker is an excellent strategy to support staff well-being, but it does not provide the opportunity for staff to have autonomy and influence in their work, and it may make more experienced staff members feel like they carry a heavier burden than the novices.

104. B: It is best practice for social work supervisors to collaboratively develop the agenda with the supervisee for each supervision session. However, the supervisee is responsible for bringing to the supervisor all questions and concerns related to social work practice, regardless of their participation in a formal agenda-setting process. The National Association of Social Workers (NASW) Practice Standards for Social Work Supervision specify that the supervisor and supervisee should document each supervision session and maintain liability insurance (or ensure that their agency has sufficient insurance on their behalf). The standards also specify that the research and selection of evaluative tools for the supervision process and the supervisee are the responsibility of the supervisor.

105. D: Most responses to trauma are naturally occurring coping efforts that allow the individual to maintain functional behaviors in work, relationships, and other areas of life. This means that they are psychologically effective, even though they are often distressing. A relatively small subset of trauma victims develops mental illness such as depression or anxiety. The need for clinical intervention is now understood to be less frequent than was previously believed. Although social workers tend to work with individuals at risk for more severe trauma responses, many survivors of trauma are in fact resilient and have coping strategies and systems of support that sufficiently support their recovery from trauma.

106. A: Vicarious trauma can occur when a social worker works closely with victims of trauma. It can lead to changes in a social worker's beliefs, behaviors, and thought processes, often without the social worker's awareness. For example, a social worker who is working with female victims of interpersonal violence could develop an unconscious belief that relationships are not worth the risks involved and subsequently discourage clients from dating or making new friends. The other answer choices all have the potential of negatively impacting professional objectivity, but they are more likely to be within the social worker's conscious awareness and are therefore able to be addressed.

107. B: Consistent mistakes by several members of a team indicate a training issue, rather than mere forgetfulness or human error. An experiential training session that allows staff to see, hear, and apply the correct procedure for completing intake paperwork will meet the learning needs of those that are visual, auditory, and/or hands-on learners. It is preferable to retrain the team before adding a new, additional review by the supervisor. Reminding staff to complete the documents or reformatting them (another form of reminder) will also not fix a training issue, but this can be used to support the training implementation.

108. C: Although all of the answer choices intersect with the client's sociohistorical context, the client's age will provide the most impactful lens through which to view this context. The history of LGBTQ individuals' experiences is rife with discrimination, trauma, illness (the AIDS epidemic), and shifting levels of societal acceptance. Therefore, the years/decades in which an LGBTQ individual has lived have a significant impact on their fears, hopes, and preferences regarding the coming-out process. In general, LGBTQ individuals that are in mid- to later life have significantly more concerns compared to LGBTQ youth because they have lived experience with the AIDS epidemic, widespread violence against the LGBTQ community, workplace discrimination, and higher levels of societal rejection. It is therefore critical that social workers gain knowledge regarding the history of the LGBTQ community's experience in this country.

109. B: Self-efficacy refers to the degree to which an individual can implement behaviors to achieve goals or desired states—for example, the degree to which an individual can build a healthy marriage or parent with empathy. Family life education programs pursue this goal by providing education, but they move beyond mere instruction in order to build self-efficacy. Without self-efficacy to apply what was learned, an individual will not be able to achieve a goal. Prevention is ultimately the hoped-for outcome of many family life education programs, but it cannot occur without the individuals involved having the self-efficacy to apply what they have learned. Reflection is one tool that is used to develop knowledge and self-efficacy.

110. B: The social worker must respect the client's decision to forgo treatment per her son's report. Because the son has been named as his mother's medical power of attorney, he has legally been delegated the authority by his mother to make medical decisions on her behalf when she is not in the capacity to do so, as demonstrated by her change in mentation. The son has been informed regarding the treatment and the consequences of stopping dialysis, and he therefore reserves the right to advocate for his mother's decision to forgo treatment as an extension of the ethical principle of self-determination (autonomy). If the client had not assigned her son as medical power of attorney, he would not be legally allowed to speak on her behalf.

111. B: The Social Work Code of Ethics explains that a social worker may terminate services due to nonpayment after doing three things: making the financial contractual arrangements clear, assessing if the client poses an imminent danger to self or others, and explaining the clinical and other consequences of the current nonpayment status. Professional judgment may then indicate that one of the other answer choices is a wise course of action; however, only answer option B is required by the Social Work Code of Ethics. It is best practice to refer any client in need of continued services to another service provider before terminating services. Answer D is vague because "risk" could mean a variety of things, including but not limited to the "imminent danger" described in the Code of Ethics. In this scenario, if one of the clients were an imminent danger to self or others, the social worker could not ethically terminate services until they had ensured that the safety of the client (and others) is restored and that appropriate supports are in place.

112. D: A research summary is a compilation of all recent research within a practice area. For example, a research summary related to treatments for bipolar disorder is a compilation of all recent research on all of the known effective treatment options. A systematic review is an observational study in which researchers identify and analyze previous studies on a topic. Although reading a systematic review is much more efficient than reading each individual study, it is still less comprehensive than a research summary. A meta-analysis is the quantitative synthesis of data from multiple studies. It is used to identify average effects across studies, differences in the results of each study, and potential reasons for these differences. Meta-analysis is fairly comprehensive; however, it is less comprehensive than a research summary. A critical appraisal is not a resource type; rather, it describes a thorough review of a research study or systematic review to identify possible biases that may distort the conclusions drawn from the results of the study. Critical appraisal of the research/evidence found is the third step of EBP.

113. B: In this situation, the social worker should set boundaries by calmly explaining to the client that the call cannot continue with the client's current use of profanity. If the social worker does not set this boundary, it allows the client to think that it is appropriate to communicate in this manner with the social worker, which could provide the opportunity for the behavior to continue or escalate in the future. Although alerting the supervisor to the client's hostile behavior during the phone call can be helpful, it does not set a boundary with the client during the call.

114. A: Social workers are responsible, per the NASW Code of Ethics, to advocate for policies and programs that support those in need in their communities, regardless of whether they work specifically within the context being impacted. Because this policy would decrease the support that is required to maintain the health and safety of those who suffer from substance use disorders across the state, social workers should work to educate and advocate with lawmakers.

115. B: Evidence-based practice (EBP) is a process of inquiry that guides a professional to integrate research, clinical perspective, and client needs/values so the most effective course of treatment can be determined. It is not an intervention model or a description of a type of intervention, although this is often how the phrase is used. EBP did originate in the field of medicine, but it was not modified for use in the social work profession. It is a decision-making model, but it is not prescriptive, nor does it have a bias toward psychosocial interventions.

116. B: The background information learned from clients during the course of solution-focused therapy is less detailed when compared to narrative therapy. In narrative therapy, the client will be sharing many thoughts and experiences, whereas solution-focused therapy is likely to involve more targeted conversations. Therefore, over the course of time, it is likely that a social worker using narrative therapy will learn more background details. The demographics presented should be thorough in both cases, to ensure that the assessment and treatment reflect appropriate cultural considerations. It is commonly thought that narrative therapy is simply allowing the client to tell their story, when, in fact, many different techniques and interventions can be used. Narrative therapies and solution-focused therapies are both effective with children and adults.

117. C: Although many of the newer developmental theories do focus on the coming-out process, this is best understood as a weakness because the coming-out process is merely one aspect of the human development process for LGBTQ individuals. However, the nuanced description of the internal and external developmental processes is a strength. Few, if any, of the newer, established theories represent the experiences of transgender individuals, although some research has begun in this area. Developmental theories that assume heterosexuality continue to help us understand human development, despite their limitations. Due to the incredible complexities of human development, all developmental theories are limited in one way or another.

118. D: In this scenario, the social worker should not hold the meeting with the family that day due to the lack of an interpreter. The parents have the right to an interpreter in order to understand the questions being asked and to have the ability to ask questions themselves. Attempts to reschedule the meeting while the family is there in person may prove difficult without an interpreter present. The social worker should call the family later, with the interpretation service, to reschedule and provide the opportunity to answer any questions about the issue.

119. C: The social work value of service speaks of serving those in need, whereas the social work value of social justice involves challenging injustices for oppressed and vulnerable populations. Although both values work to address social change, they differentiate in the target of their efforts.

120. B: Emails, conferences, meetings, and professional social media connections are all different ways of networking. The director is in need of quick rapport-building with other providers. Because of this, the best option is for the director to meet with the providers directly to explain the partnership that the new agency is interested in beginning.

121. C: The social worker should immediately report the suspected verbal abuse, per the mandated reporter rules, regardless of the administration's policies for discharge. It is not for the short-term rehabilitation social worker to investigate and confirm the validity of the statements provided, nor is it sufficient to have ongoing home-based visits to ensure the client's safety.

122. A: This question provides two clues that solution-focused therapy is the focus: short duration (six sessions) and the identification of an exception, or a time that things were different and better. With these clues in mind, the actions and responses to one another during this exception would be explored to identify how they contributed to the feelings of connection and pleasure. A plan to enact similar actions/responses in the coming week would then be developed. The specific activities and experiences are not as important, and it is not realistic that a couple on the verge of divorce will be able to develop more positive or constructive assumptions/perspectives so quickly.

123. A: FLE programs seek to build many of the components of the dignity and worth of a person, including self-determination, the capacity and opportunity of individuals to change, and the ability of individuals to address their own needs. This is the ultimate aim of all FLE programs, regardless of topic. Some FLE programs are designed to benefit not only the individual, but also those they are in relationships with, those they are responsible for parenting, and the broader society. FLE programs such as pre-marriage classes, marriage classes, and conflict resolution parenting classes reflect the social work value of the importance of human relationships. But many other common FLE programs, such as financial literacy, sexual health, and resource management, do not reflect this value. Some FLE programs—such as those focusing on vulnerable and oppressed individuals and those that address unemployment—reflect the value of social justice. However, FLE programs have a history of not reflecting the cultural needs and values of a diverse population and of perpetuating oppressive ideas related to gender roles. Self-determination is not a social work core value.

124. A: Individuals with somatic symptom disorder experience physical symptoms that are a result of a mental illness, but those symptoms look/feel very similar to symptoms of a physical disorder. These individuals are often not aware that their physical symptoms are psychiatric in origin, and, for that reason, it can be very difficult to build acceptance of the role that their mind and/or emotions have in their symptoms. The prevalence of a dualistic view of the mind and body in Western societies is a key reason for this difficulty because the body is thought to be independent from the mind. Psychosocial treatment modalities would seem to be a waste of time, when in fact they are the very treatments that are most likely to be successful. Without such interventions, individuals with somatic symptom disorder are likely to keep requesting medical tests and treatments for their physical symptoms. Although the connection between body and mind plays an important role in bipolar disease and in substance use disorders, a dualistic view of the body and mind is not a primary barrier to treatment. Those with factitious disorder are aware of their deceptive behavior but may have little awareness of why they are inducing illness. They also typically resist treatment, but this is due to a desire to maintain the role of a sick patient, not a lack of insight regarding the mind and body.

125. C: Burnout is the result of chronic levels of work-related distress over the course of time. First, chronic occupational stress leads to a high level of distress, resulting in a decrease in compassion, energy, and hope. When this distress continues, physical and emotional exhaustion develop, leading to burnout. Research has identified three components of burnout: emotional exhaustion, depersonalization (negativity, cynicism, and detachment from clients and colleagues), and a reduced sense of accomplishment/effectiveness (which includes feeling unappreciated and without passion or purpose).

126. B: Of the answer options provided, it is best for the supervisor to ask reflective questions so they can assess the newly hired social worker's awareness of their performance during the session. This can help create "buy-in" for the mindfulness strategies that would be helpful to work on next. To first ask about the social worker's trauma history is not a good strategy for a number of reasons: it assumes a great deal about the social worker's reaction, it is a very personal question, and the supervisor does not need to know this information in order to assess and address staff performance. Reviewing the requirements of an intake session may not be needed because the social worker may have known the information needed but was unable to apply that knowledge due to their mental distractions triggered by the client's trauma description. Whether it is required or not, the social worker will be better able to process these administrative details and consider their application with clients after having a reflective conversation about what occurred during the session.

127. D: Review of the treatment process serves several purposes, including remembering what has been accomplished and examining the status of treatment goals. It is important to do this first because the status of treatment goals may influence the renegotiation of the treatment duration and therefore shift attention from termination interventions back to treatment. If the termination phase continues, the service intensity can decrease gradually throughout the phase. Answer choices A and B are important aspects of the termination phase of treatment, with answer B typically being completed before answer A.

128. A: This interaction is an opportunity for the social worker to provide psychoeducation to the newly diagnosed student. The social worker should not assume that the individual has any experience or prior knowledge with the bipolar disorder diagnosis. Explaining how this diagnosis can affect her functioning will provide the student with the understanding and appropriate expectations required to be successful. The student should not be led to believe that she will be cured by medication and should be made aware that she will continue to experience symptoms. Inquiring about medication adherence is not relevant at this time.

129. D: There is increasing evidence that social influence is a very strong factor in the occurrence of NSSI. When students are stressed, they look to peers for support and for coping strategies. If anyone in the peer group is using NSSI to cope, others in the group are much more likely to consider and use it, particularly if they lack positive regulating and coping skills. The spread of NSSI in this way is called social contagion. Although the other answers may play a role in the occurrence of NSSI, the rate of this behavior in a student population is most accurately understood by examining peer groups and the occurrence of social contagion.

130. B: Hesitant group members may have input that could be used to modify the three selected issues in a way that everyone can accept. A debate of the pros and cons has already been completed in the process of narrowing the list to these three. Asking each member to share their opinion may be a productive approach at this time but asking them to specifically describe the anticipated positive impacts assumes that the three chosen priorities will have positive impacts, whereas the facilitator should maintain neutrality (except in the case of bias or oppression). Consensus does not require unanimity, but rather that all group members are willing to accept the group's decision. In this case, a member may continue to state that an alternative issue should be a priority, but would be comfortable addressing the issue through another avenue, or perhaps proposing it as a priority the next year.

131. C: Supporting the clients in reflecting on their experience with the social worker, progress made, and additional needs and goals will help them build motivation to continue in the program with a new social worker. Encouraging the clients to share this information with the new social worker provides a tangible action for the clients to take in the first session with the new social worker and encourages ownership of their experience and progress. Highlighting successful approaches for the new social worker can support continuity of services, but this is less important than helping the clients get to that first appointment with the new social worker. Sharing information about the new worker is also helpful, but again, not as helpful as answer C. Telling the clients what is good for them is generally not helpful.

132. A: A didactic approach is used specifically to educate, which is a focus of psychoeducation but not of MI. Psychoeducation is used widely across all formats. Although MI is most commonly used with individuals, it is also effective with families and/or groups that have a common problem or concern to address. MI and psychoeducation can support family engagement with a child welfare caseworker by helping the family understand how they could benefit from engagement, either to meet a goal (e.g., get the case closed) or to build the family's support system and access resources related to mental health, trauma, or substance use (a key focus of psychoeducation). In both methods, the social worker intentionally uses a collaborative approach that honors the client's knowledge and strengths, rather than acting as an authoritative expert.

133. C: Multifactorial conditions are caused by a mix of factors, including genetic mutations (unique to the individual or inherited) and environmental factors. The most common multifactorial conditions are neural tube defects (causing spina bifida and anencephaly) and hip dysplasia. Neural tube defects are much more likely to occur if the mother is deficient in folic acid (an environmental factor). Women of reproductive age are therefore encouraged to take a multivitamin because the issue occurs before most women are aware that they are pregnant. Alcohol consumption has not been linked to this type of genetic condition. Prenatal testing would not have prevented the condition. Future children are at risk, but the risk is low (3–6%).

134. D: A boundary violation is reflected in this scenario because the social worker is inappropriately using self-disclosure by sharing personal information with the client that is not beneficial to the therapeutic process. Countertransference is when a therapist projects either positive or negative emotions onto the client based on a familiar trait that the client represents. Transference is when a client projects positive or negative emotions toward the therapist, such as from a past relationship. A dual relationship does not describe this situation because the client and therapist do not know each other outside of this setting.

135. B: Overrepresentation among suicide victims is identified by comparing the rate of suicide within the demographic group to the group's percentage within the total population. Native Americans are the most overrepresented because they represent 18% of suicide victims and only 8.5% of the total population (+9.5% difference). Seniors (ages 65+) are next, representing 20% of suicide victims and 13% of the total population (+7% difference). Veterans represent 13.5% of all suicides, and just 7.9% of the population (+5.6% difference). In contrast to these examples of overrepresentation, Hispanic/Latino individuals represent only 8% of all suicides and 18% of the total population (−10% difference).

136. C: Self-care includes activities or exercises that someone can do to reduce stress and increase overall well-being. The student is experiencing overall stress, not just stress in one area (e.g., school, finances). Meditation has a positive effect on physical, emotional, and mental health. If the student chose to focus on meditation daily, the short- and long-term effects would provide a decrease in her overall stress.

137. C: Children younger than the age of 1 experience the highest rate of physical abuse compared to other age categories and compared to the incidence of neglect in the same age range. Answers A, B, and D are all true statements.

138. D: The social worker only reviewed the policy verbally and did not obtain a legal signature from the client to reflect his understanding of the payment expectations. At the next session, the social worker should review the policy again and obtain the client's signature. It is ethical to terminate services for nonpayment—if the client does not pose a threat to himself or others.

139. C: Young adults with severe intellectual disabilities rely heavily on family or caregivers for their basic and other needs. These caregivers will need to be involved with most, if not all, treatment strategies, or else the client may not be able to access them outside of the therapy appointment. Although teenagers and youth discharged from a residential facility often benefit from family/caregiver collaboration, most are able to implement mental health treatment strategies independently to some degree. Recently adopted children do not necessarily need the collaboration of family/caregivers, although it may be quite beneficial depending on the needs of the child.

140. C: The degree to which an individual has become institutionalized has a significant influence on their ability to reintegrate into society. Although many factors influence the process of reintegration, age upon entry to prison is one of the most influential. Youth and young adults have not yet fully developed the ability and expectation to control their own life choices or to think for themselves, making them uniquely vulnerable to the norms of prison, such as constant external controls, a chronic lack of safety, and the normalization of violence. Younger inmates are more likely to be violent, a tendency difficult to change once they are back out in the community. They also have less (or no) experience living in society as an adult. Social support upon reentry is also a significant factor in the success of reintegration. Therefore, answer C represents the person who is the most at risk, having entered prison at the age of 18 and having been released at a relatively young age with only the support of an elderly grandparent. The other answer choices represent people who are less at risk due to a combination of their older age upon entry, the number of years served, and/or the strength of their support system.

141. C: Simulations and experiential activities are an effective way to encourage learners to engage in problem solving and critical thinking. Lectures do not facilitate the development of insight because learners must focus on the receipt and comprehension of information, facts, and concepts rather than reflect upon them. Similarly, they do not effectively support skill building, which requires application of the information or concepts. Application (and therefore skill building) is best suited for exercises, demonstrations, and role-playing sessions. Case discussions do not include a thorough review of any particular topic, so they are not designed to support comprehension of complex material; lectures are better suited for this.

142. D: Every child in foster care has been removed from their family/caregivers, which is in itself a trauma warranting assessment, in addition to the trauma(s) that may have occurred prior to and since their removal. Research has shown that many children in foster care feel as if they were kidnapped, and, sadly, many (25%) are victims of additional abuse while in foster care. If someone has symptoms of anxiety, depression, and/or post-traumatic stress disorder, this does not mean that they meet the criteria for these diagnoses or that they warrant a full trauma assessment. They should have a trauma screening completed first, and should only have a trauma assessment if the screening demonstrates a need for it.

143. B: The social worker should not engage in a dual relationship and should therefore stop attending the book club because it is a voluntary, optional membership. A dual relationship can occur when there are multiple roles that a social worker and client share. Although in some small community settings this type of relationship cannot be avoided (e.g., seeing a client at a local grocery store), in this case, it can be avoided simply by the social worker no longer attending the book club. The social worker should allow the client to lead the interaction upon first realizing the connection, and should not attempt to speak with the client at the book club meeting about setting boundaries for their interactions unless the client initiates such a conversation.

144. A: A CLSI includes three stages, the first of which involves the development of coalitions and goals. A feedback loop during this stage, based on evaluation of the process and events that have occurred, could reveal that the identified goals do not reflect the scope of the coalition's priorities. Research, program development, and engagement of civic leaders are not components of the first stage of a CLSI.

145. C: An event offered to the community is a mezzo-level practice. The inclusion of fun activities, food, and access to resources will provide support to all types of families, including those without any current risk factors for child maltreatment, making this a primary intervention strategy. Parenting classes at the community center (mezzo level) are focused on a group of parents that are at risk for child maltreatment (secondary prevention). The parent coaching programs work one-on-one with parents (micro level) that are at risk (secondary prevention) or potentially have already engaged in child maltreatment (tertiary prevention). The weekly educational program for pregnant teen mothers is a mezzo-level, secondary prevention strategy because it is serving an at-risk population.

146. C: In order to get breast/chest surgery or genital surgery, a referral from a qualified mental health professional is required. The social worker must complete a health screening and psychosocial assessment, the results of which are detailed in the referral documentation of support for surgery. Although the client may opt to engage in psychotherapy prior to surgery, it is not a requirement. The social worker can decline to provide a referral for surgery, despite the client's request. A social worker must always consider their competence level regarding a client's unique characteristics and needs.

147. D: Cognitive interventions help clients identify specific thoughts and beliefs. Of the choices provided, it is MOST important to help the client identify the thoughts that occur when they are met with an opportunity to use. Once these are identified, the client can learn to produce new thoughts that will support abstinence. Identifying the reasons for substance use behaviors may include identification of the specific thoughts experienced, but answer A does not specify this. Supporting the client in identifying their thoughts and feelings about, and the impact of, substance use is an important strategy to build the client's motivation to change, but these factors are less important than the thoughts that occur precisely when the client is presented with the opportunity to use.

148. D: Selective incivility theory describes the decision-making process used when individuals decide who to discriminate against. Minority stress impact theory focuses on the way that stress impacts minority populations in different ways. Intersectionality theory helps us understand the way that a person's many facets of identity may influence their experience of discrimination, but not why people choose to enact discrimination against them, specifically. "Human dynamics theory" is not a standard term.

149. D: A social worker's personal disclosure that results in the client sharing expert advice with the social worker is not within the bounds of social work best practices. For example, if a client is a professional plumber and the social worker has a leaky kitchen faucet, the social worker may mention this issue in the hopes of gathering information to help fix the faucet. Doing so, however, is ethically problematic in two different ways. First, the power difference in the social worker–client relationship may influence the client to provide expert advice for free, when they should instead be paid for providing this service. Second, whether the advice is given for free or the social worker does pay, this exchange creates a dual relationship.

Some personal disclosures may be client-centered and ethical yet also bring a social worker a sense of personal satisfaction. It is unethical for a disclosure to be solely motivated by the social worker's personal satisfaction. During the termination phase of treatment, it can be helpful to deintensify the social worker–client relationship with appropriate personal disclosures, such as having a pet and exchanging pet stories with the client. In the event of a serious illness, a social worker may need to go on leave. When the social worker informs a client of this, even if details of the illness are not provided, the client may feel concern for the social worker. This is generally not an issue, although the social worker must assess the potential impact of personal disclosures to ensure that no harm could occur to the client.

150. A: The social worker's professional boundaries are first and foremost established by their words and actions. At the beginning and throughout their work with each client, social workers must clearly define their roles and responsibilities, set and maintain limits on behavior, and help the client know what is expected of them. Although the supervision and training received play a significant role in this communication, they do not guarantee that it is done properly. A social worker's mental health status also may or may not influence their communication about or maintenance of boundaries.

151. C: During treatment planning, social workers must select treatment modalities that reflect the available research, information about the client's problem(s), and client characteristics. A social worker must only implement intervention strategies that are commensurate with their professional competence. If the social worker determines that the most appropriate treatment strategies are not within their areas of competence, the social worker must explain this to the client and refer them to another professional who can competently implement the treatment. The consent process is not limited to the typical topics discussed at the onset of services, such as confidentiality and mandated reporter information; it also includes subsequent conversation(s) related to the recommended treatment options, rationale for selection, and risks related to treatment.

152. A: Misattribution is an example of poor reflective functioning, a caregiver characteristic that has been found to be a reliable predictor of child mistreatment. Although the other characteristics are observed in many caregivers that mistreat children, research has found them to be correlated to, but not predictive of, child maltreatment. Caregiver behaviors that indicate poor reflective functioning, lacking empathy, and having unresolved trauma have been found to be more likely to lead to maltreatment.

153. B: The person-in-environment theory stresses the importance of internal and environmental aspects of an individual's context, contending that assessment and interventions addressing both of these contexts are the focus of social work practice. Since the beginnings of the social work profession in the 1920s, the prevalence of direct practice, including case management and therapeutic individual and family interventions, has time and again drawn the profession to focus on the micro level and away from community organization and social action at a mezzo or macro level. Psychodynamic, constructivist, and psychoanalytic theories all predominantly focus on the individual and their internal experience. The rise of each of these theories has also impeded the full integration of the person-in-environment theory to social work practice.

154. C: The social worker should explain to the niece that if her uncle maintains competency, she cannot force him to use support services or go to the doctor. The niece can continue to discuss her concerns, provide the uncle with resource options, and increase natural supports through other family members, friends, or neighbors.

155. A: The school social worker should connect with the student and her parents to discuss the concerns and make a plan of action. The person-in-environment theory suggests that individuals are highly influenced by the environments within which they spend the most time (e.g., home, church, work, or friend groups). By working with the student to identify a positive environment for her to increase connections within, the school social worker is using person-in-environment theory to increase protective factors for the student during this difficult time at home. Disclosing this information to the student's teachers would be inappropriate. Although the student may enjoy working in her favorite teacher's classroom or spending more time with her classmates, it would be up to the student to decide what type of club or activity she would like to participate in to increase positive connections.

156. A: During the termination phase of treatment, collaboratively processing the treatment experience has been shown to result in more positive client reactions. For example, it provides the opportunity to address any issues or concerns that would impede a sense of closure for the therapeutic experience. It also provides an opportunity to remember the challenges that were overcome and the gains that were accomplished. A strong therapeutic relationship, while being incredibly important, has been found to increase the likelihood of difficult and/or negative client reactions as they process the ending of this valuable relationship. Similarly, treatment that has supported positive changes can also increase the likelihood of negative reactions. Although it would seem that terminating treatment on the timetable initially discussed and anticipated throughout the course of the therapeutic relationship would be helpful during termination, this has not been identified as a strategy to reduce negative client reactions. "On time" termination of services may often more likely occur when the therapeutic relationship is strong and/or the treatment resulted in positive changes.

157. C: Resistance is the term that is used in psychoanalysis to describe a client's effort to avoid the uncomfortable thoughts and feelings that are getting "close to the surface." In this vignette, the client became aware of thoughts or feelings that felt threatening to explore further and changed the topic to avoid these thoughts or feelings. It seems that the client does not want to talk about the upsetting experience further and is likely feeling uncomfortable (answer D, discomfort). The client shifts the topic of conversation (answer B, distraction) and seeks to avoid further discussion (answer A, avoidance). These feelings and actions are all indications of resistance according to the psychoanalytical perspective.

158. D: Before being approved by the licensing board, the candidate must first meet state requirements for the license. After being approved by the licensing board, the candidate can then register with ASWB to take the test. Having passed the test, the candidate can then apply for the license.

159. B: The social worker has violated HIPAA by opening up the electronic medical record of a client whose care he is not directly involved in. The social worker must inform his supervisor of this violation. It would be considered a dual relationship for the social worker to be assigned to the client, making answer D inappropriate.

160. A: When working with individuals with intellectual and developmental disabilities (IDD), occupational therapists develop strategies to support their participation in the community and activities of interest. They also have expertise related to activities that meet sensory needs, such as weighted blankets/objects, swinging, music, water, and other experiences that could provide enjoyment and a sense of grounding and that could ease symptoms of anxiety or depression. With the IDD population, psychotropic medications are only indicated when social or behavioral measures have not adequately addressed symptoms and behaviors of concern; therefore, a psychiatrist would not be the primary collaboration. A speech-language pathologist is not indicated for this client's needs. An intervention specialist is a professional working with students with IDD in the school system. This client, as a young adult, aged out of the school system at 21.

161. C: Social work practice informed by client-centered theory places a significant focus on the relationship between the social worker and client, rather than on therapeutic techniques. The social worker's congruent words, tone, and actions communicate their empathy and unconditional positive regard (respect) for the client. Congruence is also conceptualized as being authentic or genuine. The other answer options include some of the correct answers along with incorrect answers, such as openness, professional use of self, and reflective questioning.

162. C: Feedback loops can occur at any stage of an intervention, from planning and goal formulation to evaluation. Feedback loops involve reflective evaluation on what has been done, learned, and accomplished thus far to inform the current and next steps. Answer B is incorrect because it describes reflection only on the intervention results. Feedback loops can involve feedback from community members but encompass many other elements.

163. B: This group supervision, led by an experienced social worker, will provide emotional support, practice oversight, and opportunities for professional collaboration and networking. This range of support is critical for a relatively new social worker practicing in a new city. Although answer C would provide the practice oversight needed, the social worker will be at greater risk for burnout without a wider network of professional support. The peer consultation group related to SFBT is a great resource for learning and support, but it lacks the oversight and experience that a supervisor provides. Although consultation with a child psychologist may at times be beneficial as related to a specific case, it does not provide the support or clinical oversight needed by this social worker.

164. D: The age of the social worker is not a key factor that is found to influence treatment engagement for children. Frequent assessment throughout the treatment process provides opportunities for youth to provide input and even influence the treatment process, as well as build buy-in that the treatment process is effective. An integrated service environment, in which other professionals such as nurses or psychiatrists are available to provided needed services, helps children and youth more easily access the services they need. This ease is found to increase their overall engagement of services. Finally, understanding the research base for an intervention, paired with insight regarding how it could be or is currently of benefit to the youth, contributes to continued treatment engagement.

165. D: In this answer, the social worker prioritizes the tasks that must be completed within the next business day. First, the social worker should spend his working hours meeting with the family about concerns of neglect. This allows him time to make an adult protective services report. Next, the social worker should discuss the required discharge paperwork with the respite facility. He should then schedule the new-patient appointment because it needs to be completed within the next 24 hours. Finally, the social worker makes time to complete the report of all home visits provided because this report is late. The social worker chooses to wait to complete the home visit because it can be completed by the end of the week.

166. B: When completing a trauma assessment, it is not necessary or even best practice to assess in detail all aspects of the trauma(s) experienced. This degree of detail is best delayed until the social worker and client have developed further rapport and trust. It is also important that the client has time to develop coping strategies to support them as they review and disclose such difficult memories and feelings. Similarly, the assessment does not need to include every experience of trauma that the client can remember. Although many different assessment tools are available, their use is not required. Answer D includes some important elements of a trauma assessment but is missing a vital component: the symptoms and impact that the client is experiencing as a result of the trauma(s).

167. C: The social worker must first complete a needs assessment in order to collect data and determine if the community is lacking youth program services. The social worker will then identify goals for the program and create a planning team. Once these steps are in place, a time line can be determined for the start of services and goals can be implemented within the community.

168. D: Although a stipulation regarding modalities of treatment is in conflict with several of the core values listed, a blanket rule that a social worker must provide service to all clients in a particular zip code focuses the conflict to the value of competence. A requirement to serve all clients based in a zip code does not take into consideration the client characteristics or needs that may be better met by another social worker at the agency.

169. A: Although each of these demographic characteristics influences an individual's vulnerability to psychosocial problems, age-related physical and psychological changes can increase this vulnerability for people of any race, gender, and zip code. During adolescence and in later years (ages 65+), hormonal changes can occur that can significantly impact mood (including mental health) and brain and body functioning. Cognitive changes impact memory and critical thinking, which can significantly influence relationships and independence. Changes in mobility also commonly result from these hormonal and physical changes, impacting independence and ability to work and increasing social isolation. Organs and other body structures are prone to disease as they age.

170. D: An MOU must be included with a grant application if any other entities will be responsible for the provision of services funded by the grant. An MOU demonstrates that collaborative planning has occurred and that the two entities have reached an agreement regarding the details listed in answer D. In this scenario, the social service agency cannot use the MOU to compel the hospital's collaboration because the MOU is not a legally binding document. Although it does include the details listed in answer C, many other details are also involved. The rationale for the health screenings and presentations may be included in the grant application, but it would not be specifically included in an MOU.

LCSW Practice Tests #2 and #3

To take these additional practice tests, visit our bonus page:
mometrix.com/bonus948/swclinical

How to Overcome Test Anxiety

Just the thought of taking a test is enough to make most people a little nervous. A test is an important event that can have a long-term impact on your future, so it's important to take it seriously and it's natural to feel anxious about performing well. But just because anxiety is normal, that doesn't mean that it's helpful in test taking, or that you should simply accept it as part of your life. Anxiety can have a variety of effects. These effects can be mild, like making you feel slightly nervous, or severe, like blocking your ability to focus or remember even a simple detail.

If you experience test anxiety—whether severe or mild—it's important to know how to beat it. To discover this, first you need to understand what causes test anxiety.

Causes of Test Anxiety

While we often think of anxiety as an uncontrollable emotional state, it can actually be caused by simple, practical things. One of the most common causes of test anxiety is that a person does not feel adequately prepared for their test. This feeling can be the result of many different issues such as poor study habits or lack of organization, but the most common culprit is time management. Starting to study too late, failing to organize your study time to cover all of the material, or being distracted while you study will mean that you're not well prepared for the test. This may lead to cramming the night before, which will cause you to be physically and mentally exhausted for the test. Poor time management also contributes to feelings of stress, fear, and hopelessness as you realize you are not well prepared but don't know what to do about it.

Other times, test anxiety is not related to your preparation for the test but comes from unresolved fear. This may be a past failure on a test, or poor performance on tests in general. It may come from comparing yourself to others who seem to be performing better or from the stress of living up to expectations. Anxiety may be driven by fears of the future—how failure on this test would affect your educational and career goals. These fears are often completely irrational, but they can still negatively impact your test performance.

Elements of Test Anxiety

As mentioned earlier, test anxiety is considered to be an emotional state, but it has physical and mental components as well. Sometimes you may not even realize that you are suffering from test anxiety until you notice the physical symptoms. These can include trembling hands, rapid heartbeat, sweating, nausea, and tense muscles. Extreme anxiety may lead to fainting or vomiting. Obviously, any of these symptoms can have a negative impact on testing. It is important to recognize them as soon as they begin to occur so that you can address the problem before it damages your performance.

The mental components of test anxiety include trouble focusing and inability to remember learned information. During a test, your mind is on high alert, which can help you recall information and stay focused for an extended period of time. However, anxiety interferes with your mind's natural processes, causing you to blank out, even on the questions you know well. The strain of testing during anxiety makes it difficult to stay focused, especially on a test that may take several hours. Extreme anxiety can take a huge mental toll, making it difficult not only to recall test information but even to understand the test questions or pull your thoughts together.

Effects of Test Anxiety

Test anxiety is like a disease—if left untreated, it will get progressively worse. Anxiety leads to poor performance, and this reinforces the feelings of fear and failure, which in turn lead to poor performances on subsequent tests. It can grow from a mild nervousness to a crippling condition. If allowed to progress, test anxiety can have a big impact on your schooling, and consequently on your future.

Test anxiety can spread to other parts of your life. Anxiety on tests can become anxiety in any stressful situation, and blanking on a test can turn into panicking in a job situation. But fortunately, you don't have to let anxiety rule your testing and determine your grades. There are a number of relatively simple steps you can take to move past anxiety and function normally on a test and in the rest of life.

Physical Steps for Beating Test Anxiety

While test anxiety is a serious problem, the good news is that it can be overcome. It doesn't have to control your ability to think and remember information. While it may take time, you can begin taking steps today to beat anxiety.

Just as your first hint that you may be struggling with anxiety comes from the physical symptoms, the first step to treating it is also physical. Rest is crucial for having a clear, strong mind. If you are tired, it is much easier to give in to anxiety. But if you establish good sleep habits, your body and mind will be ready to perform optimally, without the strain of exhaustion. Additionally, sleeping well helps you to retain information better, so you're more likely to recall the answers when you see the test questions.

Getting good sleep means more than going to bed on time. It's important to allow your brain time to relax. Take study breaks from time to time so it doesn't get overworked, and don't study right before bed. Take time to rest your mind before trying to rest your body, or you may find it difficult to fall asleep.

Along with sleep, other aspects of physical health are important in preparing for a test. Good nutrition is vital for good brain function. Sugary foods and drinks may give a burst of energy but this burst is followed by a crash, both physically and emotionally. Instead, fuel your body with protein and vitamin-rich foods.

Also, drink plenty of water. Dehydration can lead to headaches and exhaustion, especially if your brain is already under stress from the rigors of the test. Particularly if your test is a long one, drink water during the breaks. And if possible, take an energy-boosting snack to eat between sections.

Along with sleep and diet, a third important part of physical health is exercise. Maintaining a steady workout schedule is helpful, but even taking 5-minute study breaks to walk can help get your blood pumping faster and clear your head. Exercise also releases endorphins, which contribute to a positive feeling and can help combat test anxiety.

When you nurture your physical health, you are also contributing to your mental health. If your body is healthy, your mind is much more likely to be healthy as well. So take time to rest, nourish your body with healthy food and water, and get moving as much as possible. Taking these physical steps will make you stronger and more able to take the mental steps necessary to overcome test anxiety.

Mental Steps for Beating Test Anxiety

Working on the mental side of test anxiety can be more challenging, but as with the physical side, there are clear steps you can take to overcome it. As mentioned earlier, test anxiety often stems from lack of preparation, so the obvious solution is to prepare for the test. Effective studying may be the most important weapon you have for beating test anxiety, but you can and should employ several other mental tools to combat fear.

First, boost your confidence by reminding yourself of past success—tests or projects that you aced. If you're putting as much effort into preparing for this test as you did for those, there's no reason you should expect to fail here. Work hard to prepare; then trust your preparation.

Second, surround yourself with encouraging people. It can be helpful to find a study group, but be sure that the people you're around will encourage a positive attitude. If you spend time with others who are anxious or cynical, this will only contribute to your own anxiety. Look for others who are motivated to study hard from a desire to succeed, not from a fear of failure.

Third, reward yourself. A test is physically and mentally tiring, even without anxiety, and it can be helpful to have something to look forward to. Plan an activity following the test, regardless of the outcome, such as going to a movie or getting ice cream.

When you are taking the test, if you find yourself beginning to feel anxious, remind yourself that you know the material. Visualize successfully completing the test. Then take a few deep, relaxing breaths and return to it. Work through the questions carefully but with confidence, knowing that you are capable of succeeding.

Developing a healthy mental approach to test taking will also aid in other areas of life. Test anxiety affects more than just the actual test—it can be damaging to your mental health and even contribute to depression. It's important to beat test anxiety before it becomes a problem for more than testing.

Study Strategy

Being prepared for the test is necessary to combat anxiety, but what does being prepared look like? You may study for hours on end and still not feel prepared. What you need is a strategy for test prep. The next few pages outline our recommended steps to help you plan out and conquer the challenge of preparation.

STEP 1: SCOPE OUT THE TEST

Learn everything you can about the format (multiple choice, essay, etc.) and what will be on the test. Gather any study materials, course outlines, or sample exams that may be available. Not only will this help you to prepare, but knowing what to expect can help to alleviate test anxiety.

STEP 2: MAP OUT THE MATERIAL

Look through the textbook or study guide and make note of how many chapters or sections it has. Then divide these over the time you have. For example, if a book has 15 chapters and you have five days to study, you need to cover three chapters each day. Even better, if you have the time, leave an extra day at the end for overall review after you have gone through the material in depth.

If time is limited, you may need to prioritize the material. Look through it and make note of which sections you think you already have a good grasp on, and which need review. While you are studying, skim quickly through the familiar sections and take more time on the challenging parts. Write out your plan so you don't get lost as you go. Having a written plan also helps you feel more in control of the study, so anxiety is less likely to arise from feeling overwhelmed at the amount to cover.

STEP 3: GATHER YOUR TOOLS

Decide what study method works best for you. Do you prefer to highlight in the book as you study and then go back over the highlighted portions? Or do you type out notes of the important information? Or is it helpful to make flashcards that you can carry with you? Assemble the pens, index cards, highlighters, post-it notes, and any other materials you may need so you won't be distracted by getting up to find things while you study.

If you're having a hard time retaining the information or organizing your notes, experiment with different methods. For example, try color-coding by subject with colored pens, highlighters, or post-it notes. If you learn better by hearing, try recording yourself reading your notes so you can listen while in the car, working out, or simply sitting at your desk. Ask a friend to quiz you from your flashcards, or try teaching someone the material to solidify it in your mind.

STEP 4: CREATE YOUR ENVIRONMENT

It's important to avoid distractions while you study. This includes both the obvious distractions like visitors and the subtle distractions like an uncomfortable chair (or a too-comfortable couch that makes you want to fall asleep). Set up the best study environment possible: good lighting and a comfortable work area. If background music helps you focus, you may want to turn it on, but otherwise keep the room quiet. If you are using a computer to take notes, be sure you don't have any other windows open, especially applications like social media, games, or anything else that could distract you. Silence your phone and turn off notifications. Be sure to keep water close by so you stay hydrated while you study (but avoid unhealthy drinks and snacks).

Also, take into account the best time of day to study. Are you freshest first thing in the morning? Try to set aside some time then to work through the material. Is your mind clearer in the afternoon or evening? Schedule your study session then. Another method is to study at the same time of day that you will take the test, so that your brain gets used to working on the material at that time and will be ready to focus at test time.

STEP 5: STUDY!

Once you have done all the study preparation, it's time to settle into the actual studying. Sit down, take a few moments to settle your mind so you can focus, and begin to follow your study plan. Don't give in to distractions or let yourself procrastinate. This is your time to prepare so you'll be ready to fearlessly approach the test. Make the most of the time and stay focused.

Of course, you don't want to burn out. If you study too long you may find that you're not retaining the information very well. Take regular study breaks. For example, taking five minutes out of every hour to walk briskly, breathing deeply and swinging your arms, can help your mind stay fresh.

As you get to the end of each chapter or section, it's a good idea to do a quick review. Remind yourself of what you learned and work on any difficult parts. When you feel that you've mastered the material, move on to the next part. At the end of your study session, briefly skim through your notes again.

But while review is helpful, cramming last minute is NOT. If at all possible, work ahead so that you won't need to fit all your study into the last day. Cramming overloads your brain with more information than it can process and retain, and your tired mind may struggle to recall even previously learned information when it is overwhelmed with last-minute study. Also, the urgent nature of cramming and the stress placed on your brain contribute to anxiety. You'll be more likely to go to the test feeling unprepared and having trouble thinking clearly.

So don't cram, and don't stay up late before the test, even just to review your notes at a leisurely pace. Your brain needs rest more than it needs to go over the information again. In fact, plan to finish your studies by noon or early afternoon the day before the test. Give your brain the rest of the day to relax or focus on other things, and get a good night's sleep. Then you will be fresh for the test and better able to recall what you've studied.

STEP 6: TAKE A PRACTICE TEST

Many courses offer sample tests, either online or in the study materials. This is an excellent resource to check whether you have mastered the material, as well as to prepare for the test format and environment.

Check the test format ahead of time: the number of questions, the type (multiple choice, free response, etc.), and the time limit. Then create a plan for working through them. For example, if you have 30 minutes to take a 60-question test, your limit is 30 seconds per question. Spend less time on the questions you know well so that you can take more time on the difficult ones.

If you have time to take several practice tests, take the first one open book, with no time limit. Work through the questions at your own pace and make sure you fully understand them. Gradually work up to taking a test under test conditions: sit at a desk with all study materials put away and set a timer. Pace yourself to make sure you finish the test with time to spare and go back to check your answers if you have time.

After each test, check your answers. On the questions you missed, be sure you understand why you missed them. Did you misread the question (tests can use tricky wording)? Did you forget the information? Or was it something you hadn't learned? Go back and study any shaky areas that the practice tests reveal.

Taking these tests not only helps with your grade, but also aids in combating test anxiety. If you're already used to the test conditions, you're less likely to worry about it, and working through tests until you're scoring well gives you a confidence boost. Go through the practice tests until you feel comfortable, and then you can go into the test knowing that you're ready for it.

Test Tips

On test day, you should be confident, knowing that you've prepared well and are ready to answer the questions. But aside from preparation, there are several test day strategies you can employ to maximize your performance.

First, as stated before, get a good night's sleep the night before the test (and for several nights before that, if possible). Go into the test with a fresh, alert mind rather than staying up late to study.

Try not to change too much about your normal routine on the day of the test. It's important to eat a nutritious breakfast, but if you normally don't eat breakfast at all, consider eating just a protein bar. If you're a coffee drinker, go ahead and have your normal coffee. Just make sure you time it so that the caffeine doesn't wear off right in the middle of your test. Avoid sugary beverages, and drink enough water to stay hydrated but not so much that you need a restroom break 10 minutes into the test. If your test isn't first thing in the morning, consider going for a walk or doing a light workout before the test to get your blood flowing.

Allow yourself enough time to get ready, and leave for the test with plenty of time to spare so you won't have the anxiety of scrambling to arrive in time. Another reason to be early is to select a good seat. It's helpful to sit away from doors and windows, which can be distracting. Find a good seat, get out your supplies, and settle your mind before the test begins.

When the test begins, start by going over the instructions carefully, even if you already know what to expect. Make sure you avoid any careless mistakes by following the directions.

Then begin working through the questions, pacing yourself as you've practiced. If you're not sure on an answer, don't spend too much time on it, and don't let it shake your confidence. Either skip it and come back later, or eliminate as many wrong answers as possible and guess among the remaining ones. Don't dwell on these questions as you continue—put them out of your mind and focus on what lies ahead.

Be sure to read all of the answer choices, even if you're sure the first one is the right answer. Sometimes you'll find a better one if you keep reading. But don't second-guess yourself if you do immediately know the answer. Your gut instinct is usually right. Don't let test anxiety rob you of the information you know.

If you have time at the end of the test (and if the test format allows), go back and review your answers. Be cautious about changing any, since your first instinct tends to be correct, but make sure you didn't misread any of the questions or accidentally mark the wrong answer choice. Look over any you skipped and make an educated guess.

At the end, leave the test feeling confident. You've done your best, so don't waste time worrying about your performance or wishing you could change anything. Instead, celebrate the successful completion of this test. And finally, use this test to learn how to deal with anxiety even better next time.

> **Review Video: Test Anxiety**
> Visit mometrix.com/academy and enter code: 100340

Important Qualification

Not all anxiety is created equal. If your test anxiety is causing major issues in your life beyond the classroom or testing center, or if you are experiencing troubling physical symptoms related to your anxiety, it may be a sign of a serious physiological or psychological condition. If this sounds like your situation, we strongly encourage you to seek professional help.

Additional Bonus Material

Due to our efforts to try to keep this book to a manageable length, we've created a link that will give you access to all of your additional bonus material:

mometrix.com/bonus948/swclinical